# Institutional Ethics Committees and Health Care Decision Making

$T \xi^A$

# Institutional Ethics Committees and Health Care Decision Making

Edited by
Ronald E. Cranford, M.D.
A. Edward Doudera, J.D.

Published in Cooperation with
the American Society of Law & Medicine

Health Administration Press
Ann Arbor, Michigan
1984

Copyright © 1984 by the Foundation of the American College of Healthcare Executives except for chapter 5, copyright © 1983 by George J. Annas, and chapter 7, copyright © 1983 by John A. Robertson. Printed in the United States of America. All rights reserved. This book or parts thereof may not be reproduced in any form without written permission of the publisher.

Copyright previously held by the Regents of The University of Michigan.


**Library of Congress Cataloging in Publication Data**
Main entry under title:

Institutional ethics committees and health care decision making.

"Section I consists of the papers, audience discussions, and panel discussion . . . first nationwide conference on institutional ethics committees, held in Washington, D.C., in April of 1983 under the sponsorship of the American Society of Law & Medicine"—Introd.
Bibliography: p.
Includes index.
1. Medical ethics—Congresses.  2. Medical care—Decision making—Moral and ethical aspects—Congresses.  3. Medical laws and legislation—United States—Congresses.  I. Cranford, Ronald E.  II. Doudera, A. Edward, 1949–     .  III. American Society of Law and Medicine. [DNLM: 1. Ethics, Professional.  2. Health Facilities.  3. Professional Staff Committees.  4. Decision Making.  WX 159 I595]
R724.I56   1984        174'.2        84–14640
ISBN 0–914904–98–1


Health Administration Press
A Division of the Foundation of the
American College of Healthcare Executives
1021 East Huron Street
Ann Arbor, Michigan 48104-9990
(313) 764-1380

*To Adam, Brian, and Erika, with love.*

# Contents

## SECTION III: SAMPLE GUIDELINES AND POLICIES

# Contributors

GEORGE J. ANNAS is Edward R. Utley Professor of Legal Medicine at Boston University School of Medicine, Professor of Health Law at Boston University School of Public Health, and Chief of the Health Law Section of Boston University School of Public Health. He received his undergraduate degree in 1967 from Harvard College, his law degree from Harvard Law School, and his M.P.H. from Harvard School of Public Health. Professor Annas received the first Joseph P. Kennedy Foundation Fellowship in Medical Ethics and has authored or coauthored a number of books, including *The Rights of Hospital Patients* and *Genetics and the Law*, volumes 1 and 2. He formerly served as Editor-in-Chief of *Medicolegal News* and Co-Editor of *Nursing Law & Ethics*, which were consolidated into *Law, Medicine & Health Care*, of which he is currently Editor-in-Chief Emeritus. Professor Annas serves on the Board of Directors of the American Society of Law & Medicine.

MILA ANN AROSKAR is Associate Professor in the Program in Public Health Nursing at the University of Minnesota School of Public Health. She received a B.A. in religion from the College of Wooster, a B.S. and masters degree in nursing education from Columbia University, and an Ed.D from the State University of New York at Buffalo. Professor Aroskar has performed extensive research on ethical issues in public health nursing and has served as a consultant to the Institute of Society, Ethics, and the Life Sciences at the Hastings Center, Hastings-on-Hudson, New York.

SISTER CORRINE BAYLEY is Vice President for Bioethics at Sisters of St. Joseph of Orange Health System in Orange, California. She received her undergraduate degree from St. Joseph College, a masters in hospital administration from St. Louis University, and a masters in religion and medical ethics from the Pacific School of Religion. Sister Bayley is currently the chair of the California Association of Catholic Hospitals.

She also serves on the ethics committees of Saint Joseph Hospital, Santa Rosa Hospital, and the Children's Hospital of Los Angeles.

DAVID N. BUCHALTER is currently completing his medical studies. Dr. Buchalter received his undergraduate degree in biochemistry from Brandeis University in 1978, and his medical degree from the University of Medicine and Dentistry of New Jersey at Rutgers. Dr. Buchalter's internship was at Saint Vincent's Hospital in New York City, and he expects to pursue a residency in orthopedic surgery.

ALLEN E. BUCHANAN is Professor of Philosophy and Lecturer in the Division of Social Perspectives in Medicine at the University of Arizona. He received his undergraduate degree in 1970 from Columbia University and his Ph.D. five years later from the University of North Carolina. Dr. Buchanan served as the staff philosopher for the President's Commission for the Study of Ethical Problems in Medicine and Biomedical and Behavioral Research from January 1, 1982, to January 1, 1983. Dr. Buchanan served as a member of the Ethical Crisis Committee of the Children's Hospital and Health Center in Minneapolis.

ALEXANDER MORGAN CAPRON is Topping Professor of Law, Medicine and Public Policy at the University of Southern California. Professor Capron received an undergraduate degree from Swarthmore College in Pennsylvania and an LL.B. from Yale Law School. From 1980 to 1983, he was the Executive Director of the President's Commission for the Study of Ethical Problems in Medicine and Biomedical and Behavioral Research, which issued sixteen volumes of findings. Professor Capron is the author or editor of six books and more than sixty articles or chapters in professional journals, books, and general publications. He also serves on the Board of Directors of the Hastings Center and the American Society of Law & Medicine.

CLAUDIA COULTON is a Professor in the School of Applied Social Sciences at Case Western Reserve University in Cleveland, Ohio. Dr. Coulton is a graduate of Ohio Wesleyan University. She received an M.S.W. from Ohio State University and a Ph.D. in Social Welfare from Case Western Reserve University.

RONALD E. CRANFORD is Associate Physician in Neurology and Director of the Neurological Intensive Care Unit at Hennepin County Medical Center in Minneapolis, Minnesota, and Associate Professor of Neurology at the University of Minnesota. He received his undergraduate degree in 1962 from the University of Illinois and his M.D. from the University of Illinois College of Medicine. Dr. Cranford serves as the Chairperson of the American Society of Law & Medicine's Institutional Ethics Committees Advisory Board and as the Chairperson of the Ethics and Humanities Committee of the American Academy of Neurology. He is also the Chairperson of the Biomedical Ethics Committee of the Hennepin County Medical Center.

A. EDWARD DOUDERA is Executive Director of the American Society of Law & Medicine. He received a B.S. in business administration from Boston University in 1972 and a J.D. from Suffolk University School of Law. Mr. Doudera is Executive Editor of both the *American Journal of Law & Medicine* and *Law, Medicine & Health Care.* He has coedited several texts, including *Legal & Ethical Aspects of Treating Critically & Terminally Ill Patients* and *Defining Human Life: Medical, Legal, and Ethical Implications.* Before joining the American Society of Law & Medicine in 1977, Mr. Doudera was Associate Administrator for Research at Tufts-New England Medical Center.

JOAN M. GIBSON is Associate Professor of Philosophy at the University of Albuquerque, and Adjunct Associate Professor at the University of New Mexico Schools of Law and Medicine. Dr. Gibson graduated from Mount Holyoke College and received a Ph.D. in philosophy from the University of California, San Francisco. Dr. Gibson has written extensively on the physician-lawyer relationship in medical education, and on right-to-die issues.

LEONARD H. GLANTZ is Associate Director of the Public Health Program and Associate Professor of Health Law at the Schools of Medicine and Public Health at Boston University. Mr. Glantz received his undergraduate degree in psychology from Boston University. In 1973, he earned his J.D. from Boston University School of Law. He has authored a large body of articles on medicolegal issues and has coauthored a number of books, including *Informed Consent to Human Experimentation: The Subject's Dilemma* and *The Rights of Doctors, Nurses and Allied Health Professionals.* Professor Glantz serves on Boston University's Clinical Research Review Committee which reviews experimentation on human subjects.

MICHAEL A. GRODIN is Assistant Professor of Pediatrics at Boston University School of Medicine and Adjunct Assistant Professor of Social and Behavioral Science at the School of Public Health. He is Director of Pediatric and Emergency Services and Intensive Care at Boston City Hospital. In 1982, Dr. Grodin received a National Endowment for the Humanities grant for a study of ethics and public policy in health care. Dr. Grodin is a graduate of the Massachusetts Institute of Technology, and received his medical training at Albert Einstein College of Medicine in New York. He is also a member of the Board of Directors of the American Society of Law & Medicine.

ANGELA R. HOLDER is Counsel for Medicolegal Affairs at Yale–New Haven Hospital and Yale University School of Medicine, and Clinical Professor of Pediatrics (Law) at the School of Medicine. Ms. Holder graduated from Newcomb College of Tulane University and Tulane University Law School. In 1975, she received a masters in law from Yale Law School. She has published a number of books, including *Legal Issues in Pediatrics and Adolescent Medicine*, and is a regular contributor to a number of prestigious journals. At Yale, Ms. Holder serves on the Medical School's Human Investigation Committee. Professor Holder is a member of the American Society of Law & Medicine's Executive Committee.

DAVID L. JACKSON is currently the Director of the State of Ohio Department of Health. Dr. Jackson received an A.B., a Ph.D. with distinction, and an M.D. from Johns Hopkins University. After completing an internship and residency in medicine, Dr. Jackson was a White House Fellow in the Department of Neurology at Johns Hopkins. Prior to his present appointment, Dr. Jackson was Director of the Center for the Critically Ill at the University Hospitals of Cleveland and Associate Professor of Neurology at Case Western Reserve University. Dr. Jackson currently serves on the Ethics and Humanities Committee of the American Academy of Neurology.

BARBARA W. JUKNIALIS is a Research Associate at the Center for the Critically Ill in Cleveland, Ohio. Ms. Juknialis received her undergraduate degree and a masters degree in Russian studies from Case Western Reserve University. Ms. Juknialis assists the Center in psychosocial research, developing surveys and questionnaires, interviewing subjects, and performing data analysis. Ms. Juknialis was a member of the research team that studied institutional ethics committees for the President's Commission on the Study of Ethical Problems in Medicine and Biomedical and Behavioral Research.

THOMASINE KUSHNER obtained a masters degree in philosophy from the University of Miami, did graduate work at the Sorbonne and at Stirling University in Scotland, and received her Ph.D. in philosophy from the University of Florida. She has taught at Florida International University and currently is a faculty member at the University of Miami School of Medicine, where she lectures in bioethics and participates in residency training and ethics rounds for pediatric surgery. She contributes to professional journals in aesthetics, as well as ethics, and her book, *Anatomy of Art,* has recently been published by Warren H. Green.

JOANNE LYNN is Assistant Clinical Professor of Geriatric Medicine in the Department of Health Sciences at George Washington University. From January 1981 until its disbandment, Dr. Lynn served as the Assistant Director for Medical Studies for the President's Commission for the Study of Ethical Problems in Medicine and Biomedical and Behavioral Research. Dr. Lynn is a graduate of Dickinson College in Carlisle, Pennsylvania, and the Boston University School of Medicine. Since 1979, she has been the Medical Director of the Washington Home Hospice, has authored numerous contributions to the medical and ethical literature, and has made a number of presentations on a wide range of ethical issues to national audiences.

RUTH MACKLIN is Associate Professor of Bioethics at Albert Einstein College of Medicine of Yeshiva University in the Bronx. Dr. Macklin received a B.A. in philosophy from Cornell University and an M.A. and a Ph.D. from Case Western Reserve University. Dr. Macklin's publications have addressed a broad range of bioethical issues, including health care for children, mental retardation and sterilization, and the ethics of behavioral research. She is a coeditor of *Moral Problems in Medicine,* and participates in several ethics committees in New York City.

WILLIAM S. MARKLEY is Assistant Director for Administrative Services at Boston City Hospital. Prior to assuming that position, he was Senior Administrative Analyst for Inpatient Services. Mr. Markley received a graduate degree in psychology from West Virginia University and an M.B.A. and M.P.H. in planning and regulation from Boston University. Since 1980, Mr. Markley has been a member of the Board of Directors of the North Cottage Program, a multibranched residential rehabilitation program.

ANNE E. MCDONALD is Special Assistant Corporation Counsel to the City of Boston's Department of Health and Hospitals. She is also Associate Director of the city's Family Development Center. Ms. McDonald is a graduate of Trinity College in Washington, D.C., the Boston College Graduate School of Social Work, and Suffolk University Law School. Ms. McDonald is a contributor to *Child Abuse: Intervention and Treatment,* and has presented numerous classes on child abuse at hospitals throughout Massachusetts.

RUSSELL L. MCINTYRE is Director of the Programs in Health Care Humanities at the University of Medicine and Dentistry of New Jersey, and is Assistant Professor of Environmental and Community Medicine at Rutgers Medical School. Reverend McIntyre received an undergraduate degree from Wagner College in New York, a B.D. from Lutheran Theological Seminary in Pennsylvania, an S.T.M. and an M.R.E. from Wittenberg University in Ohio, and a Th.D. from the University of Toronto. Reverend McIntyre has served on a number of institutional review boards, and is a consultant in Biomedical Ethics to Middlesex General Hospital in New Brunswick, New Jersey.

FATHER JOHN J. PARIS is Associate Professor of Social Ethics at College of the Holy Cross in Worcester, Massachusetts, and Adjunct Associate Professor of Medicine at the University of Massachusetts Medical School. In 1983, he received a fellowship from the Hastings Center Institute of Society, Ethics and the Life Sciences. Father Paris graduated from Boston College in 1959, and received graduate degrees from Harvard University, Weston College, Boston College, and the University of Southern California. He has published on ethical issues related to the withholding of treatment and life support in a number of prestigious journals, including the *New England Journal of Medicine*.

JOHN A. ROBERTSON is Professor of Law at the University of Texas School of Law in Austin, Texas. He is a graduate of Dartmouth College and Harvard Law School. Professor Robertson is the author of *The Rights of the Critically Ill*. From 1975 to 1978, he was a consultant to the National Commission on Protection of Human Subjects in Biomedical and Behavioral Research. He has written and lectured extensively on institutional review boards and on ethics committees.

LESLIE STEVEN ROTHENBERG is Adjunct Assistant Professor of Medicine in the Department of Medicine at the University of California, Los Angeles, School of Medicine. He received a B.S. from Northwestern University, a master's in political science from Stanford University, and a J.D. from UCLA. Professor Rothenberg is cochair of the Joint Committee on Medical Ethics of the Los Angeles County Bar and Medical Associations. He also chairs the Committee on Medical Ethics of the California Perinatal Association.

ROBERT M. VEATCH is Professor of Medical Ethics at the Kennedy Institute of Ethics at Georgetown University. From 1970 to 1979, he was a Senior Associate at the Hastings Center Institute of Society, Ethics and the Life Sciences. Dr. Veatch received a B.S. in pharmacology from Purdue University, an M.S. in pharmacology from the University of California Medical Center in San Francisco, a B.D. from Harvard Divinity School, and an M.A. and Ph.D. in religion and society from Harvard. Dr. Veatch is the author of *Death, Dying, and the Biological Revolution*, and an editor of *The Teaching of Medical Ethics*.

STUART A. WESBURY, JR., is the President of the American College of Hospital Administrators. Dr. Wesbury received an undergraduate degree in pharmacy from the Temple University School of Pharmacy in Philadelphia. In 1960, he received an M.H.A. with High Distinction from the University of Michigan, and in 1972 received a Ph.D. in economics and business administration from the University of Florida. He is the author of a number of articles on health care delivery and administration, many of which have focused on ethical decision making and the need for education within institutions. Dr. Wesbury is a member of the Board of Directors of the American Society of Law & Medicine and is the Chairman of the Board of the Association of University Programs in Health Administration.

STUART J. YOUNGNER is Acting Director of the Center for the Critically Ill at the University Hospitals of Cleveland, and holds an appointment in the Department of Psychiatry at Case Western Reserve University. He is a graduate of Swarthmore College and Case Western Reserve University School of Medicine. Dr. Younger was Co–Principal Investigator of a national survey of hospital ethics committees supported by the President's Commission for the Study of Ethical Problems in Medicine and Biomedical and Behavioral Research. He has been a member of the Critical Care Advisory Committee at the University Hospitals of Cleveland since 1978.

# Acknowledgments

Publishing a book based on the papers and proceedings of any conference devoted to a topic of current interest to health care professionals, lawyers, and ethicists is a painstaking task. This was especially so for the April 1983 conference that gave rise to this book. That meeting, held in the midst of the Infant Doe controversy, was the first national conference devoted to institutional ethics committees and their potential for assuring that reasonable and fair health care decisions would be made for those unable to decide for themselves, especially handicapped infants. The conference faculty, many of whom have contributed chapters to this book, explored various roles and functions for ethics committees, discussed their genesis and prognosis, and generally focused national attention on the concept. Our thanks go to all who participated in the conference—as faculty, as attendees, or as tireless staff— and especially to Professors George Annas and Robert Veatch for their insightful suggestions on the program and to Julie Canny, then Assistant Executive Director of the American Society of Law & Medicine, for a well-run and well organized conference.

Progress on the manuscripts coincided with legal and political developments in the Infant Doe case and subsequently in the Infant Jane Doe case, and an increased interest in institutional ethics committees. When possible, such developments were noted in the text. Equally important, in an effort to make this book a practical resource for those involved in setting up or serving on an institutional ethics committee, two attendees at the conference were stimulated to organize, coordinate, and edit a series of descriptions of existing ethics committees on key questions. Our special thanks go to Drs. Thomasine Kushner and Joan Gibson, for the collection of the materials in Section II.

Thanks and acknowledgments must also go to the many health care institutions and associations that agreed to have their guidelines, policies, or statements included in Section III. Taken together, this collection provides a unique resource for those who must confront and resolve complex and emotion-laden health care dilemmas.

Lastly, we must give thanks to the contributions of Betty Barrer, Managing Editor of *Law, Medicine & Health Care,* and the research assistants of Boston University School of Law. Truly, without their efforts in editing, cite checking, and proofreading, this book would not exist.

R.E.C.
A.E.D.

April 1984

# Section I

# Perspectives on Institutional Ethics Committees

## INTRODUCTION

Section I consists of the papers, audience discussions, and panel discussion that together constitute the first nationwide conference on institutional ethics committees, held in Washington, D.C., in April of 1983 under the sponsorship of the American Society of Law & Medicine. The section is divided into four parts. Part I focuses on the technological and social developments that gave rise to the institutional ethics committee as a mechanism by which health care dilemmas can be rationally and equitably addressed. The functions and responsibilities of IECs, as defined by the President's Commission for the Study of Ethical Problems in Biomedical and Behavioral Research, are discussed in the second chapter. The last three chapters in Part I examine the various ethical and legal concerns of IECs.

Part II provides several perspectives on the functioning and effectiveness of institutional ethics committees that are already in place. Chapter 6 presents the results of a study designed to examine patients' awareness of ethics committees in their hospital and their opinion about the appropriate roles of such committees. Alternative models of ethics committees, based on their possible roles and responsibilities, are outlined in Chapter 7. The next two chapters focus on the experiences of those serving on IECs, Chapter 8 through a summary of self-descriptive reports and Chapter 9 through a survey of institutional committees in New Jersey, the first state to authorize their establishment. Chapter 10 presents a retrospective audit of the cases handled by an informal, multidisciplinary team of hospital staff members. The last chapter in Part II clarifies the similarities and differences between institutional ethics committees and institutional review boards.

Part III examines the process of implementing IECs, and how they carry out the roles generally assigned to them: education, policy development, consultation, and decision review.

The first two chapters in Part IV examine two of the practical problems that are often brought before institutional ethics committees: withdrawal of life-sustaining treatment, illustrated by the case of California physicians Barber and Nejdl; and mechanisms for decision making for incompetent patients. Finally, Chapter 18 analyzes the relationships among the various health care professionals who typically serve on IECs, and proposes three ethical principles that should underlie those relationships.

# Part I

## An Introduction to Institutional Ethics Committees

# The Emergence of Institutional Ethics Committees

## Ronald E. Cranford and A. Edward Doudera

The institutional ethics committee—an entity that many believe can solve a number of the medical, legal, and ethical problems that exist in modern health care—was the focus of a conference held in April 1983. This milestone event convened a faculty of distinguished scholars from a variety of disciplines to discuss various aspects of ethics committees and to try to develop some consensus on what these committees are and what they should be. Their papers form the first section of this book.

Utilized sporadically since the early 1970s, ethics committees began to receive renewed and heightened attention in 1982 and 1983. Cases such as that in Los Angeles, where two physicians were charged with first-degree murder for heeding the family's request to remove intravenous feeding tubes from a comatose, severely brain-damaged patient,[1] the *Infant Doe* case from Bloomington, Indiana,[2] and the more recent case of Baby Jane Doe from New York State,[3] have generated an enormous amount of interest and publicity and provided a new impetus for institutional ethics committees.

Perhaps the most compelling impetus has been the final "Infant Doe" regulations promulgated by the United States Department of Health and Human Services (HHS) after a public comment period during which 16,739 comments were submitted—96.5 percent of which supported the rule.[4] The regulations, following the recommendation of the American Academy of Pediatrics and other organizations, strongly encourage, but do not mandate, that hospitals caring for newborn infants establish infant care review committees—committees whose suggested functions are: (1) to develop hospital policies and guidelines for management of specific types of diagnoses; (2) to monitor adherence through retrospective record review; and (3) to review specific cases on an emergency basis when the withholding of life-sustaining treatment is being considered.[5]

Another force toward this increased interest in ethics committees (and we use this term broadly here) was a major report released in early 1983 by the President's Commission for the Study of Ethical Problems in Medicine and Biomedical and Behavioral Research.[6] The report, *Deciding to Forego Life-Sustaining Treatment*, suggests:

> Health care institutions . . . have a responsibility to ensure that there are appropriate procedures to enhance patients' competence, to provide for the designation of surrogates, to guarantee that patients are adequately informed, to overcome the influence of dominant institutional biases, to provide review of decision making, and to refer cases to the courts appropriately.[7]

The President's Commission concluded that courts should generally be used as decision makers for incompetent individuals requiring medical treament only as a last resort. The Commission's premise was that informal procedures involving the responsible physician and family members are preferable to formal mechanisms for most routine matters regarding the determination of incapacity and subsequent decision making.[8] Nonetheless, the Commission also noted that "there are enough possibilities for error in the process of decision making for incapacitated persons that at least some decisions made by families and practitioners should be subject to review."[9] The need for this "review" is highlighted by the Commission's conclusion that a "surrogate decision maker" be designated and utilized when a patient is considered by his or her attending physician to be incapacitated. Thus, the President's Commission concluded that in order to protect the interests of patients who lack decision-making capacity and to ensure their well-being and self-determination,

> [t]he medical staff, along with the trustees and administrators of health care institutions, should explore and evaluate various formal and informal administrative arrangements for review and consultation, such as "ethics committees," particularly for decisions that have life-or-death consequences. . . .[10]

We believe that ethics committees can serve as a reasonable and valid institutional endeavor to increase understanding among all concerned—health care providers, families, patients, and society—as well as to resolve many of the ethical, legal, and medical dilemmas facing those who care for critically and terminally ill patients. That is the premise of this chapter, and the overwhelming conclusion of the chapters that follow.

For our purposes, we would like to broadly define an ethics committee as a multidisciplinary group of health care professionals within a health care institution that has been specifically established to address the ethical dilemmas that occur within the institution. At the present time, these dilemmas frequently concern the treatment or nontreatment of patients who lack decision-making capacities. Many other definitions or descriptions are available. For example, the President's Commission used the term to refer to those committees that have the potential to become involved in decision making in particular patients' cases.[11] The American Medical Association recorded its support for committees that

> . . . offer[ed] assistance to parents, physicians, and all other members of the treatment team in making critical treatment decisions. Such committees could provide a free and open forum for all parties to exchange views and information on a particular case and also provide a valuable educational role on options available for treatment and subsequent care.[12]

The idea of an ethics committee is a relatively new concept, in large part stemming from the 1976 decision of the New Jersey Supreme Court in the case of Karen Ann Quinlan.[13] In that landmark decision, the court quoted an article by Dr. Karen Teel which suggested that the way to improve medical decision making was for each hospital to establish an "Ethics Committee composed of physicians, social workers, attorneys, and theologians . . . which [serves] to review the individual circumstances of ethical dilemma[s] and which [provides] much in the way of assistance and safeguards for patients and their medical caretakers."[14] Dr. Teel saw such a committee as being "advisory" rather than "enforcing,"[15] but the New Jersey court in the *Quinlan* case gave it a greater role: if the hospital ethics committee agreed "that there is no reasonable possibility of Karen's ever emerging from her present comatose condition to a cognitive, sapient state," the request of the parents, guardians, and attending physicians to remove life-sustaining treatment could be acted upon without fear of civil or criminal liability.[16] Yet somehow the concept was not a practical success, and few hospitals created such committees. A recent article in the *Hastings Center Report* attributes the failure to adopt ethics committees after the *Quinlan* decision to "a reluctance to disturb the status quo, together with a sense of confusion over what an ethics committee could accomplish. . . ."[17]

As mentioned earlier, it was the Bloomington, Indiana, case of Infant Doe, and the ensuing federal regulatory response,[18] that may have had the most significant effect on the movement towards establishing bioethical review committees for infants and, ultimately, ethics committees for all patients. The development of local ethical review boards by hospitals and their staffs was recommended or supported by many organizations in their responses to the proposed Infant Doe regulations. The American College of Hospital Administrators, the American Hospital Association, the American Medical Association, the American College of Physicians, the American Society of Law & Medicine, the National Association of Children's Hospitals and Related Institutions, and many others expressed their belief that such committees could play a positive role in assuring that reasonable medical decisions would be made for handicapped infants.[19] The American Academy of Pediatrics made the most specific proposal, urging that HHS require, as a condition of participation in the Medicare/Medicaid programs,[20] that institutions caring for handicapped infants create infant bioethical review committees.[21] The Academy's proposal was substantially adopted by HHS, and with the publication of the final federal rules on January 12, 1984, infant care review committees (ICRCs) have come into existence.[22] In the section of the regulations that describes the "Model Infant Care Review Committee," HHS states its view of the purpose of the ICRC as follows:

> [To] facilitat[e] the development and implementation of standards, policies, and procedures designed to assure that, while respecting reasonable medical judgments, treatment and nourishment not be withheld, solely on the basis of present or anticipated physical or mental impairments, from handicapped infants who, in spite of such impairments, will benefit medically from the treatment or nourishment.[23]

While HHS regulations apply only to handicapped infants, physicians, nurses, and others are recognizing the intrinsic value of open multidisciplinary discussion when clinical dilemmas arise. As such, a number of organizations have begun to advocate the formation of ethics committees in situations other than the neonatal unit. For example, the California Medical Association Council has advised each acute care hospital in California "to establish and support an ethics committee."[24] In its *Guidelines on Hospital Ethics Committees*, the Association states that "the purpose of the committee would be to facilitate communication between concerned parties regarding treatment decisions, to assist in the decision-making process when ethical conflicts occur, and to retrospectively review decisions for the purpose of establishing guidelines."[25] This movement towards ethics committees has been echoed by Samuel R. Sherman, M.D., the chairman of the Judicial Council of the American Medical Association. Dr. Sherman recently predicted that "before very long, all hospitals will have ethics committees."[26] He also urged that they be allowed to "evolve slowly according to the needs expressed at the local level" and that questions as to their role "be resolved locally through the establishment of local guidelines and following local needs."[27]

Currently, the number of ethics committees around the country is small but growing. In a survey conducted for the President's Commission, Dr. Stuart Youngner and his colleagues found only 17 committees in the 400 hospitals with more than 200 beds that they surveyed.[28] Combining this with their survey of 202 hospitals with fewer than 200 beds—where they found no ethics committees—Youngner and his group estimated that approximately 1 percent of the country's hospitals have ethics committees in place.[29] It should be noted, however, that Youngner utilized a very narrow definition of an ethics committee, i.e., a committee having the "potential" to participate in the making of a clinical decision.[30] Perhaps this can explain the variance with the findings of another study which found that of 396 responding hospitals in New York, New Jersey, Connecticut, and Massachusetts, 16.4 percent had ethics committees.[31] Nonetheless, the Youngner survey found that these committees facilitated decision making by clarifying important issues, providing legal protection for hospital administration and staff, making consistent hospital policies, and providing a forum for the airing of professional disagreements.

The Catholic Health Association recently conducted a survey of its member institutions and found that 41 percent had committees that met its definition of an ethics committee.[32] Nineteen percent reported committees that functioned as "decision-making groups," and 17 percent reported committees that functioned as "policy-making groups."[33] The authors also reported a regional variation: in the Pacific and mountain states, 55 percent of respondents had ethics committees, whereas only 30 percent of the hospitals studied from the north central and east south central states had committees.[34]

Whatever the current incidence of institutional ethics committees, it seems certain that their numbers will increase in the years ahead, and it is important at this formative stage to strive to understand their benefits, functions, and problems.

## BENEFITS

A number of benefits have been asserted by the proponents of ethics committees. First, ethics committees will satisfy the need for a more systematic and principled approach to the contemporary dilemmas of medical/ethical decision making within our hospitals and long-term care facilities. It is quite likely that the *Infant Doe* case in Bloomington, Indiana, and the California criminal case involving Drs. Barber and Nejdl would have been handled quite differently had an active ethics committee been involved—doing its best to insure that all appropriate factors were taken into consideration. As those who serve on such committees know, just having a group of interested and knowledgeable health care professionals discuss the case in an open forum will help insure a more considered and reasonable decision.

This benefit has been acknowledged by both the President's Commission and HHS. The President's Commission emphasized that good decision-making practices are an obligation of the institution and that ethics committees are one way to encourage institutions and their staffs to develop good decision-making practices.[35] The position of HHS, as expressed in the final Infant Doe regulations, is that although it cannot accept such committees as a substitute mechanism for enforcing Section 504, they "can be very valuable . . . in bringing about informed, enlightened and fair decision making regarding these difficult issues."[36]

The importance of this multidisciplinary forum is evidenced in the overwhelmingly one-sided comments of nurses on the proposed Infant Doe regulations, promulgated July 5, 1983. Of these nurses, 97.5 percent favored the proposed rule.[37] This may be due to their feeling that they have nowhere to go when confronted by ethical dilemmas, and that the regulations provide an avenue for action.

Another benefit, one closely related to the first, is that institutional ethics committees can serve as a link between societal values and the actual developments occurring in the institutions that care for and treat the particular patients whose cases manifest these dilemmas. This is an important role for institutional ethics committees: translating general considerations into specific cases. Similarly, the ethics committee can serve as a means to channel information on new developments, such as the President's Commission's reports, federal regulations, court decisions, newly developed medical standards or guidelines, and surveys of public opinion, to institutional officials and health care personnel.

As an example, consider the question of whether, or to what extent, cost should be a consideration in health care decision making. Dr. Joanne Lynn believes that ethics committees may provide the necessary responsive forum for resolving this dilemma,[38] and a medical-policy committee of Blue Cross-Blue Shield of California has recommended that all of its participating hospitals adopt ethics committees[39] (perhaps in response to allegations that cost containment had been a motivation of Drs. Barber and Nedjl in stopping treatment on Clarence LeRoy Herbert, a patient at the largest HMO in the country).[40] Allegations of improper concern about cost will impair the trust and confidence that patients and families have in health care professionals, and we need to develop some means for maintaining trust and confidence in the decision-making abilities of physicians and nurses. In addition, we have to ensure that the rights of individuals, as well as societal interests, are protected. Lastly, we must adopt procedures for principled and open decision making. Ethics committees can serve an important role in fulfilling these needs.

A third potential benefit of ethics committees and the network that they will develop will be to help us distinguish between those ethical dilemmas where a consensus seems to exist and those where no consensus seems achievable, at least in the foreseeable future. For example, in this decade we have moved toward a consensus that the death of the brain is the death of the individual; that concept is now endorsed by 36 states through legislation and by two others through state supreme court decisions.[41] The ethics committee could help educate medical staff members and families about this trend and aid them in recognizing and accepting the standard of brain death.

Another area where consensus is beginning to develop is the appropriateness of written resuscitation and nonresuscitation policies. A decade ago, few hospitals had any form of "no-code" or "do-not-resuscitate" (DNR) policies in place. Today, written DNR policies are fairly routine in most hospitals, and it now becomes necessary to decide for each patient whether to resuscitate or to withhold cardiopulmonary resuscitation. A multidisciplinary ethics committee could help health care practitioners feel more secure about the appropriateness of their decisions and help assure patients of their rights.

There are many areas, however, where consensus does not yet exist. Two of these are treatment for handicapped newborns and the provision of fluids and nutrition to the hopelessly ill. Although ethics committees cannot resolve problems on which there is no societal agreement, those institutions having ethics committees will at least be able to address such dilemmas in an open and constructive manner. The ethics committee can also assist health care providers to differentiate the circumstances of various controversial cases that arise outside the institution but are discussed within it. For example, in the *Conroy* case, the trial judge held it permissible to remove a nasogastric tube from an elderly, severely demented person in a nursing home;[42] yet in the *Barber/Nedjl* case in California, the physicians were charged with murder for performing a similar act.[43] It is essential that providers recognize the determinative factors that exist in such cases, and the ethics committee can fulfill this role.

## FUNCTIONS

Three general functions have been suggested for institutional ethics committees—education, development of policies and guidelines, and consultation and case review. When one examines the descriptions or the charters of existing ethics committees, one is impressed by the multiplicity of contexts in which they operate and the functions which they perform.[44] Frequently, these functions overlap each other and may even produce contrary mandates to committee members. Professor Robert Veatch, in analyzing the ethical principles that may be adopted by ethics committees, even argues that the variety of tasks may "create real, probably insurmountable problems" for many committees.[45] Clearly, ethics committees must be able to identify what they want to achieve.

EDUCATION

The educational function involves improving the understanding of the institution's staff and serving as a focal point for multidisciplinary discussion and education on medicolegal and bioethical issues. Most committees assume this role and engage in a variety of activities aimed at filling this need. In the report on the Catholic Health Association's survey of committees, the authors write, "the committees are generally proactive and educational, rather than reactive, or problem oriented."[46] But before ethics committees can effectively fill this role, they must focus first on the education of committee members, expanding their knowledge and experience with the pertinent issues. The committee members can achieve this goal by reading relevant materials, by attending conferences, and simply by talking among themselves.

In addition to educating its own members concerning alternative points of view, the hospital ethics committee can assume the responsibility for educating the medical and nursing staffs about the various considerations and the proper procedures to be followed when, for example, orders not to resuscitate are issued.[47] An example of this function is found in the activities of the committee at the Hennepin County Medical Center[48] in Minneapolis, which developed a DNR policy in 1977–78. After the policy was formally adopted by the institution, the ethics committee assumed responsibility for educating hospital personnel on the meaning and scope of the guidelines. Continuing education, consisting of one or two conferences each year, has focused on the DNR guidelines and their application to the specific cases the staff has experienced. The result has been a more informed and uniform application of the policy.

DEVELOPMENT OF POLICIES AND GUIDELINES

The President's Commission concluded that health care institutions "should adopt clear, explicit, and publicly available policies regarding how and by whom decisions are to be made for patients who lack adequate decision-making capacity."[49] This is a role for which ethics committees seem highly suited and one which many committees have performed. The Catholic Hospital Association survey, for example, indicated that approximately 80 percent of the committees in that study advised administrators and recommended policy for their facilities.[50] In addition to being the facilitators of the development of policies for decision making for incapacitated patients, ethics committees could also propose, review, and recommend administrative policies and guidelines on such problems as the determination of death, orders not to resuscitate, foregoing life-sustaining treatment, supportive care, and treatment of handicapped newborns. Moreover, in conjunction with its educational role, the committee could review guidelines and policies in light of the newest information. Thus, when Susanna E. Bedell and her colleagues published their study on survival after CPR,[51] the ethics committee could have reviewed the institution's DNR guidelines with their medical and nursing staffs and discussed the implications of the data. The multidisciplinary ethics committee is especially well suited to the task of developing and revising general policies or guidelines, and the ethics committee may frequently be charged with overseeing the implementation of newly developed institutional guidelines.

CONSULTATION AND CASE REVIEW

This function is served by having the committee or its individual members available to discuss the ethical and social concerns of interested parties, and by having the committee provide advice to parties that seek it. In this role, the ethics committee or its members would help patients, families, attending physicians, and other health care providers to face and resolve the ethical dilemmas presented to them by modern health care. The committee would serve as a resource with specialized training, understanding, and experience within the institution—be it a hospital or a nursing home—for staff and families.

   Case review may also have a broader, more intrusive objective, i.e., "to ensure that the interests of all parties, especially those of the incapacitated person, have been adequately represented, and that the decision reached lies within the range of permissible alternatives."[52] This type of involvement is controversial and has, in fact, been rejected in many ethics committee charters. For example, "[t]he committee would not make medical decisions nor become involved in clearcut cases of surrogates or guardians of incompetent patients refusing medical treatment."[53]

   Currently, most proponents of ethics committees would suggest that they not be the final decision makers but that they strive to emphasize the role of attending physicians and surrogates as the primary decision makers for incapacitated patients. However, to be effective, an institutional ethics committee might require authority to postpone actions based on decisions it counseled against or to initiate judicial review of such decisions. This role, which makes many health care providers apprehensive, is, in the opinion of Alexander Morgan Capron, the one special task of ethics committees.[54] Professor Capron sees the role of ethics committees to be that of considering issues prospectively in the hospital, with the perspective that there is often a range of ethically acceptable decisions.

## PROBLEMS

Ethics committees are not without their problems, and we need to recognize them. One problem stems from the term *ethics committee* itself. As many commentators note, and as the titles of various existing ethics committees evidence, these committees are not confined to ethical issues. Some argue that such committees should address only medical questions, and thus HHS's title, "infant care review committee," removes all reference to ethical decisions. Others object to the term *ethics committee* because of its presumed focus on morals and because of the possibility that the committee will impose its values on the medical staff and the patients whom it is supposed to assist.[55]

While the problems of definition and of determining the ethical focus are difficult, we believe that the solution is not to deny that these committees are involved in ethical decisions, ethical education, and ethical consultations. The heart of the matter is that we are faced with ethical dilemmas, and ethics committees can help us cope with them. If these problems were purely medical ones, we would have developed committees with special medical expertise—for example, the New Jersey and the Washington state prognosis committees. It would be misleading to avoid the term *ethics committees*, because that would belie the nature of the problem—and the workings of these committees. Indeed, the contributions to this book illustrate clearly that these committees are dealing with fundamental ethical dilemmas.

This confusion or disagreement has also been fanned by the inaccurate naming of committees charged with specific tasks, for example, confirming a patient's prognosis. Thus, while the *Quinlan* court placed significant power in the hands of what it called the "hospital ethics committee,"[56] that committee was specifically charged with making a medical determination that confirmed the attending physician's prognosis that the patient would not return to a cognitive, sapient state. This is a medical or clinical function, not an ethical one.[57] This distinction, in fact, was made by a Washington state decision from 1983, *In re Colyer*.[58] In discussing the proper way in which medical decisions should be made for those unable to decide for themselves, the court cited with approval the ethics committee of the *Quinlan* case—but more because of its function than its name. The Washington court specifically rejected the concept of multidisciplinary composition, and held that the committee's task was limited to that of confirming a medical prognosis of an incurable disease or inability to return to cognitive, sapient life.[59] After a patient's prognosis was confirmed unanimously by the committee, life supports could be withheld or withdrawn, without judicial intervention.[60]

The confusion about the name and function of ethics committees may explain the differing results of studies concerning their incidence. For example, in New Jersey, where the state attorney general and the director of the health department, along with the state medical and hospital associations, promulgated nonbinding guidelines concerning the role and function of prognosis committees,[61] two recent surveys produced varying results. Of the hospitals responding to the survey conducted by Professor Russell McIntyre and Dr. David Buchalter, 64 percent had committees.[62] However, in a brief filed in the case of Claire Conroy, the counsel for the New Jersey Hospital Association revealed different data that resulted from a poll of its member acute care hospitals.[63] She reported that the vast majority of hospitals do have committees that were formed pursuant to New Jersey's voluntary guidelines; of 101 hospitals represented by the association, only 16 did not have such a committee.[64]

Another problem that has been suggested is that the ethics committee, which is supposed to be multidisciplinary and representative of a diversity of views and interests, may be dominated by one individual, discipline, or point of view. Thus, Father John Paris suggests that we add a member of the institution's maintenance or housekeeping staff to the ethics committee to bring in views and values not shared by the "professionals."[65] This has been done in a number of committees; for example, Rose Medical Center in Denver, Colorado, currently has two lay members, a secretary and a carpenter, both of whom are employed by the hospital.[66] To be effective, such committees must continue to be open to all perspectives and be ever-vigilant to domination—whether by paternalistic, aggressive physicians or by legal counsel concerned only with protecting the institution from liability and adverse publicity.

Another problem is the lack of a clear understanding of the relation that the committee has or should have to actual decisions on specific cases in the institution—questions such as, when do we go to court? when do we let families decide? This uncertainty is quite significant and is attributable, at least in part, to the current "grass-roots" approach toward ethics committees. While many of those recommending "ethics committees" specifically state that such committees "would not make medical decisions,"[67] it is hard to believe that a committee's recommendation would not carry weight. Professor John Robertson expands upon this when he discusses the types of authority that these committees can have.[68] He notes the different results that will occur depending on whether a committee has mandatory or optional authority to review problems, and whether it is optional or mandatory for health care providers to adhere to the results of the committee's deliberations (i.e., the recommendation or decision). As Robertson notes: "Clearly, the review procedures for mandatory and optional IECs are quite different."[69]

Lastly, there is the very practical problem of insufficient time, personnel, and other institutional resources. The vast majority of hospitals do not have personnel who are experienced and knowledgeable about medical/ethical dilemmas, even though this expertise is the key ingredient of a successful ethics committee. Self-education, as well as participation in meetings and in a communication network with others in similar situations, can help develop a group of concerned and committed committee members. Of course, their involvement in committee activities must be recognized as an important contribution to the institution, and sufficient resources need to be devoted to the committee's work. The need for these resources has become greater because of the final Infant Doe regulations which suggest that ICRC meetings called to review individual cases "will be convened within 24 hours (or less if indicated). . . ."[70] Given the demands upon the time of all health care professionals, such an objective may frequently create difficulties, but we must not let a lack of time limit the effectiveness and potential value of our institutional ethics committee.

## The Future

The future holds much potential. For infant-focused committees, their existence, composition, and activities will be the focus of much attention. The American Academy of Pediatrics released its guidelines on Infant Bioethics Committees in the spring of 1984, and various educational meetings will be devoted to the role of IBCs in medical decision making for handicapped infants. The American Academy of Pediatrics and the American Society of Law & Medicine will cooperate in various activities to educate and inform committee members, as well as the attorneys, administrators, and general medical and nursing staffs at institutions having committees. It is essential that we follow and study the ethics committees that develop in order to document their effects upon and contributions to health care decision making.

In nonpediatric settings, it seems likely that ethics committees will, in general, have an undirected process of development. These committees will be subject to numerous forces and factors, and information sharing and communication among committees will be essential. For example, the *Ethics Committee Newsletter*, first published by the American Society of Law & Medicine in the fall of 1983, has a mailing list of over 1,200 individuals who are forming or serving on institutional ethics committees, and its number grows weekly. A recently formed National Center for Institutional Ethics Committees, sponsored by the Society and the Institute for Public Law of the University of New Mexico in cooperation with the Division of Medical Ethics in the School of Medicine at the University of California, San Francisco, will focus on four primary objectives:

1. promoting and facilitating communication and sharing ideas and information, including the publication of the *Ethics Committee Newsletter*

2. creating and maintaining a resource library of educational and case-oriented materials for use by institutional ethics committee members

3. creating and maintaining a clearinghouse for consultants and speakers available for assisting institutions in creating committees, for helping committees to educate themselves or their staffs, or for consulting on cases

4. conducting research and surveys on institutional ethics committees

Information from the National Center can be obtained by writing to the American Society of Law & Medicine, 765 Commonwealth Avenue, Sixteenth Floor, Boston, Massachusetts 02215.

While the National Center will help develop the needed network of involved institutions and individuals, this work also needs to be accomplished on the local level. In 1982, for example, an informal network was started among local ethics committees in the Minneapolis/St. Paul area. The more established committees help the newer committees and those institutions that are currently forming committees. This network has a newsletter, holds regular educational meetings, and discusses common needs and problems. It serves as a sort of interinstitutional ethics committee network to coordinate the policies and procedures of the intrainstitutional committees that see the actual cases. A related development is the formation of the Twin Cities Committee for Neonatal Life Support Policy, which has prepared guidelines on the withholding of medical treatment from severely handicapped newborns.[71]

Lastly, the value of such committees will increase if we can avoid adversarial situations. Specifically, we feel that governmental regulation should be avoided, and that we should follow the example of hospice care in this country, which developed as local and independent, but connected, entities in the health care system, rather than following the path of institutional review boards, which were created by federal regulation to protect the subjects of human biomedical experimentation.[72] If concerned individuals in our health care institutions—be they pediatric, acute care, or geriatric—work to establish an effective means to protect the rights of patients and insure that reasonable and fair decisions are being made for those unable to decide for themselves, the prospects of governmental regulation will be diminished, and the possibility of improving patient care will grow stronger.

Ethics committees present a challenge and an opportunity to physicians and nurses, health care administrators, lawyers, families, and others to take the initiative and to develop this means to insure that reasonable and fair decisions are made by those who should make them —patients, physicians, and families.

## Notes

1. Barber v. Superior Court, 195 Cal. Rptr. 484, 486 (Cal. App. 1983). *See also* Paris, J.J., ch. 16 of this text.
2. *In re* Infant Doe, No. GU 8204–00 (Cir. Ct. Monroe County, Ind., April 12, 1982), *writ of mandamus dismissed sub nom.* State *ex rel.* Infant Doe v. Baker, No. 482 S 140 (Indiana Supreme Court, May 27, 1982) (case mooted by child's death).
3. Weber v. Stony Brook Hosp., 52 U.S.L.W. 2267 (N.Y., October 28, 1983); United States v. University Hosp., CV83–4818 (E.D. N.Y., November 17, 1983).
4. *Nondiscrimination on the Basis of Handicap; Procedures and Guidelines Relating to Health Care for Handicapped Infants; Final Rule*, 49 Fed. Reg. 1622, 1623 (January 16,1984) (to be codified at 45 C.F.R. §84.55).
5. 49 Fed. Reg. 1623–24.
6. President's Commission for the Study of Ethical Problems in Medicine and Biomedical and Behavioral Research, Deciding to Forego Life-sustaining Treatment: Ethical, Medical and Legal Issues in Treatment Decisions (U.S. Gov't Printing Office, Washington, D.C.) (March 1983) [hereinafter referred to as Deciding to Forego Treatment].
7. *Id.* at 4.
8. *Id.* at 6.
9. *Id.*
10. *Id.* at 5.
11. *Id.* at 161, note 122.
12. American Medical Association, Comments on Nondiscrimination on the Basis of Handicap; Procedures and Guidelines Relating to Health Care for Handicapped Infants (American Medical Association, Chicago) (August 26, 1983) at 17.

13. *In re* Quinlan, 355 A.2d 647 (N.J. 1976). *See* Veatch, R. M., *Hospital Ethics Committees: Is There a Role?*, HASTINGS CENTER REPORT 7(3):22 (June 1977); Levine, C., *Hospital Ethics Committees: A Guarded Prognosis*, HASTINGS CENTER REPORT 7(3):25 (June 1977).

14. *In re* Quinlan, *supra* note 13, at 668, *quoting* Teel, K., *The Physician's Dilemma—A Doctor's View: What the Law Should Be*, BAYLOR LAW REVIEW 27:6, 8–10 (Winter 1975) [hereinafter referred to as Teel].

15. Teel, *supra* note 14, at 8.

16. *In re* Quinlan, *supra* note 13, at 671.

17. Randal, J., *Are Ethics Committees Alive and Well?*, HASTINGS CENTER REPORT 13(6):10, 10 (December 1983).

18. Nondiscrimination on the Basis of Handicap; Procedures and Guidelines Relating to Health Care for Handicapped Infants; Final Rule, 49 Fed. Reg. 1621–54 (January 16, 1984) (to be codified at 45 C.F.R. §84.55), *amending* Proposed Rules, 48 Fed. Reg. 30,846 (July 5, 1983); Interim Final Rule, 48 Fed. Reg. 9630 (March 7, 1983); Notice to Health Care Providers, 47 Fed. Reg. 26,027 (May 18, 1982). *See* American Academy of Pediatrics v. Heckler, 561 F. Supp. 395 (D.D.C., April 14, 1983).

19. *See* U. S. MEDICINE, p. 3 (November 15, 1983). *See also* 49 Fed. Reg. 1623–24; Committee on the Legal and Ethical Aspects of Health Care for Children, *Comments and Recommendations on the "Infant Doe" Proposed Regulations*, LAW, MEDICINE & HEALTH CARE 11(5):203 (October 1983).

20. Conditions of Participation; Hospitals, 42 C.F.R. §405.1011–1041.

21. Comments of the American Academy of Pediatrics on Proposed Rules Regarding Nondiscrimination on the Basis of Handicap Relating to Health Care for Handicapped Infants (Pierson, Ball & Dowd, counsel) (September 1983).

22. 49 Fed. Reg. 1622, 1651.

23. *Id.* at 1652.

24. California Medical Association, *Guidelines on Hospital Ethics Committees* (approved by the California Medical Association Council, October 1, 1983), *reprinted in* Section III of this text [hereinafter referred to as *CMA Guidelines*].

25. *Id.*

26. *AMA Judicial Chairman Sees Emergence of Hospital Ethics Panels as an Inevitability*, FEDERATION OF AMERICAN HOSPITALS REVIEW 16(6):30,30 (November–December 1983).

27. *Id.*

28. Youngner, S. J., *et al.*, *A National Survey of Ethics Committees*, in DECIDING TO FOREGO TREATMENT, *supra* note 6, at 446.

29. *Id.*

30. *Id.* at 445.

31. Guido, D. J., *Hospital Ethics Committees: Potential Mediators for Educational and Policy Change*, DISSERTATION ABSTRACTS INTERNATIONAL 43(11):3529–B (1983).

32. Kalchbrenner, J., Kelly, M. J., McCarthy, D. G., *Ethics Committees and Ethicists in Catholic Hospitals*, HOSPITAL PROGRESS 64(9):47, 47 (September 1983) [hereinafter referred to as *Ethics Committees in Catholic Hospitals*].

33. *Id.*
34. *Id.* at 49, 50.
35. *See* DECIDING TO FOREGO TREATMENT, *supra* note 6, at 160–70.
36. 49 Fed. Reg. 1624.
37. *Id.* at 1623.
38. Lynn, J., ch. 2 of this text.
39. San Francisco Chronicle (February 12, 1983).
40. For a discussion of the *Barber/Nejdl* case, see Paris, J. J., ch. 16 of this text; Barber v. Superior Court, *supra* note 1.
41. Alexander M. Capron, Presentation on Brain Death Legislation, at Maintenance of a Cadaver Donor for Multiple Organ Procurement, workshop under the auspices of the National Institutes of Health, Arlington, Va., January 21–22, 1984.
42. *In re* Conroy, 457 A.2d 1232, 1233 (N.J. Super. 1983).
43. Barber v. Superior Court, *supra* note 1, at 486.
44. *See* descriptive summaries, Section II of this text. *See generally* DECIDING TO FOREGO TREATMENT, *supra* note 6, at 160–70 (discussion of various roles and problems).
45. Veatch, R. M., ch. 4 of this text.
46. *Ethics Committees in Catholic Hospitals, supra* note 32, at 49.
47. *See* Bayley, C., Cranford, R. E., ch. 12 of this text.
48. *See* descriptive summary, Hennepin County Medical Center Biomedical Ethics Committee, Section II of this text.
49. DECIDING TO FOREGO TREATMENT, *supra* note 6, at 5–6.
50. *Ethics Committees in Catholic Hospitals, supra* note 32, at 49.
51. Bedell, S. E., *et al., Survival after Cardiopulmonary Resuscitation in the Hospital,* NEW ENGLAND JOURNAL OF MEDICINE 309(10):569–76 (September 8, 1983).
52. DECIDING TO FOREGO TREATMENT, *supra* note 6, at 164.
53. *CMA Guidelines, supra* note 24.
54. Capron, A. M., ch. 15 of this text.
55. *See generally* Veatch, *supra* note 45 (discussion of committees' moral values).
56. *In re* Quinlan, *supra* note 13, at 671.
57. *See, e.g.,* Annas, G. J., *Reconciling* Quinlan *and* Saikewicz: *Decision Making for the Terminally Ill Incompetent,* AMERICAN JOURNAL OF LAW & MEDICINE 4(4):367, 378–79 (Winter 1979) ("a more accurate description would be 'prognosis committee,' because that is the only issue on which the participants would be asked to consult"). *See also* McIntyre, R., Buchalter, D., ch. 9 of this text.
58. *In re* Colyer, 660 P.2d 738 (Wash. 1983).
59. *Id.* at 749.
60. *Id.* at 751.
61. *New Jersey Guidelines for Health Care Facilities to Implement Procedures Concerning the Care of Comatose, Non-Cognitive Patients* (January 27, 1977), *reprinted in* Section III of this text.
62. McIntyre, Buchalter, *supra* note 57.

63. Affadavit of Mary K. Brennan, Counsel to the New Jersey Hospital Association, *In re* Conroy, No. A-2483-82-T (N.J. Supreme Court, April 29, 1983).
64. *Id.*
65. *See* Glantz, L. H., ch. 11 of this text.
66. *See* narrative description of Rose Medical Center Ethics Committee, Section II of this text.
67. *CMA Guidelines, supra* note 24.
68. Robertson, J. A., *Ethics Committees in Hospitals: Alternative Structures and Responsibilities*, QUALITY REVIEW BULLETIN 10(1):6–10 (January 1984).
69. *Id.* at 10.
70. 49 Fed. Reg. 1653.
71. *See* Section III of this text.
72. *See* U.S. MEDICINE, p. 3 (November 15, 1983) (the American Medical Association argued that ethics committees should "remain a local option and not become a uniform requirement imposed by the federal government or hospital accrediting bodies").

# 2

## Roles and Functions of Institutional Ethics Committees: The President's Commission's View

Joanne Lynn

The President's Commission for the Study of Ethical Problems in Medicine and Biomedical and Behavioral Research has recommended that institutions develop internal mechanisms, including ethics committees, to review treatment decisions for patients who lack decision-making capacity.[1] The recommendation, which gives institutions wide flexibility in establishing these committees, arises from a particularly troublesome group of problems that the Commission felt ethics committees could resolve.

Traditionally, health care decisions have been made almost exclusively by physicians; doctors were nominally obliged to share this authority with patients, but the degree to which decision sharing actually occurred rested largely with the particular doctor. The patient was often without authority. Furthermore, only when doctors made serious errors, or when the issues involved moved doctors to invoke court action, were courts involved in decision making. Therefore, doctors, and in rare instances courts, held the real authority over decision-making procedures.

For a variety of reasons, including an awareness of the institution's responsibility for assuring that good decision-making procedures exist,[2] physicians are increasingly collaborating with their patients in making decisions. There is much more disclosure about medicine, medical prognoses, and available options than there was some time ago.[3] By and large, doctors are taking more responsibility for helping patients make decisions that are correct from the patient's perspective.

But there is still excessive liability for errors, and there is very little possibility of correcting errors before their harmful effects have occurred. Especially troubling is the fact that physicians can ignore patients—their need for information, for control, and for input into decisions. It is very difficult for the patient or anyone else to correct physicians' behavior, unless their actions are so outrageous that correction and punishment are sought in court.

On the other hand, doctors who take their obligations regarding decision making seriously find that they have very few guidelines as to what they really ought to be doing. Doctors looking for protocols to help them resolve difficult situations find that there is no format that regularly produces quality decisions. Therefore, physicians are regularly placed at the risk of being second-guessed in court. Physicians do not generally take up the challenge of defining and assuring high-quality decision making. Instead, they look for someone else to decide whether the patient is competent or not, and who should make decisions if the patient is deemed incompetent. In trying to secure help with the responsibility of decision making, physicians generally find their only recourse to be the courts.

## The Problem with Courts

Courts offer a complementary set of difficulties. Involving a judge in the process does not regularly lead to better decision making. First, judges are as likely as physicians to impose their own values, and there is no evidence that this is any better for patients than the imposition of doctors' values. Although there are very good cases marked by careful reasoning, there is also a plethora of very badly decided cases—a situation that seems unlikely to improve if the courts are flooded with a vast new array of cases. Second, the judicial process is very expensive. As an example, consider a recent case in Washington, D.C., involving a patient who needed a simple, uncontested guardianship order (a family member was willing to serve as the guardian). This simplest guardianship proceeding cost $400. Certainly, that $400 could have better served the patient than it did in funding a court process granting her son the authority which in times past he would routinely have been granted without a proceeding.

Also, the court process is, virtually by its nature, slow. Lawyers are very proud when they can bring anything to conclusion within a week —and very few medical circumstances will wait even that long. Furthermore, the court's accountability rests largely upon the fact that its process is public. Contesting someone's competence in court must therefore be a public issue. To contest the appropriateness of the surrogate, all the family's "dirty linen" may have to come into public view. Sometimes that is a substantial cost.

Finally, the court process is intrinsically adversarial. Presenting conflicting points of view, each with a different account of the truth, is supposed to allow a neutral party to see the actual truth. However, at its best, the medical decision-making process is collaborative—it is concerned with mutual obligations rather than competing rights. The imposition of an adversarial process places people at odds, which is likely to distort relationships to such an extent that a more ideal collaborative process becomes impossible.

So, leaving things completely in the hands of doctors without any review has its flaws. And regularly using courts, the only available mechanism for review, has serious flaws. The President's Commission sought an effective and efficient alternative that could serve the patient's needs without imposing so many burdens on all concerned. The appeal of having health care institutions act as responsible parties in this endeavor was obvious. The health care institution is a ready-made moral community, or at least could be. The people present are usually concerned about the patient's welfare, are educated or at least educable about the decision-making process, and can be held accountable for their behavior. They can develop a process to achieve the principled decisions that are the hallmark of court process while maintaining reasonable privacy; they can respond quickly and responsibly to changing circumstances; and they can perform these duties fairly inexpensively.

## Involving the Institution in Decision Making

Social recognition of the responsibilities of health care institutions has been growing over the past few decades. The hospital of 30 or 40 years ago was largely a hotel in which doctors provided treatment. The hospital employed some people with very special skills, mostly nurses and a few other professional groups, but even these were present primarily to see that the hospital worked well and that the doctors' plans were carried out. But the institution itself had the same responsibilities that would apply to a hotel: i.e., to hire well-trained people and to have certain essential items available. Hospitals were certainly not held responsible for decision making, which was entirely the province of doctors.

More recently, hospitals have sometimes been asked to take responsibility.[4] In addition, the pressures are building for hospitals to make tough allocation decisions, which will require them to be active in patient care decisions. Hospitals cannot allow physicians, or any other somewhat independent health care providers, to make decisions as if costs were irrelevant, because hospitals will bear the brunt of the shortfall between costs and collections. The hospital is thus being forced to take a responsible and active role.

In this context the term *hospital* should mean not only acute care hospitals, but all health care institutions, because virtually all institutions are in a morally comparable position. (The institutions most in need of special attention in this realm are long-term care facilities.) The Commission's model of intrainstitutional responsibility for review and regulation of decision making is applicable to all health care institutions.

Medical care has come to be provided predominantly in institutions. The overwhelming majority of patients now die in institutions; and even those who do not die in an institution are likely to have been subject to major treatment decisions made there. Very few people with substantial illnesses have not, at some point, been cared for by an institutional provider. Even the individual practitioner who practices largely outside of hospitals probably identifies strongly with some institution that could be used to assure quality outpatient care. Therefore, having institutions bear the responsibility for decision making offers an obvious advantage.

## THE COMMISSION'S SOLUTION

Despite the preceding discussion, the Commission's recommendations fall short of a wholehearted endorsement of ethics committees.[5] The Commission has recommended that there be a formal procedure for intrainstitutional review of health care decision making. Such a procedure should be available at least for contested and "high-risk" cases, and possibly for other types as well. The procedures should be formal and explicit. The Commission called on hospitals to examine which cases should come before a formal review and which responsibilities should rest with others (most notably courts and doctors).

The Commission recognized many different functions that might be served by an intrainstitutional review process, but did not decide which are most appropriate. Among these possible functions are: (1) to determine what issues are actually central in a particular case; (2) to ensure the reliability of the prognosis that a physician has given; (3) to ensure correct determinations of competence; (4) to judge whether the designated surrogate is best situated to speak for an incompetent patient; (5) to protect the competent patient's authority to decide whether or not to undertake a treatment; and (6) to protect the incompetent patient's interests. This last function would often entail finding and honoring such a patient's advance directives.

Internal review (instead of court involvement) could protect the discretion of all parties concerned. Institutional policies regarding decision making could themselves come under review, as could other community decisions regarding decision making (funding, court cases, public education). Review committees could educate people within the institution and, to some extent, the community. Adequate procedures could guarantee that appropriate cases are taken to outside authorities —the courts and social service agencies. Institutions and their committees can always serve as *amici* if not principals in court cases, and can ensure that all the relevant information is presented to the judge. Finally, ethics committees can provide responsive consideration of the role of costs in health care decision making.

The Commission felt that it would be premature to recommend any one model of internal review mechanism, including the hospital ethics committee such as Dr. Cranford described.[6] Although the Commission cited reasons for believing that such committees may work well, very little data have been published concerning the utility of these committees: the Commission found only five published reports[7] other than its own.[8] The Commission did make the following recommendations: (1) that review be multidisciplinary except when the issue is solely prognosis, in which case the function could be provided by physicians; (2) that, at the very least, it should involve people from different social groups within the institution and, if possible, from the community as well; (3) that it have clear authority within the institution; (4) that its relationship with other parts of the institution be carefully developed and articulated; (5) that it adopt clear procedures as to who can bring a case, who can be present during review, what the institution's stance will be regarding discovery of evidence under court process, and whether publication of summary or individual case results will be allowed; and (6) that every hospital and other institution that sets up a committee (or something of the sort) be concurrently involved in research on how it works, what works best, and what problems it encounters, and share the results of the research with other institutions.

Models other than an ongoing ethics committee may suffice.[9] Some hospitals have been working with ad hoc committees consisting of representatives of the institution's staff who have certain professional backgrounds, rather than naming particular persons. Other institutions might use external review mechanisms, while still others might rely upon internal consultants. No one knows how well those methods work, especially in comparison with regularly established ethics committees.

Some risks attend the establishment of mechanisms for intrainstitutional review, and the absence of data about the import of those risks caused the Commission to stop short of fully endorsing them. For example, routine review might absolve everyone of the responsibility of decision making. The doctor might leave decisions to the committee;

the surrogate might feel that he or she has lost the power to make decisions and rely upon the committee; and a committee, as committees often do, may flounder and never come to a collective decision. If this were to occur, review might ultimately reduce the efficiency of decision making and result in harm to patients. It might also increase costs, especially if the vast majority of decisions are already being made correctly. If regular intrainstitutional review adds another layer of review in these instances, the extra effort may lead to unnecessary costs in both time and money. No one knows how likely that outcome is.

In addition, review might well invade privacy. How will patients feel (and should they be consulted) when their case receives this sort of review? As noted, one of the major problems of going to court is the necessary diminution of the patient's privacy; a similarly undesirable reduction of privacy might occur if the patient's history and situation are reviewed by people other than the patient's care givers. How privacy concerns should be addressed is a very difficult question, and probably varies by state law, since there may be ways to protect some proceedings from discovery.

Furthermore, review might increase legal liabilities for all concerned. Liabilities might arise directly for those who are involved in the review process. For example, if a group of people talked together and decided that Infant Doe[10] should not be treated, they might be susceptible to indictment for conspiracy to commit murder—a possibility that will certainly give people involved with ethics committees some pause! This issue needs to be addressed clearly. Hospitals quite reasonably will be reluctant to perform the review if they are likely thereby to increase their civil, criminal, or financial liability.

These review processes may be so appealing that they will be implemented widely without concurrent research. Then, in five or ten years, one or another of these hazards will materialize and no one will know how best to rectify the problem. From the very beginning, then, there should be a solid commitment to ongoing research on the activities of every committee. The experience of the institutional review boards (IRBs) is very instructive. Most of the research community was eager to have them and there was a clear mechanism to require them. They were quickly established in all sorts of different ways. Even now, however, very little research exists on what IRBs are doing and at what cost. Though the evidence is scant, most observers believe that they are performing important and valuable work. However, there are all sorts of different models whose comparative virtues and problems are unknown. It would have been very instructive if, at the same time the regulation requiring IRBs was imposed, there had been concurrent research on them.

An even greater hazard arises if those involved in ethics committees or other intrainstitutional review processes come to be viewed as ethical experts. In medicine, practitioners are prone to say, "If a renal specialist says that this is XYZ disease of the kidney, that must be right, because he's the expert." The development of ethically sound medical care would be stymied if practitioners were to say, "The ethical expert says that this is an XYZ problem and therefore it's not our concern— the experts are right." Part of the function of these committees must be to educate the whole community so that people can make these decisions more effectively themselves.[11] Practitioners and patients should be able to understand the issues that are at stake rather than relying on a group of moral arbiters. One especially harmful potential effect of relying on experts would be to limit the range of choices offered to patients. If the ethics committee unreasonably considers only one kind of outcome as correct, that fact creates another hurdle that the patient who prefers a different outcome may have to surmount.

Another risk is that ethics committees might become a powerful voice in limiting the consideration of cost. One of the concerns that has been missing from the debate on medical ethics in the past is serious consideration of the fact of limited resources. Ethics committees might help define the legitimate range of cost concerns, but they might also decide that cost is always an illegitimate consideration and become a lobbying force to keep costs from impinging upon patient care. That would be a troublesome move for society, although a potentially comfortable one for the ethics committee.

One of the outcomes of the continuing controversy over Infant Doe regulations may well be that the Department of Health and Human Services (HHS) may begin to look for better ways of solving the problems that arise in medical decision making. HHS could sponsor conferences on the topic, promote information gathering, help support a newsletter, and issue grants on the decision-making process.

On the other hand, HHS could come forward in two weeks with a requirement that every hospital establish an ethics committee, that it be composed of certain types of people, that it meet every other Tuesday, and that it keep records in elite type. Those who are concerned about how review procedures develop need to be attentive to this sort of overregulation because it would stymie growth and innovation.

The Commission did discuss the application of ethics committees and similar review processes to three concrete situations taken up in the report on life-sustaining treatment.[12] The applications were illustrative of the kinds of functions the Commission saw as being appropriate for ethics committees. For permanently unconscious patients, the Commission saw ethics committees as being useful for resolving disputes among care givers and family, and for ascertaining whether the prognosis has been reliably demonstrated. Beyond that, the ethics committee's functions would be (1) to protect the prerogative of the family to make decisions and (2) to establish institutional policy. However, the committee would not be involved in the decision making.

On the other hand, regarding newborns, the Commission said that every case involving foregoing life-sustaining treatment for a newborn should be brought before a formal intrainstitutional review, because these patients are regularly at risk of poor decision making. The Commission recommended including retrospective decisions when there has not been enough time for prospective review. The first issue for the committee to decide is what sort of case it is reviewing, especially to determine whether there is a clearly beneficial treatment available. If there is, the ethics committee should, like the doctor, see that the child receives the treatment. That responsibility includes being a party to court action or child abuse proceedings before an agency. If, however, the only available treatment is futile, then the ethics committee has a role in establishing institutional policy. For example, it might decide that the institution will not provide long-term respirator care for a severely anencephalic child (thereby denying resources to other children who could be saved), or that the institution will not yield to parents' wishes that a child be repetitively resuscitated when the child has an inevitably fatal lesion.

Finally, and perhaps most importantly, the Commission felt that the intrainstitutional review process should define and defend for parents a range of choice in ambiguous cases. Where reasonable people differ on whether treatment might be beneficial, one role of the ethics committee is to decide whether this is the sort of case in which the parents should have the authority to decide. This is a function of ethics committees that is unlikely to be well served in the courts.

When the Commission considered orders against resuscitation, it was discussing a situation that is present only in an institution; that is, only in such a setting would one be faced with an automatic order to resuscitate. Therefore, institutions have a special responsibility to establish policies to protect those patients who should not be resuscitated. The committee should serve to ensure informed policies and adequate review for contested decisions.

These are the considerations that the Commission studied in determining how intrainstitutional review processes should function. Ethics committees may well be the best model. It cannot be overstated that all those involved need to be collecting and publishing data on the functioning of the committees, and establishing forums in which those data can be discussed adequately. Intrainstitutional review boards for research presently operate in only a few hundred universities and other institutions in the country that do clinical research. Ethics committees would be needed in the country's 8,000 hospitals and in most of the 20,000 other health care institutions. The implications for health care costs and the potential danger of establishing erroneous procedures mandate caution for all concerned.

## NOTES

1. PRESIDENT'S COMMISSION FOR THE STUDY OF ETHICAL PROBLEMS IN MEDICINE AND BIOMEDICAL AND BEHAVIORAL RESEARCH, MAKING HEALTH CARE DECISIONS, vol. 1 (Report) and vol. 2 (Empirical Studies of Informed Consent) (U.S. Gov't Printing Office, Washington, D.C.) (October 1982) [hereinafter referred to as MAKING HEALTH CARE DECISIONS] at 187–88.
2. PRESIDENT'S COMMISSION FOR THE STUDY OF ETHICAL PROBLEMS IN MEDICINE AND BIOMEDICAL AND BEHAVIORAL RESEARCH, DECIDING TO FOREGO LIFE-SUSTAINING TREATMENT: ETHICAL, MEDICAL AND LEGAL ISSUES IN TREATMENT DECISIONS (U.S. Gov't Printing Office, Washington, D.C.) (March 1983) [hereinafter referred to as DECIDING TO FOREGO TREATMENT] at 103–6.
3. *See* MAKING HEALTH CARE DECISIONS, *supra* note 1, at 34–36.
4. Darling v. Charleston Community Memorial Hospital, 50 Ill. App. 2d 253, 200 N.E.2d 149 (1964), *aff'd*, 211 N.E.2d 253 (Ill. 1965).
5. *See* DECIDING TO FOREGO TREATMENT, *supra* note 2, at 160–70.
6. Cranford, R. E., Doudera, A. E., ch. 1 of this text.
7. Freedman, B., *One Philosopher's Experience on an Ethics Committee*, HASTINGS CENTER REPORT 11:20 (April 1981); Stalder, G., *Ethical Committees in a Pediatric Hospital*, EUROPEAN JOURNAL OF PEDIATRICS 136:119 (1981); Levine, C., *Hospital Ethics Committees: A Guarded Prognosis*, HASTINGS CENTER REPORT 7:25 (June 1977); Esqueda, K., *Hospital Ethics Committees: Four Case Studies*, THE HOSPITAL MEDICAL STAFF 7:26 (November 1978); Veatch, R., *Hospital Ethics Committees: Is There a Role?*, HASTINGS CENTER REPORT 7:22 (June 1977).
8. Youngner, S. J., *et al.*, *A National Survey of Hospital Ethics Committees*, in DECIDING TO FOREGO TREATMENT, *supra* note 2.
9. DECIDING TO FOREGO TREATMENT, *supra* note 2, at 161.
10. *In re* Infant Doe, No. GU 8204–00 (Cir. Ct. Monroe County, Ind., April 12, 1982), *writ of mandamus dismissed sub nom.* State *ex rel.* Infant Doe v. Baker, No. 482 S 140 (Indiana Supreme Court, May 27, 1982) (case mooted by child's death).
11. *See* Cranford and Doudera, *supra* note 6.
12. DECIDING TO FOREGO TREATMENT, *supra* note 2, at 160–70.

# 3

# Trends in Ethical Decision Making

Stuart A. Wesbury, Jr.

Let me share with you a few basic concerns that we in hospital administration must address. In particular, I am bothered by the focus of ethics committees and by their role in hospitals as perceived by others—that is, institutional ethics committees seem to focus only on the patient and the issues surrounding the individual patient. I suggest that another set of issues is developing that will move us to consider the broader community because of the emerging and greater concern about resource allocation.

Today, the abiding force, the real initiative behind changes in the health industry, is cost containment. This is true because of significant constraints on the number of dollars being spent in the health care system.[1] Decisions about cost containment will have an ethical dimension —for example, a decision concerning which programs we provide and which programs we choose not to provide. More important, the decision may concern the programs that the hospital will stop providing; this decision is anathema to any administrator. These issues are part of the broader picture that we should examine when we consider ethical decision making.

Another of my concerns is that the institution and its governing body must become involved in institutional ethics committees if they are to be effective. In this regard, I urge academics and ethicists to write for journals that are directed toward administrators and members of hospital governing bodies. We need a cross-disciplinary exchange of ideas among persons who have responsibility for ethical decision making.

As we look at the increasing importance of cost containment in hospital administration, it is clear to me that the outlook for the future is not bright. Growing financial pressures on hospitals, ranging from cutbacks in third-party reimbursement and competition to an acute shortage of capital, signal the potential of rationing health care in this country—a very serious issue. As an administrator, I see that today's health care institution is working hard to balance demands from physicians, governments, special interest groups, and the community at large in order to do what is—in the institution's judgment—in the best interests of the patient and the community. The patient is of great concern, but so is the community. We can talk about the patient and about the specifics surrounding his or her case. But soon we will be forced to deal with the broader issue of the interest of the community at large.

What can we as hospital administrators do to meet some of these challenges? I have several suggestions.

First, we must keep in mind that the patient is the only reason for the hospital's existence. We must make sure that full and open communication with the patient occurs. Patients, or their parents or guardians, must be aware of and involved in decisions surrounding their care. Informed consent is the foundation of that patient-provider trust. Our responsibility is to ensure that our patients are informed and that patients' concerns are heard.

In a new journal, an author speaks of patients' growing dissatisfaction with "paternalistic health care providers."[2] We are now in an era of growing health care consumerism. This means that health care providers must aid in the creation of an environment of greater mutual participation. The physician will increasingly act as an "agent, consultant, and information conduit, guiding the individual through the complex health delivery system."[3]

This view is shared by another author in a recent issue of the *New England Journal of Medicine*. He stated that the patient should be given the benefit of the doubt when important decisions are contemplated.[4] That means we must assume that the patient is capable of becoming a full partner in the decision-making process. Thus, health care providers must surrender the prerogative of making life-and-death decisions alone; instead, they will get involved in "the less glamorous and more time-consuming process of exploring options and outcomes."[5] For example, the providers will have to inform patients about how a hospital's policies might limit their choices of treatment. Whether these policies are rooted in religious, moral, or economic concerns, patients and their families need to know about them. In addition, patients and their families need time to make intelligent, informed decisions about their care.

Second, hospital policy must clarify the practices that are or are not acceptable in the institution. Of course, acceptable practice is determined at the highest levels, but all appropriate parties, regardless of their roles in the organization, should be invited to participate in the policy-making process. During this process, we must let our personal and institutional values rise to the surface and become integrated into our decisions.

This participation means more than simply developing mission statements and codes; it means that we must constantly test and confront both our own values and those of our institution. Increasingly, I believe, administrators will take a leadership role in facilitating discussion in their institutions. They will discuss ethical issues openly and frequently, with a variety of people, and they will create forums for the discussion of anticipated ethical problems as well as possible solutions and outcomes.

Above all, hospital administrators must ensure that an organized decision-making process, reflecting multiple interests, exists in their hospitals, simply because no one person or group of people or any one profession can control or dominate this process. This challenge could be answered through a standing institutional ethics committee composed of board members, administrators, physicians, nurses, attorneys, social workers, community representatives, and others.

But this is only one possible solution. Too frequently in our society, we create what we think are solutions and then try to find applications for those solutions in a particular institution without knowing whether there is a real problem in that institution. In developing institutional ethics committees, I am concerned that we develop both expected outcomes and a process that will assure that we logically reach those outcomes. If we were coaches discussing football, it would be silly to say that "T-formations" are the only way you can win football games —or that the "single wing" or the "shotgun" is the best. One must evaluate the situation after defining the problem; then one can decide on the best way to reach one's goals. So, the best answer could be an institutional ethics committee.

Even with a system in place, the administrator has no assurance that ethical decisions will be either simple or automatic. Conflicts are inevitable. Moreover, ethical issues evolve, for they are products of the dynamic nature of technology, changing attitudes, shifting health care needs, and increased fiscal restraint. Even when administrators, hospital committees, or governing bodies resolve ethical issues, these decisions must be reviewed regularly. Values may change, and we must be willing to reassess how these changing values are applied.

No one method, no one set of prescriptions, is effective in every health care institution. Each institution must develop its own processes and procedures, drawing on the resources and input of the community and its board. A correct policy for one hospital may not be appropriate for another. What is imperative is that administration take a leadership role as facilitator and advocate in upholding the values of the institution, safeguarding the rights of patients, and promoting a full and fair discussion of the issues.

But just as the patient is our reason for existence, so the patient must be the final decision maker. Whatever the committee or system, its only purpose is to improve the patient's ability to make better decisions—legal, informed, and able to be implemented. That's our job—and our challenge. Working together, we can meet it.

## NOTES

1. *See* Iglehart, J. K., *The New Era of Prospective Payment for Hospitals*, NEW ENGLAND JOURNAL OF MEDICINE 307(20):1288 (November 11, 1982); Richards, G., *Special Report: Congress Gives Hospitals a Target Rate Per Case*, HOSPITALS 56(20):76 (October 16, 1982).
2. Easthaugh, S. R., *Placing a Value on Life and Limb: The Role of the Informed Consumer*, HEALTH MATRIX 1(1):5, 17 (Winter 1983).
3. *Id.*
4. Kassier, J. P., *Adding Insult to Injury: Usurping Patients' Prerogatives*, NEW ENGLAND JOURNAL OF MEDICINE 308(15):898 (April 14, 1983).
5. *Id.* at 900.

# 4

# The Ethics of
# Institutional Ethics Committees

Robert M. Veatch

Institutional ethics committees deal with ethics. They are created to confront some of the most difficult ethical questions faced by patients and their agents in hospitals and other health care facilities. They often participate in ethical dilemmas faced by physicians, nurses, and other health professional decision makers as well. What quickly becomes apparent to any participant in a hospital ethics committee is that the committees themselves pose ethical questions.

The idea of hospital ethics committees has been with us for over a decade.[1] After this period of development, it makes sense that we pause to see if we can gain some understanding of the ethical mandate that governs these committees and the ethical problems they may confront in bearing out their mission. This, then, is the beginning of an ethic for ethics committees.

Some of the problems are close to the surface. Often, the committees have been created to deal with the problems of caring for terminally ill patients. Any such committee will soon be in the thick of controversies surrounding the ethics of euthanasia—whether there is an ethical difference between stopping a treatment and not starting it in the first place, whether it is as justifiable to stop an IV or antibiotics as to stop some complicated gadget like a ventilator or a hemodialysis machine. Those, of course, are questions that patients, families, and health care professionals faced long before committees ever existed. When a committee speaks on one of these questions, however, it may give a false sense of closure to questions that are really not yet settled in the moral community. It may even relieve other decision makers of a sense of responsibility about the grave questions they face.

In an early article suggesting the idea of ethics committees, San Antonio physician Karen Teel offered as one of the justifications for such committees the fact that the committee might diffuse the awesome burden of responsibility that is placed on an individual decision maker.[2] Actually, the committee might leave no one with the sense that he or she is responsible for the way a patient dies. Upon reflection, it is not clear that such an effect, if it occurs, is good or morally acceptable.

Confidentiality is the second ethical question raised by any committee that deals with individual patient decisions about care. The idea of a hospital ethics committee often conjures up the image of a large, amorphous, often anonymous committee of health professionals and even of laypeople who are reviewing the details of an individual patient's case. Committees may include members from outside the hospital and health care system, who may have access to the patient's record. Confidentiality problems are likely to arise at two points: when the committee gains access to information about the patient and when the committee approaches family members and others for clarification about the decision. All of the contemporary professional and lay codes of medical ethics are in agreement that confidentiality is a right of the patient or the agent for the patient.[3] That means that committee members should have no access to information about a patient's case without the patient's approval, and that any scheme that involves hospital ethics committees without the knowledge of the patients is a clear violation of this moral standard. There was a day when physicians could violate confidentiality when they thought in good faith it was in the interest of the patient to do so. Some have interpreted the Hippocratic Oath in that way, but every current code now rejects that move. Moreover, there is logically no ethical way that the committee can consult with the family about decisions for a patient unless the patient or the patient's agent has approved of the disclosure of information about the patient's case. Hospital ethics committees, like computerized information-retrieval systems, should be added to the list of newfangled technologies that pose new kinds of threats to the confidentiality of the patient-physician relationship.

These are important ethical problems, but ones that in principle can be overcome. The committee should be alert to the possibility that it may have the effect of lessening the sense of responsibility of patients and health professionals for the moral decisions they make, but a committee sensitive to this problem need not have that effect. Committees need to be aware that when they gain information about individual cases they are gaining privileged information. They have the right of access only with the patient's permission and can transmit it to others, such as members of the patient's family, only with further permission. Still, in principle, these are ethical requirements that a good committee should be able to meet.

Hospital ethics committees also raise ethical questions at a somewhat different, more profound level. Any institutional ethics committee, if it is to function well, must understand consciously and explicitly how its mission relates to what I shall refer to as a theory of medical ethics. It must have in place, and must consciously orient to, a set of general ethical principles that will guide its actions and shape its decision making. The closest cousin to the institutional ethics committee, the institutional review board (IRB) for the protection of human subjects, must by federal regulation adopt a set of ethical principles under which it operates.[4] The same kind of formal commitment to a set of principles should be required for an IEC. For ethics committees, in fact, I want to go even further. I want to suggest that it will be impossible for an ethics committee to carry out its various tasks without some ethical frame of reference. When we examine how a set of ethical principles might operate, I think we will quickly discover that the tasks that are often assigned to ethics committees are simply incompatible with any plausible set of ethical principles that a committee might adopt. More critically, and more practically, once a committee has adopted a set of principles, it may discover, if it constitutes itself to fulfill one set of tasks oriented to certain ethical mandates, that it will by that very fact be incapable of fulfilling other tasks. Let me suggest what such an ethical framework might look like and then examine the impact it would have on the way the committee constitutes itself and goes about its tasks.

## ETHICAL PRINCIPLES FOR HOSPITAL ETHICS COMMITTEES

Anyone analyzing the nature of an ethical framework within which an ethics committee might operate faces an immediate problem. Some people working in medical ethics have begun with the assumption that a professional group may generate its own code of ethics or ethical principles. This presents serious problems, however. Professional groups may well hold unique positions on the ethics of professional obligation that are not shared by laypeople with whom the professionals will be interacting. Any unilateral imposition of a code or set of principles may disenfranchise the patient population, the very group that will be most affected by the ethical code being adopted. Moreover, a philosopher or professional analyst of ethical systems is not in a much better position to articulate a code or set of principles for the lay-professional relation. He or she may also be part of a special tradition or hold special commitments. This has forced many to the conclusion that the structure of the ethical framework for a medical ethic must be generated by a complex process involving the active participation of both laypeople and health professionals. It must be the result of an understanding, a contract, or a covenant between laypeople and professionals established in three different stages.[5] It must begin with an understanding about the most basic moral commitments operating in our community. At the second stage, there has to be an understanding between laypeople and professionals about the nature of the roles that each party will assume; and, finally, there must be room for maneuvering at the level of individual decision making where both the layperson and the professional are given maximum freedom to be guided by their own consciences. This means that in principle I will not be able to set out one set of ethical principles that will be definitive for all hospital ethics committees. I would assume, for example, that the ethics committee at the local Catholic hospital might operate on a moral mandate that differed somewhat from that of the city hospital or the Jewish hospital. Still, given our general knowledge of ethical theory as it has evolved over the last decade, we can say something about the general content of any set of ethical principles governing the work of a hospital ethics committee.

It seems clear that any such set of principles will include the recognition that the health care team, including the ethics committee, should strive to serve the welfare of the patient. This is simply good old-fashioned Hippocratic ethics.[6] What is new in research work in medical ethics in the last decade, however, is the recognition that the old Hippocratic ethic of benefiting the patient must be placed within severe constraints. Two important kinds of ethical constraints have emerged. First, if the only moral mandate were to serve the welfare of the individual isolated patient, several important medical activities would immediately be immoral. Research medicine, where the objective is to serve the welfare of society more generally, would be ethically unacceptable. The institutional review board for the protection of human subjects must be an example of a kind of hospital-based ethics committee that supplements the old Hippocratic ethic with a more general principle of beneficence that takes into account the welfare of others in the society.

There is a second, more substantial, kind of limit to be placed on the old Hippocratic ethic of patient benefit. We have increasingly recognized in medical ethics that even in cases where there is no potential conflict between the welfare of the individual and the welfare of society, moral limits must be placed on the idea that health care professionals should always benefit their patients. To paraphrase the opening of a now famous book by Robert Nozick, patients have rights and there are certain things that health care professionals and hospital ethics committees cannot do to them without violating their rights.[7] Increasingly, a consensus is emerging that there is a small set of ethical principles that must supplement—indeed, take precedence over—the principle that we must serve the welfare of the individual and the welfare of society in individual cases. The *Belmont Report* of the National Commission for the Protection of Human Subjects is the only official public document at the federal level ever to endorse a set of ethical principles. In addition to beneficence, it acknowledges respect for persons, including autonomy, as a second principle, and justice in the distribution of resources as a third principle.[8] A number of other people would add the principles of truth telling and promise keeping—notions that the National Commission apparently includes under the rubric of respect for persons.[9] Finally, I have argued elsewhere that the principle of avoiding killing human beings has to be understood as an additional independent principle of medical morality.[10]

There will be some debate at the edges about precisely which principles should show up on any such list. Controversy will continue over the exact content of the list. What is striking, however, is that there is a substantial and very broad consensus that some such list is the basis for medical morality. Moreover, that list includes beneficence, doing good for people and avoiding evil, but it also includes certain other important moral considerations such as autonomy and justice—and probably truth telling, promise keeping, and avoiding killing.

There is also continuing disagreement about why these items are chosen and exactly what function they serve. Some people, now referred to in the jargon as rule utilitarians, say that these principles are fundamental characteristics of actions that deserve high claim on us because they tend to produce good consequences.[11] The deontologists among us say that these are inherently right-making characteristics of actions, whether or not they produce good consequences. That tension can and probably will remain in the future of debate in medical ethical theory. What is important is that both camps agree on some such short list. They must also agree that these considerations be given substantial weight in any medical ethical deliberation. To shift language somewhat, they suggest correlative rights claims that people have that are to be given substantial independent ethical weight. None of these considerations can be overridden by mere ad hoc situational claims that the consequences for the patient or for society would be better if these rights were overlooked in a particular case.

While not everyone will accept this kind of framework for an ethic for ethics committees, the notion that there are basic ethical principles and rights derived from them is a view held very widely in our society. It is, in effect, the moral framework used by just about everyone writing in medical ethics today. It is the framework used by our courts when they adjudicate disputes about the rights of patients, health care professionals, and society. It is also the framework used in all of the relevant American codes of health professional ethics. Such a framework has been the basis of the American Nurses' Association code for many years.[12] In June of 1980, when the American Medical Association revised its principles of ethics, it also abandoned its more traditional framework and began using rights language and referring to autonomy, honesty, and other core ethical principles as if they were to be given this fundamental independent status.[13] When a hospital ethics committee decides to adopt a basic set of ethical principles for its deliberations, when it consults with patients, health care professionals, and members of the community for guidance about what its core ethical framework ought to be, it will adopt this kind of set of ethical principles. The real question then becomes, what does this set of ethical principles mean when an institutional ethics committee sits down to work?

## ETHICAL PRINCIPLES AND THE
## TASKS OF ETHICS COMMITTEES

One possibility is that a hospital-based ethics committee could have before it this full agenda of ethical principles, and would move from task to task, balancing autonomy and justice on one occasion, truth telling and patient welfare on another. That turns out, however, in the eyes of most people, to create real, probably insurmountable problems. It is the nature of ethical problems that different ethical tasks will emphasize different ethical principles, depending on the fine points of one's ethical theory and how different principles are related to one another. An ethical problem may be one primarily of autonomy or of justice or of truth telling. To the extent that it is a real problem, it will often involve a conflict between two or more principles. Normally, however, the full range of ethical principles need not come into play.

The problem is related to one that Weberian sociologists would recognize as the problem of legitimation. If an institutional ethics committee is to function effectively within a health care setting, it will have to be conscious of its legitimation, of its claim to be taken seriously by virtue of having the appropriate skill and authority to deal with the tasks at hand. Should a small concerned group within the hospital simply appoint itself to be the institutional ethics committee and proceed to press its ethical agenda on the institution, such a committee is likely to face serious problems of legitimation. Patients and health care professionals are likely to ask who these people are and where they think they got the authority to make pronouncements on ethical issues. For the institutional ethics committee to be viewed as legitimate, that is, as having appropriate authority to carry out its function, it will have to be able to demonstrate that it has the necessary skills and moral stature for the task at hand. It will have to be able to show that it was duly authorized for this task by those holding the authority for the decisions to be made, whether that be the patient, the health professional, the administration, or the general public. It will also have to show that it can avoid any serious conflicts of interest that would compromise its ability to carry out its task.

I am increasingly convinced that institutional ethics committees can plausibly be legitimated for only one ethical task at a time. Some committees may be constituted for the purpose of assisting patients in making autonomous decisions. Others may take on the ethical responsibility of promoting justice in resource allocation. Still others might face the complex task of balancing the welfare of the patient and the welfare of the society in decisions about research involving human subjects. It is very difficult, if not impossible, for a single institutional ethics committee to have more than one ethics agenda.

The idea of committee legitimation is closely related to the question of to whom the committee is accountable. If the committee is accountable to physicians on a hospital staff, then the committee will take on the ethics agenda of that medical staff. It will be viewed as legitimate to the extent that the physicians are convinced that it is really helping the medical staff make decisions based on its ethical framework. On the other hand, if the committee is accountable to patients, then it will turn to patients for its legitimation. Other committees might see themselves as accountable to the administration of the hospital, the board of trustees, or the broader community that has created the hospital, whether that be a city government or a church.

In order to show how these things might play themselves out in the different ethical tasks of institutional committees, let me take three significantly different ethical mandates for ethics committees, each of which requires a different ethical principle as the guiding principle for the committee's work. These three different ethical mandates could cut across the four major functions of committees discussed in this volume: education, consultation, guideline formation, and case review.

We can structure different possible mandates for hospital ethics committees by looking more carefully at the implications of the ethical principles that place constraints on the traditional Hippocratic ethic that the health care professional is to act always so as to benefit his or her patient. These constraints, which were discussed earlier, suggest ethical mandates for possible ethics committees. One of those constraints would remain patient-centered. It insists that those in clinical roles recognize both the rights and the welfare of the patient as primary. It would see clinicians as operating under a mandate of respecting persons—promoting their autonomy, keeping promises, dealing with them truthfully, and so forth. Thus, one ethical mission for ethics committees might simply be to extend this patient-centered ethical mandate, acting so as to promote the rights of the patient.

## AUTONOMY AND INDIVIDUAL PATIENT DECISIONS

No matter how much we would like to escape it, it is clear that the first task people think of for an institutional ethics committee is participation in individual patient care decisions. The usual problem is that of a terminally ill patient where the ethical question is whether it is appropriate to stop or continue treatment. Exactly the same moral structure would apply for any other kind of individual-case-oriented clinical decision. The early suggestions for hospital ethics committees, such as those made by Karen Teel and by the Massachusetts General Hospital Committee, saw the committees participating in clinical decisions, either making the actual decision or providing advice and counsel to the decision makers.[14] In the simple and straightforward case these are fundamentally patient-centered problems. We want to know not only how to promote the welfare of the patient, but also how to do right by the patient. If we begin by considering the competent patient or the formerly competent patient whose wishes are known, these are fundamentally problems of autonomy and the related ethical principles needed to preserve autonomy—that is, truth telling and promise keeping. If there is an ethical problem at all, it is whether the health care professional or anyone else is ever justified in infringing upon the autonomy of the individual patient as a decision maker about his own health care. I am for the moment not considering cases where we might want to restrict medical care for purposes of conserving scarce resources, but only those cases where the welfare of the patient is the decisive consideration. The ethical problem is one of whether some other decision maker might, on paternalistic grounds, attempt to promote the welfare of the patient in violation of the patient's own autonomy. I take it as a conclusion of both law and ethics resulting from the last decade's debate that there is considerable agreement now that in such a simple case the principle of autonomy must dominate. The competent patient has the right to consent to treatment or refuse treatment on any grounds whatsoever, provided that treatment is offered for the patient's own good.[15] Thus, one possible ethical mandate for a committee is to be patient-centered, not focusing exclusively on the welfare of the patient in Hippocratic fashion, but on the rights of the patient, as well as on helping the patient preserve his or her autonomy in decision making.

The implications for an institutional ethics committee are radical. If the principle of autonomy is the dominant ethical principle, and the patient is the primary decision maker, then the institutional ethics committee for this kind of case must be accountable to the patient and must function as the agent of the patient, helping the patient clarify available alternatives and the ethical justifications for and against the treatment alternatives under consideration.

Several implications follow immediately from this conceptualization of the task as one of promoting autonomy. First, any committee that enters a patient's case without the knowledge of the patient is surely in violation of its mandate. If the health care professional, the physician, nurse, chaplain, or social worker, believes that the case is complex enough to require assistance from an ethics committee, that individual should approach the patient and ask the patient for permission to bring the committee in contact with the patient.

Second, the composition of the committee should be governed by the task at hand. People should be placed on the committee for their skills in counseling and analyzing ethical alternatives and in clarifying to the patient the medical and social implications of alternative therapies. Since patients are unique and operate with quite distinctive systems of beliefs and values, a standing committee at the hospital may discover that some of its members should step aside to be replaced by trusted counselors and advisors whom the patient might introduce to the committee. For example, if the standing committee included the hospital chaplain, it might be appropriate for the chaplain to step aside in favor of the patient's own clergyperson so that the spiritual counsel received could be based upon the patient's religious heritage.

Third, insofar as the promotion of autonomy is the ethical mission of the institutional ethics committee, it should be clear that in principle it is not possible to create a protocol that would provide substantive guidance for hospital staff about when to treat or when to stop treatment. The old Massachusetts General Hospital scheme that would classify all patients in four treatment groups solely on the basis of diagnosis and prognosis makes no sense.[16] Attempting to classify all patients solely on the basis of medical criteria violates the autonomy of the patient. Likewise, any protocol to decide which patients should be resuscitated would be ethically unacceptable if that protocol attempted to make substantive judgments based solely on the medical criteria of diagnosis and prognosis. Any guidelines created for institutional ethics committees, insofar as they are performing the task of promoting the autonomy of the patient, will necessarily be procedural. The guidelines might indicate who should be consulted, at what points patients should be asked to consent or refuse to consent to DNR and "no-code" orders, and so on. The guidelines should never, however, spell out substantively which patients to treat and which patients not to treat.

JUSTICE, SOCIAL ETHICS, AND
RESOURCE ALLOCATION DECISIONS

A second, radically different task is sometimes envisioned for an institutional ethics committee. It requires the abandonment of the exclusively patient-centered perspective. The second kind of ethical constraint on the Hippocratic ethic of benefiting the patient grows out of social considerations of the welfare of others in the society and the promotion of justice in the distribution of goods. A committee at New Britain, Connecticut, General Hospital was formed on the basis of these concerns.[17] Suppose, for example, that a hospital needed to decide whether to spend a large bequest to build an expanded intensive care unit or to open a walk-in, holistic preventive medicine clinic. This is the kind of question that raises ethical issues that might be referred to an institutional ethics committee. It is obvious, however, that the ethical principle of autonomy will not get us very far. Presumably, patients who are candidates for an ICU would favor the intensive care unit, whereas those in the local community who are active promoters of holistic health care would autonomously decide for the preventive medicine clinic. An institutional ethics committee that takes on these kinds of questions is functioning in the realm of the ethical principles of justice and social welfare.

The same kind of ethical question arises when a committee is asked to participate in decisions about allocation of scarce medical beds or to create guidelines about such allocation. These questions cannot be answered by asking individual patients and by assisting them in expressing their autonomous decisions. It is important to realize that this ethical mandate, rooted in the principles of justice and social welfare, would not necessarily limit a committee to larger questions of hospital policy and macro-allocation. A justice problem would arise if an ethics committee were asked to participate in policy-making decisions about when to limit expensive but marginal medical care for a terminally ill patient. For example, whether to permit a 93-year-old comatose patient in end-stage renal failure to be dialyzed is not a question to be answered under the rubric of the principle of autonomy; it is a problem of justice. The problem for an ethics committee is whether it can take on the patient-centered tasks of promoting the rights and welfare of the patient and simultaneously be expected to make social ethics judgments based on justice and social welfare in which the rights and welfare of the individual patients must be compromised. It is sometimes maintained that individuals can operate from time to time under two different moral mandates, shifting hats, as it were, as the role dictates. A physician may, for example, be patient-centered while delivering clinical care and then abandon the patient-centered perspective when administering a clinic or research program. Others have argued that it is extremely difficult psychologically for individuals to shift moral mandates in this way. It is, in fact, impossible to act faithfully on both mandates at the same time.

If it is difficult for an individual to shift ethical principles, it is even more difficult for a committee—a corporate person—to do so. If an ethics committee is to take on these questions of justice and social welfare, it must be accountable to a much larger social unit. It needs to be accountable to the hospital as an institution and, ultimately, to the moral community to whom the hospital itself is accountable, that is, to a government or church or other sponsoring agency.

An ethics committee that is to take on these questions of justice and social welfare will require skills different from those required of a committee whose ethical mandate is to further patient autonomy. The committee will need not only expertise in the technical aspects of medicine and nursing involved in the decision, but also the capacity to represent the ethical and other values of the group to which the committee is accountable—the government, church, or other sponsoring community. By contrast, a committee whose purpose is to facilitate autonomous patient choice has much less reason to be so representative of the sponsoring group. In fact, for choices rooted in the moral principle of autonomy we could say that if the committee successfully reflects the moral consensus of the community and thereby entices the patient into a choice based on that consensus, then it has failed. The committee charged with the responsibility of basing choices on justice and social welfare, on the other hand, may not want to simply mirror the community values; rather, the committee must be very conscious of those values and should articulate its sense of what is just when communicating with the community.

I am forced to the conclusion that it is extremely difficult, if not impossible, for one committee to work under the conflicting mandates of promoting patient-centered rights and promoting justice in the distribution of resources. At the very least, if the committee sees as its task the placing of limits on patients' rights and welfare in cases where justice requires devoting scarce resources to others, the patient has to be informed that that is the committee's conception of its task.

An IRB for protecting human subjects is similar in many ways to ethics committees involved in social welfare determinations. It is clear that its sole ethical responsibility is not—in spite of its name—the protection of human subjects. If that were its only task it could simply ban all nontherapeutic research and thereby provide maximum subject protection. It must trade off the welfare of the subject against the welfare of the society, determine whether subjects are treated justly, and decide whether the risks of research so violate the ethic of the institution that the collective moral sense cannot tolerate them. This is social ethics much like the resource allocation questions in hospital policy planning, hospital bed allocation, and cost containment. The IRB (rather than the institutional ethics committee dealing with individual clinical decisions emphasizing the principle of autonomy) might be a better committee for these problems. On the other hand, while the perspective may be similar, the IRB may require different specialized skills—expertise in research methodology, statistics, and the like. In the end a social ethics committee may be as different from an IRB in its ethical task and skill requirements as it is from the clinically oriented committee whose ethical mandate is promotion of autonomy.

### INCOMPETENTS AND PATIENT-CENTERED BENEFICENCE COMMITTEES

This drives us to a rather startling conclusion. There is virtually no area of work for which a committee should take as its mandate making a choice that will most benefit the patient. Promotion of patient autonomy is one legitimate ethical mandate. Much committee education work will be justified under this rubric, as will be counseling with patients and families as well as with health professionals. Promotion of justice and social welfare is also a legitimate ethical mandate for some institutional ethics committees. Neither of these types of committees, however, should see itself as making substantive decisions to benefit individual patients.

There is, however, one type of committee involvement where patient-centered welfare might appear to be the real ethical mission. This occurs in cases where someone has to make individual patient care decisions and the patient is simply incompetent to participate as an autonomous decision maker: where the patient is too sick, too young, or too senile. Here someone else must make a decision. In those cases where we have no idea what the patient would prefer—when the patient has not expressed himself or herself while competent—the only basis for the decision is what someone else considers to be best for the welfare of the patient. Is it here, finally, that the institutional ethics committee is able to act on the classical Hippocratic principle of doing what it can to try to benefit the patient? Perhaps here it finally can, but only in a most attenuated way.

Normally, someone is designated to be the agent of an incompetent patient. By a law just passed in the state of Virginia, any competent person may designate someone for this role.[18] By law in several jurisdictions, the next of kin is the presumed agent in cases where no one has been so designated. In other cases, such as that of a parent of a minor child, there is a presumption of guardianship whereby the agent—but not necessarily an ethics committee—has the task of attempting to make a decision that will serve the interest of the patient. This patient agent, however, does not have unlimited discretion. As in the case of the Jehovah's Witness parent attempting to refuse to consent to a life-saving blood transfusion, any interested party has the right to seek judicial review to determine if the agent is being reasonable. Physicians or hospital administrators often take on this task, not by acting directly on what they determine to be the patient's best interest, but by attempting to get court authorization to have someone else legitimated to give the consent.

The present arrangement is admittedly a bit chaotic. Anyone may seek review. If an individual physician chooses not to do so, however, there has been no due process and his or her judgment may be idiosyncratic. It might be good to have a committee responsible specifically for determining whether or not to seek judicial review. In such a role the committee would at least indirectly be acting out the ethical principle of promoting the welfare of the patient. It would not have the authority to authorize reversal of the agent's decision, but it would have formal responsibility for taking the first step to see whether the courts would reverse it. The committee might appear to be making this decision on the basis of the ethical principle of attempting to promote the incompetent patient's welfare. That is certainly the ethical charge to the parent or other agent who is the initial decision maker. While the committee would evaluate the case in terms of the patient's welfare, it is clear that it would not want to seek judicial review at every point at which the agent's decision appeared to deviate from the best interest of the patient. The deviation would have to appear to be substantial; it would have to be intolerable. Otherwise, we would have committees, and eventually courts, second-guessing parents on every decision they make. The agent's decision would have to appear to be beyond the realm of reason.[19] Thus, while the agent for the patient would strive to choose what is in the patient's best interest, a committee (or an individual health professional) would seek to initiate review only if the agent's decision appeared to be beyond the limits of reason.

A related question is whether the committee could be given quasi-judicial authority to overrule the agent or to affirm the agent's decision, thus granting legal protection against charges of neglect. While such an arrangement may appear attractive, it poses some problems. The committee at best will reflect the moral consensus of the institution and its sponsors. That may not be the same, however, as the moral consensus of the broader community. In fact, it is conceivable that a small minority of physicians could become aligned with a small minority of parents and other agents in approving decisions that most reasonable people would take to be seriously contrary to the patient's interest. If those physicians were clustered in a small number of hospitals, it is possible that a committee (even if it were representative of the medical staff) would also express deviant moral judgments. If even a dozen hospitals nationally had committees that routinely approved grossly deviant decisions, and if agents and professionals favoring grossly deviant decisions were clustered together at those hospitals, serious ethical infringement on the rights and welfare of patients could occur.

If the committee were so constituted that it could reflect the reasonable judgment of the community, a judgment by the committee not to have an agent's decision reviewed by the court could be taken as supportive evidence that the parents were acting within the realm of reason. Here at last the committee might begin to approach the ethical mission of making a decision based on concern for the welfare of the patient.

## CONCLUSION

Here, then, we might have the beginnings of an ethic for ethics committees. Such an ethic will not only have to deal with more mundane problems of euthanasia, confidentiality, and committee integrity, but will also have to determine whether it is dealing with decisions that raise problems primarily of autonomy, of justice and social welfare, or of patient benefit. For the most part the traditional committee involved in terminal care clinical cases will have as its ethical responsibility the promotion of patient autonomy. In other cases the ethical issues will concern justice and social welfare. Only in those rare cases where the patient is incompetent and the patient's agent appears to have exceeded the limits of reason will a committee possibly find for itself a limited role in making a decision to try to benefit the patient. Even here it will not be to directly overrule the patient's agent, but to determine whether the hospital should initiate a formal judicial review of that decision. To remain clear about these diverging ethical responsibilities, institutional ethics committees ought to begin thinking about adopting a set of ethical principles to guide their work, and they ought to determine which of those principles should govern the particular tasks they are undertaking.

## NOTES

1. Veatch, R. M., *Choosing Not to Prolong Dying*, MEDICAL DIMENSIONS (December 1972) at 8, 10; R. M. VEATCH, DEATH, DYING AND THE BIOLOGICAL REVOLUTION: OUR LAST QUEST FOR RESPONSIBILITY (Yale University Press, New Haven, Connecticut) (1976) at 60–61, 173–76; Veatch, R. M., *Hospital Ethics Committees: Is There a Role?*, HASTINGS CENTER REPORT 7(3):22–25 (June 1977).

2. Teel, K., *The Physician's Dilemma—A Doctor's View: What the Law Should Be,* BAYLOR LAW REVIEW 27:6, 9 (Winter 1975).

3. R. M. VEATCH, A THEORY OF MEDICAL ETHICS (Basic Books, New York) (1981); T. L. BEAUCHAMP, J. F. CHILDRESS, PRINCIPLES OF BIOMEDICAL ETHICS, 2d ed. (Oxford University Press, New York) (1983) at 331–32; *World Medical Association, Declaration of Geneva, reprinted in* ENCYCLOPEDIA OF BIOETHICS, vol. 4 (W. T. Reich, ed.) (The Free Press, New York) (1978) at 1749; MEDICAL ETHICS (British Medical Association, London) (1974) at 3.

4. Protection of Human Subjects, Basic Health and Human Services Policy for the Protection of Human Research Subjects, 45 C.F.R. §46.103 (9) (1) (1982).

5. *See* VEATCH, *supra* note 3, at 108–38.

6. The Oath of Hippocrates states, "I will follow that method of treatment which, according to my ability and judgement, I consider for the benefit of my patients, and abstain from whatever is deleterious and mischievous."

7. Robert Nozick's formulation of this idea is as follows: "Individuals have rights, and there are things no person or group may do to them [without violating their rights]." R. NOZICK, ANARCHY, STATE, AND UTOPIA (Basic Books, New York) (1974) at ix.

8. THE NATIONAL COMMISSION FOR THE PROTECTION OF HUMAN SUBJECTS OF BIOMEDICAL AND BEHAVIORAL RESEARCH, THE BELMONT REPORT: ETHICAL PRINCIPLES AND GUIDELINES FOR THE PROTECTION OF HUMAN SUBJECTS OF RESEARCH (U.S. Gov't Printing Office, Washington, D.C.) (1978) at 4–10.

9. VEATCH, *supra* note 3, at 179–84, 214–22.

10. *Id.* at 227–49.

11. BEAUCHAMP, CHILDRESS, *supra* note 3, at 30–33.

12. AMERICAN NURSES' ASSOCIATION, CODE FOR NURSES WITH INTERPRETIVE STATEMENTS (Kansas City, Missouri) (1976) at 1, 4, 6.

13. BEAUCHAMP, CHILDRESS, *supra* note 3, at 331–32.

14. Teel, *supra* note 2; Critical Care Committee of the Massachusetts General Hospital, *Optimum Care for Hopelessly Ill Patients,* NEW ENGLAND JOURNAL OF MEDICINE 295(7):362–64 (August 12, 1976) [hereinafter referred to as Critical Care Committee].

15. Stephenson, S. A., *The Right to Die: A Proposal for Natural Death Legislation,* UNIVERSITY OF CINCINNATI LAW REVIEW 49:228–43 (1980); Cantor, N. L., *A Patient's Decision to Decline Life-Saving Medical Treatment: Bodily Integrity versus the Preservation of Life,* RUTGERS LAW REVIEW 26:228–64 (1973).

16. *See* Critical Care Committee, *supra* note 14. For similar criteria of New York's Mount Sinai Hospital, *see* Kirchner, M., *How Far to Go Prolonging Life: One Hospital's System,* MEDICAL ECONOMICS 53:70 (July 12,1976).

17. Esqueda, K., *Hospital Ethics Committees: Four Case Studies,* THE HOSPITAL MEDICAL STAFF 7:30 (November 1978).

18. "Natural Death Act of Virginia" signed into law by Governor Robb on March 28, 1983. Virginia Code, Section 54–325.8:1 (1983) states: "[T]he General Assembly hereby declares that the laws of the Commonwealth of

Virginia shall recognize the right of a competent adult to make an oral or written declaration instructing his physician to withhold or withdraw life-prolonging procedures or to designate another to make the treatment decision for him, in the event such person is diagnosed as suffering from a terminal condition."

19. For a development of the "limits of reason" concept and its role in overriding agent decisions, see Veatch, R. M., *The Limits of Guardian Treatment Refusal: The Standard of Reasonableness*, AMERICAN JOURNAL OF LAW & MEDICINE 9(4): 427 (Winter 1984); PRESIDENT'S COMMISSION FOR THE STUDY OF ETHICAL PROBLEMS IN MEDICINE AND BIOMEDICAL AND BEHAVIORAL RESEARCH, DECIDING TO FOREGO LIFE-SUSTAINING TREATMENT: ETHICAL, MEDICAL AND LEGAL ISSUES IN TREATMENT DECISIONS (U.S. Gov't Printing Office, Washington, D.C.) (1983) at 136. The Commission concluded that in situations in which no consensus as to decision exists, the surrogate should "retain discretion to choose among a range of acceptable choices."

# 5

## Legal Aspects of Ethics Committees

George J. Annas

Ethics committees have arisen in response to new dilemmas in health care—what Guido Calabresi calls "tragic choices."[1] Previously, these dilemmas were nonexistent; the technology that underlies them had not been developed or we were constrained by law. But when the dilemmas arose, committees seemed one way to address them.

The first committees that might be termed ethics committees were set up by statutes to review abortion decisions in the 1960s.[2] At that time most states had statutes that forbade abortions. In some, an exception was made if a hospital abortion committee found that the pregnant woman's life was in danger.[3]

The next kind of committee to appear was the dialysis committee. In Seattle and at least seven other cities, lay committees were established to allocate dialysis machines by deciding which of the candidates for lifesaving hemodialysis should get it.[4] This rationing decision was not based on a general theory of justice. Rather, the notion was that some people may be more "worthy" than others to receive dialysis, and that the individual's worthiness probably should not be judged by the physician alone. As with rationales for current ethics committees, diffusion of responsibility was high on the list. As one physician member put it, "It's a lot more comfortable to play only one-fifth God, to share these decisions with other people."[5]

Another type of committee formed almost contemporaneously with the kidney dialysis committees was the institutional review board (IRB). IRBs have existed in some form since the early 1960s to review protocols for proposed research on humans, and were the subject of federal regulations[6] several years before the Karen Ann Quinlan case.[7]

More recently, ethics committees have been used in other settings, some of which involve experimental treatments. For example, two states, Oregon and California, have statutes that mandate multidisciplinary review of every person proposed to undergo psychosurgery.[8] In some individual hospitals, like Boston City Hospital, committees were used in the early 1970s to review proposed cases of psychosurgery. A similar problematic example was the procedure developed to select the recipient of the artificial heart in Utah.[9] Before Dr. Barney Clark received his artificial heart, he was personally reviewed, as were his medical and family histories, by a committee which included the surgeon, a member of the IRB, and a social worker.

Committees in one form or another have been used in medical decision making for more than two decades. What all these "ethics" committees have in common is that they are used in situations in which people feel uncomfortable. Many people, for example, feel uneasy making decisions that involve a new procedure or technology. The main role of ethics committees, at least in the past, has been to reduce the anxiety of the health care providers and hospital administrators. These committees thereby provide what some call "ethical comfort." I like that term. It implies that we somehow feel better about a decision if an "ethics committee" (whatever we call it) agrees that the patient should receive, or stop receiving, a treatment. In the wake of Judge Gessell's ruling on the Baby Doe notices,[10] for example, many newspapers published editorials urging the federal government to stop encouraging use of the hotline and instead to rely on ethics committees to review problem cases in neonatal intensive care units.[11]

## COMMITTEE ROLES: PROTECTING INSTITUTION AND PATIENTS

Committee roles can be defined in many different ways—for example, on ethical principles: autonomy, justice, helping the patient. I think the best way to approach an understanding of ethics committees, however, is to categorize them on the basis of their primary function, a taxonomy that is a bit different from Robert Veatch's.[12] Their primary function is usually either to protect the institution (and the people who work at the institution) or to protect patients. We have seen both kinds, although the ones designed to protect institutions are more prevalent.

The first question is: What do institutions need protection against? The answer is primarily protection against legal liability. The institution or its staff or employees may be liable in criminal or civil law for certain actions. An example of this kind of committee is the one approved by the New Jersey Supreme Court in the Karen Ann Quinlan case, which allows the physicians and the hospital to arrive at a decision to terminate treatment with legal immunity.[13] The abortion committees were established for similar reasons, i.e., to prevent any criminal liability on the part of physicians for performing abortions. Such committees had as their primary function the protection of the institution. It is a legitimate function, but one cannot accurately label it an "ethics" committee; it is really a "risk management" or "liability control" committee.

The second kind of committee is one in which individuals are so uncomfortable about the patients in their institution that they set up a committee to help protect them. One example is the patients' rights committees established by institutions for the mentally retarded.[14] Other examples are legal services committees and other types of committees established by institutions for mentally ill patients. The institution's rationale for these committees is that they have populations at special risk who, because of their vulnerability, need extra protection.

In summary, committees have historically been set up with the primary purpose of reducing anxiety in the hospital staff either with regard to their own liability, or with regard to the way they feel about taking care of particularly vulnerable patients.

## COMMITTEE GOALS

To determine what kind of a committee to set up, or who will be on it, or what kind of authority it will have, or what kind of procedures the committee should follow, we must first articulate the goals of the committee.

Generally the goal of all these committees is to modify behavior in some way: to encourage the staff to share information with patients; to develop standards upon which decisions should be made, such as orders not to resuscitate and brain-death standards; to make decisions on whether to remove life-support systems in individual cases; or to decide on certain allocations either on a "micro" level (e.g., Johnny Jones will not receive open-heart surgery at this hospital) or on a "macro" level (e.g., this hospital will not perform open-heart surgery). The goal of the committee will depend upon what the institution wants. But one committee cannot accomplish all of these functions. Different agendas require different types of committees with different procedures and different compositions.

The second consideration is how these committees can actually change the behavior of staff members. Behavioral theorists posit that there are three ways to change human behavior. The first is to convince individuals that changing their behavior is in their own best interest. This is almost impossible to do. It is like telling somebody that he or she is a bad driver. It is very insulting to suggest that someone doesn't know what his or her own best interests are, and one can seldom change behavior that way.

The second way to alter behavior is to change the norms of the profession, to change the rules of the game. This is generally termed the educational model. In this model, the main function of the committee is to educate the hospital staff so that they take into account in their decision making certain values—for example, autonomy, equity, justice—that they may have overlooked in the past. This is important. Obviously, I cannot argue against education, as it is what I spend most of my time doing. It is, however, long-term strategy, and its effects are difficult to measure.

The third way to change behavior, and the one that is arguably the most effective, is coercion. This method is one with which most lawyers are comfortable. Basically, it consists of changing the incentives: "If you don't do this, you're going to jail." One can also do it in a positive way. To paraphrase the *Quinlan* court: "If you follow this procedure (i.e., go through an ethics committee) you're not going to jail, and there is no way that anybody can ever sue you for doing this." So another consideration for ethics committees is how to go about accomplishing their goals. The job of ethics committees is to change the institution by changing the behavior of the decision makers in the institution. It is a form of social engineering, engineering designed to change the way decisions are made in the hospital.

## Committee Constituencies

In deciding the sorts of behavioral changes wanted, in order to determine the focus of the committee, it is useful to look at the types of patients in the institution. Corresponding to the types of patients are three basic types of committees: (1) those that deal with competent patients, (2) those that deal with incompetent patients, and (3) those whose primary function is to enhance patients' rights.

### AUTONOMY COMMITTEES

The first type of committee can be termed an *autonomy committee*, a committee established to review a decision of a competent patient. An example of this type is the abortion committees, previously mentioned, which were set up in the 1960s to review the decision made by a woman and her physician that she should have an abortion.

On a moral level, autonomy is an important goal which is translated, on a legal level, into the right of privacy. Individuals have a fundamental constitutional right to make important decisions concerning their own bodies, from the decision of whether or not to reproduce to the decision to refuse even lifesaving or life-sustaining treatment. It is both unconstitutional and a deprivation of liberty to require committee approval of a competent patient's acceptance or refusal of treatment.

Of course, the Constitution only applies to state hospitals or hospitals involved in state action. A constitutional right of privacy does not apply to private hospitals. Thus, a private hospital might be able to have a committee that makes such decisions. But there could not be a statute that says, for example, that no one can refuse lifesaving treatment unless a committee reviews it; such a requirement would be unconstitutional. It would also be unethical (if not illegal) for private hospitals to institute such a statute. If the institution wants to promote autonomy based on an individual's values, you do not have a committee review the individual's decision; you simply honor that decision.

There are exceptions to the unconstitutionality of these review committees, and they involve experimentation. California enacted a statute, for example, requiring a review committee to interview possible psychosurgery patients to make sure that they are competent and understand the risks and benefits of psychosurgery before they can undergo the procedure.[15] A California court ruled that even though the patient has a right to privacy, the state has a compelling interest to ensure that no one undergoes this experimental, highly intrusive, irreversible procedure unless he or she is competent and makes an informed decision.[16] The constitutional right to privacy does not mean that one can impose no conditions on decision making. It means that the state must demonstrate a compelling interest before it gets involved. These are very rare cases. The Barney Clark artificial heart implant constituted such a case because it concerned a highly unusual, highly intrusive, experimental procedure. Generally, however, ethics committees have no business reviewing the decisions of competent patients.

## INCOMPETENT PERSON REVIEW COMMITTEES

The second type of review, and the most popular one, is for incompetent patients. Ethics committees might review the treatment of patients like Karen Ann Quinlan—patients in a persistent vegetative state, who have no hope of recovery. The New Jersey Supreme Court used the idea of ethics committees as a solution to the perplexities of determining treatment in the Karen Ann Quinlan type of case for only one reason: the influence of legal liability on doctors' decisions. In its decision, the court stated that the main reason underlying the New Jersey doctors' refusal to turn the ventilator off was the fear that they might be criminally and civilly liable.[17] If that was seen as the problem, the solution was to ensure that doctors would not be criminally and civilly liable. This is the real genesis of the modern ethics committee. The court held that if an ethics committee reviews the case and agrees with the prognosis—i.e., that there is no reasonable possibility of the patient's returning to a cognitive, sapient state—then the decision to withdraw life-support systems can be made with legal immunity. This exemplifies the third way to modify behavior: change the incentive system.

If one believes that doctors do not make ethically sound decisions because they are afraid of the law, one can effectively "take the law away." At least that was the *Quinlan* solution. More recently, courts and others have commented that what was at stake in the *Quinlan* case was not an ethics decision, but concern over liability for acting upon a medical prognosis. Thus, the committee created by the New Jersey Supreme Court had only one task: to confirm the prognosis. In New Jersey, and in the state of Washington which has just adopted this model,[18] health care providers do not rely upon a multidisciplinary "educational" group, but upon a group of physicians (usually three neurologists or neurosurgeons) to confirm the prognosis. This makes perfectly good sense because these are the only people who have any expertise concerning neurological prognosis. The point is that the Quinlan-type committees are not properly considered "ethics" committees; they are prognosis committees constituted exclusively by physicians who are there only to confirm a medical prognosis. The committees are used, at least in New Jersey and Washington, because the courts have given health care providers an incentive: legal immunity.

In addition to the comatose patient, there are other major types of legally incompetent patients: the mentally ill and neonates. No one knows how to make decisions in neonatal intensive care units, and many institutions want to try ethics committees to aid in decision making. However, if the ethics committee is to make a decision about whether a particular child is to be treated or not, the committee must meet the requirements of basic due process. The ethics committee would have to act like an administrative agency that is set up to make decisions usually made by the courts. Again, the institution would be using the ethics committee as a substitute for going to court.

Of course, one is always free to go to court. But if one does not want to go to court and yet wants to act in a manner that will be socially acceptable, then one must build due process into an alternative method. The people involved must know the rules of the game—both the substantive rules that are used to make the decisions and the procedural rules. They must know whether the committee is concerned with prognosis (as in the *Quinlan* case) or with something else, and whether the decision will be based on burden to the child, burden to the family, or some other factor. Whatever the rules, they must be made clear to all. Second, there must be some provision for representation of the child. I am not sure how formal it needs to be, whether a lawyer needs to be involved, but someone must act as advocate for the child. Since the parents are probably refusing to consent to treatment, someone else must present the argument in favor of treatment if the procedure is to be seen as fair to the child. Finally, the institution establishing such an ethics committee needs a mechanism for appeals. Obviously, one can always go to court, but if the committee's purpose is to avoid judicial proceedings, the institution's administrators should set up an internal appeals mechanism that can be used.[19]

PATIENTS' RIGHTS COMMITTEES

The third type of committee, with which we have had almost no experience, is set up primarily to enhance patients' rights. Rather than call them ethics committees, I prefer to call them *human rights committees*; it is a better description of what they do. These committees would not try to usurp the rights of competent patients, or to review the decisions of others for incompetent patients, but instead would help competent patients implement their decisions. It is one thing to say that everybody is autonomous in the hospital, and that the institution respects the rights of individual patients to make decisions pertaining to their treatment; it is quite another for sick or dying patients in a hospital to make their desires known, and to make sure they are implemented. Most often, patients do not have that type of power or authority, and there is no mechanism in the hospital to help patients implement their desires. I have been involved with two such committees; one was in a state facility for the retarded in Massachusetts, the Fernald School, where a human rights committee was started in 1972.[20] The second was begun recently in conjunction with an experimental prepaid managed health plan in Boston for severely disabled adults.

The committee at Fernald had residents as members. If a committee is devoted to promoting patients' rights, it must have patients on it. This is impossible for most general hospitals, because the average length of a stay for patients is under eight days. But I think committees like this are appropriate and needed in nursing homes, facilities for the retarded, mental institutions, and all other settings where patients stay for a significant period of time. We are deluding ourselves if we establish committees to enhance patients' rights that do not include patients or former patients, or both, as members.

The second main setting which needs a patients' rights committee to protect patients is the prepaid health care setting. When the health care provider has a financial incentive to reduce the level of services, as is the case in any prepaid or managed health care plan, the patients' right to care and treatment may conflict directly with the provider's desires. A very simple case which came up recently in a managed care setting in Massachusetts involved a woman who had gone into a coma and could be kept alive almost indefinitely on a ventilator. Her prepaid group was very small, and her expensive care had the potential to literally "break the bank" of that group each year she survived. There was a tremendous financial incentive to turn off the respirator. The physicians believed that the respirator should be removed and that she probably would have wanted that, although she had never indicated her wishes. This situation was much more complicated than the Karen Ann Quinlan case, in which the doctors had no financial incentive to keep Karen on the respirator or take her off it. The doctors in this situation had a tremendous financial incentive. Not only would money be taken out of their pockets, but it would also jeopardize their entire program. It could go bankrupt. That case was "solved" by the courts by having Medicaid assume financial responsibility. But patients of this type need some sort of mechanism, perhaps an ethics committee, for protection in situations where their physicians, theoretically looking out for their best interests, are also the insurers, and where their medical decisions will affect them financially.

## SUMMARY

Committees have served a variety of purposes over the past two decades. They have come into existence when we have encountered novel problems on which there is little societal agreement. In addition, ethics committees are formed when individuals feel uncomfortable. In the past, discomfort has stemmed primarily from the fear of health professionals that they might be legally liable, either criminally or civilly, for making certain decisions. Some have felt that they could insulate themselves from this legal liability by interposing a committee. On occasion, courts like the *Quinlan* court have agreed with this. When dealing with competent patients, however, courts have ruled as a matter of constitutional law that committees cannot overrule decisions made by competent patients and their doctors.

We should look not only at committees that protect the institutions, but also at committees that protect patients. Settings in which patients are staying for a long time, or prepaid programs with a group of identifiable patients, should have human rights committees. Membership on these committees should include representatives from the patient group. Finally, procedures should be developed so that the patients can use these committees to enhance their ability to implement their decisions.

Today, ethics committees mean many things to many people; they can have many different functions in the same setting; and one hospital may have a variety of ethics committees. The ethics committee in a nursing home could be quite different from the ethics committee in a home for the retarded or in a general hospital. In ethics committees, we have the luxury of experimentation and we can afford to pursue a variety of strategies. The law gives committees only limited guidance. Mainly, the law demands that the committee respect the wishes of the competent patient. Committees may be useful to help protect the rights of individuals who are at serious risk, who may not be able to speak for themselves, and who may not be protected under the usual mechanisms that are now in place. As long as their role is clearly defined, and their substantive rules and procedures are known, followed, and fair, they stand a reasonable chance of contributing both counsel and comfort to medical decision makers.

## NOTES

1. *See* G. CALABRESI, P. BOBBITT, TRAGIC CHOICES (Norton Co., New York) (1978) at 22.
2. *See, e.g.*, Doe v. Bolton, 410 U.S. 179, 184 (1973).
3. *Id.* at 183.
4. *See* R. FOX, J. SWAZEY, THE COURAGE TO FAIL (University of Chicago Press, Chicago) (1978) at 208.
5. *Id.* at 254.
6. HHS Policy for Protection of Human Research Subjects, 45 C.F.R. §§46.101, 46.102(h).
7. *In re* Quinlan, 355 A.2d 647 (N.J. 1976), *cert. denied*, Garger v. New Jersey 429 U.S. 922 (1976).
8. *See* Annas, G. J., Glantz, L. H., *Psychosurgery: The Law's Responses*, BOSTON UNIVERSITY LAW REVIEW 54:249, 263–65 (1974).
9. For a discussion of other problems concerning the IRB's role in this case, see Annas, G. J., *Consent to the Artificial Heart: The Lion and the Crocodiles*, HASTINGS CENTER REPORT 13(2):20–22 (April 1983).
10. American Academy of Pediatrics v. Heckler, 561 F. Supp. 395 (D.D.C. 1983).
11. *See* Boston Globe (November 11, 1983) at 18; New York Times (November 11, 1983) at A30.
12. *See* Veatch, R. M., ch. 4 of this text.
13. *In re* Quinlan, *supra* note 7, at 671.
14. Allen, D., Annas, G. J., Katz, B. F., Promoting the Rights of the Institutionalized Retarded (unpublished manuscript)(1974) at 2–6.
15. *See* Annas, G. J., *Informed Consent and Review Committees*, THE PSYCHOSURGERY DEBATE (E. S. Valenstein, ed.) (Freeman, San Francisco) (1980) at 494–98.
16. Alden v. Younger, 129 Cal. Rptr. 535, 548 (Cal. App., 1976).
17. *In re* Quinlan, *supra* note 7, at 666–67.
18. *In re* Colyer, 660 P.2d 738, 749–50 (Wash. 1983).
19. *See* Robertson, J., ch. 7 of this text.
20. *See generally* Allen, Annas, Katz, *supra* note 14.

# Audience Discussion

## A. Edward Doudera, Moderator

A. EDWARD DOUDERA, J.D.: Before we have our first question, Dr. Ronald Cranford has a few comments.

RONALD E. CRANFORD, M.D. (conference faculty): I think it is important to note that our committee at Hennepin County Medical Center has existed for 11 years, and during that time we have sort of felt our way along. We were—and you will be—faced with a dilemma: we need experts and knowledgeable people on our committees, but how many institutions have them available? What is needed is a lot of self-education and a willingness to tackle problems as we go along. For example, we have not yet adopted formal procedures for our committee, largely because we lacked knowledge and expertise in this area. Now we see the need for them. It's a circular process: we need to develop that expertise and yet have a committee in place to draw on.

GEORGE ANNAS, J.D., M.P.H. (conference faculty): Ron, can you articulate the goals of your committee? Have you come that far?

DR. CRANFORD: The goal of our committee[1] is to deal with the ethical dilemmas that confront our hospital staff. We have never become more formal than that. Our committee started because we felt there was a need for ethical reflection on policies and practices. Cases came before our committee when our colleagues recognized that they were unsure of the appropriate course of action and needed guidance in a certain situation—an "ethical dilemma."

RONALD MILLER, M.D. (St. Joseph Hospital, Orange, California): I have two questions. First, do we really need different committees, or do we need different resource people sitting on a single committee? Second, how do you balance the extent to which we need to maintain the continuity of the committee (e.g., to develop and maintain experience to deal with problems) against the need for change to bring in new ideas and perspectives?

ROBERT M. VEATCH, PH.D. (conference faculty): Considering the variety of tasks that both George Annas and I have described, you might envision a kind of bureaucratic nightmare with different committees for each of these different tasks. I am convinced, however, that many of the tasks I have described—health policy, institutional policy, research, resource allocation, and cost containment—require the same ethical mandate and the same ethical principles. One committee could easily handle all these issues. It might be called the ethical policy committee or the equity committee. The committee should be highly diverse, representing the community the hospital serves.

The main distinction that I wanted to press for was a difference between a committee that would focus on these more policy-oriented resource-allocation questions and one that focuses on individual patient problems. I do not see this patient-centered committee as strictly one that would fight legally to protect the patient's right to decide. This second kind of committee would come together to help the patient work through a very difficult set of questions, questions he or she has never faced before. Its task is to constitute itself as a support network committed not only to the well-being but also to the dignity and autonomy of the patient. It should be made up of the people most capable of offering that support.

The thing that troubles me most is the possibility that the same committee would also be charged with saving money for the hospital or allocating resources among patients. I would keep these functions quite separate. Thus, maybe we need to talk about two kinds of committees.

PROFESSOR ANNAS: Bob, did you say that you do not necessarily want to help patients implement their decisions, rather only help them with counseling?

PROFESSOR VEATCH: I think it is wonderful to have the committee assist the patient in executing a decision once it is well formulated and firm, but I think often the problem is that the patient has not reached a decision. He or she needs help in sorting out what the options are, what the alternatives are; and this means psychological help for some patients, spiritual help for others. It also means just explaining what the options mean.

S. BRYANT KENDRICK (Department of Pastoral Care, North Carolina Baptist Hospitals, Winston-Salem): One of the assumptions I have heard thus far is that ethics committees arise to deal with anxiety; I think Dr. Veatch used the phrase "an individual diffusion of responsibility." If that is the case—and I think it probably is true for both health care professionals and family members who do not want to be responsible for decisions laden with guilt—are there alternatives other than the establishment of an ethics committee? We might, for example, want to deal with the question of anxiety on a broader basis than the institutionally based response. How, in fact, will the members of an ethics committee free themselves of this problem?

PROFESSOR ANNAS: My answer to that is that it depends on the source of the anxiety. If the source of the anxiety is, "Is our prognosis accurate?," then I think you could set up a consulting system, a "prognosis committee" that would consult with the attending physician. If, however, the source of anxiety is concern that someone may someday sue you, or that you'll be charged with murder, then you are in a different ballgame. If you really need a guarantee against those occurrences, there are two things you can do. One is to try to work out in your own mind the fact that you do not really need a 100 percent guarantee of immunity. As long as you are convinced that what you are doing is professionally correct, and your patient wants it done, you are on pretty solid legal ground and would probably prevail in any court. Having reached that position, you go ahead and follow your best judgment. But if you need the 100 percent immunity guarantee then you have to go to court. That's the alternative. What we are really talking about is an alternative to the present system of going to court, and there are two ways to do that: one is to make it easier to go to court; the other is to try to figure out a way to get people to understand that they do not have to go to court in all cases.

PROFESSOR VEATCH: I think we have to be clear on whether diffusion of anxiety is a good thing or a bad thing. My remarks implied that I am very nervous that such committees may achieve the result of diffusing decision-making responsibility. One of the worst things that could happen would be for an ethics committee to convey to the family, "you don't really have to take this responsibility; we'll take it off your hands and do the dirty work for you." I have never been impressed with the argument that families should not be involved in decision making because it is hard work. There are many things involved in being a good family member that are hard work. That fact alone cannot be a justification for shifting authority to a committee. Nonetheless, I am certain that there are times when a family member just does not understand what the options are or when a physician is worried about legal liability, and that committee can remove this false or unnecessary anxiety.

PROFESSOR ANNAS: I might note that in the hospital setting, the person who traditionally has the authority is the attending physician, since he or she is the one that has to take ultimate legal responsibility for the decision. The ethics committee notion challenges all that, and it may be the main reason why many physicians see ethics committees as a very threatening thing. Many physicians are not worried about diffusing authority, they are not worried about going to court; they are worried about losing their own autonomy and authority as physicians.

ROBERT FRASER (National Institutes of Health, Rockville, Maryland): My comment is that all the parties who are interested—the institution, the medical staff, the patient and his or her family—may all be experiencing conflict between different ethical principles such as truth telling, justice, and beneficence. As a member of an IRB, I see the need to facilitate a decision-making process which reflects the interest of all these different parties. And the interest of those parties might not always need protection. Rather than talking of having multiple committees as Professor Veatch suggested, might we not talk about characterizing the role of the committee in terms of various stages of involvement in the process, and also in terms of the parties or agents the IEC is representing or mediating for at a given time? I mean, at a given time the primary interest at issue might be the cost and its effect on the institution, and at another point in time it might be the interest of the family. I see a multiplicity of interests here and at different stages in the process, of perhaps the IEC functioning as a mediator and a consultant for these different bodies. I'd be interested in your response.

DR. CRANFORD: Before Bob answers, let me second what you said. That is precisely what I see ethics committees doing; not representing one discipline, or one point of view, or one ethical principle, but mediating between many, and trying to resolve conflicts and dilemmas as they arise. I think we are dealing with the heart of the strengths and the weaknesses of such committees, because the committees cannot represent exclusively the institution or the patients or the doctors. They have a multiplicity of interests to represent. If you focus entirely on one single task, be it economics or justice, or whatever, you are defeating the very purpose of an ethics committee.

PROFESSOR VEATCH: I would not disagree that there are often times when there are such conflicts. What I was pressing for was the recognition that there are different kinds of problems that have been proposed to be brought before ethics committees. One very large class of problems is problems where the real objective is helping the patient or the agent for the patient reach a decision about what ought to be done. Once that has been worked through, the hospital staff will be willing to concur, whether it is a yes or a no decision. That is the autonomy model that I am proposing. The job is not simply to shout and affirm patient autonomy, but to mobilize a support network for helping the patient or the agent for the patient work through the problems.

There are other kinds of problems where autonomy is not the issue at all. For example, consider a situation where we know very well what the patient wants: the patient wants the treatment to continue. The problem is that it is going to cost the hospital $100,000. The question might be whether it is appropriate to spend those resources. This problem is quite different in structure. It involves more than mediating between conflicting interests. I have been suggesting today that I believe it is very difficult for one committee to take on both of these tasks.

This is simply an extension of my belief that, in general, clinical professionals should be exempt from resource-allocation and cost-containment decisions when they conflict with the interests and welfare of their patients. I am making the same argument with respect to committees. Consider the case of a Catholic hospital in a heavily Catholic community. If the problem is how to allocate scarce resources, it is reasonable that the committee be made up heavily of people capable of reflecting a Catholic perspective. If, however, the committee were asked to assist a patient who was Jewish and wanted help in determining whether refusal of a treatment was compatible with the Jewish tradition, to the extent that the committee was structured to reflect a Catholic perspective, it would have difficulty performing its job. It cannot be made up to do both jobs well.

STUART YOUNGNER, M.D. (Case Western Reserve University, Cleveland): It seems to me that there is a more obvious conflict for a committee considering economic, allocation, or legal matters, as well as looking after patients' interests. It is not so obvious to me that there is a conflict between promoting what is best for the patient and promoting the patient's autonomy. A committee may serve as a forum for health professionals who are not sure whether the patient's autonomy has been honored, or where there is disagreement among health care professionals about which course is in the patient's best interest. Would you disagree that what you call the "autonomy committee" could help health professionals deliver care in the patient's best interest and simultaneously honor the patient's autonomy? My opinion is that these functions should not be artificially separated, because patient autonomy does not exist in a clear, readily identifiable form in the hospital. You refer to ethics committees as being products of technology, but you're also advocating a kind of specialization of ethics committees which may preclude an opportunity for dialogue in a complicated psychosocial, as well as moral, framework. And I don't think that it is just a platitude to say that things are complicated in hospitals.

PROFESSOR VEATCH: Fortunately, in the normal case, promoting the patient's autonomy also promotes the patient's best interest, and promoting the patient's best interest promotes the patient's autonomy. Some, like John Stuart Mill, argue that promoting liberty is the most efficient, reliable way of promoting welfare. As long as we see the two as converging, we do not need to resolve this issue.

Unfortunately, there is a long history in medical ethics of people perceiving a conflict between the two; for example, where a health professional perceives course A as the autonomous choice of the patient but deems course B as that most likely to best promote his or her welfare. Where the two diverge, we have got to bite the bullet and decide whether patient benefit or patient autonomy is the objective of the committee. I do not see how we can simply say, "we've got to have a little bit of both and we'll have to compromise." To talk about rights, which I believe we are at this level of discourse, the committee is going to have to constitute itself to pursue one or the other, even if we recognize that the other option might be a means to the first.

DR. YOUNGNER: Why do you assume that we're just talking about rights? Whose assumption is that?

PROFESSOR VEATCH: At least as long as we're talking about cases where the only thing at stake is patient-centered decision making, that is the assumption of the legal system in every case where these issues have been discussed. It is the assumption of virtually every philosophical or ethical discourse on the subject in the last decade and, to make it complete, it is also the official opinion of the American Nurses' Association, the American Medical Association, and every professional organization that has spoken on the issue. If we block off what the philosopher would call the harm principle—cases where the patient's decision has third-party effects—and it is a straight, head-on conflict between the welfare of the patient and the autonomy of the patient, we are as close to a societal consensus as we've ever been. Even the AMA's *Principles of Ethics* on this subject uses "rights" language.[2]

PROFESSOR ANNAS: This discussion of rights begs one question (and I'm not prepared to say whether it should or shouldn't yet)—that is, whether the ethics committee should have some role in determining the patient's competence. We all say a competent adult patient has the right to refuse treatment, but it is very problematic, at least on the border, how to determine, outside of the judicial setting, whether or not a patient is competent. If that is a big issue at a particular hospital, it may be worthwhile to let its ethics committee develop some standards or even, on occasion, make competence decisions.

HOWARD BELL (Abbott Northwestern Hospital, Minneapolis): I come out of the clinical setting, and in that setting it seems as though the multidisciplinary team will routinely discuss a case without permission from the patient. With physician consultations, you permit medical review without the patient's permission. My question for Dr. Veatch is, what legal or ethical principle leads to such a strict interpretation of confidentiality that would distinguish between an ethics committee and clinical consultation?

PROFESSOR VEATCH: The only basis for allowing collegial consultation that I know of is for the patient to consent to having information transmitted to others. If I ask myself, "If I were a patient entering a hospital that I knew had an ethics committee, would I give blanket permission for my medical record, including problems about decisions, to be referred to this committee without my being consulted," my answer would be no. I think I would at least like to know if they are going to discuss my case, especially if recommendations about my life-and-death decisions are to be made in that committee. I take the principle of confidentiality very seriously, and if there are times when routine collegial consultation falsely presumes the consent of the patient, then everything I said about confidentiality for committees would also apply to those consultations as well.

PROFESSOR ANNAS: The legal answer to that turns on another question: what is the reasonable expectation of a patient? At this point, when very few hospitals have something called "ethics committees," it is certainly not the reasonable expectation of patients coming to hospitals that their case is going to be discussed by an ethics committee. Therefore, no discussion of individual patients should take place with an ethics committee without the patient's knowledge and consent.

DR. CRANFORD: I guess my practical experience differs from that of Bob and George. A lot of our cases, maybe 100 cases over the past ten years, are extremely difficult. They were brought to the committee, or to individual members of the committee, in an informal fashion by clinicians, and we discussed the ethical dilemmas presented by the individual cases. Practically, it was important for those professionals involved to be able to discuss these things before going to the family. Don't misunderstand me—one of the main objectives of an ethics committee is to draw in the family, and then to draw on their support systems to help them resolve the dilemma. But as a practical matter, one of the valuable purposes served by an IEC is to have health care professionals feel free to come to the committee for education, for consultation, for discussion before they talk to the patient or family.

PROFESSOR VEATCH: I think it depends on whom you view as the primary decision maker. I have been quite explicit in that I see the patient, or the agent for the patient (the family member, or whoever it may be), as the presumed decision maker in these cases. I hope that ethics committees think of themselves as accountable to the patient or family member or agent. The patient or his or her surrogate should be the one who brings these questions to the committee. If that is the case, the problem of confidentiality disappears since it is the patient who asks the committee to review the case. The health professional should not disclose the patient's case to others unless he or she can correctly presume that the patient would consent to such disclosure. That cannot be presumed for ethics committees.

RICHARD BERQUIST, PH.D. (College of Saint Thomas, Saint Paul, Minnesota): I have a very brief legal question for Professor Annas concerning the right of the competent patient to refuse treatment and the constitutional right of privacy. Does the right to privacy mean that a court could not order treatment even if the patient's refusal of a lifesaving treatment amounted to suicide?

PROFESSOR ANNAS: It's hard to answer that question absolutely. Generally, I would think yes. Certainly, if a patient is terminally ill. The courts have said that the constitutional right to privacy gives way under certain circumstances to compelling state interests—e.g., sanctity of human life, prevention of suicide, interests of innocent third parties. The problem is that there has never been a case where a court has overruled a competent adult's decision to refuse treatment on the basis of any of those things (outside of the childbirth and prisoner cases).[3]

THOMAS SMITH, M.D. (St. Mary-Corwin Hospital, Pueblo, Colorado): I would like to hear the panel discuss their feelings about the ethical implications of the new diagnosis related groups and their new incentives for our health care delivery system.[4]

PROFESSOR ANNAS: I don't have the answer, but I agree that a whole new set of incentives will exist—for instance, having the doctor be the insurer or have a stake in the insurance (in the sense that he or she gets some of the money saved) really changes the incentives. That's why it's been done, it's supposed to change the incentives so that hospitals and doctors conserve money. The question is: Can this be done without endangering patients? I don't think we know the answer to that yet. We must now discuss the implications and try to develop mechanisms to help alleviate the problem of potential conflicts between good patient care and cost-effective patient care.

PROFESSOR VEATCH: I take it that the relevant dimension is that somebody is going to have to make decisions to put limits on care or, at least, to accept that incentives will push in that direction. I happen to think that is an appropriate, understandable, and responsible action for a society that has potentially infinite demand on its resources. It is the kind of task that can be undertaken as long as there is full public participation in deciding what the criteria are for limits. That might best be done at the insurers' level with the full participation by the insured in deciding what gets covered and what does not. It will also be done at the hospital level, and that is the kind of justice and resource allocation committee task that I was describing. In order to make such choices it is crucial that there be due process; that there be fair and equal treatment for all patients in similar categories; and that patients be fully represented in the choices that are made. In addition, and I think this is more controversial, I would strongly favor exempting health care professionals from the responsibility of deciding to cut off care for their patients. I would like to insulate the clinical professional so that he or she is free within the autonomy framework to pursue the rights and best interests of the patient. Others must take on the responsibility for the resource allocation judgments.

PROFESSOR ANNAS: Isn't that the problem now? Isn't the problem that doctors are now insulated from that type of decision making? The only way we can continue to insulate them and save money is to say we are not going to cover certain types of things, e.g., heart transplants.

PROFESSOR VEATCH: Well, my scheme, for instance, would in principle exclude a local hospital policy that mounts a little campaign telling doctors to be as cost-conscious as possible. It would exclude saying to physicians, "When you think your intervention is only going to help the patient a little bit, try to exclude it and save money for us."

PROFESSOR ANNAS: What about just a simple provision in a prepaid plan run by physicians where they share in the "surplus" at the end of the year? You would object to that scheme, I take it? In other words, all of the physicians share in the money that's saved at the end of the year by their own actions in cutting costs and reducing lengths of stay.

PROFESSOR VEATCH: I am aware of the problem you suggest. For now, let me say that if there is to be that kind of an incentive, at the very least it needs to be adopted by full patient participation. I would prefer to have the cost-containment incentives push in some other direction so that my clinician would be free to do everything that was possible within his or her power to pursue my interest, even if it is quite trivial. The limits would more appropriately be put in place by an ethics policy committee, the hospital trustees, or the government agency responsible for the hospital.

## Notes

1. *See* narrative report on Biomedical Ethics Committee, Hennepin County Medical Center, Section II of this text.
2. American Medical Association, *Principles of Medical Ethics, reprinted in* JOURNAL OF THE TENNESSEE MEDICAL ASSOCIATION 73(11):780 (November 1980).
3. *See, e.g.*, Jefferson v. Griffin Spalding County Hospital Authority, 247 S.E.2d 457 (Ga. 1981) (state's interest in viable fetus outweighed maternal right to refuse cesarean section on religious grounds); Commissioner of Corrections v. Myers, 399 N.E.2d 452 (Mass. 1979) (prisoner required by prison commissioner to undergo treatment for kidney disease). *See generally* Annas, G. J., *Reconciling* Quinlan *and* Saikewicz: *Decision Making for the Terminally Ill Incompetent,* AMERICAN JOURNAL OF LAW & MEDICINE 4(4):367–96 (Winter 1979); Note, Jefferson v. Griffin Spalding County Hospital Authority: *Court-Ordered Surgery to Protect the Life of an Unborn Child,* AMERICAN JOURNAL OF LAW & MEDICINE 9(1):83–101 (Spring 1983).
4. Social Security Act Amendments of 1983, 43 U.S.C. §1395x (1983). Under this prospective payment system, Medicare reimbursement to hospitals is based on patients' diagnoses. This provides an incentive to cut costs because a hospital will strive to spend no more on a patient's care than what it expects to receive from Medicare, based on the patient's diagnosis.

# Part II

## Review of Existing Institutional Ethics Committees and Comparison with "Prognosis" and Research Committees

# 6

## Patients' Attitudes toward Hospital Ethics Committees

Stuart J. Youngner, Claudia Coulton,
Barbara W. Juknialis, and David L. Jackson

There is a growing concern in our society about the proper application of life-sustaining medical treatments. This concern has been stimulated by both the explosion in medical technology and the increasing emphasis on patients' rights and autonomy in clinical decision making. Technological progress enables us to prolong or sustain life, even when its "value" or "quality" is questionable. There is also increased concern, both within and outside the medical community, about the optimal process for making decisions to withhold or withdraw treatment.

Hospital ethics committees have been suggested as a possible solution to this problem. Although few hospitals have actually adopted ethics committees, and little is known about the way they function or their effectiveness, there have been some recent efforts to study these issues.[1] Despite the increasing recognition of patients' wishes to know more about and influence their medical care,[2] there have been no reports about patients' attitudes toward the role of ethics committees in decision making.

This study is the first known attempt to determine the extent of patients' knowledge about their hospitals' ethics committees, as well as their opinions regarding the general role of such committees.

### BACKGROUND

As the decision-making process in critical care medicine has come under increasing scrutiny, it has been suggested that physicians in medical institutions may have interests and values which differ from those of their patients.[3] Final decisions must therefore rest with the patient, if he or she is competent. Other commentators note that the ideal concept of autonomy is subject to the limitations imposed by serious illness and medical emergencies.[4]

This work was supported in part by a grant from the Cleveland Foundation.

This problem is magnified when the patient is clearly incompetent, as in the cases of comatose adults and severely handicapped or premature infants. Who in such situations should represent the patient's interests? The family seems a logical choice, but problems can arise when family members disagree among themselves, or when the family has interests which might conflict with those of the patient. In fact, this last possibility has become a painful issue with respect to some defective newborns. Living wills have been one attempted solution for adults, although there have been problems; vague terminology has been open to varying interpretation, and some physicians have refused outright to comply with the terms of living wills.[5] Another suggested solution is that a "neutral" guardian be appointed to represent the interests of an incompetent patient. Although the courts must remain the final arbiters of such decisions, there seems to be a growing consensus that their regular involvement in decision making would be cumbersome and inefficient.[6] Furthermore, the adversary system might not provide the optimal setting for resolving the majority of these painful, complicated, and personal dilemmas.

Hospital ethics committees first appeared in the mid-1970s, partly in response to the New Jersey Supreme Court's decision in the much-publicized Karen Ann Quinlan case.[7] An early report on one such committee at Massachusetts General Hospital suggested that its main benefits had been "clarification of misunderstanding about the patient's prognosis, reopening of communication, reestablishment of unified treatment objectives and rationales, restoration of the sense of shared responsibility for patient and family, and above all, maximizing support for the responsible physician who makes the medical decision. . . ."[8]

Others have voiced concern about ethics committees. As outlined in the *Quinlan* decision, their purpose and function are vague. Are they supposed to determine prognoses, make final decisions, or only give advice? Are they primarily a source of "legal comfort" to physicians,[9] or do they have a more vital role in protecting or promoting the patients' best interests? How much access should patients, their families, and other health professionals (e.g., nurses) have to such committees? The most current and comprehensive discussion of these problems appears in the report of the President's Commission for the Study of Ethical Problems in Medicine and Biomedical and Behavioral Research, *Deciding to Forego Treatment*.[10]

A recent national survey estimated that only 1 percent of United States hospitals have ethics committees that become involved in decision making for specific cases.[11] Recent reports have at least tentatively suggested an important role for hospital ethics committees. For example, according to the President's Commission, "ethics committees and other institutional responses can be more rapid and sensitive than judicial review: they are closer to the treatment setting, their deliberations are informal and typically private . . . and they are able to reconvene easily or delegate decisions to a separate group of members."[12] However, the President's Commission recommends that institutions report on the successes and failures of ethics committees, and that any increase in their use should be accompanied by "rigorous study."[13]

## METHODOLOGY

This study was designed to elicit patients' opinions about two issues: (1) how decisions should be made concerning the application or withdrawal of heroic or extraordinary treatments, once all concerned individuals are aware of the medical facts; and (2) the appropriate role of ethics committees in the decision-making process.

The ethics committee at the large, urban, university hospital that we studied had been created six years earlier by a task force of representatives from the departments of nursing, medicine, and administration. The committee was supposed to serve everyone (i.e., health professionals, patients, and families) involved in making the clinical decision to withdraw life support. In addition to helping with difficult decisions, the committee had an educational function. In short, the committee would have met John Robertson's criteria for an "optional/optional" committee.[14] People brought cases to the committee voluntarily, and received only recommendations and advice. The committee guidelines stated that anyone involved in patient care, including patients and families, could bring cases to the committee and attend its meetings.

After the committee had been operating for five years, we decided to study its impact. We developed a structured questionnaire and used it in interviewing a large cross-section of the hospital community (including staff physicians, social workers, intensive care nurses, and third-year medical students) regarding the committee's effectiveness and the functioning of such committees in general.

We also wanted to study 120 patients, and decided to interview them using a structured, multiple-choice questionnaire asking patients whether they had ever heard about ethics committees, whether they knew that the hospital had one, and how they felt about ethics committees and decision making in critical clinical situations. Before we could begin the study, we needed approval from the institutional review board (IRB). In our hospital, a study is initially reviewed by an IRB subcommittee from the sponsoring department. Since this study came from the department of psychiatry, five psychiatrists reviewed and approved it. The physician chairman of the IRB was concerned about the adverse effect these questions might have on patients, and argued that discussing these issues with patients would be tremendously upsetting and cause them undue suffering. We requested a second review by the subcommittee, which again approved the study. Although five psychiatrists knowledgeable about emotional injury to patients had approved these questions twice, and although the interviews would be completely voluntary and patients would not have to participate, the chairman still refused. He even attempted to deny us access to the members of the IRB, to prevent our discussing the issue with them. Fortunately, the medical administration was not as prejudiced and insisted that we be allowed to present our case to the IRB. We were then grudgingly allowed to pretest the interview—but only on individuals who were not patients!

After interviewing ten cooperative and interested individuals who worked in the housekeeping department at the hospital, we were given permission to talk with patients who "were not too sick." We thus studied 120 outpatients in three different settings affiliated with our large, urban, teaching hospital: a medical staff clinic providing care to an indigent, inner-city population; a suburban outpatient medical clinic staffed by the hospital's clinical faculty; and an ambulatory oncology clinic. IRB approval was contingent upon our having a psychiatrist on emergency call who could intervene if any of the questions caused patients acute psychiatric distress. All 120 patients gave written informed consent to participate in the study. Patients who were critically or terminally ill at the time of the study were not included because their responses might have differed from those of less severely ill patients and because they might have been more likely to become upset by the interview.

A structured interview schedule was developed and pretested by a trained interviewer. To examine test-retest reliability, 20 respondents were interviewed twice, with a one-week interval between interviews. At least 80 percent of the respondents provided identical answers to all items on both administrations of the test. The interview schedule was therefore considered to have adequate test-retest reliability.

Interviews were conducted during routine office hours until 40 patients from each setting had participated. Although the sample was not random, there were no known differences between the patients included in the study and those seen on other days during the same time period.

Response distributions were analyzed and described for the sample as a whole. The responses were analyzed to determine whether differing beliefs and attitudes were associated with various types of health care delivery.

The following background statement was read to all patients to establish the context for the study's questions:

> Many new medical treatments and machines can be used to prolong a person's life, sometimes without improving its quality. This means that physicians, patients, and family members must make difficult decisions about giving such treatments to those who are critically ill. This interview is part of University Hospital's study of the community's attitudes about these issues. These general questions concern all of us, even though we are not in such a situation. In answering these questions, you should assume that the patient is conscious and able to communicate.

The concept of ethics committees was then introduced and the following definition was given: "Some hospitals have formed committees of health professionals and other concerned individuals to help make difficult life-and-death decisions. These committees are often called *ethics committees*."

## RESULTS

The first part of the survey attempted to discern patients' attitudes toward ethics committees. In response to the question, "Do you think such committees could be useful?," 76 percent replied affirmatively, 4 percent replied in the negative, and 20 percent answered that they did not know.

When asked about the ideal purpose of such a committee, the overwhelming majority (76 percent) picked the answer "provide consultation and advice." Only 12 percent felt that an ethics committee should "make the final decision." Thirty-eight percent of the subjects felt that the committee should have a role in all cases involving life-and-death decisions; 43 percent felt that the committee should become involved in cases only "where there is disagreement or uncertainty."

In response to the question, "Who should be able to ask the committee to review a case?," the greatest number of respondents chose the patients' physician (85 percent), the patient's family (84 percent), and the patient (78 percent). The patient's nurse (32 percent), social worker (38 percent), and clergyperson (36 percent) were less frequently chosen (see Table 1).

When asked who should serve on institutional ethics committees, subjects most frequently chose physicians (96 percent). Nurses (74 percent), clergypersons (58 percent), and social workers (55 percent) were chosen less frequently. Thirty-two percent of the subjects felt that the committee should have some sort of lay representation; 21 percent picked the general heading "people without medical training," and another 11 percent specified particular laypersons, i.e., ethicists,

Table 1:  Who Should Ask the Committee to Review a Case?
(*N* = 120)

| Description | % Choosing Response* |
|---|---|
| Patient | 78% |
| Patient's family | 84% |
| Patient's doctor | 85% |
| Patient's nurse | 32% |
| Social worker involved in case | 38% |
| Member of clergy | 36% |
| Other doctors who may know about case | 31% |

*Multiple responses possible.

Table 2:  Who Should Serve on Ethics Committees?
(*N* = 120)

| Description | % Choosing Response* |
|---|---|
| Doctors | 96% |
| Nurses | 74% |
| Clergy | 58% |
| Social workers | 55% |
| People without medical training | 21% |
| Lawyers | 42% |
| Others | 11% |

*Multiple responses possible.

patients' families, "friends," "people with the same illness," "people who have been ill," "a politician," and "friends of the patient" (see Table 2).

There was little awareness of the existence of the hospital's ethics committee. Only 9 (8 percent) of the 120 subjects said they knew there was an ethics committee in the hospital associated with the clinical setting in which they were interviewed. Of these nine, none correctly perceived the committee's actual function. However, 76 percent of the subjects felt all patients and families should automatically be informed about the committee's existence at the time of their admission to the hospital.

The study also attempted to ascertain general attitudes toward decision making and control. The subjects were asked the question, "Once all concerned individuals are aware of the medical facts, who should be responsible for making the final decision?" Sixty-one percent chose the patient, 9 percent the physician, and 6 percent the family. Other choices included various combinations of the above (see Table

Table 3:  Who Should Be Responsible for Final Decision on
Life Support?

| *Description* | *% Choosing Response** |
|---|---|
| Patient | 61% |
| Physician | 9% |
| Family | 6% |
| Patient, family, and physician | 12% |
| Judge in court | 0% |
| Other | 12% |

Collapsed Categories:

| *Patient Involvement in Decision:* | | *No Patient Involvement in Decision:* | |
|---|---|---|---|
| Patient | 61% | Physician | 9% |
| Patient, family, and physician | 12% | Family | 6% |
| Other | 10% | Other | 2% |
| | 83% | | 17% |

3). If categories in Table 3 are collapsed, 83 percent of the subjects felt that the patient should have some involvement in the final decision about life-and-death treatment. Yet, 17 percent excluded the patient entirely from decision making. No one chose "a judge in court" as the final decision maker.

Some informal observations about the study are also worth reporting. Because the physician head of the IRB was concerned about patients being unduly upset by the nature and subject of the questions, all subjects were asked at the conclusion of the interview if it had been upsetting to them in any way. The response to this question was uniformly negative. In fact, many subjects spontaneously thanked the interviewer for consulting them about a matter which they felt was important.

Some people who reviewed the study, especially those in the staff clinic, felt the questions were likely to be "too sophisticated" and the subject "too esoteric" for many patients. Again, these concerns proved to be unfounded. Patients in all three treatment settings were interested in, and informed about, the issues. They often mentioned having thought about and discussed these issues with family or friends.

## DISCUSSION

While hospital ethics committees remain relatively rare, unproven, and controversial, the recent literature, including the report of the President's Commission, suggests that they may have a useful role in resolving difficult dilemmas involving medical ethics. Consistent with this viewpoint, 76 percent of the patients in our study thought ethics committees could be useful.

The vast majority of our research subjects felt that ethics committees should only provide consultation and advice (76 percent), and that patients should be involved in making final decisions (83 percent). This suggests that most patients saw ethics committees as facilitating rather than replacing patients' decisions. We agree, and feel that many potential committee functions (e.g., clarification of treatment goals and prognoses, improvement of communication, and moral support of health professionals) are likely to promote patients' best interests without usurping their decision-making authority. The ethics committee at our hospital has, on occasion, ensured that a patient's competence is assessed and that a competent patient's wishes are honored.

It is important to note that a significant minority of respondents wanted the ethics committees to "make the final decision" (12 percent). In another question, 17 percent entirely excluded the patient from the decision-making process (see Table 3). This finding corroborates the clinical observation that some people, especially when they are critically ill, want others to make decisions for them. This minority view cannot be ignored in individual clinical situations, but should not become an excuse for generally paternalistic policies.

More problematic is the fact that only 8 percent of the patients in the study knew the hospital had an ethics committee and that none of these patients correctly perceived its function. This finding is even more significant because the ethics committee in this particular hospital had met 32 times in four years, making it eight times as active as the average committee in the national survey.[15] The hospital studied has no mechanism for informing inpatients about either the existence or the function of the ethics committee. Therefore, the fact that the sample group contained only outpatients is not significant; polling hospitalized patients would most likely yield similar results. Neither of the detailed reports on functioning ethics committees[16] indicates any policy of routinely informing patients about the committees' existence or function—although one committee's stated objective was to "provide counsel and support for those caring for terminally ill patients, the families of these patients, and *the patients themselves.*"[17]

The "Model Bill to Establish Hospital Ethics Committees," published as an appendix to the President's Commission's report, recommends: "The hospital shall inform all patients admitted to the hospital about the committee and its functions and the means of patient access to the committee."[18] The overwhelming majority of the patients in this study favored informing all patients and families about a committee's existence automatically upon patients' admission to the hospital.

The ethics committee at our hospital was established to give advice and help in difficult clinical situations. The written hospital policy explicitly states: "In no event should the physician discontinue or not initiate therapy if the patient (if able to understand and concur, otherwise the next of kin substituting for the patient) does not understand the implications or does not concur with the decision." Clearly, this policy recognizes the primacy of informed consent and patient autonomy in decision making. The formal guidelines and actual function of the committee allowed access to the committee by patients, family, and any staff member caring for the patient. Yet, no formal or routine effort was made to publicize or educate either the inpatient or outpatient populations about the committee's existence and purpose. Furthermore, there is no indication that any of the ethics committees described in the literature routinely publicizes its existence to the population of patients which it could potentially serve. It follows that control of, and access to, these committees rests with those health professionals who know about them, and the selective groups of patients and/ or families which they choose to inform.

We will briefly comment on the possible rationale for, and the significance of, decisions not to publicize committees to patient populations. The implications of changing these policies will then be discussed.

SIGNIFICANCE OF POLICIES

Staunch patients' rights advocates will undoubtedly deplore the failure to routinely inform patients about hospital ethics committees. At best, they would view this failure as another example of unjustified paternalism—i.e, health professionals using institutional ethics committees to help themselves make the best decisions *for* their patients. At worst, patients' rights advocates would see such institutional ethics committees as sinister cabals, intent upon protecting the legal, financial, or political interests of their institutions, often at the patients' expense.

On the other hand, some physicians will view ethics committees, even those which do not widely publicize their existence, as unwelcome and destructive intrusions into the traditional doctor-patient relationship. They will object to having physicians from other departments (to say nothing of nurses and other health professionals) question or challenge their authority or judgment. For them, publicity about an ethics committee's existence would give patients, families, and other health professionals a routine, accepted, and convenient way to bypass, overstep, or even undermine the traditional authority and responsibility of physicians.

Finally, patients themselves have differing views on how much they should participate in decisions to stop or withhold treatment (see Table 3).

IMPLICATIONS OF CHANGING POLICIES

If patients and their families are uniformly informed of the existence and purpose of their hospital's ethics committee, they will have much greater access to it; this may enhance their autonomy and role in decision making. This ideal scenario, however, is not likely to develop freely in most hospitals, where traditional authority structures will resist such changes. Therefore, such a policy should be adopted only after full and open discussion with important hospital personnel, such as heads of clinical and nursing departments, hospital administration, and attending medical staffs. Without the support and agreement of these people, resentment, political discord, and dysfunction would result. In our estimation, most hospitals are not ready to adopt or support such a change. In fact, the data indicate that 99 percent of them have not yet adopted ethics committees, and that the committees that have been established are controlled by health professionals and are not publicized to the patient population.[19]

## CONCLUSION

A few hospitals have been gingerly feeling their way by establishing ethics committees—poorly defined, unproven entities. Such committees may find growing support among those health professionals who feel threatened by increasing judicial, legislative, and federal administrative involvement in the clinical decision-making process.

Although hospital ethics committees are controlled by health professionals and are generally inaccessible to patients and families, they may be an acceptable step toward patient autonomy. Patient autonomy could be clearly stated as a governing principle in committee deliberations. Patients and families could be routinely informed about relevant committee meetings. Access to committee deliberations could be provided through limited attendance at meetings or verbal reports from the patient's physician or a committee member. Patient autonomy can also be protected by means other than committees, including patients' rights advocates and staff orientation to the importance of patient autonomy.

The patients in this study saw institutional ethics committees as potentially helpful to both patients and health professionals who must grapple with difficult treatment decisions. As the President's Commission and speakers at a recent national conference on institutional ethics committees suggested,[20] more study of these committees is needed. It would be interesting to see what might result if a hospital took the bold step of informing *all* patients about its committee's existence. The patients in this study would support such a step. We would all learn from the experience.

In establishing a hospital ethics committee, one must be mindful of the social and political realities of modern hospitals. We agree with those commentators who have advocated research of existing committees so that all may learn from each others' experiences and mistakes. The problems we faced when initiating this study may provide insight into the attitudes and prejudices that may influence or even impede any effort to establish hospital ethics committees or make them effective.

Although the story of how the study was approved by the IRB is amusing in retrospect, it was very irritating at the time. Many people in the hospital supported the study, including the chief of staff. There were others, however, who did not approve of increased patient involvement in decision making. Depending upon the individual institution, there will be more or fewer of these people, and their power and prestige will vary. Similarly, as our study shows, any hospital patient population will have different opinions about the right way to do things, who should make decisions, and how they should be made. Thus, one must take into account the political realities inside the hospital, as well as the different needs and wishes of its patients.

## Notes

1. Youngner, S. J., *et al.*, *A National Survey of Hospital Ethics Committees*, CRITICAL CARE MEDICINE 11(11):902–5 (November 1983); PRESIDENT'S COMMISSION FOR THE STUDY OF ETHICAL PROBLEMS IN MEDICINE AND BIOMEDICAL AND BEHAVIORAL RESEARCH, DECIDING TO FOREGO LIFE-SUSTAINING TREATMENT: ETHICAL, LEGAL AND MEDICAL ISSUES IN TREATMENT DECISIONS (U.S. Gov't Printing Office, Washington, D.C.) (March 1983) [hereinafter referred to as DECIDING TO FOREGO TREATMENT]; Cohen, C. B., *Interdisciplinary Consultation on the Care of the Critically Ill and Dying: The Role of One Hospital Ethics Committee*, CRITICAL CARE MEDICINE 10(11):776–84 (November 1982) [hereinafter referred to as *The Role of One Committee*].
2. *See, e.g.*, Faden, R. R., *et al.*, *Disclosure of Information to Patients in Medical Care*, MEDICAL CARE 19(7):718–33 (July 1981); Haug, M., Lavin, B., *Public Challenge of Physician Authority*, MEDICAL CARE 17(8):844–58 (August 1979); Brody, D. S., *The Patient's Role in Clinical Decision Making*, ANNALS OF INTERNAL MEDICINE 93(5):718–22 (November 1980).

3. *See generally* R. M. VEATCH, DEATH, DYING, AND THE BIOLOGICAL REVOLU-
   TION (Yale University Press, New Haven, Ct.) (1976).
4. *The Patient's Role in Clinical Decision Making, supra* note 2, at 721; Jackson,
   D. C., Youngner, S. J., *Patient Autonomy and "Death with Dignity,"* NEW
   ENGLAND JOURNAL OF MEDICINE 301(8):404–8 (August 1979); Siegler, M.,
   *Critical Illness: The Limits of Autonomy,* HASTINGS CENTER REPORT
   7(5):12–15 (October 1977); Ackerman, T. E., *Why Doctors Should Intervene,*
   HASTINGS CENTER REPORT 12(4):14–17 (August 1982); Cassem, N., *When
   to Disconnect the Respirator,* PSYCHIATRIC ANNALS 9:84–93 (1979).
5. Eisendrath, S. J., Jonsen, A. R., *The Living Will: Help or Hindrance?,* JOUR-
   NAL OF THE AMERICAN MEDICAL ASSOCIATION 249(18):2054–58 (April
   1983); Note, *The California Natural Death Act: An Empirical Study of Physicians' Practices,* STANFORD LAW REVIEW 31:913, 940 (May 1979).
6. *See, e.g.,* Suber, D. G., Tabor, W. J., *Withholding of Life-sustaining Treatment
   from the Terminally Ill, Incompetent Patient: Who Decides?, Parts 1, 2,* JOURNAL
   OF THE AMERICAN MEDICAL ASSOCIATION 248(18, 19):2250–51, 2431–32.
7. *In re* Quinlan, 355 A.2d 647 (N.J. 1976).
8. Critical Care Committee of the Massachusetts General Hospital, *Optimum
   Care for Hopelessly Ill Patients,* NEW ENGLAND JOURNAL OF MEDICINE
   295(7):362–64 (August 12, 1976).
9. Annas, G. J., *In re* Quinlan: *Legal Comfort for Doctors,* HASTINGS CENTER
   REPORT 6(3):29–31 (June 1976); Hirsch, H. L., Donovan, R. E., *The Right
   to Die: Medico-Legal Implications of* In re Quinlan, RUTGERS LAW REVIEW
   30(2):267–76 (Winter 1977); Levine, C., *Hospital Ethics Committees: A
   Guarded Prognosis,* HASTINGS CENTER REPORT 7(3):25–26 (June 1977);
   Veatch, R. M., *Hospital Ethics Committees: Is There a Role?,* HASTINGS CEN-
   TER REPORT 7(3):22–25 (June 1977).
10. DECIDING TO FOREGO TREATMENT, *supra* note 1, at 160–70.
11. Youngner *et al., supra* note 1, at 903.
12. DECIDING TO FOREGO TREATMENT, *supra* note 1, at 168–69.
13. *Id.* at 170.
14. Robertson, J., ch. 7 of this text.
15. Youngner *et al., supra* note 1, at 904.
16. *The Role of One Committee, supra* note 1; *Optimum Care for Hopelessly Ill
    Patients, supra* note 8.
17. *The Role of One Committee, supra* note 1, at 777 (emphasis added).
18. DECIDING TO FOREGO TREATMENT, *supra* note 1, at 442 (emphasis added).
19. Youngner *et al., supra* note 1, at 904.
20. Keenan, C., *Ethics Committees: Trend for Troubling Times,* HOSPITAL MEDICAL
    STAFF 12(6):2–8 (June 1983).

# 7

## Committees as Decision Makers: Alternative Structures and Responsibilities

John A. Robertson

Should hospitals create ethics committees and give them a role in the practice of clinical medicine? If so, how should such committees be constituted and how should they function?

Before an institution can decide to form an ethics committee, it must know what one is. Since there is no official definition, I offer the following:

> A hospital ethics committee is an institutionally authorized or designated group of persons that, on an optional or required basis, will advise, discuss, or consult with a physician, patient, or family about ethical issues that arise in clinical care.

This definition is, of course, incomplete; many aspects of the ethics committee remain unspecified. The remarks that follow attempt to fill in the gaps, and thus to provide a firmer basis for determining what hospital policy toward ethics committees should be.

### BACKGROUND AND ORIGINS OF THE INSTITUTIONAL ETHICS COMMITTEE

The use of a committee structure for decisions in the practice of medicine is not especially novel. Hospital medical affairs have traditionally been governed by various committees: credential, tissue, mortality, records, and others. Ethics and disciplinary committees have been an integral feature of medical societies' regulation of medicine. The earliest precursor of committees regulating clinical decisions is found in the sterilization legislation spawned by the eugenics movement of the early twentieth century. An institutional committee of three or four professionals had first to find that the person was "feebleminded" before sterilization could be performed.[1] Another precursor was the therapeutic abortion committee of the 1950s and 1960s which played an important role in facilitating exceptions to a highly restrictive abortion policy.[2]

An ethics-type committee also played an important role in allocating scarce dialysis machines for persons with end-stage renal disease before Medicare funding in 1973 made dialysis available to all who needed it.[3] Professional standards review organizations (PSROs) are another committee-type structure that has played a regulatory role in the clinical setting. The most immediate ancestor, however, is the institutional review board (IRB) system of review of research with human subjects. As the cornerstone of federal research policy, it is a model most administrators and physicians are familiar with, and upon which they may draw in devising institutional ethics committees.

The institutional ethics committee, then, though not novel, is nevertheless unique, in that its area of concern extends beyond a few limited or specialized issues such as research or abortion to the numerous, more comprehensive ethical issues that arise in the care of critically and terminally ill patients. Beginning in the late 1960s and continuing through the 1970s, the realization that medical technology was able to extend the life of critically ill and dying patients moved the debate on death and dying from an exclusively medical realm to a social, ethical, and legal one. As the nonmedical, normative nature of many decisions became clear, many felt that the community should be involved in questions of prolonging or refusing to prolong life, and that legal rules specifying standards and the authority of various actors were needed. The first official mention of an ethics committee in this context arose in the *Quinlan* case in New Jersey. The New Jersey Supreme Court, in appointing Karen Quinlan's father as guardian and authorizing him to remove her from a respirator, held that immunity from suit for such decisions would be provided if a hospital ethics committee reviewed and confirmed the prognosis.[4] Since then, a number of other court cases have mentioned committees.[5] Recently, the President's Commission for the Study of Ethical Problems in Medicine and Biomedical and Behavioral Research has recommended that ethics committees function as part of an intrainstitutional review system for nontreatment decisions.[6]

Although the *Quinlan* case gave great impetus to the idea of committees in clinical medicine, that impetus was, ironically, based on two faulty assumptions. First, the court called the committee an "ethics committee," although the group it described was actually charged with confirming the physician's judgment that the patient was irreversibly comatose.[7] Second, the court relied on a structure that it presumed existed in nearly every institution, even though, as now, ethics committees existed in very few hospitals. Rather than adding to an existing mechanism for reviewing clinical decisions, the ethics committee concept of the New Jersey Supreme Court entailed the creation of a new regulatory body.

At the present time neither legislation nor court decisions require that hospitals create and operate institutional ethics committees, or that physicians consult them. In New Jersey and a few like-minded states, review and approval by an institutional ethics committee will provide immunity from civil and criminal liability. In others such as Massachusetts, where only a court can provide advance immunity,[8] resort to an institutional ethics committee will show a physician's good faith and reasonableness, and may give a de facto immunity. Since creation of an ethics committee is an institution's option, the clinical role of institutional ethics committees depends on the judgment of hospital administrators, attorneys, and physicians.

## OPTIONAL REVIEW BY INSTITUTIONAL ETHICS COMMITTEES

What follows are some observations and suggestions on how an institutional ethics committee might operate. If you are a hospital administrator, a hospital attorney, a chief of medical staff, or another concerned actor, I would recommend that your institution at least set up an "optional/optional" ethics committee for consultation by physicians and others on ethical issues arising in clinical practice.[9] By an optional/ optional committee, I mean that the physician has the option of consulting the committee on ethical matters, as well as the option of choosing whether to follow its advice. The main reason for creating such a committee would be to assist doctors, nurses, and others in wrestling with the ethical dilemmas that increasingly arise in medical practice. We expect physicians and nurses to be sensitive to ethical concerns and to respond to them in socially acceptable ways. Yet most physicians are neither well equipped to handle nor comfortable in handling these value questions, even if they have had a medical school or undergraduate course in medical ethics. While realistically we may hope that providers will be sensitized to recognize ethical issues when they arise, it is another matter to expect them to reach ethically acceptable results on their own.

Short of a committee structure, other resources, such as the in-house ethicist, moral philosopher, or clergy who function as ethical consultants in many institutions, could help physicians with this task. But ethicists are not always available, and many problems require a wider-ranging discussion and perspective than a single ethicist can provide. A committee more representative of the several competing interests can be useful in identifying a greater range of options, in reflecting representative community values, and in providing different professional perspectives.

Indeed, one may catalogue several functions or jobs that an ethics committee can perform for an institution and the doctors, staff, and patients served by it. One function is to facilitate analytic moral inquiry by identifying conflicting interests, rights, and duties, and aiding in the reconciliation of competing goals. A second, closely related function is the educative one. Just as IRBs help educate investigators about ethical norms in research, an optional ethics committee can help educate physicians and others about the moral issues and conflicts that arise in clinical practice, and acceptable ways of resolving them.

The third function is a supportive one. Decisions to terminate treatment often excite profound and complex emotions, and may generate conflict with family members and staff. An institutional ethics committee can help doctors and nurses deal with the stress of ethical dilemmas by allowing them to ventilate their positions and by providing information, support, and some assurance that their actions are in line with community standards.[10]

A fourth function would be to resolve disputes among staff members, and between staff and patients and their families, over nontreatment decisions. Since such disputes may produce acrimonious feelings, it is important to have an in-house forum for resolving disputes rather than to have resolution accomplished, for instance, by fiat of the most senior member of the medical team, or by complaints to law enforcement officials. An in-house forum may prevent disputes about hospital procedures from spilling over into the criminal justice system, as occurred in the *Edelin* case in Boston,[11] the Danville, Illinois, Siamese twins case,[12] and the Kaiser-Permanente physicians' murder case in California.[13]

Finally, from a pragmatic standpoint, such a committee would protect physicians, nurses, institutions, and patients. By making physicians aware of the snares and traps of legal liability, an ethics committee may forestall the initiation of lawsuits or other disciplinary action. If a suit or disciplinary action is brought, the fact that the physician had consulted an ethics committee for advice would tend to show that he or she had acted reasonably and in good faith, which a physician acting alone might be hard pressed to show. Since physicians are unlikely to be found criminally liable for withholding care if they have acted on a "good faith" judgment that is not "grievously unreasonable" by medical standards,[14] resort to an institutional ethics committee should lessen the risk of adverse legal consequences. The ethics committee can thus function as an ethical risk management team to protect the institution and the physician as well as the patient and family.[15]

OPERATIONAL AND PROCEDURAL ISSUES

How would a consultative committee actually operate in a hospital? Just as in architecture form follows function, so the form of an ethics committee should follow the functions that we ascribe to it. The operational questions of most concern are jurisdiction, authority, composition, and procedures. The answers to these questions for an optional/ optional ethics committee readily suggest themselves. For example, the issue of jurisdiction is resolved by a decision to make the committee available to any physician or other designated member of the institution. The institution may also want to give families and patients or their representatives access to this forum. As for authority, since the purpose of such a committee is to advise, clarify, and facilitate management of ethical issues, it functions in a consultative capacity and has no decision-making authority of its own.

The matter of composition needs some discussion. Should the committee include lawyers, ethicists, clergy, and former patients, as well as physicians and nurses? To simplify matters, the institutional review board model having at least five persons, one of whom is not from the institution, would be a sufficient base on which an institution could build a workable committee.[16] It would be desirable to have someone with training in ethics on the committee. However, if an ethicist is not available, many ethics committee functions can still be served simply by having members of the local "moral community" review the case.

The question of operating procedures can also be answered by reference to the functions of an optional/optional committee. As an optional/optional advisory body, the committee's proceedings need not be formal. Unlike the case of institutional review boards, nothing written need be submitted, and no records need be kept. There is no reason for this procedure to be public or open because it is simply an advisory mechanism for members of the health care team. Nor would a committee with the optional/optional format have to notify the patient, much less get his or her permission to consider the case, though it may be desirable to do so. If consultation with the committee is viewed as another form of the consultation that physicians engage in for the benefit of the patient, the explicit consent of the patient would not be required, for consultations are part of the implied contract between physicians and patients.

A final point about operating procedures concerns the liability of institutional ethics committee members and the admissibility and discoverability of its records. While a negligently conducted review leading to patient or physician injury could result, in theory, in institutional ethics committee liability, most states have statutes that give hospital or medical staff review committees immunity from liability, and make their records confidential.[17] Taking the applicable Minnesota statute as a representative example,[18] it is reasonably clear that in Minnesota an optional/optional committee functioning as an official hospital or medical staff committee to review ethical issues that arise in medical practice would be immune from liability and its records privileged against discovery and admission into evidence.

OBJECTIONS

There are, naturally, some objections to the formation of an institutional ethics committee, even an optional/optional one, that may arise. One is that it would be costly to operate. However, since an ethics committee would not be as active or as elaborate as an institutional review board, at least initially, operational costs may not be a serious concern. Perhaps more important is the fear that the committee will interfere with clinical judgment in the doctor-patient relationship. This objection has a great deal of force in the context of institutional ethics committees with mandatory review and decisional authority. But since activation of the optional/optional committee, as well as the decision of whether or not to follow its advice, are entirely dependent upon the physician, it is hard to see how the committee would intrude on the doctor-patient relationship. Even if nurses, patients, or families could activate review, clinical judgment—though perforce exposed to other views of the case—remains intact, for the physician is not obligated to follow the committee's advice.

Indeed, the main problem with an optional/optional committee might be that it would not be intrusive *enough*, in that it would not be consulted on the full range of cases where its advice is needed. Achieving the goals and functions of an institutional ethics committee requires that cases be brought to it. Thus, leaving this decision optional with physicians will result in institutional ethics committees being greatly underutilized, for doctors will be reluctant to bring cases to them. Data about existing ethics committees confirm this fear. Not only have physicians not pushed for the creation of such committees, but when they exist, they have seldom been used. A survey for the President's Commission for the Study of Ethical Problems in Medicine and Biomedical and Behavioral Research found that no hospital with fewer than 200 beds had an institutional ethics committee.[19] Moreover, only 1 percent of hospitals with more than 200 beds had an institutional ethics committee, and seven of those were in New Jersey where, after the *Quinlan* case, the creation of prognosis confirmation committees (counted in the survey as institutional ethics committees) might have been expected. When an institutional ethics committee existed, it was used on an average of once a year.

This low rate of utilization can be explained by such factors as the relative newness of the committee as a resource, ignorance on the part of the medical staff concerning its utility, and the fact that there is no strong incentive for using it. An additional factor that may be impeding the development of even optional/optional committees is an ideological or sociological bias toward independence and self-reliance in clinical decision making. A well-established physician from Johns Hopkins Medical School, in a personal communication with the author on the usefulness of an optional/optional ethics committee, remarked that "in 30 years of practice, I never had a case that I could not handle on my own." This remark typifies an attitude toward individual responsibility which institutional ethics committees must confront and overcome if they are to penetrate the hospital. Since an optional/optional ethics committee is strictly consultative and advisory, it is the type that is least threatening to medical independence.[20]

## MANDATORY REVIEW BY INSTITUTIONAL ETHICS COMMITTEES

The reluctance of physicians to use optional institutional ethics committees raises the question of whether ethics committee review should be mandatory in certain cases. The main issues here involve identifying situations of sufficient complexity and conflict to justify the intrusiveness of mandatory review. Another question is whether the institutional ethics committee review should be "mandatory/optional" or "mandatory/mandatory." In the mandatory/optional form physicians would have to consult the ethics committee in certain cases, but would not be required to follow its advice. In the mandatory/mandatory form, the physician would be required both to consult the committee and to follow its advice. This, in effect, transforms the institutional ethics committee into a decision maker in those cases. There are arguments supporting each form.

When a committee is optional/optional, and physicians choose not to use it or not to follow its advice, poor, unacceptable, or ethically indefensible decisions may still result. This may be because of the difficulty in communicating norms, confusion about what a rule requires in a particular case, pressures to ignore the rule and advance other interests, and the low visibility of the whole process. A supplemental procedure to make sure that physicians are actually considering the ethical implications of a case may then be necessary. Indeed, such concerns led to the creation of the IRB system for human subject research, a form of mandatory/mandatory review. The idea for the IRB system was born when it became clear that researchers sometimes advanced their own interests at the expense of their subjects. An implementing structure or mechanism was necessary to make sure that researchers would be aware of applicable rules, such as those relating to informed consent, and would follow them in practice. Human subjects research, however, is not the only area in medicine where conflicting interests generate pressures to ignore ethical considerations. Thus, there may be a need for supplementary mechanisms such as mandatory review committees elsewhere as well.

When should review be mandatory? A general guideline would be to consider the need for mandatory review whenever there is a likelihood that a clinical decision will implicate important nonmedical interests that the physician and family or patient should not have the sole right to decide. The scope of mandatory review thus depends upon a prior value judgment of the relative importance of the interests at stake and the likelihood that competing interests may skew the results of clinical judgments. Human subjects research is a paradigm of ethical conflict that reappears in many other settings. Sterilization of the retarded, for example, presents the possibility that the doctor and the family will ignore the interests of the retarded person, and this justifies mandatory review. While many physicians or hospitals may refuse to sterilize a retarded person without a court order,[21] a less costly alternative to judicial review would be review by an institutional ethics committee to ascertain whether the sterilization can in fact be justified as being in the retarded person's interests.

Another compelling case for mandatory review would be one involving bone marrow or other transplants from minors. Still another case is the defective newborn situation. Whenever parents and their physician are planning to withhold lifesaving treatment from a child with Down's syndrome or spina bifida, there should be a mandatory in-house review, as the President's Commission has recommended.[22] One might also consider mandatory review when treatment is withheld from incompetent but non–terminally ill patients, such as Karen Quinlan and Earle Spring, or for particular subclasses of such decisions.

While review should be mandatory in some cases, the question is whether to rely on a mandatory/optional process or to go further and make it a mandatory/mandatory process. Will it be enough simply to require that the physician consult an institutional ethics committee, leaving it up to him or her whether or not to follow its advice? Or should we require both review and compliance with the ethics committee's decision, as occurs with IRB review of human subject research? The IRB does not simply advise the physician about the ethics of proposed research, but decides whether the research can be done at all. If the IRB disapproves, the physician cannot ignore its decision and go forward with the research.[23]

Other situations may be so fraught with ethical risks as to require that the institutional ethics committee have final decision-making power. For example, it should not be sufficient that the physician and family have consulted an ethics committee in deciding to use their four-year-old daughter's marrow for another member of the family, if they then ignore its decision that it would be unethical. A difficult issue in the ethics committee debate will be to define those cases in which review should be mandatory, and where ultimate decisional authority is given to the ethics committee.[24]

Since form follows function, the form and procedures of a mandatory ethics committee will differ in some important respects from those of the optional/optional committee. When the committee is optional/optional, it functions as a consultant. It is there to facilitate the physician's independent moral inquiry. However, when it becomes mandatory, the committee functions more like a decision maker applying preset norms or rules to each case. Although some ethics committees will function as policymakers for the institution, and actually draft rules and standards to be applied to particular cases, a mandatory/mandatory institutional ethics committee will usually apply rules and norms given by some other authority (such as courts, legislatures, or the institution), rather than create them itself.

Questions of jurisdiction and authority will be resolved in the decision to make institutional ethics committee review mandatory/optional or mandatory/mandatory. With respect to composition, the mandatory committee could have the same composition as the optional committee. However, an important difference between mandatory and optional committees would be in the procedures followed. When the mandatory/mandatory nature of review turns the institutional ethics committee into the decision-making authority, there is an obligation to inform patients and to involve them or their representatives in the decision-making process. Just as the physician who is denied staff privileges has a right to be notified of that decision and to participate in it, or an investigator whose protocol is turned down has the right to appear before the IRB and present his or her views, due process requires that when the committee review is mandatory/mandatory, the patient has the right to notice and participation. By the same token, when the mandatory committee has decision-making authority, it functions more like a public body. Its operations should then be open and available to public scrutiny.

CONCLUSION

This brief survey of some of the salient issues surrounding institutional ethics committees suggests that the time has come for every health care institution to consider designating a body of persons to be available for ethical consultation on an optional basis. It also suggests that, in a narrow category of cases, institutions should require some kind of mandatory in-house review. A new forum, growing out of the IRB model, is ready to help physicians, nurses, patients, and administrators wrestle with the ethical issues that our technological magic continues to present us. I commend the ethics committee form to you.

NOTES

1. *See, e.g.*, Buck v. Bell, 274 U.S. 200 (1927).
2. *See* B. SARVIS, H. RODMAN, THE ABORTION CONTROVERSY, (Columbia University Press, New York) (2d ed. 1974) at 36–40.
3. *See* J. KATZ, A. M. CAPRON, CATASTROPHIC DISEASES: WHO DECIDES? (Russell Sage Foundation, New York) (1975) at 191–92.
4. *In re* Quinlan, 355 A.2d 647 (N.J. 1976).
5. *See, e.g.*, *In re* Eichner, 426 N.Y.S.2d 517 (N.Y. 1980); *In re* Colyer, 660 P.2d 738, 749 (Wash. 1983).
6. PRESIDENT'S COMMISSION FOR THE STUDY OF ETHICAL PROBLEMS IN MEDICINE AND BIOMEDICAL AND BEHAVIORAL RESEARCH, DECIDING TO FOREGO LIFE-SUSTAINING TREATMENT: ETHICAL, MEDICAL AND LEGAL ISSUES IN TREATMENT DECISIONS (U.S. Gov't Printing Office, Washington, D.C.) (March 1983) [hereinafter referred to as DECIDING TO FOREGO TREATMENT].
7. *Quinlan, supra* note 4, at 671. The Washington Supreme Court in *In re Colyer* recognizes this problem and calls explicitly for a prognosis committee.
8. Superintendent of Belchertown State School v. Saikewicz, 370 N.E.2d 417 (1977); *In re* Spring, 405 N.E.2d 115 (Mass. 1980).
9. The institution, if it follows its designated governance procedures, has ample authority to create institutional review committees, and even to require that they be consulted or decide how particular cases are to be managed. For a discussion of the legal authority of institutions to regulate the professional activities of staff, see Robertson, J., *The Law of Institutional Review Boards*, U.C.L.A. LAW REVIEW 26:484 (1979).
10. The supportive function was mentioned in the description of an ethics-type committee for ICU decisions at the Massachusetts General Hospital. *See* Critical Care Committee of the Massachusetts General Hospital, *Optimum Care for Hopelessly Ill Patients*, NEW ENGLAND JOURNAL OF MEDICINE 295(7):315 (August 12, 1976).
11. 359 N.E.2d 4 (Mass. 1976).
12. *See* Robertson, J., *Dilemma in Danville*, HASTINGS CENTER REPORT 11(5):5 (October 1981).

13. Magistrate's Findings, People v. Barber and Nejdl, No. A 025586 (Los Angeles Municipal Court, Los Angeles County, Calif., March 9, 1983).
14. *See In re* Spring, *supra* note 8, at 122.
15. By helping to assure that the physician acts lawfully, the ethics committee is also likely to protect the interests of patients and families.
16. Annas, G. J., remarks at the Conference on Institutional Ethics Committees and Health Care Decision Making, sponsored by the American Society of Law & Medicine, Washington, D.C., April 1983.
17. *See, e.g.,* N.Y. EDUC. LAW §6527(3) (McKinney Supp. 1982–1983). However, to qualify for such protection, the committee may have to be constituted as an official hospital or medical staff committee.
18. MINN. STAT. ANN. §§145.61–.67 (West Supp. 1983).
19. Youngner, S. J., *et al., A National Survey of Hospital Ethics Committees,* in DECIDING TO FOREGO TREATMENT, *supra* note 6, at 446–47.
20. The question of whether resort to an optional/optional committee could change it into an optional/mandatory committee is complex and beyond the scope of this paper. Briefly, the committee's decision or advice—if there is clear advice—would not necessarily define reasonableness, and therefore need not necessarily be followed by the physician. The physician may therefore have it both ways: gaining legal protection from consulting the committee, without having to take its advice. The ultimate legal issue will be the reasonableness of the physician's action, which will not necessarily be determined by the committee's view of the situation.
21. *See, e.g., In re* Grady, 405 A.2d 851 (1979). As with review of nontreatment decisions by ethics committees, a court order is not usually legally required, though when obtained, it provides immunity.
22. DECIDING TO FOREGO TREATMENT, *supra* note 6, at 227–28.
23. Protection of Human Subjects, 45 C.F.R. §46.109 (1981).
24. One form of mandatory/mandatory review would have the ethics committee identify those cases in which the institution or physician should go to court to have a guardian appointed to make decisions on behalf of the patient. *See* DECIDING TO FOREGO TREATMENT, *supra* note 6, at 227.

# 8

## Institutional Ethics Committees Speak for Themselves

Thomasine Kushner and Joan M. Gibson

The burgeoning number of institutional ethics committees is testimony to the fact that more and more institutions are responding to a need to find internal means of dealing with the increasingly complex array of ethical dilemmas. Paralleling the geometric progression of their growth are the questions that arise as to how these committees are faring and functioning.

To facilitate an exchange of this information,[1] we asked representative committees from different kinds of institutions and from a variety of geographical locations to submit self-descriptive reports that would serve as portraits of their particular committees. The resulting narratives, and supplemental commentaries, differ from the growing body of statistical information in a vivid way. The sharing of their histories, growing pains, successes, and shortcomings provides a practical and realistic account of IECs.

The needs of institutions are necessarily different, and the committees reflect the range of those differing needs in the scope of their attempted solutions. This is only as it should be; and in analyzing the reports we have been more interested in providing an overview of the variety of models and approaches used by committees than in trying to reduce the diversity of experiences to their commonalities.

While not wanting to discourage a description of each committee's unique qualities, for the sake of continuity, and to lend some symmetry to the reports, we suggested that an outline be followed covering some basic topics, such as the history of the committee; its structure, function, and activities; and its position within the institution (see the complete form preceding the descriptive reports, in Section II of this text).

From the start, the information received from responding committees addressed three primary areas of interest: (1) institutional ethics committees in the 1970s, (2) current profiles (the early 1980s) and (3) trends and predictions. Each of these will be discussed below.

## INSTITUTIONAL ETHICS COMMITTEES IN THE 1970s

Most of the committees represented in the self-descriptive reports are quite recent in origin, the oldest having been formed in 1971. If data from questionnaires submitted by participants at the ASLM conference are representative, the growth of the committees during the 1970s was comparatively slow. According to the questionnaires, only 18 committees were started during this decade, as opposed to 47 new committees since 1980. From January to April of 1983, 15 committees were formed—almost as many in a four-month period as in the whole previous ten years. This recent proliferation is part of a trend that seems to be nationwide. It would not be unreasonable to speculate that the President's Commission, and its subsequent series of reports, has had some bearing on this burst of interest and growth.

Of those committees established during the mid-1970s, many report that they were responding to specific problems in determining appropriate care—both physical and psychosocial—for dying patients and their families. In so doing, they focused on such topics as withholding treatment, termination of mechanical life-support systems, care in crisis, and the Karen Ann Quinlan case. Even prior to Karen Ann Quinlan, however, committees were concerned that "dying patients and their relatives were not receiving proper treatment" (North Shore University Hospital).[2] Because questions of death and dying were primary, it was not unusual for committees to call themselves "thanatology committees" in this early period.

Certainly the publicity surrounding the *Quinlan* case increased the number of such committees, as well as the variety of purposes they serve. For example, the Morris View Nursing Home Ethics Committee was established for the sole purpose of dealing with its newly admitted client, Karen Ann Quinlan; and establishment of the Critical Care Advisory Committee of the University Hospitals of Cleveland was "prompted by administrative concern following the Karen Ann Quinlan case, coupled with a desire to handle ethical issues in the most optimal way possible." It was common for committees established for these purposes to be staffed mostly by physicians, and to engage actively in consultation with individual health care providers, normally in an advisory capacity only.

This same period saw committees established for other reasons as well. Some reacted to specific ethical dilemmas such as abortion or allocation of scarce resources. Others recognized the need for broad education—self-education, institution-wide education, and community education—covering a truly interdisciplinary range of issues. Committees established for the latter reason were the forerunners of current committees that are either forming for the first time or restructuring themselves in major ways. Whereas early thanatology committees normally offered consultation services, most education-oriented committees did not.

In the late 1970s, many of the consulting committees suspended this activity in order to engage in serious self- and institution-wide education programs, and to redefine their mission and role in a way that would reflect a broader range of issues and activities. Symbolic of these early attempts to expand committees' roles is the deletion of the word "moral" from many names and the substitution instead of the word "ethical" or "bioethical." The intent was to broaden the focus of the committee to include a fuller range of ethical and interdisciplinary issues. This expansion is summed up by the Biomedical Ethics Committee of the Hennepin County Medical Center, Minneapolis:

> The main reason for disbanding the thanatology committee and forming a new Biomedical Ethics Committee was because many members of the thanatology committee, as well as others in our institution, felt that the scope of the committee's work should be broadened to include more than just issues related to death and dying—as we became increasingly aware of recurrent bioethical themes that covered many ethical dilemmas and not just termination of treatment. Also, we felt there was a need to expand the committee to make it more truly representative of the views and interests of the hospital. The thanatology committee usually had about ten members, and we felt that that was probably not sufficient to adequately represent the views of the hospital.

Thus, by 1980, restructured (and often renamed) thanatology committees, early ethics education committees, and ethics committees being formed for the first time shared a remarkably common view of their purpose and potential effectiveness: education first, policy making second, and consultation third (but only after sufficient time for education had elapsed, and even then with caution).

## CURRENT PROFILES: THE EARLY 1980s

Current profiles of committees whose self-descriptions follow can be grouped in three categories: single-issue or consult-only committees, education and policy-making committees, and committees that consult in addition to developing educational programs and institutional policies.

Single-issue/consult-only committees maintain such a focus either because of the continuing influence of the initial mandate (as in the case of the Morris View Nursing Home Ethics Committee) or because of the unique circumstances of the institution. For example, the Hebrew Home of Greater Washington, serving as it does a clientele whose needs and conditions are more homogeneous than those of an acute care facility, explains why it has moved away from policy making and concentrates on consultation only: "At first the committee was educational, but now it is largely consultive. We have found that each case is so different that we could not set policies down on paper, although in a more subtle way, policies have been shaped by the discussions and consensus reached at meetings."

Committees engaging only in education and policy making emphasize the need for self-education above all. They advise careful preparation: "Words of advice: Start quietly, slowly. Develop your own member bonds and expertise. Keep a multidisciplinary membership." (Biomedical Ethics Committee, University of Minnesota Hospitals and Clinics, Minneapolis). Some committees that express reluctance to initiate consultation have effective pastoral care or counseling services already in place. Their desire not to duplicate these activities is understandable. "It is our opinion that we ought to avoid individual care responsibility where at all possible. To date, no case referrals have been received. We believe that a working dialogue between patient (where possible), family, nursing staff, doctors, and pastoral care providers is the best solution when dealing with the individual problems and decisions" (Medical Ethics Committee, St. Joseph Hospital, Albuquerque).

Virtually all of the reporting multipurpose committees have developed strong educational and/or policy-making roles as necessary support for what is usually a low-key, advisory-only ethics consultation service. "The Committee's role is definitely advisory. However, because committee members are well educated with regard to legal issues, physicians have recently looked to the committee for a 'current standard of medical practice' kind of legal approval before taking definite steps, e.g., withdrawal of life-support equipment" (Mount Sinai Bioethics Committee, Mount Sinai Hospital, Minneapolis).

A committee's position within the institutional hierarchy, no matter which of the three types it may be, is revealing. The majority of those reporting function as subcommittees either of the Medical Staff Committee or of the Administration/Hospital Committee—the two most powerful institutional forces. The next most usual arrangement is for a committee to report to either a human services or a social services department. Responses were also received from a Board Committee, a Medical/Administrative Joint Committee, and an ad hoc committee which was not a part of the institutional flow chart. It is interesting that even in these latter situations, the committee reportedly enjoyed strong support from either the medical staff or administration or both. The ad hoc committee has received implicit administrative support and is gathering medical staff support. For those committees reporting, (1) their status within the institution is seen as legitimate and stable; and (2) long-term growth and even survival may depend, at least in part, on the strength of the relationship between a committee and its institution.

There is no issue on which there is greater diversification among committees than the amount of structure a group feels is needed to carry out its function. At one end of the spectrum is the Biomedical Ethics Committee of Hennepin County Medical Center which, from its inception, has considered informality a desirable feature:

> We have never formally stated in writing the exact purpose or purposes of our committee but have decided to proceed in an informal manner. This was deliberate on our part because we felt that if we became too formal in our stated procedures, there might be negative repercussions from the physicians and others in our hospital who have a misunderstanding of the function of our committee. We felt that to formalize our objectives might be counterproductive to the work of our committee.

This committee continues to define itself as it grows in response to needs and to resist being hampered by what it sees as the rigidity imposed by more specific delineations.

This fluidity is in sharp contrast to committees who assume as their initial task precise mapping of their direction and aims. Notable is the Ethical Advisory Committee of Holy Cross Hospital, Silver Spring, Maryland. Because of its corporate structure, this committee began its work with a statement of purpose that described the function of the committee; proposed goals; defined the issues to be addressed, ranking them according to priority; and assigned the resulting categories to appropriate subcommittees.

Both of these committees, so different in their initial approaches, agree on the usefulness of subcommittees to address recurring ethical dilemmas for which policies and appropriate means of decision making need to be developed. In the words of the Hennepin County Medical Center Bioethics Committee, "We believe subcommittees are useful in providing mechanisms, procedures, or other means for decision making in the frequently faced issues; e.g., when respirator-dependent patients who are alert and competent request termination of treatment, how should the distress that follows that discontinuation be treated? A subcommittee can make an important contribution by making specific recommendations as to appropriate medications to give." However, subcommittees may offer more than just an effective means of dealing with a single topic. When their membership is expanded to include others of the hospital and medical staff, as in the case of the Ethical Advisory Committee of Holy Cross Hospital (Silver Spring, Maryland), they also can be very successful in promoting awareness and interest in committee work throughout the institution.

Regarding their successes and strengths, the committees respond in a variety of ways. For the committee brought together solely for the purpose of the Quinlan deliberations, success is measured in the narrowest way—its continued existence and its current plans to reexamine its role. Remaining committees gauge their success by some combination of the following factors: increased number of meetings and requests for consultations, growth in credibility and visibility within the institution, support from physicians who once saw the committee as threatening, acceptance of the committee's policies and guidelines, continued existence as a forum for the exchange of ideas among diverse disciplines, and the growing ability of committee members to recognize and think through an ethical issue. However, the theme repeated most often involves the changes brought about through the educational functions of committees, which heighten and maintain awareness of ethical issues: "By raising the consciousness of the staff to ethical issues, much more consideration is given to problems of competency, consent, promotion of autonomy, etc. We are aware of cases which have been redirected by staff members asking, 'What do you think the Ethics Committee would say about this projected course of therapy?'" (Ethics and Human Values Committee, Rose Medical Center, Denver). The same committee offers the ultimate definition of success: "True success would be such widespread knowledge and sensitivity that there would be no need for such a group."

From the time of the early committees to the present, there has been a general shift in the kinds of problems committees encounter with respect to their own structure and function. Originally, in the 1970s, difficulties were primarily internal, as committees struggled to define their role and establish a sense of purpose. In the 1980s, however, committees have achieved more agreement and understanding within themselves as to their proper identity. As a consequence of this change, the problems facing committees are more likely to be external ones—for example, time constraints and inadequate funding.

The lack of adequate time routinely plagues committees in two ways: (1) unfortunate curtailment of committee discussions and (2) insufficient time to properly educate committee members and hospital staff. This second difficulty is viewed as a critical element in optimum committee functioning. Committees also complain about a lack of financial resources to promote committee activities, provide administrative and clerical help, and support visits by outside speakers.

The most pervasive and frustrating difficulty, however, involves distorted perceptions and suspicions about committee activities on the part of administration and staff. Administration's resistance to change takes the form of, "what we have now works fine." At a large county teaching hospital familiar to one of the authors, a multidisciplinary group sought administration's support in establishing an IEC. The request was met with the concern that more problems might be created than alleviated, but there was agreement that a committee would be formed to study the question. When after six months the investigative committee was not yet functioning, an ad hoc "ethics study group" began gathering, not to advise, consult, or make policy, but only to meet the participants' own needs to explore pressing ethical dilemmas. The study group is entirely outside official sanction, but is attracting increased interest within the institution and offers an alternative until administrative approval, if not enthusiasm, can be secured.

In addition to administrative reluctance, there is also the perennial distrust on the part of physicians that their traditional decision-making powers will be threatened. Typical of this concern is the comment by the Ethics Committee of the Hebrew Home of Greater Washington, that "staff physicians are reluctant to bring cases to the committee since they see it as a loss of control and they do not like a committee 'looking over their shoulders' and asking 'Why?'" Growing committee credibility has served to allieviate such concerns, as evidenced by the Medical Moral Committee of St. Joseph Hospital, Mt. Clemens, Michigan: "The greatest fear seemed to be that the committee would be telling the M.D.s what they could or could not do. This group is beginning to see the committee as a strong support."

## TRENDS AND PREDICTIONS

Assuming that medical, legal, and social events will continue to demand attention and resolution—and there is good reason to expect that they will do so in increasingly visible and striking ways—the future of IECs is virtually guaranteed. How they shape their own future, however, is another issue. We offer the following observations and predictions, drawn from our own experience as well as from the material included in this volume, for use by institutions considering establishing an IEC, by newly formed committees whose identity is still evolving, and by well-established committees who recognize the value of self-examination, not only for the health care providers with whom they consult, but also for themselves as a committee.

INCREASE IN THE NUMBER OF COMMITTEES

The safest prediction is that the number of IECs will increase dramatically over the next decade, at least in part for the reasons listed below. At all levels within institutions there is a growing awareness of urgent, complex problems whose resolutions are beyond the capabilities of individuals acting alone. (For example, the Ethics and Human Values Committee at Rose Medical Center, Denver, has been requested by the hospital administration to study the ethical issues involved in a proposed *in vitro* fertilization program, and at the University of California, San Francisco, the Medical Ethics Committee was asked by the Chief of Medical Services to explore questions in the treatment of AIDS.) Even where such a realization may not be supported by first-hand experience, relentless bombardment by the media makes total ignorance of these issues nearly impossible. A genuinely attractive feature of most IECs is the extent to which their structure mirrors the interdisciplinary reality of the issues and decisions brought for review.

INCREASING ADMINISTRATIVE PRESSURE

There is good reason to expect, as legal and regulatory constraints on institutional activities increase, that administrators will look to legitimate and effective internal groups to develop policies and to monitor individual situations. IECs are ideally suited for this, and we expect increased pressure from administrators, agencies, and government to establish such committees where none exist, to determine which policies shall be developed, and to decide how mandatory review procedures for certain types of cases will be established (e.g., withdrawing treatment from permanently unconscious patients, and treatment decisions for seriously ill or defective newborns). Committees will have to pay serious attention to the nature of their response to such pressures.

INCREASING PRESSURE FOR CONSULTATION

Although recent trends have shown a reluctance on the part of most committees to concentrate only on their consultative, single-case-review activities, there is no question that as these committees develop sound interdisciplinary expertise, and as they become more visible within their institutions, they will be asked to consult even if they do not invite such activity. A number of committees that do not yet consult report that they are being urged to do so. And committees already providing such services have recently experienced a sizable jump in the number of requests.

EMPHASIS ON EDUCATION

Committees that have been formed or have restructured themselves during the past three years identify the same activity as having top priority for their committee: education, beginning with self-education. A remark by the Medical Moral Committee of St. Joseph Hospital, Mt. Clemens, is representative: "When we started we knew very little, but through workshops and reading we grew." Since most members assume their committee roles without any expertise in dealing with ethical dilemmas, and few committees have access to professional ethicists, groups recognize a need for self-education before turning to other activities. One group determined that "without some formal background in normative ethics there simply continued to be an expression of personal reaction" (Committee on Ethics and Human Values, Rose Medical Center, Denver). The Mount Sinai Bioethics Committee, Minneapolis, thought this initial step so vital that it took approximately two years to educate committee members, so that they would feel qualified to handle consultations. For the Clinical Ethics Committee of the Royal Victoria Hospital, Montreal, the process took longer:

> . . . with respect to the functions of consultation and education the committee early adopted the philosophy that they would first have to educate themselves and develop a "feel" for ethical issues before they could presume to consult on problems or educate others. Three years of discussion on various topics, reading, exchange of information, and input by knowledgeable members have perhaps brought us to the point where it is felt that the committee could make a significant contribution in these areas.

To assist in self-education, University of Minnesota Hospitals and Clinics advises committees to "develop a data base for ethical issues, advancing medical technology and its implications, sponsor talks, provide a network of communication for local, state, and national seminars." Hennepin County Medical Center makes the strong point that even consultations are most accurately viewed as part of their educational activities: "We have found the most effective way to educate is through our consultations. In consulting we are, at the same time, educating." Whether or not committees subsequently assume policy-making and/or consultative roles, they recognize that interdisciplinary self-education is needed to a greater degree than any of them had realized.[3]

Self-education may also serve as a valuable tool in helping individual committee members to arrive at their own reasoned decisions rather than succumbing to the will of more forceful committee members. Surgeon General C. Everett Koop, when recently asked his opinion of IECs, expressed to one of the authors his concern that rather than working together to arrive at rational decisions, committees may simply reflect the views of the dominant members. As an example, Dr. Koop cited his own experience in an institution where certain treatment policies had been changed as a direct result of his strong influence. Dr. Koop suggested that entirely different policies would be effected in another institution where the dominant persons were of another mind. The Hebrew Home of Greater Washington also reports having experienced this problem: "One very strong, articulate individual is sometimes able to sway the group (not the same individual at each meeting). Rabbis tend to have more influence than other disciplines. Doctors are the next most influential group." However, Dr. Koop expressed the belief that if a committee of hospital staff members (physicians, nurses, administrators, etc.) were augmented by members of the community—for example, parents of a disabled child, disability experts, or representatives of a disability advocacy group—the committee would have the means to come to satisfactory decisions about infant care.

Rather than seeing the possibility that the committee will be dominated by one or more powerful members as an inherent weakness of IECs that attentuates their effectiveness, it would seem more reasonable to take these examples as strong arguments for self-education. The purpose of education is to learn how to think through an ethical dilemma, not merely to support a particular view or espouse a specific position, no matter how cleverly or convincingly it is proposed. This involves developing an approach to ethical problems in medicine which liberates the person from relying simply on emotion, intuition, spontaneous decision making, or the beliefs of powerful authority figures. Education of this kind—whether for the committee, members of the institutional community, or the community at large—aims at empowering those closest to and responsible for a decision with the ability to make the best decision possible.

## NOTES

1. The study was undertaken in response to requests from participants at the conference on institutional ethics committees sponsored by the American Society of Law & Medicine, Washington, D.C., April 1983.
2. The self-descriptive reports of all committees cited in this chapter are provided in Section II of this text.
3. Self-education materials for committees are presently being compiled by the authors.

# 9

# Institutional Committees: The New Jersey Experience

Russell L. McIntyre and David N. Buchalter

Advances in the technologies of medicine have provided greater control over life, disease, and, especially, the process of dying. Prior to the development of life-support technologies, chemotherapy, and the transplantation of viable organs, physicians generally perceived their duty to be that of making every conceivable effort to prolong life. With the development of these new technologies, however, serious questions have arisen as to what may constitute "acting in the best interest of the patient."[1]

In the care of the terminally ill, the choice has become increasingly difficult because physicians are realizing that in many cases, extraordinary measures "only prolong suffering, isolate the family from their loved one . . . or result in economic ruin for the family."[2] The New Jersey Supreme Court, in the Karen Ann Quinlan case, recognized the difficult and complex nature of medical decision making regarding the irreversibly ill and dying patient. In that decision, the court acknowledged that to ask a court "to confirm such decisions . . . would [generally] be . . . [an] encroachment upon the medical profession's field of competence."[3] The court also rejected judicial review because it would be impossibly cumbersome.

The court suggested, instead, that "[d]ecision making within health care, if it is to be considered as an expression of a primary obligation of a physician . . . should be controlled primarily within the patient-doctor-family relationship."[4] Not wanting to encourage the seeking of judicial determinations regarding the care of hopelessly ill patients, the court suggested that local hospital-based "ethics committees"[5] be used to sanction the removal of life-support technologies, presumably allowing the hopelessly ill patient to die rather than to be maintained in a chronic vegetative state.

The *Quinlan* decision made two important contributions to medical decision making for the permanently unconscious patient, which together form the backdrop for the *New Jersey Guidelines*.[6] First, the court said that the decision concerning treatment should focus on the prognosis of the patient. To paraphrase the court, when the patient's prognosis begins to worsen and when the patient is beyond being restored to a cognitive, sapient state, then the state's interest in protecting and preserving life begins to be overshadowed by the patient's right of privacy and right to refuse further treatment. Second, the court said that the focus of that decision ought to rest with the family.[7] In the fall of 1976, responding to these directions by the court, the attorney general of New Jersey, the president of the New Jersey Board of Medical Examiners, and the state health commissioner convened a special committee for the purpose of establishing guidelines to permit the formation and functioning of "prognosis committees" to review cases similar to that of Karen Ann Quinlan.

Three things should be noted about the *Guidelines* themselves. First, the *Guidelines* encompass all health care facilities, both hospitals and nursing homes. Second, the *Guidelines* were not promulgated as regulations and therefore do not have the force of law; nor do they require any health care facility in New Jersey to establish such a committee. Finally, the *Guidelines* were intended to spell out one way in which a health care facility might comply with the directions of the New Jersey Supreme Court in the Karen Ann Quinlan case.[8] Health care facilities were free to form or not to form a committee based upon either the *Guidelines* or the more general description found in the *Quinlan* decision, which suggests that nonmedical personnel have a role in such committees. As we shall see, hospitals in New Jersey use both models.

## PROGNOSIS COMMITTEE GUIDELINES

### ACTIVATION OF THE COMMITTEE

There are a variety of ways that the committees in New Jersey can become activated, because of their voluntary nature. The *Guidelines* refer to two ways. In the first, the physician approaches the prognosis committee with the concurrence of the family or guardian.[9] In the second, "[t]he patient's family or guardian, or the attending physician acting on behalf of the family may, in writing, request the health care facility's chief executive officer (administrator) to activate the Prognosis Committee to begin its work on a case."[10] As shown in the second part of this chapter, the committees active in New Jersey have diverse methods of initiating review.

## COMPOSITION OF THE COMMITTEE

Committees formulated according to the *Guidelines* would be staffed by physicians only. The *Guidelines* call for a "core" medical group consisting of a general surgeon, an internist, a neurologist or neurosurgeon, and an anesthesiologist. If the patient is a child, then a pediatrician must be a part of the core group. The *Guidelines* suggest, but do not require, that all core group members be board-certified in their fields.

The *Guidelines* also stipulate that at least two physicians from outside the facility be selected by the board of trustees of that health care facility to serve as members of the committee. In addition, the family (or the attending physician) may designate two physicians, one of whom is a specialist for purposes of consultation, and one of whom is to be present throughout the committee's deliberations. None of these participants should have had any previous association with the case. The *Guidelines* do allow for the possibility of regionalized committees where several health care facilities might jointly staff a committee.[11]

## FUNCTIONS AND REPORTING REQUIREMENTS

After being activated by the administrator, the committee is to review all relevant medical records. It is authorized to seek additional medical or nursing information as appropriate and to assign members to examine the patient. Once all information is available, the committee is to meet, deliberate, and come to a consensus. When this happens, the chairman bears the responsibility of summarizing and reporting the committee's conclusion in writing to the chairman of the hospital's board of trustees, the attending physician, the administrator, and, finally, the patient's family.

Throughout the process, the *Guidelines* recognized the continuing responsibility of the primary care physician:

> It should be recognized from the foregoing that the function and responsibility of the Prognosis Committee is limited to the application of specialized medical knowledge to a particular case in order to arrive at a determination of concurrence or nonconcurrence with the prognosis of the attending physician. Once that determination has been made and reported, the Committee has thereby discharged its responsibility. The attending physician, guided by the Committee's decision, and with the concurrence of the family, may then proceed with the appropriate course of action and, if indicated, shall personally withdraw life-support systems.[12]

Before describing the conditions set forth in the *Guidelines*, let us respond to a frequent objection: that permitting a committee to review a case is, in reality, a "diffusion of responsibility," and that this procedure "can lead to arbitrary and lethal decision making," the result being that "when everyone is responsible, no one is. . . ."[13] Yet, under the *Guidelines*, responsibility is clearly vested in the primary care physician, not in the committee.[14] The committee is to consider and come to a consensus regarding the prognosis given by the primary care physician; it is not supposed to arrive at a decision by itself. As we shall see below, some hospitals have given greater responsibility to the committee than the *Guidelines* propose. We will return to this problem later. The purpose of the *Guidelines*, nevertheless, is very clear, i.e., to keep the responsibility with the primary care physician.

LEGAL PROTECTION

The *Quinlan* decision stipulated that immunity from both civil and criminal liability would be given to all who participate in the discussion of the case and in the removal of the life-support measures if the committee has concurred with the prognosis that the patient is beyond being restored to a cognitive, sapient state.[15] While the *Guidelines* do not provide such immunity, they clearly have been developed to fill the *Quinlan* requirements for medical prognosis committees. Many New Jersey hospitals, however, have not followed the *Guidelines* and have included nonmedical persons on their committees. Thus, it could be asked whether these hospitals are protected in the same way as those hospitals that formed their committees on the basis of the "prognosis committee" *Guidelines*. It is reasonable to speculate that to achieve the immunity protections, the hospital would have to demonstrate that the composition and functioning of its more broadly based "ethics committee" actually protected the interests of the patient in the same way the "prognosis committee" created under the *Guidelines* is intended to protect them. In the six years since they were issued, the New Jersey courts have yet to deal with a single challenge to the "prognosis committee" *Guidelines*.

THE NEW JERSEY EXPERIENCE:
RESPONSES TO THE QUESTIONNAIRE

During March and April 1983, the authors of this paper undertook a mail survey of all 101 hospitals in New Jersey to inquire about their experience with an "institutional ethics" or "prognosis" committee. The study provides a broad base for understanding the diversity of experience of New Jersey's hospitals: the results combine the experiences of more than 50 hospital committees coping with at least 221 patients. In this section we note some of our findings.

Table 1:  Activity of Responding New
Jersey Committees

| *No. of Hospitals* | *No. of Cases Considered* | *Total No. of Cases* |
|---|---|---|
| 8 | 0 | 0 |
| 5 | 1 | 5 |
| 4 | 2 | 8 |
| 7 | 3 | 21 |
| 8 | 4 | 32 |
| 6 | 5 | 30 |
| 3 | 6 | 18 |
| 3 | 8 | 24 |
| 1 | 9 | 9 |
| 1 | 10 | 10 |
| 2 | 12 | 24 |
| 2 | 20 | 40 |
| 50 | 80 | 221 |

Of the 101 possible returns, 84 questionnaires were returned, a response rate of 83 percent. Fifty-four hospitals, or 64 percent of those responding, stated that they had these committees, while 30 hospitals (36 percent) did not. The authors are aware that higher projections have been reported,[16] but our figure is larger than that reported in the national survey conducted by Stuart J. Youngner, M.D., and David L. Jackson, M.D., for the President's Commission for the Study of Ethical Problems in Medicine and Biomedical and Behavioral Research.[17] Their work led them to project that less than 1 percent of the hospitals in the United States have an ethics committee.[18] It should be mentioned that we found no statistically significant difference between the responses of hospitals with religious affiliations and those of nonsectarian hospitals.

Of the 30 hospitals that said that they did not have a committee, ten (33 percent) planned to form one within the next year. Of the 54 hospitals that had committees, 27 considered their committees as "standing" or "formal" committees within the hospital structure; 27 said that their committees were "ad hoc."

The first question attempted to determine the number of times that each committee met to consider the prognosis of a patient. The results are shown in Table 1.

Four hospitals with functioning committees did not give the number of patients considered by the committees, but they did inform us of the number of times per year that they met. The average response was six meetings per year. When we ignore the partial information from

Table 2:  Composition of Hospital Ethics Committees

| Types of Professionals | No. of Hospitals | Percent* |
|---|---|---|
| Neurologist/neurosurgeon | 42 | 78 |
| Administrator | 29 | 54 |
| Other physician | 25 | 46 |
| Pediatrician | 23 | 43 |
| Clergy | 19 | 35 |
| Attorney | 17 | 31 |
| Surgeon | 11 | 20 |
| Nursing personnel | 10 | 19 |
| Anesthesiologist | 6 | 11 |
| Social service personnel | 6 | 11 |
| Psychiatrist | 3 | 6 |
| Hospital trustee | 1 | 2 |

\* % of the 54 hospitals with committees.

these four hospitals, we can note that 17 committees apparently had relatively little experience, each having considered zero to two patients. Twenty-seven, or over half of the hospital committees, had greater experience, as each of these considered from three to eight patients.

Of the total number of cases before the committees that concerned the prognosis of a patient, 93 percent involved adult patients, while 7 percent involved children. In 63 percent of the cases the family had been involved in the discussion with the committee.

With respect to the composition of the committees, we asked for data regarding the number of hospitals that use specific types of persons as regular members of the committee. The data are given in Table 2.

According to the responses, many of the committees examined in this survey seem to be composed primarily of physicians. Indeed, 18 hospitals indicated that their committees had no nonmedical members, which seems to indicate that they are following the staffing suggestions of the *New Jersey Guidelines* for prognosis committees.

Our study also attempted to ascertain the kinds of medical cases in which the committees intervened. The survey provided five possible answers, of which three were more often identified by hospitals: trauma (25 of 54 respondents); terminal cancer (15); and senility-dementia (6). Cited much less frequently were neonatal cases (2) and obstetrical cases (1). Several hospitals chose to describe other cases as: irreversible coma (4), which we take to mean the persistent vegetative state; post-cardiopulmonary arrest (4); multiple-system failure on life supports (3); strokes (2); and cardiovascular accidents (2). From the variety of responses, as well as the somewhat vague and confusing language, we infer that these hospital committees encounter a wide range of cases and that there is some confusion about the scope of their duties.

We also wanted to find out why the hospitals used the committees. A majority of the responding hospitals agreed with three basically different reasons: to insure that all possible options have been explored; to minimize liability; and to facilitate a decision. Some hospitals offered other reasons; 13 percent mentioned that the committees provide support to the families; 9 percent stated that they support the physician. In the follow-up phone calls, these were the most common answers when we asked about the most important reasons for using the committees. Again, it is apparent that hospitals use committees for enormously varying reasons—some of which seem to conflict.

The survey inquired about the experiences of committees that were asked to confirm the prognoses made by attending physicians. The responses to our survey indicate that in 97 percent of the cases, the committee agreed with the prognosis of the primary care physician. Of the 54 responding hospitals with committees, 49 reported that their committees had agreed in all cases with the prognosis of the primary care physician. One of the hospitals that reported less than 100 percent agreement stated that when the committee disagrees with the physician's prognosis for the patient, it stipulates conditions of the patient's status that must be met before life-support technologies may be removed.

The lack in New Jersey of any legislation or case law that defines legal death as brain death seems to leave many hospitals and their committees in a state of confusion. This confusion became apparent when we asked about the committee's role in determining brain death. While 30 of the 54 hospitals with committees stated that they routinely use the EEG to define death, the other hospitals had other ideas about brain death and the committees' roles. In 79 percent of the cases considered, EEGs were performed to evaluate whether there was brain death. Nine hospitals stated that the committees only meet to confirm the patient's flat EEG. One committee chairman added: "If there is any sign of brain activity, the committee would not dare meet." Again, the responses show the wide range of these committees' activities and knowledge.

The respondents were asked to rate their experience with their committees on a scale from 1 (most negative) to 7 (most positive). The 46 hospitals with active committees answered the question, and the responses are summarized in Figure 1.

Figure 1:  Respondents' Ratings of Experience With Ethics
Committees

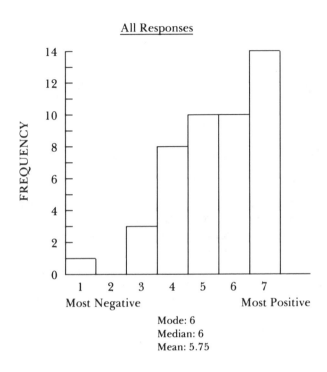

All Responses

Most Negative                    Most Positive

Mode: 6
Median: 6
Mean: 5.75

The chart clearly indicates positive evaluations. Moreover, it is
important to note that all the hospitals that rated their experience at 3
or less had used their committees less than four times. The single hospital that rated its committee "most negative" had used it only once. In
a follow-up phone call, that committee's chairman indicated that in that
case, the patient's family situation was so horrendous that the committee would have had to get involved in tracking relatives living outside
the United States. The committee therefore chose not to make a decision because of possible legal consequences.

From the responses to the questionnaire, as well as the more thorough follow-up telephone conversations, it is clear that the more experience the committee had, the easier it was for the committee to function effectively and the more positive was its evaluation of its own
experience. One chief of medicine, who serves as the chairman of his
hospital's committee, commented, "I don't know how we survived
without this committee before we had it." Several of the hospitals that
have used the committee less than four times told us that it was difficult

for them to get physicians to bring cases before the committee or to get physicians to serve on the committee.

OTHER COMMENTS

In addition to the responses discussed above, several hospitals reported unique experiences, and it might be instructive to look at these briefly in the expectation that other hospitals currently forming committees might share similar concerns. Information that would be helpful is not always disseminated or used. At one hospital, for example, the chairman of the committee admitted to not being familiar with the 1977 *Guidelines*; her committee was structured on the basis of several articles that she "had read in medical and hospital journals."

*Withdrawing Treatment*

Issues surrounding the withdrawal of treatment are frequently the source of much of a committee's work. One hospital said that it uses the committee as a "consultant" whenever a physician wishes to write a "no-code" order for a patient. Three hospitals stated that they would assist the family in changing physicians if their own physician refused to disconnect life supports after the committee found such an action appropriate. Although "living wills" are technically not legal documents in New Jersey, one committee, if presented with a living will, follows it as "an absolute directive" for decision-making purposes.

*The Role of the Family*

Involvement of the family seems to be extremely important. All 46 hospitals with committees that have considered at least one case indicated that they require a written statement from the family or guardian before they will consider the case. Moreover, several hospitals have provisions allowing or encouraging family representatives to meet with the committee. One hospital administrator indicated that the committee expects the family to meet with it, and stated: "This is a very serious matter that is being discussed, and if the family can see how the committee functions, it will help them deal emotionally with the matter." One hospital commented that the committee not only takes the family's wishes into consideration, it tries to evaluate their motives in requesting the termination of treatment and/or the removal of life-support technologies. However, one hospital indicated that regardless of the wishes of the family, it does not permit the committee to consider a case if the attending physician does not agree to call the committee into action. One hospital imposed a seven-day waiting period between the time the family makes the request and the time the committee first meets.

CRITICISMS

Only two major criticisms of the hospital committees were encountered in this study.

First, many hospitals reported a serious problem finding "outside" physicians to serve on the committee. Most hospitals tried for a short time, but eventually abandoned the idea, believing they could find physicians on their own staff who would be unfamiliar with the case and objective in evaluating the prognosis data.

Second, several hospitals commented on the time lag that occurs in trying to set a meeting time. Three hospitals made statements to the effect that once the family members have decided to submit the case to the committee, they seem to expect that the committee "will be able to meet in the next 20 minutes." A number of hospitals stated that it usually takes 24 to 72 hours to convene the committee.

## Conclusions

New Jersey hospitals have had considerable experience with institutional ethics committees in the eight years since the Karen Ann Quinlan case. The experience, however, is not uniform, and while the overwhelming majority of hospitals report a very positive experience, problems do exist. The problems most frequently mentioned by the responding institutions were:

— continued fear of liability

— confusion regarding the proper role of the committee in decision making

— the reluctance of many attending physicians to submit "hopeless" cases to the committee or to withdraw life supports even when approved by the committee

— the cumbersome use of "outside" physicians

— the time lag between the time the family makes the request and the time the committee can finally meet

We received strong testimony from our hospitals that it was extremely important to keep the courts out of terminal care decisions. There was considerable agreement that the courts do have a role in establishing guidelines, procedures, and safeguards on the review and decision-making processes, but not in the actual decision making in an individual case. Such a decision, our respondents told us, ought to remain a medical decision focusing on the prognosis of the patient. Another significant fact is that the committee chairmen who responded to our survey see the family as the proper locus for decision making.

They suggest that relatives do, in actuality, have the patient's best interest at heart, are able to understand the medical prognosis or lack of one, and are able to make appropriate decisions.

The majority of the chairmen, in our follow-up telephone calls, stressed the need for widespread education regarding the existence and role of the committee. Education is often provided at staff meetings, quarterly and annual meetings of the medical staff, nursing conferences, and grand rounds. There is a continuing need to increase awareness among all physicians, nurses, social workers, patient representatives, chaplains, and other hospital personnel, as well as to educate patients and their families. From the beginning, it is extremely important that committee members read and share perspectives on articles describing how such committees function. Continuing discussion on policy matters and further education help to facilitate increased trust among committee members.

Finally, the best indicator of the success of these committees is whether the hospitals would recommend the committee to other hospitals. The last question on our questionnaire was: "New Jersey is still the only state to authorize such a committee for health care institutions. On the basis of your experience, should the New Jersey Guidelines become a precedent for other states?" Of the hospitals with active committees, 89 percent said yes, 3 percent gave no response, and 8 percent said no. Clearly, the reaction of the 54 responding New Jersey hospitals that have institutional ethics committees was strongly positive.

## NOTES

1. *See* Superintendent of Belchertown State School v. Saikewicz, 370 N.E. 2d 417, 423 (Mass. 1977).
2. Lewis, H. P. *Machine Medicine and Its Relation to the Fatally Ill,* JOURNAL OF THE AMERICAN MEDICAL ASSOCIATION 206(2):387 (October 7, 1968).
3. *In re* Quinlan, 355 A.2d 647 (N.J. 1976), *cert. denied,* Garger v. New Jersey, 429 U.S. 922 (1976).
4. *In re* Quinlan, *supra* note 3, at 669.
5. For the first suggestion of the idea of a hospital "ethics" committee, see Teel, K., *The Physician's Dilemma: A Doctor's View: What the Law Should Be,* BAYLOR LAW REVIEW 27:6 (Winter 1975), *cited in In re* Quinlan, *supra* note 3, at 668.
6. While the *Quinlan* court used the term "ethics committee," many commentators have noted that since its only function is to confirm an attending physician's prognosis, "prognosis committee" would be a more accurate name. *See New Jersey Guidelines for Health Care Facilities to Implement Procedures Concerning the Care of Comatose Non-Cognitive Patients* (January 27, 1977) [hereinafter referred to as *Guidelines*]. The *Guidelines* are printed in Section III of this text.

7. *In re* Quinlan, *supra* note 3, at 669.

8. *See Guidelines, supra* note 6.

9. *Id.* at 1.

10. *Id.* at 2, §C.

11. *Id.* at Part B.

12. *Id.* at Part E.

13. Annas, G. J., In re Quinlan: *Legal Comfort for Doctors*, HASTINGS CENTER REPORT 7:29, 31 (June 1976).

14. *See Guidelines, supra* note 6.

15. *In re* Quinlan, *supra* note 3, at 672.

16. In an affadavit filed in *In re* Conroy, 457 A.2d 1232 (N.J. Super. 1983), Mary K. Brennan, general counsel of the New Jersey Hospital Association, cites a survey indicating that 85 out of 101 acute care hospitals in New Jersey had ethics committees. This information was provided through a telephone survey to hospital administrators. The general counsel did not, apparently, talk with the committees' chairpersons.

17. Youngner, S. J., *et al., A National Survey of Hospital Ethics Committees*, in PRESIDENT'S COMMISSION FOR THE STUDY OF ETHICAL PROBLEMS IN MEDICINE AND BIOMEDICAL AND BEHAVIORAL RESEARCH, DECIDING TO FOREGO LIFE-SUSTAINING TREATMENT: ETHICAL, MEDICAL AND LEGAL ISSUES IN TREATMENT DECISIONS (U.S. Gov't Printing Office, Washington, D.C.) (March 1983) at 443–57. *See also* Youngner, S. J., *et al.*, ch. 6 of this text.

18. Youngner, *et al., National Survey, supra* note 17, at 448.

# 10

# A Team Approach to Medicolegal and Ethical Dilemmas in a Teaching Hospital

Michael A. Grodin, William S. Markley, and Anne E. McDonald

The increasing organizational and technological complexity of hospital-based medical practice has brought with it a new set of moral, legal, and administrative problems. The evolving nature of patient-physician-hospital relationships has frequently created ambiguity, ambivalence, and conflict. After therapeutic options and modalities are examined in an attempt to answer the question, "What can be done medically for a patient?," a moral discourse often ensues regarding what *ought* to be done ethically. The realization that these questions are neither synonymous nor mutually exclusive can create feelings of uncertainty and fallibility in individual members of the medical team and is often the basis of conflict. As issues regarding life, death, and the withholding of life-sustaining treatment become matters of public as well as private concern, society grapples with both substantive and procedural dilemmas.[1] The patient's legal and moral right to respect and autonomy often conflicts with the paternalistic stance of the medical community.[2] With the incompetent patient, one must question not only what should be done but also who should decide. The principles of justice and the need to consider allocation of resources demand policies, rules, and bureaucratic solutions.[3]

Several approaches have been suggested to deal with these moral dilemmas. Respect for the concept of a confidential and private relationship between physician and patient is almost universal. However, a belief that there are occasions when the participation of other parties in medical decision making is appropriate has gained wide acceptance in recent years. Federal and state regulatory agencies, as well as various legislative bodies, have mandated that administrators of health care facilities implement rules and guidelines for decision making.[4] A number of courts have acknowledged the role of institutional committees in resolving patient care conflicts and in ensuring that a high standard of professional practice is maintained. The establishment of abortion review committees was discussed by the United States Supreme Court in its decision in *Doe v. Bolton*, although the Court concluded that the state statute at issue in the case, which mandated review of all abortions by these committees, was "unduly restrictive."[5] In the now-famous *Quinlan* case, the Supreme Court of New Jersey suggested the use of prognosis committees to determine appropriate care for incompetent patients.[6] In *Superintendent of Belchertown State School v. Saikewicz*, the Supreme Judicial Court of Massachusetts recognized the usefulness of "medical ethics committees" in resolving these cases, but issued a reminder that courts are still the appropriate forum for the ultimate decision making in problematic cases.[7] Finally, the President's Commission for the Study of Ethical Problems in Medicine and Biomedical and Behavioral Research encouraged hospitals to consider the role that ethics committees might play in the resolution of patient care dilemmas.[8]

One percent of hospitals in the United States now have established formal ethics committees.[9] Other hospitals have ad hoc committees or individuals who carry out the functions outlined for these officially sanctioned or institutionalized ethics committees.[10] It should be noted that there is considerable variation among institutions in terms of the committees' composition, purpose, and authority. Referral to a committee might be optional for certain types of cases, while in other situations (for example, withholding of life-sustaining treatment) referrals might be mandatory. Similarly, the recommendations of such committees might be adopted as hospital policy in specific cases, but considered optional or merely advisory in others.[11] Committee activities generally include some or all of the following: identification of rights and duties; education; formulation of guidelines and policies; assessment of prognosis; support of staff and patients through difficult decisions; risk analysis of potential liabilities; conflict resolution; and decision review.[12]

## BACKGROUND INFORMATION

Boston City Hospital (BCH) is a 469-bed municipal hospital which had 17,389 admissions and 143,120 outpatient visits in fiscal year 1983. BCH is a part of Boston's Department of Health and Hospitals and serves all city residents, regardless of their ability to pay. Because of their age and socioeconomic status, many of the patients who seek care are unsophisticated in their understanding of the medical establishment and how to gain access to services. They tend to be unaware of their options for treatment or their rights as patients. In addition, a large number of incompetent patients with fragmented support systems and a paucity of family are cared for by BCH. All these factors contribute to the increasing number of administrative and medical dilemmas which confront the hospital's staff.

Prior to 1981, morally difficult cases were dealt with primarily by physicians who consulted the hospital's legal counsel when conflicts could not be resolved. In 1981, out of the need for a more formalized approach to conflict resolution, a multidisciplinary team was formed in an attempt to improve the quality, nature, and form of such conflict resolution. Although this team is not an established committee, its primary function is to review specific cases upon request and to help solve problems. The team is composed of three individuals: a physician with advanced training in ethics, a member of the hospital legal staff who is also a licensed social worker, and an administrator with degrees in both business and public health.

## METHODOLOGY

A retrospective audit has been made of the cases handled, either individually or collectively, by the team members over the 18-month period from July 1981 to December 1982. Data have been collected with respect to case number, category, medical service of origination, final resolution, and team member participation. This retrospective analysis attempts to answer the following questions:

1. How many moral/legal/medical cases have been presented to the team?
2. Which types of cases were referred?
3. How might such a team function and assist in conflict resolution?
4. How many cases require the involvement of the court and how many can be internally resolved?

## RESULTS

The cases that were studied cover a wide range of medicolegal issues which are most commonly encountered in a hospital setting. They include do-not-resuscitate (DNR) orders, brain death, termination of life support, public health, involuntary restraint, fetal-maternal units, religious conflict, disposition (a problem regarding appropriate discharge), refusal of treatment, inpatient consents, and Pediatric Walk-In

Clinic (PWI) consents. Of the types of cases discussed by the team, only consents and DNR orders are guided by formal hospital policies. While consents numerically constitute the bulk of the cases which involve the team, they generally present straightforward issues which are easily resolved.

Table 1 shows team participation in the cases, excluding those concerning consents, during the 18-month period. All cases originated with the treating physician and were directed to any of the three team members, depending on the type of issue raised (medical, legal, or administrative), the experience of the treating physician, or both. The individual team member's participation in a particular case generally followed a logical involvement based on the nature of the dilemma. For example, brain death is primarily a medical dilemma since only physicians may determine death, while disposition is more in the legal and administrative realm. In the case of DNR orders, the increased participation of administration was due to the fact that many questions arose regarding the hospital's policy and procedure on this matter. It is the administration's responsibility to assist in the interpretation and implementation of these hospital policies.

All three team members worked together in only seven cases (14 percent). Twenty of the cases (39 percent) were resolved by two team members, and twenty-four cases (47 percent) were handled by a single member. No one member was involved in all the cases.

Table 2 shows the number of cases resolved through internal mechanisms and by court adjudication. An internal resolution indicates that all parties (the patient, physicians, family, nurses, friends, as well as the team members) were in agreement regarding the appropriate course of action. It also indicates that if there were legal aspects to a case, they were not considered sufficiently compelling to warrant court intervention. The five cases that were taken to court had either failed to have total concurrence or had been deemed to have legal implications requiring judicial intervention. Table 2 also shows resolution of the case in terms of action taken, regardless of whether the case went to court.

Inpatient consents refer to cases where a procedure is medically necessary, the patient is thought to be incompetent, and no next of kin can be located. In such cases, the hospital has a formal procedure which requires that the administrator on duty be consulted. Once called, the administrator has the responsibility to see that: (1) a psychiatrist has been consulted and has concluded that the patient is incapable of providing informed consent to treatment; (2) every reasonable effort has been made to contact known relatives; and (3) there is general agreement that the treatment proposed is nonexperimental and is the best alternative for the patient. Other team members are called in if neces-

Table 1:  Team Participation in Cases

| Type of Case | # | % | Participants | | | Individual Resolution* | | | Group Resolution† | | | |
|---|---|---|---|---|---|---|---|---|---|---|---|---|
| | | | Legal | Med. | Adm. | Legal Only | Med. Only | Adm. Only | Legal & Med. | Legal & Adm. | Med. & Adm. | Entire Team |
| DNR | 11 | (22%) | 3 | 3 | 9 | — | 2 | 6 | — | 2 | — | 1 |
| Brain death | 4 | ( 8%) | 2 | 3 | 2 | — | 1 | 1 | 1 | — | — | 1 |
| Termination of life support | 14 | (27%) | 6 | 13 | 2 | 1 | 8 | — | 3 | — | — | 2 |
| Public health | 3 | ( 6%) | 2 | 2 | 0 | 1 | 1 | 1 | 1 | — | — | — |
| Involuntary restraint | 5 | (10%) | 4 | 1 | 3 | 1 | — | 1 | 1 | 2 | — | — |
| Fetal-maternal units | 1 | ( 2%) | 1 | — | — | 1 | — | — | — | — | — | — |
| Religious conflict | 2 | ( 4%) | 2 | — | 2 | — | — | — | — | 2 | — | — |
| Disposition | 8 | (16%) | 8 | 1 | 8 | — | — | — | — | 7 | — | 1 |
| Refusal of treatment | 3 | ( 6%) | 3 | 2 | 3 | — | — | — | — | 1 | — | 2 |
| Totals | 51 | (100%) | 31(61%) | 25(45%) | 29(57%) | 4(8%) | 12(24%) | 8(16%) | 6(12%) | 14(27%) | 0 | 7(14%) |

*N = 24 (47%).
†N = 20 (39%).

Table 2: Type of Resolution and Action Taken

| Type of Case | # Cases | Type of Resolution | | Action Taken |
| | | Internal | Court | |
| --- | --- | --- | --- | --- |
| DNR | 11 | 11 | 0 | DNR order written: 9<br>DNR order not written: 2 |
| Brain death | 4 | 4 | 0 | Not broken down by action taken since these were problems of definition and/or family acceptance |
| Termination of life support | 13 | 13 | 0 | Treatment continued: 12<br>Treatment terminated: 1 |
| Public health | 3 | 2 | 1 | Patient treated: 3<br>Patient not treated: 0 |
| Involuntary restraint | 5 | 5 | 0 | Patient restrained: 4<br>Patient released: 1 |
| Fetal-maternal units | 2 | 1 | 1 | Unit treated: 2<br>Unit not treated: 0 |
| Religious conflict | 2 | 0 | 2 | Patient treated: 2<br>Patient not treated: 0 |
| Disposition | 8 | 8 | 0 | Not broken down by action taken since placement of disposition patients is often a very long process; some have been hospitalized for several years |
| Refusal of treatment | 3 | 2 | 1 | Patient treated: 0<br>Patient not treated: 3 |
| Totals | 51 | 46 (90%) | 5 (10%) | |

sary, but most of the concerns are procedural and can be resolved administratively without additional team input. Of the 215 inpatient consents, four patients (2 percent) were determined to be competent and thus able to give informed consent. In twenty-three cases (11 percent) a previously unknown or unavailable family member was contacted to represent the patient's interests. In five cases (2 percent), the original procedure proposed was determined to be inappropriate. Three cases (1 percent) were taken to court. Finally, 180 cases (84 percent) were approved by administrators, with or without consulting other team members. In such cases, the administrator concurs and signs the consent indicating that there are no administrative or legal obstacles to providing treatment.

Pediatric Walk-In consents are considered separately from the others for several reasons. First, although the PWI is the pediatric emergency floor, it also serves as a site for primary care for many nonemergency patients; thus, the care provided often does not meet the statutory requirements for emergency care. Second, although the age of majority in Massachusetts is 18, state law permits certain minors to give consent to their own treatment. Third, the only next of kin who may approve treatment for minors are the parents. Finally, since the formalized procedure for PWI consents was instituted in August 1982, the period covered by the audit is only four and one-half months (August 15, 1982, through December 31, 1982) and thus the statistics for PWI consents are not comparable to the other statistics. During this time a total of 124 cases were seen where parents were not present or easily available to give consent for their children's treatment. Seventy-one of the minors (57 percent) were classified as meeting state law requirements to consent to their own treatment. Parents were located in two of the cases (2 percent). Five (4 percent) of the minors were refused treatment as the parents could not be located, the children did not meet state standards for self-consent, and their conditions were determined to be nonemergent. Forty-six minors (37 percent) received administrative authorization for treatment in accordance with the hospital's policy for providing emergency care when parents are unavailable and the minors are unable to consent for themselves.

## DISCUSSION

Ever-increasing medical technology has brought burdens as well as blessings, one of which has been the advent of an often bewildering array of choices for patients and physicians. In the wake of these choices, questions arise. How are the wishes of patients and families to be balanced against the ethical and professional responsibilities of medical care givers? Who is to choose for patients who cannot choose for themselves? Our team gathered together to address these and related dilemmas as they are experienced in an inner-city public hospital.

The team evolved naturally; no one consciously decided to establish such a group. It began in 1981 with increased collaboration between the administrative and legal offices in an effort to better resolve issues of consent to medical care in cases of questionably competent patients. The medical component was added when the need for assistance in interpreting medical records and determining possible alternative methods of treatment was realized. This multidisciplinary approach proved helpful in consent determinations and was eventually used in assessing other dilemmas involving patient care presented to one or more members of the team. The existence of the team has been noted with approval by the hospital's medical executive committee.

The team is an ad hoc gathering of three individuals representing the administrative, legal, and medical services of the hospital. In addition to the designated job responsibilities, each team member has training in another area or specialty which enriches the base of knowledge available within the admittedly small group. (The dual interests of the team members were fortuitous; in all likelihood, the team would include more people if this were not the case.)

The team exists to provide reasonable resolutions to patient care dilemmas when assistance is required. Such requests are usually made by one or more physicians involved in a particular patient's care. The initial request for assistance is usually made to a single member of the team identified by the requesting party as the person most likely to provide the answer. The team member consulted decides whether to involve one or both of the other members. In this respect, the team differs substantially from the traditional institutional review team or ethics committee in that all team members do not participate in all decisions.

Certain requests that the team receives require nothing more than a single team member's telephone interpretation of existing hospital policy. More complicated cases obviously require more extensive involvement of the team. In the typical complicated situation, the entire team will first review the medical record and discuss the case with the physicians and nurses caring for the patient. The team will then meet with the patient and attempt to ascertain his or her wishes and beliefs. The patient's family and friends are consulted if the patient is questionably competent or unable to communicate. (Many of the patients seen by the team can be described as vulnerable because they are elderly and poor, and have no relatives or friends to act in their behalf. The preponderance of cases brought to court involves patients in this category.)

With particularly difficult decisions, it has also proved helpful to call in senior specialists from other areas within the hospital. Their participation frequently serves to clarify issues and to resolve conflicts by providing information which neither the ward staff nor the team could furnish. This process is again a departure from the usual procedures of hospital committees.

Interestingly enough, the team has experienced little staff resistance to either the notion of a team intervention or the involvement of senior specialists from other fields. Although the team anticipated complaints about unwarranted interference in the physician-patient relationship and "turf" issues between specialties, by and large they have not materialized. Probably this is because the team does not seek out cases. The people requesting assistance want help in making a decision and will generally accept it from whatever source with good grace.

Decisions are ultimately made by considering all available information in the light of the patient's wishes and the hospital's responsibilities. Sometimes conferences are called to ensure that all parties in a case have a chance to air their views. When all relevant material has been assessed, the team reaches a conclusion and issues its opinion. Here, again, the team's approach differs from the manner in which the opinions of most ethics committees are rendered. Theirs are usually retrospective or advisory.[13] The opinions of this team are always prospective and, in some instances, binding on the institution and its employees and staff. The obligatory nature of some of these opinions stems from a concern about potential liability. The team cannot reasonably sanction either clear violations of hospital policies or questionable treatment choices which expose the institution or its employees to a great likelihood of liability. However, in cases where the team recommends what it believes to be the better of two proposed courses of action, both of which are acceptable, staff are free to reject the team's opinion.

## CONCLUSION

The work of this team has led the authors to conclude that formally established ethics committees are not the only possible vehicle for resolution of problematic issues of contemporary medicine. A less structured interdisciplinary collaboration to resolve problems as they arise may be a pragmatic alternative which better serves the needs of certain health care facilities and their patients.

The information gained in the audit we conducted suggests that for such an informal arrangement to prove workable, the core group of participants must have the acceptance of the institution's medical executive committee plus the ability to draw upon the expertise of all disciplines and specialties within the institution as needed. The team's distinguishing characteristic is its ability to expand and contract accordion-fashion in response to various situations. Whenever possible, the wishes and beliefs of patients and their families are ascertained by the team and considered with respect. Conflicts which cannot be resolved in this forum, whether between a patient and the institution or among staff members treating a patient, are brought to the attention of the appropriate court for resolution.

Initially, the team was drawn together by the need to resolve thorny problems that went beyond the bounds of any one discipline. In the course of collaboration, the team members have grown to appreciate each other's skills and have supported each other in making difficult choices. The self-imposed mandate has been to protect the hospital and its staff from liability while fostering the rights of privacy and autonomy for patients and their families. Experience has led us to believe that these two seemingly disparate goals are actually quite harmonious.

## NOTES

1. *See generally* T. BEAUCHAMP, J. CHILDRESS, PRINCIPLES OF BIOMEDICAL ETHICS (Oxford University Press, New York) (2d ed. 1983); T. BEAUCHAMP, L. WALTERS, CONTEMPORARY ISSUES IN BIOETHICS (Wadsworth Publishing Co., Belmont, Calif.) (2d ed. 1982); ENCYCLOPEDIA OF BIOETHICS (W. Reich, ed.) (Free Press, New York) (1978); ETHICS IN MEDICINE: HISTORICAL PERSPECTIVES AND CONTEMPORARY CONCERNS (S. Reiser, A. Dyck, W. Curran, eds.) (M.I.T. Press, Cambridge, Mass.) (1977).
2. *See* J. CHILDRESS, WHO SHOULD DECIDE? PATERNALISM IN HEALTH CARE (Oxford University Press, New York) (1982).
3. *See* M. SHAPIRO, R. SPECE, BIOETHICS AND LAW (West Publishing Co., St. Paul, Minn.) (1981).
4. *See* Fost, N., *Putting Hospitals on Notice*, HASTINGS CENTER REPORT 12(4):5–8 (August 1982). *See also* Nondiscrimination on the Basis of Handicap, 48 Fed. Reg. 30,845 (1983) (to be codified at 45 C.F.R. § 84.61).
5. Doe v. Bolton, 410 U.S. 179, 198, *reh. denied*, 410 U.S. 959 (1973).
6. *In re* Quinlan, 355 A.2d 647 (N.J. 1976), *cert. denied sub nom.* Garger v. New Jersey, 429 U.S. 922 (1976).
7. Superintendent of Belchertown State School v. Saikewicz, 370 N.E.2d 417, 434 (Mass. 1977).
8. PRESIDENT'S COMMISSION FOR THE STUDY OF ETHICAL PROBLEMS IN MEDICINE AND BIOMEDICAL AND BEHAVIORAL RESEARCH, DECIDING TO FOREGO LIFE-SUSTAINING TREATMENT: ETHICAL, MEDICAL AND LEGAL ISSUES IN TREATMENT DECISIONS (U.S. Gov't Printing Office, Washington, D.C.) (March 1983) at 160–70 [hereinafter referred to as DECIDING TO FOREGO TREATMENT].

9. Youngner, S. J., *et al.*, *A National Survey of Hospital Ethics Committees*, in DECIDING TO FOREGO TREATMENT, *supra* note 8, at 443–49.

10. DECIDING TO FOREGO TREATMENT, *supra* note 8, at 161.

11. Levine, C., *Hospital Ethics Committees: A Guarded Prognosis*, HASTINGS CENTER REPORT 7(3):25–27 (June 1977). *See also* Robertson, J., ch. 7 of this text.

12. Veatch, R. M., *Hospital Ethics Committees: Is There a Role?* HASTINGS CENTER REPORT 7(3):22–25 (June 1977).

13. Youngner *et al.*, *supra* note 9, at 447.

# 11

# Contrasting Institutional Review Boards with Institutional Ethics Committees

Leonard H. Glantz

The question of the similarities and differences between institutional review boards (IRBs) and institutional ethics committees (IECs) is largely hypothetical because there are so few ethics committees to examine and because they perform so many different functions. The question is further muddled by the fact that although we know a good deal about IRBs, there is still a lot that we do not know.

My data on IRBs come from two sources: (1) my personal observations over the years, from being on two IRBs and attending dozens of meetings where I talked to other people who have been on IRBs; and (2) the *Appendix to Report and Recommendations: Institutional Review Boards* from the National Commission for the Protection of Human Subjects of Biomedical and Behavioral Research (IRB Report).[1]

The roles and functions of IRBs need some clarification. In general, IRBs review research project proposals developed by staff members of the institutions in which they sit. For the most part, they are creatures of federal regulation.[2] As a result, a good deal of what IRBs do, as well as the way they are constituted, is determined by federal regulations. Unlike IECs, which may set rules for the institution, IRBs apply rules developed by others. They are part of a larger bureaucracy, one that exists outside of the institution, and are designed, to an extent, to help investigators obtain funding, since they serve as intermediaries between the funding agencies and the investigators. Thus, even if IRBs are perceived as bothersome, they are a useful and necessary bother, since the researcher needs their approval before he or she can get a project funded.

## The Composition of IRBs

The membership of an IRB is dictated in part by federal regulations. These regulations do not describe exactly what an IRB must look like, but they do prescribe certain minimum guidelines. Thus, there must be no less than five members; at least one member has to be a nonscientist; the board must include both men and women, and they cannot all be from one profession; and at least one member must not be affiliated (apart from his or her membership on the IRB) with the institution.[3] Therefore, a board consisting of four male researchers from the institution and one female nonscientist from outside the institution would presumably meet the regulatory guidelines.

The regulations, however, also require that IRB members be qualified in diverse areas, and be familiar with certain racial and cultural concerns, so that their advice and counsel will be respected. Finally, the regulations require that the IRB have the necessary professional competence to review the kind of research that will come before it.[4] The data in the IRB Report indicate that in 1975, 71 percent of the people on IRBs were either "biomedical scientists" or "behavioral and social scientists." These terms were relatively strictly defined, for they excluded hospital administrators, nurses, statisticians, social workers, physical scientists, and lawyers, all of whom may nonetheless work for and be an integral part of the institution.[5] To determine whether or not the composition of the board is appropriate for that institution, and adequate to protect the rights of potential human subjects of research conducted in that institution, an external review of the qualifications of those appointed to the boards is conducted by the federal Office for the Protection of Research Risks.

### THE INDIVIDUAL CONCERNS OF BOARD MEMBERS

The study for the National Commission found that different committee members had different research concerns. The overall list of concerns, in order of greatest to least concern, was informed consent, the balance of risks with benefits, privacy and confidentiality, the appropriateness of subject selection, and the contribution that the research will make to scientific knowledge and scientific design.[6] Different groups had different primary concerns; for example, biomedical scientists were more interested in the contributions to knowledge and scientific design than were the other groups. Social scientists were less concerned with the appropriateness of subject selection than were other members. (This finding seems to be a good argument for having people from different fields on each IRB; an important consideration, though, is that no profession or group should be so predominant that certain concerns are heard more often and more loudly than other types of concerns.)

In a survey from the IRB Report, IRB members were asked to choose between two descriptions of an IRB's function. One choice was "to balance the need for protecting human subjects with the need to develop new knowledge;" the second choice was "to protect human subjects." As might be expected, a majority of the nonscientists said that the role of an IRB was to protect human subjects, while the biomedical scientists said that the chief function of the IRB was to balance protection of human subjects with the need for the development of new knowledge.[7] Another interesting finding of the survey was that the biomedical scientists were more likely to request additional information from the investigators about what the investigator was going to do. They were also the people who were most likely to request modifications in the research.[8]

The vast majority of IRB members are from the institution, and the institutional officials who appoint them may know the appointees' biases and proclivities. IRB members are also reappointed by those same individuals. It would be interesting to ask the individuals who appoint IRB members what they think constitutes a good IRB and to find out how they assess the IRB's performance.

The fact that so many IRB members come from within the institution may lead to certain problems. First, as in the case of ethics committees, IRB members will be reviewing the proposals of colleagues and friends. Those who have sat on IRBs have heard, "Oh, that's Harry's random clinical trial; that's really no problem, is it?" Certainly, there is room for skepticism as to whether such informality leads to proper decision making. Second, those who sit on IRBs know that they will have their own proposals reviewed by the same committee in the future, and that the rules they develop will be applied to them. One case from my personal experience illustrating this point concerned the question of whether human subjects should be paid for certain research. Those people on the IRB whose research would be reviewed during the next few months asked themselves, "How much will I have to pay my own subjects if we require these subjects to be paid?" The subjects ended up not being paid at all in this particular case.

So there is a sense of built-in self-interest which may be in conflict with the committee members' obligation to their colleagues and to the institution itself. IRB members are aware that IRBs can be somewhat of a roadblock, but they cannot be too much of a roadblock, especially to funding sources. Additionally, I am sure most IRB members would probably agree that it is easier to be very strict with someone who has unfunded research than with the chief of surgery who has a proposal for $2 million that is going to support forty people. So even though the IRBs are regulators, they are often friendly regulators.

## THE COMMUNITY REPRESENTATIVES

The people on the IRB who are of particular interest are the community representatives. These laypeople provide valuable services to the IRBs. For instance, if the community representatives do not understand the consent forms, the chances are that prospective subjects will not understand them either. Therefore, they serve as liaisons between the technical world and the world of the laypeople.

One observes, however, a number of things happening to the community representatives over time. First, they become more sophisticated themselves. The more they learn the professional lingo and begin to identify with the institution, the less they can serve their original purpose. Second, the community representatives sometimes become enthralled with the importance of the research, and at times become more proresearch than the scientists. Comments such as "How can you keep this potentially beneficial treatment from people in the community?" are heard. Third, the laypeople, not wanting to appear silly or uninformed, sometimes do not ask the questions that we would like them to ask. In this regard, it is interesting to note that the IRB Report found that the committees having the fewest members with graduate degrees produced the most complete consent forms. So, evidently, the community representatives serve at least one purpose that we would like them to serve.

Another important function of the community representatives is that they assess risk in a manner quite different from the investigators who conduct research. They ask, "How much does that hurt?," learn that it feels much like receiving a stitch, and respond, "A stitch! A stitch is a serious matter!" By bringing their own concerns and values to the assessment of risk and harm, the laypeople broaden the IRB's perspective.

The question of the exact role of each of the various individuals on a board has never been answered clearly, and the community representatives, in particular, tend to be uncertain about what they are supposed to do. Sometimes they are simply handed the federal regulations on IRBs, and then on-the-job training begins. This presents certain problems.

One example of the potential problems resulting from the lack of well-defined functions took place about ten years ago, in a case involving psychosurgery. In the *Kaimowitz* case,[9] a human subject was to be part of an experimental psychosurgical procedure, and two committees discussed the experiment—a scientific review committee, and an ethical review committee consisting of two scientists and one layperson. The question was whether or not it was appropriate to subject a particular person to psychosurgery. The layperson wrote a letter to the head of the ethical committee, in which he stated: "As a layman I am unqualified to comment on any of the technical aspects that are involved in the project. Therefore we must all trust the good intentions and technical competence of the hospital medical committee's psychologists, psychiatrists, neurologists, etc., who have reviewed and evaluated John Doe's case."[10] Of course, he was not qualified to review the scientific validity of the project. In fact, he was there precisely because he wouldn't understand the science; he was there to consider what the patient might feel and think. Yet, since he did not understand his function, he did not serve his intended purpose.

## THE COMPOSITION OF IECs

The composition of institutional ethics committees is much more difficult to ascertain than that of IRBs, because there is very little information about IECs. Stuart Youngner and his associates at Case Western Reserve examined 17 institutional ethics committees and found that the average IEC was composed of 5.25 physicians, 1.05 clergypersons, .58 administrators, .44 nurses, .35 lawyers, .21 social workers, and .15 laypersons.[11] (There was no category for ethicists, although members of the clergy would probably qualify as such.) The study showed that health professionals dominate IECs, while laypeople are generally excluded as insignificant. Just as in the case of IRBs, it seems that the membership of institutional ethics committees should be based on what it is they are supposed to do, and which tasks we assign to them. Granted, an IEC has to contain enough physicians to ensure that the committee has the respect of others within the institution; if it serves as a prognosis committee, as in the *Quinlan* case,[12] there may be no problem with having only physicians as members. However, if it serves as an ethics committee, a committee of persons who are supposed to apply values of some sort to a particular problem, it becomes a much more difficult issue. It is hard to determine who has expertise in applying ethical standards. If the committee, like a jury, is supposed to be the conscience of the community, then we may want to pick members by going out to the community and finding out what it is that community people think about these various ethical issues.

One objective in encouraging diversity in composition of committees, both IRBs and IECs, is to keep the committees honest. Thus, the community representatives on institutional review boards, even if they say nothing, have a distinct impact on the deliberations of those committees. For one thing, human subjects cannot be discussed disrespectfully, given the fact that representatives of potential subjects are sitting in the room. For another thing, policies and types of research performed cannot remain secret; they do not stay within the institution since members from the community can disclose what those policies are and what kinds of research are going on. Given this, it seems that if IECs are perceived as decision makers for various kinds of people, membership should be broad.

When we consider the composition of institutional ethics committees, we generally think about physicians, clergypeople, nurses, lawyers, and social workers. As a result, such committees will tend to be white, middle-class, and profoundly overeducated. They will be people who value and are concerned about intellectual life. A committee composed of ballerinas or baseball players would make different decisions than a committee made up of health care professionals. It seems to me that if the committees are going to make decisions for handicapped people, we should try to involve people who have some of those handicaps. In this manner, we can avoid making assumptions about the meaning and impact of conditions which we have not experienced. Having blind, deaf, wheelchair-bound, and mentally retarded members will make these committees more representative of the people whom their decisions will affect.

## IRBs IN ACTION

The IRB in the institution has two roles: to protect human subjects and to help research take place. We find that IRBs rarely disapprove research on grounds of protecting subjects. One likely reason for that finding is that outrageous research does not come before the IRBs to be reviewed. There is a self-education process as to acceptability that has gone on before a research project is proposed. When research is turned down, it is often with the expectation that there will be some sort of reapplication in the future.

According to the data, IRBs spend a lot of time looking at consent forms.[13] They really do not know how the consent forms are used in institutions or how the consent process actually occurs, but there is an indication that consent forms are made more readable by these committees and, if people pay attention to the consent forms, it is better to go through the committee than not.

One of the ways that IRBs help research take place is by rewriting consent forms. This activity has both good and bad aspects: it is good because the forms may be made more readable, but it is troublesome in that it indicates a problem. After the board sends the consent form back to an investigator three times for revision and the form is not improved, the board should worry about whether or not this investigator can communicate with subjects very well. An IRB should look into such a situation carefully, but often this does not happen.

Another finding is that the IRBs are generally not inclined to adopt stricter guidelines than the federal regulations require. The data in the IRB Report indicated that the more powerful an IRB becomes in terms of its role as an advocate for research subjects, the more problems it tends to run into within the institution. That is, the more active an IRB was (i.e., the more changes in consent forms that it asked for or the more requests for additional information that were sent to investigators), the less likely it was that investigators would feel that the IRB was protecting the rights of subjects, and the less likely it was that investigators would give the IRB a positive evaluation.[14]

The study showed, therefore, that there was a trade-off between the activity of the IRBs and the acceptance of the IRBs within institutions. Ethics committees will also have to deal with this problem. They will have to become accepted parts of institutions to be useful, but they will have to pay very close attention to the political problems that arise when a new layer of review is introduced into an already existing bureaucratic system.

IRBs are clearly decision makers: the federal regulations require that they decide whether certain research may be done in the institution before funding can be released to the investigators. Moreover, they are final decision makers in the sense that if an IRB says that the research should not be done, there is nobody else in the institution who is empowered to override that decision. However, if the IRB approves a research project, the institution still has the power to say that the research cannot be done in that particular institution.

There is no question, therefore, that the ultimate role for the IRB is to make a decision. Fortunately for IRBs, their guidelines for decision making are externally imposed—they come from the Department of Health and Human Services.[15] Thus, the IRB is not "the enemy." The IRB applies the rules that are sent to it from a bureaucracy in Washington. If the question is whether the informed consent form is adequate, one looks at section 46.116 to see what is required.[16] Can there be a waiver to informed consent? By looking at sections 46.111 or 46.116, one can determine whether the standards for waiver of informed consent have been met.[17] While personal biases may enter into discussions, decisions are generally shaped by these external rules.

In one recent incident illustrating the role of the regulations, a chairperson of an IRB wanted to review a research project that was clearly exempt from IRB review under the new federal rules. He ultimately accepted the fact that he could not conduct the review, since the committee had adopted the federal rules as its own and therefore had no authority to mandate review. The federal regulations keep IRBs from acting in totally arbitrary ways and let investigators know the rules of the game.

One of the most important rules of the IRB review process is that it is triggered by law. For IECs, there will be questions as to how issues get to them; it is as yet unclear what will trigger review by ethics committees. In the case of IRBs, as noted, it is a very simple question: any researcher applying for federal funds must submit his or her project to the IRB for review. As a result of that fact, IRB members do not see only those individuals who believe in the review process. Investigators who do not like IRBs still have to confront them, and that enables IRBs to serve an educational role, even for people who do not want to be educated. In contrast, ethics committees, which commonly operate on an optional basis, will tend to see people who already have some ethical sensibility about what it is they are doing.

The times that IRBs apply ethical rules are the times when they probably do their job in the least organized fashion. Before the new rules came out, when presented with a proposal for epidemiological research using retrospective record review (enabling researchers to go into the records of patients), the IRBs tried to think ethically. They asked themselves, "Is this right?" There was no guidance in the regulations, and IRBs had problems justifying the invasion of patients' privacy. This issue is going to arise in research on children as well, for IRBs are going to have to create some of their own rules, perhaps for the first time.

## CONCLUSION

Although IRBs and institutional ethics committees have some similar characteristics, they are essentially dissimilar. Perhaps the most useful purpose that IRBs can serve for IECs is to raise certain questions that IECs are going to have to address.

First, IECs are going to have to determine their own composition, unaided by federal guidelines. This is an important decision, for perception of the makeup of IECs will influence physicians' decisions as to whether to come before the committees.

Second, IECs must determine what will trigger their review. If the review process is optional, they will need to perform their function in a way that will make their constituents want to continue using them. One complication caused by optional review is that IECs will not be decision makers, like IRBs, but advisors. Therefore, it is the quality of their advice that will determine whether the personnel affected will continue to come before them.

Third, unlike IRBs, which apply already existing rules in making most of their decisions, IECs are going to have to promulgate their own rules for making decisions. In time, they will have to face the issue of whether the standards they have chosen in promulgating the rules are the proper ones, and whether the application of these rules is fair and consistent.

Fourth, if IECs are involved in making decisions, these decisions will involve individual patients. In contrast, IRBs look at research projects as a whole but are never involved with an individual subject. This makes IECs look even more intrusive than IRBs.

While the role of IRBs should not be underplayed, the function of institutional ethics committees is, in at least one respect, of greater magnitude. In many cases, they will be called upon to make life-and-death decisions in a short period of time. Therefore, it is imperative that the questions raised by IRBs are answered with certainty, but after careful deliberation.

## NOTES

1. NATIONAL COMMISSION FOR THE PROTECTION OF HUMAN SUBJECTS OF BIOMEDICAL AND BEHAVIORAL RESEARCH, APPENDIX TO REPORT AND RECOMMENDATIONS: INSTITUTIONAL REVIEW BOARDS (U.S. Gov't Printing Office, Washington, D.C.) (1978) [hereinafter referred to as IRB REPORT].
2. *See* 45 C.F.R. §46 (1981).
3. *Id.* §46.107.
4. *Id.*
5. IRB REPORT, *supra* note 1, at 1–28, 1–173 (Table VI.5).
6. *Id.* at 1–30.
7. *Id.* at 1–217 (Table XIII.1).
8. *Id.* at 1–31.
9. Kaimowitz v. Dept. of Mental Health, Civil No. 73–19434–AW (Cir. Ct. Wayne County, Mich., July 10, 1973), *reprinted in* MENTAL DISABILITY LAW REPORTER 1(2):147 (September–October 1976).
10. *See* Annas, G. J., Glantz, L. H., *Psychosurgery: The Law's Response*, BOSTON UNIVERSITY LAW REVIEW 54(1):249, 257 (1974).
11. Youngner, S. J., *et al.*, *A National Survey of Hospital Ethics Committees*, in PRESIDENT'S COMMISSION FOR THE STUDY OF ETHICAL PROBLEMS IN MEDICINE AND BIOMEDICAL AND BEHAVIORAL RESEARCH, DECIDING TO FOREGO LIFE-SUSTAINING TREATMENT: ETHICAL, MEDICAL AND LEGAL ISSUES IN TREATMENT DECISIONS (U.S. Gov't Printing Office, Washington, D.C.) (March 1983) at 450.
12. *In re* Quinlan, 355 A.2d 647 (N.J. 1976).
13. IRB REPORT, *supra* note 1, at 1–23.
14. *Id.* at 1–47.
15. 45 C.F.R. §46 (1981).
16. 45 C.F.R. §§46.111, 46.116.
17. *Id. See also* 45 C.F.R. §§46.401, 46.408.

# Audience Discussion

## Angela R. Holder, Moderator

ANGELA R. HOLDER, J.D., LL.M.: Before we take questions, and since there are three lawyers on our podium, I take the prerogative of the Chair to ask the other lawyers two questions. First, if an ethics committee had the right to make a decision in a case, say, of terminating care for an incompetent, dying patient, and the physician who has the responsibility for taking care of the patient disagrees with the decision, should one of the doctors on the committee volunteer to take over as the patient's doctor? Second, assume we have a patient who needs hospital care. What will happen if the committee says, "You cannot turn off this respirator; we think it would be unethical," but the doctor and the family sincerely believe that terminating treatment is the right thing to do? What are the rights of the physician or family in such a situation?

JOHN A. ROBERTSON, J.D. (conference faculty): Just as in living will or natural death legislation in California, Texas, and other states, if a physician does not agree with the patient's prior directive, he or she has an obligation either to follow it or withdraw from the case. For example, in a Baby Doe-type case, it seems to me that if the physician thinks that the duodenal atresia should not be repaired, and the hospital requires all such decisions to go before an ethics committee, and the ethics committee says, "We think treatment should occur in this case," the physician should withdraw from the case and a new physician should be provided. I'm not sure that the physician should be from the ethics committee since it seems to me that it ought to be possible to find another physician in the institutional community who would be willing to act in conformance with the ethics committee's recommendation. It seems to me that would be an acceptable solution to such a case.

RONALD B. MILLER, M.D. (St. Joseph Hospital, Orange, California): I think there is a dilemma posed by the way you suggest that patients be represented on institutional committees. In your example, where blindness was involved, one might think that having a blind individual on the committee would avoid bias. However, some people adapt to blindness very well and others adapt very poorly. My concern is that you're likely to take the person who has adapted successfully and to remove from consideration and deliberation the point of view of those who do not adapt well to their handicap.

LEONARD H. GLANTZ, J.D. (conference faculty): That is a very good point; nonetheless, I think the question is, do you get better representation by making this kind of mistake and including the wrong kind of blind person, or by excluding blind people altogether? Also, I would imagine that if I had to choose between those two, I would choose the person who has successfully adapted to being blind if for no other reason than that the belief or the feeling that being blind is a very terrible thing would be adequately represented by the people on the committee who have sight.

DR. MILLER: I am sympathetic to your point of view, but it presumes that the committee would not consider the point of view of blind persons unless a blind person were there.

MR. GLANTZ: I am not saying that they would not consider it; what I'm saying is that there is a gut level that the sighted cannot approach. Sighted people who fear losing their sight have a different view of blindness than do blind people who have lost their sight and who have adapted.

MARGARET A. GRANT, ESQ. (Lutheran General Hospital, Park Ridge, Illinois): I have a question for John Robertson. Throughout your paper you referred to physicians initiating the contact with the ethics committee. Could you comment on a situation where a nurse would perceive that a case presents an ethical dilemma and she or he raises the issue with the ethics committee? Secondly, how are you going to implement a decision of the ethics committee in light of the fact that the physician was not the initiator?

MR. ROBERTSON: In my definition of ethics committees I have tried to include physicians, nurses, and others. Obviously, however, this is a major policy decision to be made; but if the committee is to perform some of its functions—dispute resolution, development of policies, education—it would seem essential to have persons other than physicians able to bring cases to the committee. This being so, the question becomes, how do you implement the committee's recommendation? It goes to the basic question of the authority that you're willing to grant the committee. Suppose the committee thinks that what the physician is doing is unacceptable. Is the institution willing to allow the committee to be the arbiter of disputes? Since such a course might lead to medical opposition and difficulties for the committee, it may be sufficient that the physician has been informed of or even participated in the discussion before the ethics committee, leaving it up to him or her to follow its advice.

BENJAMIN FREEDMAN, PH.D. (Westminster Institute for Ethics and Values, London, Ontario): Both speakers have presumed a fairly sharp distinction between ethics committees which would have mandatory jurisdiction and those which would not. Mr. Glantz noted a distinction between IRBs and ethics committees in that IRBs automatically have access to problems that occur. In the real world, if the committee is open to everybody, then my own experience suggests that maybe half of its cases will be brought by a nurse or an administrator, most frequently by a nurse who is troubled, not by her own conduct, but by the conduct of a physician—for example, somebody working in a neonatal intensive care unit who is distressed at the treatment being given a particular handicapped baby.

I think the point is that peer pressure, even that resulting from a purely optional committee, becomes very strong. The physician is pressured to appear at and to participate in the committee's deliberations. Experience suggests that they come, kicking or screaming sometimes, but they do come. Thus, the idea that only very sensitive people might approach an optional/optional committee is not, I think, necessarily true. There is almost a kind of feedback where very insensitive people cause other people to bring cases to the ethics committee. This, it seems to me, would represent a natural way for an optional committee to evolve in the direction of a mandatory one.

MR. GLANTZ: The people who come kicking and screaming—how do they feel when they leave?

DR. FREEDMAN: In the one case that I remember most vividly, the person who feared that the committee would be the tool of the individual who asked for the meeting discovered the committee to be most objective. He benefited from the experience.

MR. ROBERTSON: I just want to agree with your perceptive analysis of the situation wherein the optional/optional committee may simply evolve through informal peer institutional pressures into a committee of a more mandatory nature. You need not get so formalized about requiring review except maybe in a very few complex cases.

VALERIE GRASSO (University of Rochester Medical Center, Rochester, New York): My comment concerns our IRB at Rochester, which is quite diverse in terms of its membership and the type of protocols we review. One of the big problems we had was the often conflicting regulations of DHHS, FDA, and other federal agencies. Now that these agencies seem to have coordinated their efforts we have a good sense of where we are headed.

My second comment is that our committee members do not care, nor do they rely on, what the guy in the next seat is going to think about them at the next committee meeting, or what the investigator may think. This is, I think, because the committee's remarks are confidential and only summarized for the researcher. So there is no fear of intimidation.

MR. GLANTZ: My point was not that IRBs don't work or that they are unrepresentative; rather, that IRBs are made up in a very different way than you would expect an institutional ethics committee to be. Additionally, while there are certain requirements that IRBs must meet— for example, to consider when subjects get paid—there's no guidance in the regulations as to what's too much or how much is enough or under what circumstances people should get paid. The question of who decides too much is an interesting thing, and the answer will be determined in part by the kind of people who sit on that review committee. That seems to me to be something of an ethical question. My guess is that if you went to different IRBs, you would get different opinions of how much is too much. If you asked the subjects or if you asked others in the subjects' community, "How would you like to make $500 to participate?" you would get a very different answer than if you offered only a dollar. And it is not clear to me that they would think incorrectly about it. My point is simply that the makeup of the IRB will determine the outcome of that type of question.

PETER MCSHANNON, JR., J.D. (Keck, Mahin & Cate, Washington, D.C.): My question is for Mr. Robertson. As I understood your description and recommendation for the optional/optional ethics committee, it would be optional to bring a case before it and optional to follow its recommendations. As I understood it, you said no records need be kept and very few procedures would need to be established. You then cited the fact that many states provide immunity for various hospital review boards by means of specific statutes. While I have not researched fully such statutes, I do not understand them to grant immunity to committees with the characteristics of your so-called optional/optional committee. Would you comment?

MR. ROBERTSON: The question, of course, depends upon the statutory language of each state.

MR. MCSHANNON: I realize that, but you quoted the Minnesota statute which referred to a "review board."

MR. ROBERTSON: It refers to a "review organization." Let me read you some statutory language: "Review organization means a committee whose membership is limited to professionals and administrative staff."[1] Thus, if you're a "review organization," you have immunity from liability, and your records are confidential and cannot be subpoenaed or searched.

It seems to me that if our optional/optional committee were composed of "professional and administrative staff" members only, such a statute would apply so long as your function was defined so as to be included within the scope of the statute, which is so broad that many ethics committee functions would fall within it.[2]

MR. MCSHANNON: Without arguing about the language, let me just suggest that if the committee is too loose and too optional it is unlikely that any such immunity statute would apply.

MR. ROBERTSON: I agree; it's very important for people starting to set up hospital ethics committees to involve their hospital counsel to ensure compliance with whatever provisions apply. That's the same with IRBs. In many states, IRBs would fit within the protective provisions of these statutes if they're set up in a certain way; that requires your lawyer.

WALTER J. TARDY, M.D. (President of the Medical Board, Queens Hospital Center, New York): My question for Mr. Robertson relates to a concept he raised—"ethical risk management." Risk management is concerned with the protection of physicians and the institution, which often is in conflict with the interests of the patient. I'd like you to expand on that conflict, if you will.

MR. ROBERTSON: In discussing ethical risk management, I was simply suggesting that having an ethics committee available for people to consult for help with complex decisions may forestall trouble later on; it may forestall people from going to court or going to the prosecutor's office. Risk management, if you will, is simply calling attention to the institution's management problem areas so proper action can be taken to avoid recurrences of these problems.

DR. TARDY: Are you suggesting that a hospital risk management committee could simply expand and look at ethical issues?

MR. ROBERTSON: No, I think you want a different group of people and a different committee, even though the institutional goals may be somewhat similar.

UNIDENTIFIED SPEAKER: It seems to me that the primary function of an ethics committee ought to be to render quality moral decisions. If that's our goal, it seems to me that you would put people on the committee who were skilled in rendering ethical decisions. I don't think it is sufficient to simply have interesting, demographically diverse groups of people participating; that will not insure that you are going to have high-quality moral decision making.

MR. ROBERTSON: You're probably right; by all means, if you have an ethicist, someone trained or learned in medical ethics, include him or her, just as you should on your IRB. The objective, at least for the optional/optional committee, which I think would be the first form that an ethics committee would take, is to help the physician or nurse or whoever needs or wants help to wrestle with a clinical problem. Even if you don't have an Immanuel Kant or John Rawls available, there may still be useful progress made, some benefits achieved from having a less expert committee that's willing to sit down and facilitate a discussion of the issues and try to analyze or understand that moral problem.

MR. GLANTZ: It seems to me that the question really has to do with what you want the ethics committee to do. If the goal is to make high-quality moral decisions, then we probably want moral philosophers to sit on it. The composition of the committee must, at least in part, be based on what it is you want the committee to decide. Accordingly, it's also not clear to me that the term *ethics committee* is what we should use.

WILLIAM F. FINN, M.D. (North Shore University Hospital, Manhasset, New York): For the past nine years, I have been chairman of a medical ethics committee at a 600-bed hospital on Long Island. Last year, I was one of the doctoral advisors to Doris Guidi, professor of health sciences at C. W. Post Center. Dr. Guidi received 316 responses to approximately 700 questionnaires directed to hospitals in the Northeast and Middle Atlantic states. Fifty-three of the respondents stated that they had a medical ethics committee. Twenty-nine, or 55 percent, were merely prognosis committees and hence were excluded. Twenty-four, or 45 percent, were committees whose purposes were educational, consultative, or guideline advisors, but not decision making. So approximately 7 percent of the hospitals in the states stated that they had medical ethics committees.[3] This difference from Dr. Youngner's 1 percent is due to the fact that he restricts medical ethics committees to merely cessation of treatment decisions.

STUART J. YOUNGNER, M.D. (conference faculty): That is correct. The discrepancy between your 40 percent figure and our 1 percent figure points out the need to specify exactly what is meant by an ethics committee. For our study, we defined ethics committees in a very narrow sense—"a formally appointed group of hospital and professional personnel with the potential to become involved in the decision-making process in specific cases of critical illness." Many more than 1 percent of the approximately 600 hospitals we surveyed initially responded that they had ethics committees. When we asked more detailed questions, however, it was revealed that most of these "ethics" committees dealt with matters of education or policy, or reviewed cases of alleged moral misconduct by physicians. This is not to say that such functions are unimportant. The point is that the term *ethics committee* must be defined to prevent its being confused with very different purposes, methods of functioning, and policy implications.

UNIDENTIFIED SPEAKER: My question is for Dr. McIntyre. As I understand your statement, the legal mandate was to determine when the interests of the state in preserving life should succumb to the patient's privacy interests and the right not to be abused. Is it actually the patient that's being abused, and in what way, if he or she is comatose? While I'm not in disagreement with the general principle, I wonder, if you followed such a position to its logical conclusion, whether it's not our sensibilities or some sense of humanity that's being abused, as opposed to the patient?

RUSSELL L. MCINTYRE, PH.D. (conference faculty): My sense is that once it has been determined by the primary physician that the patient cannot be returned to a cognitive, sapient state, then, at least by extrapolation, you've decided that continued treatment is simply delaying the dying process. It is at that point that the patient's right of privacy begins to overshadow the state's interest in preserving life; at that point, continued treatment would serve no purpose.

PREVIOUS SPEAKER: I certainly agree it would serve no purpose; but I also do not see how it really affects the right of privacy of a patient who is unaware of any insult or intrusion on privacy.

ROBERT M. VEATCH, PH.D. (conference faculty): I would like to ask Russell McIntyre about the widely expressed consensus that the prognosis committee is the one area where a membership that is made up entirely of medical or scientific professionals would be appropriate. Presumably that is based on the belief that determining prognosis is a pure fact problem, and it therefore need not have the input from a wide variety of community representatives. The problem is that, on the basis of work in the philosophy of science, we increasingly recognize that there is no such thing as a pure, value-free "fact." This problem is especially serious when the mandate is to determine something as nebulous as "a reasonable hope of recovery." This claim—that apparently factual judgments often incorporate evaluations—is supported by your testimony that one committee apparently would not meet if the physician did not agree to stop treatment, and that another apparently spelled out the conditions under which treatment could be stopped. Has this idea of prognosis being a pure medical fact been controversial in the "prognosis committees" in New Jersey? And do you think that we should try to force the prognosis committees back into the realm of pure fact, admitting ideally that it is impossible? Or alternatively, should we open up prognosis committees, make them more like the ethics committees that we are talking about at this conference, make them more representative of the community, and confess that we cannot do value-free factual determination of prognosis?

DR. MCINTYRE: I'm not sure I have an answer to your first question. Our questionnaire did not give us that kind of data. My sense is that the committees that function purely in terms of prognosis find that their responsibilities are a lot easier to handle. They think that since they're making factual determinations, it is a medical decision, only physicians can truly understand all the data, and therefore it ought to be left in their hands.

In my own relationships with hospitals in New Jersey, I have helped four hospitals form committees. My advice has been to use the prognosis guidelines as a starting point, but to broaden the responsibilities in a sort of consultative way, to include clergy, to include nursing. I urge the committees to actually talk with the family, to find if there are conditions or reasonable facts to be considered before the committee makes its final decision. I personally agree with you that there are a lot of outside conditions, nonmedical issues, that need to be dealt with, and frequently a final rendering is not simply a prognosis.

## NOTES

1. MINN. STAT. ANN. §§ 145.61–.67 (West Supp. 1983).
2. *Id.*
3. Guidi, D. J., *Hospital Ethics Committees: Potential Mediators for Educational and Policy Change* (doctoral dissertation, Fairleigh Dickinson University, 1983) (available from University Microfilms, Inc., 300 N. Zeeb Road, Ann Arbor, Michigan 48106).

# Part III

Implementing an
Institutional Ethics
Committee:
Roles and Functions

# 12

# Techniques for Committee Self-Education and Institution-wide Education

Corrine Bayley and Ronald E. Cranford

New technology, increasing costs, the growing interest in patients' rights, and changing roles among health care professionals account for many of the ethical issues pressing for attention today. The environment has changed, and our response to it must likewise change. It is time that people in the health care professions start dealing more openly with the ethical dilemmas that they have helped create. One way to do that is to establish institutional ethics committees.

It seems logical that those most directly concerned with these issues ought to openly discuss them. Yet we have shied away from the thorny questions they present, leaving them to the courts, third-party payers, and the government. The emergence of ethics committees signals the intention of health care providers to grapple with hard questions, and to be more responsive to the concerns of their patients and of society. As ethical issues are discussed more openly, not only will their resolution be more satisfactory, but the quality of relationships among health care professionals will improve. Interdisciplinary dialogue and mutual respect are two important outcomes of probing ethical concerns in multidisciplinary efforts.

Our experience with ethics committees indicates that each institution handles things a little differently; however, there are some common threads. First, the process is slow. It takes a long time for the committee to feel as though it is accomplishing anything or making an impact on institutional attitudes and behavior. Committees with extensive experience report that it takes a few years of work before they see significant results. Ethics committees are not task-oriented like most other committees, and the issues being discussed are not subject to scientific analysis. They are, by nature, problematic, and involve profound human emotions. As such, the necessary virtues for members of ethics committees are patience, compassion, and the ability to listen well.

Second, committees may become bogged down in the establishment of too many structures, rules, and procedures for operation. The committee should be flexible enough to deal with the issues in a variety of ways, and should not establish elaborate procedures. Especially in the early formative stages, committee members should be willing to handle things in whatever way seems most efficacious for the situation at hand. It is tempting to spend time on voting procedures, the number of people required for a consultation, the type of minutes kept, attendance, and other issues. Ethics committees are too new for anyone to have a definitive answer on these matters. Besides, each institution has its own needs and personalities, and what works well for one may not work best for another. Eventually, the committee will feel more secure in handling its responsibilities flexibly. We cannot stress enough that it is a mistake to spend energy trying to establish the "right" procedures. It is far better to start discussing the issues. Operative procedures will take care of themselves once it becomes more clear how the committee can best serve the institution.

Finally, the committee will periodically struggle with its purpose, functions, and accountability. This is a natural (though frustrating) part of the evolutionary process. If the initial ambiguity can be tolerated, the results will almost certainly be rewarding.

## The Ethics Committee as Educator

In our opinion, the primary purpose of an ethics committee is its educational function. In every institution there is a great need for an in-house resource to clarify the issues, to facilitate interdisciplinary dialogue, and to improve processes for decision making. Eventually, with the support of the ethics committee, a knowledge base will build up within the institution—a result that will be of great benefit to all.

There is an old adage that "you can't give what you haven't got." The first task of the committee is to become educated itself. Techniques for this are limited only by one's imagination and, of course, time. One of the first things committee members should do is become familiar with the resources. Books, journals, and articles in the field of bioethics are increasing at a rapid rate, and their quality is likewise on the rise.[1] Two excellent sources are *Clinical Ethics*[2] and *Deciding to Forego Treatment*.[3] As a practical aside, it should be noted that some committees have read and studied these books together, discussing a chapter or two at each meeting.

Other resources are becoming more plentiful as well. Conferences, lectures, and workshops on bioethical issues can be found in increasing numbers. The committee can also locate local individuals (theologians, ethicists, physicians, nurses, economists, lawyers) who are developing expertise in one or more areas of bioethics. A roster of local authorities should be maintained. The committee should also develop a resource center—a bibliography of relevant readings, audiovisuals, and other resources—for hospital-wide or departmental education. Two excellent films that are often used are *Who Should Survive?* (Joseph P. Kennedy, Jr., Foundation, 1972) and *Please Let Me Die* (University of Texas Medical Branch at Galveston, 1974). Once the committee is formed and begins looking, a variety of resources will materialize. Many committees have established subcommittees on specific topics and have found this a good way to use time and become more knowledgeable.

One of the topics the committee should explore early in its formation is the nature of ethics and ethical decision making. You must be careful not to assume that members will have the same understanding of ethics or of what constitutes an ethical issue. Committee members will need assistance in recognizing and sorting out key ethical principles, such as justice, beneficence, nonmaleficence, and autonomy. Members should become familiar with various ethical theories and methods of moral inquiry, as well as a systematic approach to the resolution of an ethical dilemma.[4] Discussion should be focused on principles rather than on personalities. There is a vast difference between logical argumentation and rhetorical arguments or slogans.[5] Committee members should, as soon as possible, become familiar with the language and tools of ethical analysis.

In order to maximize understanding of ethical tools, it is helpful to apply them to specific cases. To talk about ethical principles without applying them to human dilemmas is empty. One of the purposes of the committee is to relate theory to practice. The analysis and resolution of cases is a very familiar technique for health care professionals, but it does not often extend to the ethical issues. The ethics committee's review of cases, either actual or hypothetical, should focus on the ethical dimensions. Over time, the committee members will learn to ask the right questions, to sort out the significant principles involved, and to suggest appropriate options. As committee members develop a common experience with the issues, they will become more aware of areas where consensus exists and areas where there is greater controversy. For example, there is general consensus that a definition of death should include the neurological standard (brain death) as well as the cardiopulmonary standard. There is also agreement that under most circumstances, there is no moral obligation to continue life-sustaining treatment for permanently unconscious patients. Examples of areas of greater controversy include the withholding or withdrawing of fluids and nutrition, and the treatment of newborns with defects.

For many committees, the central focus will be on questions related to termination of treatment. Members should become familiar with the medical and legal aspects of this issue. The committee should be familiar with case law, both in its own state and in other states.[6] Committee members should also be familiar with state legislation, if any, on definition of death, living wills, and other laws affecting decisions to forego treatment. Several medical and bar associations are now developing guidelines for the withholding of cardiopulmonary life-support systems, the initiation of DNR orders, and the determination of death. The committee should be familiar with these guidelines, as well as official statements from such groups as the American Medical Association, hospital associations, and religious groups.[7]

The committee should be aware of the ethical implications of such distinctions as killing vs. letting die, ordinary vs. extraordinary treatment, not starting vs. stopping treatment, and so on. Terms such as euthanasia, handicapped, quality of life, informed consent, and therapeutic abortion should not go undefined. To do an in-depth analysis of these and other issues, some committees have held extended workshops in which members interact with each other and one or more resource persons especially well read or experienced in the issues.

As the committee becomes more familiar with the issues and principles involved, its ability to assist other members of the hospital community in working through ethical dilemmas will increase. Members will also begin to collect and clarify institutional myths. Questions related to termination of treatment are difficult enough without the misinformation that seems to accompany them. And we all know that erroneous statements are repeated and eventually come to be thought of as established fact. Examples of such fallacies include the following: "It is against the law to write a no-code order on the chart." "A patient must be brain-dead before a ventilator can be removed." "Once treatment has started (e.g., dialysis), it can't be stopped." "The law says that there must be two flat EEGs, 24 hours apart, before a patient can be pronounced dead." If taken as true, such statements may lead to inappropriate decisions; if explored further, they will uncover important ethical, legal, and procedural issues. The ethics committee can be of enormous help in identifying and exposing commonly held assumptions. The committee, in other words, should not let statements go unexamined. As John F. Kennedy said, "The great enemy of truth is very often not the lie—deliberate, contrived, and dishonest—but the myth—persistent, persuasive, and unrealistic."

Ethics rounds, using a case-based approach, is an excellent technique for hospital-wide education. Some ethics committees have sponsored rounds in individual departments or units while others have arranged monthly ethics rounds for the entire hospital. An actual case or a composite hypothetical case is often used. Dialysis and burn units, high-risk nurseries, and the oncology and critical care departments have no lack of cases. If the committee perseveres with regularly scheduled conferences, a level of awareness and ability to deal with clinical dilemmas will gradually be increased throughout the institution.

Some committees have reported doing surveys among hospital staffs to determine their greatest concerns. Subsequently, the committee focused its educational efforts in these areas. One hospital surveyed its physicians on attitudes and behaviors toward informed consent and found several areas in need of discussion and decision.

## THE ETHICS COMMITTEE AS POLICY MAKER

Guidelines need to be formed, and the process of developing guidelines is educational in itself. Having to put guidelines and policies down on paper requires thorough study and discussion of the issues by committee members. As noted earlier, important distinctions need to be made; for example, the committee must distinguish between withholding CPR and withholding or withdrawing other forms of treatment. The two are not necessarily equivalent. These discussions can lead to the development of guidelines on foregoing life-sustaining treatment or "supportive care" guidelines which recognize another important distinction that should be made in this context, i.e., the difference between allowing to die and causing death.

For most committees, the formulation of guidelines has taken several months or longer. Once a draft is ready, it should be sent to individuals and committees throughout the hospital for review and comments. This, too, is an educational process.

Discussion on such issues as DNR orders and the involvement of patient or family is likely to be far more productive when held around a table than at a nursing desk or a patient's bedside. One ethics committee sponsored an open meeting to discuss its draft of a DNR policy. The session was multidisciplinary and the ensuing dialogue was extremely enlightening and long overdue. The guidelines are being revised and another meeting is planned.

The purpose of such sessions, then, is twofold: first, to get feedback so that the policy or guideline can be revised, if necessary; and second, to provide a directed forum for the discussion and understanding of these issues. It should be noted that the committee's draft is not completed once the guidelines are approved. For maximum effectiveness, they should be distributed to all those involved in their implementation, and they should be evaluated and revised as necessary. Some ethics committees now report being in their third generation of DNR guidelines.

Other creative methods of education have been developed around the country. In Minneapolis, for example, the Biomedical Ethics Committee at the Hennepin County Medical Center sponsors a course in medical ethics through the Medical Center and the United Theological Seminary. It has been held every other year since 1975. During 14 three-hour sessions, ethical principles are explored and applied to actual cases. Often, health care professionals involved in those cases are present for the discussion.

A new development is networking among committees within geographical areas or among committees with common bonds, such as religious affiliation or ownership. In Minneapolis/St. Paul, there are eight ethics committees in place, and nine more are in the process of being formed. These committees have begun to sponsor quarterly conferences discussing issues of common concern. The conferences are open to all health care professionals in the area. A newsletter is also being developed. The Sisters of St. Joseph of Orange Health System, with nine hospitals in California and one in Texas, sponsored a two-day conference on ethical issues for their medical staffs and personnel. Ethics committees in this system have found it helpful to share successes and failures, specific programs, and guidelines. The California Association of Catholic Hospitals sponsored workshops in the fall of 1983 for its 47 member hospitals, and plans to facilitate the development of networks among ethics committees following the workshop. The American Society of Law & Medicine, headquartered in Boston, publishes the *Ethics Committee Newsletter*. Finally, networks have been developed among specialty units. Six neonatal units in the Minneapolis/St. Paul area have collaborated on the development of life-support policies and procedures for seriously ill newborns.[8] They have also advocated the establishment of neonatal intensive care ethics committees, which will work closely with the institutional ethics committee.

Ethics education is not limited to health care professionals. Boards of trustees are becoming increasingly interested in the discussion of ethical concerns. The committee can provide them with helpful insight and resources. The committee should also consider another audience for education: patients and the public. The public is becoming increasingly aware of the controversies and dilemmas surrounding the issue of life-prolonging treatment, to name one controversial area. In the near future, patients and their families will begin asking hospitals for an explanation of their policies regarding DNR orders, the implementation of living wills, treatment of handicapped newborns, and the withholding or withdrawal of treatment under various circumstances. After the committee has been functioning for a while, it should consider letting patients and families know of its existence. Unity Hospital in Fridley, Minnesota, has done this by distributing a brochure explaining the purpose and functions of its ethics committee. As the President's Commission states, "Institutions need to develop policies because their decisions have profound effects on patient outcomes, because society looks to these institutions to ensure the means necessary to preserve both health and the value of self-determination, and because they are conveniently situated to provide efficient, confidential, and rapid supervision and review of decision making."[9]

The bioethical issues in need of clarification and discussion within health care institutions are multiplying rapidly. By educating the institution's personnel and the public on these matters, ethics committees can perform an extremely valuable service.

## NOTES

1. See Bibliography at the end of this text.
2. A. R. JONSEN, M. SIEGLER, W. J. WINSLADE, CLINICAL ETHICS (Macmillan Publishing Co., New York) (1982).
3. PRESIDENT'S COMMISSION FOR THE STUDY OF ETHICAL PROBLEMS IN MEDICINE AND BIOMEDICAL AND BEHAVIORAL RESEARCH, DECIDING TO FOREGO LIFE-SUSTAINING TREATMENT: ETHICAL, MEDICAL AND LEGAL ISSUES IN TREATMENT DECISIONS (U.S. Gov't Printing Office, Washington, D.C.) (1983) [hereinafter referred to as DECIDING TO FOREGO TREATMENT].
4. A helpful article on processes in decision making is Aroskar, M., *Anatomy of an Ethical Dilemma: The Theory*, AMERICAN JOURNAL OF NURSING 80(4):658–63 (April 1980).
5. *See* McCormick, R. A., *Rules for Abortion Debate*, in HOW BRAVE A NEW WORLD (Doubleday & Co., New York) (1981) at 176–88.
6. A few of the landmark cases are: *In re* Quinlan, 355 A.2d 647 (N.J. 1976); *In re* Spring, 405 N.E.2d 115 (Mass. 1980); Superintendent of Belchertown State School v. Saikewicz, 370 N.E.2d 417 (Mass. 1977): *In re* Severns, 425 A.2d 156 (Del. Ch. 1980); Satz v. Perlmutter, 362 So.2d 160 (Fla. App. 1975); People v. Barber and Nejdl, No. A 025586 (Superior Court of California, County of Los Angeles, May 5, 1983); American Academy of Pediatrics v. Heckler, 561 F. Supp. 395 (D.D.C. 1983).
7. Statements by the American Medical Association and the Catholic Church are reprinted in DECIDING TO FOREGO TREATMENT, *supra* note 3, at 259 (Appendix A). Other materials with which the committee should be familiar are also included in this report by the President's Commission, are *Natural Death Statutes and Proposals* (Appendix D); *Statutes and Proposals to Empower the Appointment of Proxies* (Appendix E); *Permanent Loss of Conscious-*

*ness: Expert Opinion and Community Standards* (Appendix G); *Seriously Ill Newborns: A Federal Directive and Sample State Statutes* (Appendix H); *Orders against Resuscitation: Selected Policy Statements* (Appendix I).

8. *See* Twin Cities Committee for Neonatal Life Support Policy, Decision Making for Critically Ill and Handicapped Newborns, printed in Section III of this text.

9. DECIDING TO FOREGO TREATMENT, *supra* note 3, at 4.

# 13

## Consultative Roles
## and Responsibilities

### Ruth Macklin

In considering the consultative roles and responsibilities of hospital ethics committees, one will see that a number of questions need answers. In its role as consultant, to whom is the committee responsible? Is a consultative role to be viewed primarily as decision-making or as advisory? In what ways or for what reasons do hospital ethics committees differ from one another in terms of their consultative roles and responsibilities? Is a single model for such roles and responsibilities desirable or preferable to a variety of approaches?

These central inquiries are a blend of descriptive and normative concerns. In part, these are questions posed about the actual operation of existing ethics committees—their policies and practices. But they also inquire into what *ought to* comprise the consultative roles and responsibilities of institutional ethics committees. In addressing these questions, I will include both the descriptive and normative aspects, making clear when I am describing actual functions of existing committees, and when I am proposing that the activities of such committees should proceed in certain ways.

### RESPONSIBILITIES OF INSTITUTIONAL ETHICS COMMITTEES

To begin, then, with the first question: to whom is the committee responsible? It might be thought that the answer to this question will vary, depending on individual differences among committees—their relationship with the hospital administration; the initial charge or mandate to the committee when it is first created; the extent to which patients or their families have access to the committee; the nature of the problems that come before it; and whether the committee's role is viewed primarily as advisory, as educational, or as one that comes close to decision making. Although it is likely that different hospital ethics committees perceive their responsibilities differently in regard to these factors, only one of the features just listed properly calls for a shifting or varying responsibility: that is, the nature of the ethical problems or issues brought to the committee. Since that is a rather bold prescriptive judgment, let me first offer general support for the claim before turning to a consideration of pertinent details.

Although it may sound platitudinous, I think that the proper role of institutional ethics committees is to assist in efforts to arrive at morally right solutions to hard choices in clinical decisions or problematic policy issues in the hospital. The appearance of a platitude can be quickly dispelled by suggesting a leading principle for evaluating proposed solutions as morally right. That principle can be stated as follows:

> The rights and welfare of patients should take precedence over other, competing concerns, however relevant and important: the risk of medico-legal liability for the hospital and its personnel; the autonomy and authority of physicians in the institution; conscientious moral objections by nurses or other staff; the expressed wishes of the patient's family, when those wishes conflict with the patient's rights or well-being; and financial worries relating to the cost of particular diagnostic or therapeutic procedures, the need to keep hospital beds filled, and problems of reimbursement.

Few are likely to quarrel with this principle stated as broadly as it is here. Yet its function can be easily misunderstood. The principle by no means enables us to deduce correct solutions to dilemmas in individual cases. Instead, the principle is intended to serve as a guide to the responsibilities of institutional ethics committees. Their primary responsibility is to protect the rights and welfare of patients—values that are often compromised by the complexity and uncertainty of competing institutional pressure, the fear of legal consequences, and the traditional prerogatives of different professional groups and individuals.

The principle stated here, that the primary responsibility of ethics committees is the patient's welfare, could not possibly serve the more difficult function of providing ready solutions to moral dilemmas. This can be shown by noting a few obvious facts. Sometimes the legal and moral rights of patients come into conflict with what is in their best (medical) interest. In such cases, the principle stating that patients' rights and welfare must take precedence over other institutional and professional concerns simply fails to address the dilemma. At other times, the rights or interests of various patients come into conflict with each other; this occurs in cases involving the allocation of scarce resources. In these instances, the principle also fails to suggest a solution for the relevant moral problem—a just distribution of health care resources, such as beds in the intensive care unit. Finally, and perhaps most typical of the sorts of cases that actually come before hospital ethics committees, decisions concerning the withholding or withdrawing of life supports for incompetent patients are morally perplexing precisely because of uncertainty about what constitutes the rights or "best interests" of such patients. A principle stating simply that patients' rights and welfare should take precedence over other concerns in the hospital is clearly inadequate for specifying what those rights and "best interests" are when uncertainty or disagreement prevails. The principle should thus be construed as a formal principle, which denotes the proper responsibility of an institutional ethics committee. The task of addressing the substantive issue, namely, determining the rights and best interests of patients in cases of conflict or uncertainty, is the core of the consultative role of the committee itself.

What, then, are the responsibilities of hospital ethics committees? That question is best answered not by an approach that seeks to determine to whom such committees are responsible, but rather, whose rights and welfare these committees should be responsible for protecting. No inconsistency arises from maintaining that institutional ethics committees are responsible at one and the same time to the patients about whom they are consulted, to the physicians and other health care workers who seek advice from the committees, and to the hospital administration that ultimately governs policies in the institution. A committee, like an individual person, may have simultaneous responsibilities to a number of different agencies. But a hospital ethics committee does not stand in a precise relation to any of these different agencies, as might be implied by other familiar health care models. The committee is not, strictly speaking, a collective employee of the hospital, responsible accordingly to the hospital administration. Nor does a committee stand in a fiduciary relationship with patients, as physicians are presumed to do. And, in response to a request by a physician for an ethics consultation, the committee is not bound to accept the physician's own personal values or professional commitments in fashioning its recommendations. All of these should probably remain relevant considerations in a committee's deliberations, but its primary responsibility should be viewed as seeking a morally sound solution that places patient's rights and well-being foremost among competing concerns.

## Consultative Roles

Having stipulated what I take to be the primary responsibility of hospital ethics committees, the next task is to define the details of their consultative roles. The three chief candidates for consultations by institutional ethics committees (IECs) are individual physicians or other professionals seeking advice or recommendations regarding a particular patient; a department or service looking for guidance on a matter of policy or on a range of cases of a certain type; and hospital administration seeking to arrive at a sound institutional policy on a matter of having ethical implications. Illustrations falling under the first two categories will be offered below. It should be noted, however, that not all IECs aid all of these potential users of their services; nor am I proposing that all committees should adopt the same consultative roles. Rather, these illustrations of the actual workings of different IECs are intended to show the range of possibilities open to them in providing consultations.

### IEC AS CONSULTANT TO INDIVIDUAL HEALTH CARE WORKERS

Consulting with individual physicians or other health care workers may well be the primary consultative role played by existing IECs. It certainly fits the model of the Biomedical Ethics Committee that Dr. Ronald Cranford chairs at Hennepin County Medical Center in Minnesota. Most requests for consultations at that hospital appear to come directly from attending physicians or house officers, but I assume that at Hennepin, as in other hospitals that already have bioethics committees, a significant number of consultations originate with nurses, social workers, and, less frequently, members of the patient's family. Since other papers in this volume address the relationships among IECs, patients, their families, and health professionals, and since statistics from the nationwide survey conducted by Drs. Youngner and Jackson and their associates provide additional information,[1] I will bypass discussion of those empirical data, confining my remarks to illustrative examples and agenda items from the two hospital ethics committees on which I serve.

Most individual consultations sought by physicians and other professionals focus on withholding or withdrawing life supports or on determining the appropriate level of care for a patient who is terminally ill or unable to participate meaningfully in decisions. A large percentage of cases involve a decision to remove a patient from a respirator and, often, a determination of which treatments should or should not be withheld—e.g., administration of fluids, antibiotics, IVs, nasogastric tubes, blood transfusions. Sometimes those who request consultations seek advice solely on the propriety of DNR (do-not-resuscitate) orders, an issue that remains an ethical and legal problem in the case of patients who are demented or permanently impaired because of accident, injury, or disease, and who never previously stated their wishes regarding resuscitation efforts. The problem of "no-codes" must be addressed by IECs not only in their consultative role with individual health care workers, but also in one of their more general roles: developing institutional guidelines or policies at the request of either hospital administration or a particular hospital department or service.

The consultative role of IECs may be and should be viewed more broadly than that of consultation leading to a decision. Although this is the way consultations are usually construed in medicine and other professional contexts, the consultative role of IECs can also work in a prospective fashion; the IECs are designed to give guidance for future cases raising similar ethical issues. An example from one of the committees on which I serve illustrates this role.

A hospital social worker brought the case of a 20-year-old woman who had been diagnosed as having multiple sclerosis to the committee for retrospective deliberation. Her physician, a neurologist at the hospital, felt strongly that the patient should not be informed of the diagnosis, arguing that she seemed to be in remission and that it would be soon enough to tell her the next time the disease became manifest. Other members of the team believed, with varying degrees of conviction, that she ought to be told, and the resident assigned to her care adhered to that position quite strongly. A case conference was held to discuss the matter, the paternalistic neurologist having been informed of the conference and its subject. He declined to attend. The consensus at the conference was that her diagnosis should be disclosed to the patient, but the group did not arrive at any clear plan for how to proceed. Taking the matter into his own hands, the resident told the patient of her condition.

In bringing this case to the IEC, the social worker was primarily concerned with the moral issue of full disclosure of diagnosis and prognosis to patients. That substantive issue did occupy a large portion of the committee's time, but the IEC took the discussion out of the realm of substance to that of procedure, which proved to be an appropriate and useful exercise of its consultative role. The committee itself was divided on the substantive moral judgment in this particular case of disclosure, but was in virtual agreement on the procedural issue: the resident did not take the right approach in unilaterally informing the patient, having failed to discuss his intention to do so with the group that had assembled in conference; nor had he indicated to the attending physician that he planned to defy that physician's proscription. Since there was no emergency in this case that would have indicated the patient's immediate need to know, and since informing a young woman that she has an incurable, degenerative disease is a task involving considerable sensitivity and perhaps some experience, the committee concluded that the resident had acted precipitously. Even if disclosure was the morally right course of action, the manner of its execution had been flawed.

Discussion of completed cases by IECs may thus be included in their consultative role, not with the aim of reaching a decision in a case that is already moot, but to develop guidelines for future cases. The case described here also serves to illustrate the operation of the principle of responsibility set out earlier—that the rights and welfare of patients should take precedence over competing concerns in the advice and recommendations of IECs. That principle suggests (but does not mandate) full disclosure to the patient concerning diagnosis and prognosis. The presumption in favor of disclosure shows that the committee viewed the patient's rights and interests as paramount, clearly overriding any claims the attending physician might make about his sole authority and prerogatives concerning his patient. But since the patient's "right to know" may have been at odds with her psychological welfare and emotional well-being, the time and manner of disclosure, as well as the skill and sensitivity of the person revealing the bad news, became the more pressing matter for the committee's discussion.

IEC AS CONSULTANT TO A DEPARTMENT OR SERVICE

This type of consultation can begin with a case presentation to the committee, with or without the initial aim or hope of developing guidelines or reaching a policy decision for all cases of the same type. The case may be brought by an individual professional seeking guidance, by a chairman or chief of service, or by someone acting on behalf of the director of the service or unit.

Again, one of my experiences serving on an IEC shows how one case can exemplify an ongoing problem in the hospital. The following situation was brought to the committee's attention by nurses and social workers, with the involvement of a concerned pediatrician who did not directly participate in the case at hand. The case concerned a private adoption of a child born in the hospital. In this case, as apparently in many others, the adoption had been arranged by the obstetrician and the prospective adoptive parents, with the assistance of an attorney. The nurses and social worker recited to the committee a litany of horrors: refusal by the obstetrician and some nurses to allow the natural mother to see the infant; failure to inform the mother of all her rights and alternatives in the matter; pressures applied to get the mother to sign papers, although she was ambivalent about giving up the baby at the time she entered the hospital; and other violations of her rights and interests. The mother was confused, emotionally distraught, spoke English with difficulty, and had no strong support system on the outside. No one was available in the hospital to serve as the advocate of the natural mother: the physician who was to deliver her was acting as the agent of the adoptive couple; the pediatrician could only properly view the infant as her patient; and the social workers were employees of the hospital's social service department, not clearly designated to act in the role of advocate for the natural mother. The nurses and social workers involved in this case did the best they could to serve as the mother's advocate in the absence of any hospital guidelines.

The committee discussed all aspects of the case thoroughly, and sought further information concerning private adoptions from the hospital administration and from the director of social services. Thereupon, a subcommittee formulated guidelines for private adoptions within the hospital and presented drafts for the full committee's review at two subsequent meetings. The committee eventually voted on a final draft that became hospital policy. Those guidelines significantly altered the existing practices, and served to place new restrictions on efforts by physicians affiliated with the hospital to facilitate private adoptions. The sole aim of these guidelines was to protect the rights and interests of patients and to eliminate abuses that stem from privately arranged adoptions. This example serves to illustrate how an individual case brought before a hospital ethics committee can alert the committee to a more widespread problem, and lead to the promulgation and adoption of institution-wide guidelines.

The next example shows how an individual clinical case can be transformed into a policy issue when careful scrutiny reveals the larger dimensions of the problem. The director of critical care nursing in the hospital was the first to raise the issue by bringing the case to the committee; she and others realized that other similar cases would most likely follow, thereby deepening and enlarging the problem. One of the surgical teams at the hospital had recently decided to embark on an experimental heart-lung transplant program. As part of this new program, a potential candidate for a transplant was transferred from another hospital, which had provided adequate care but could not have offered this surgical procedure. It had not yet been fully determined whether this patient was a medically suitable recipient, and she had not yet granted informed consent for the procedure. Nevertheless, she was admitted to the intensive care unit (ICU) in preparation for studies and subsequent workup. She remained in the ICU for several months awaiting a donor, but no donor emerged during that time. This patient occupied one of only ten beds in the ICU, which would otherwise have been allocated to a patient from the local community served by the hospital. Meanwhile, the potential recipient's condition deteriorated to the point where she was no longer a suitable candidate for the transplant. She was, of course, provided with the necessary care that would be granted any patient in that situation, but the prospect remained for one or more beds in the ICU to be given to this experimental program on a continuing basis.

The bioethics committee debated this issue on a policy level: Is it appropriate for one service (e.g., surgery—in particular, a heart-lung transplant team) to usurp a disproportionate share of a scarce resource in the hospital (in this case, ICU beds)? Should a new high-powered research program be allowed to displace the hospital's obligation to deliver medical services to its local community? Should this type of allocation decision be made at a higher level of hospital administration, since it clearly involves a matter of ethics in health policy? Should chairpersons or administrators of programs be required to file something akin to an "ethical impact statement" so that these developments could be analyzed and worked out before problematic cases actually arise? Predictably, the committee was sharply divided in this debate. Surgeons and others who favored continuance of the hospital's mission as a research institution with a national reputation argued for the appropriateness of allocating a scarce resource for research purposes. Others, who believed that the hospital's primary obligation lay in delivering services to needy residents of the community, held that research endeavors such as the heart-lung transplant program should not progress at the expense of caring for people in the local area.

This issue was hotly debated but never resolved by the committee. The lack of any resolution may be attributed to a number of factors. First, the case was brought to the committee by a nurse who, although she holds considerable power and prestige in her own professional hierarchy, nonetheless lacks influence with the hospital administration or even the medical personnel in charge of the ICU/CCU. Second, although the case brought to the IEC was likely to address an ongoing issue, there was no one to whom the committee could address its concerns. Third, and most distressing, such issues still seem to be decided by power plays and political machinations, thus bypassing efforts to reach just and rational decisions. Matters of health policy at the federal level will no doubt always be addressed through the political process in our country, and perhaps they should be. But the political process is incapable of facilitating just and rational solutions to the numerous moral problems the nation confronts. In contrast, a hospital can, in principle, seek to find fair and well-reasoned resolutions to difficult ethical dilemmas. One role ethics committees can play is to assist those in authority to reach policy decisions that comport with justice and fairness.

A final example illustrates the role of committees that George Annas has termed "providing ethical comfort"[2]—surely an ancillary role of IECs but one that may be wholly appropriate, given the way medicine is practiced in hospitals today. A nurse and a social worker brought a troubling case to the hospital ethics committee in the hope of gaining a clearer picture of what they might have done, and what they might do in future cases that inevitably give rise to the same problem. The problem arose on the pediatric dialysis unit of the hospital, and concerned the responses of the staff to a noncompliant 19-year-old who frequently missed his dialysis appointments and whose behavior was disruptive to other patients on the unit. Although old enough to be receiving treatments on the adult dialysis unit, Ricardo was kept in the pediatric unit because he had been receiving dialysis there for several years; he knew the staff, who had learned to tolerate his noncompliance, and he was apprehensive about leaving this setting to go to the adult unit. Because of missed appointments, Ricardo needed emergency attention when he did come in, thereby commanding all the resources of the unit, to the detriment of other patients at those times. He sometimes came to other dialysis units in the area, often in the middle of the night after a missed appointment, and was known to all nearby renal units. Because of this self-destructive noncompliance, which had brought him to the brink of death on a number of occasions, a psychiatric consultation was sought to see if the patient was genuinely suicidal, and to explore the possibility of his being temporarily hospitalized in the psychiatric unit. The psychiatrist saw no evidence of mental disorder or of suicidal intentions and, quite properly, found no reason to detain the young man. Following a missed appointment on Friday, the patient, having apparently suffered a fatal cardiac arrest, was discovered over the weekend by a relative.

The death of this patient caused grief, guilt, and anger on the part of the nurses and social workers responsible for his dialysis treatments. They were grief-stricken because they had become attached to him over the years, and had developed something akin to a parent-child relationship with him. They felt guilty in having failed to correct his noncompliant behavior. And they were angry at themselves and at him, for allowing one person to disrupt the smooth functioning of an already difficult hospital unit. Although Ricardo was unique in terms of his personality and to a considerable extent in the degree of his noncompliance, the nurses and social workers who brought the case to the IEC had identified other cases that raised similar problems, and they were concerned about the proper response to such patients. Is it ever legitimate to deny continued dialysis to a patient who is not only noncompliant, but whose behavior is so disruptive that it compromises the care of other patients on the unit? (This problem was all the more pressing because the case involved a pediatric dialysis unit, and younger children had looked up to Ricardo and emulated his behavior.) Were there other resources the personnel on the unit might have utilized, resources they might employ in future, similar cases? Was their approach to patient management flawed in some way, and could they learn by what might have been mistakes in that management?

The case engendered considerable discussion, including the issue of allocating scarce resources in a just manner, the ethics of abandoning a patient who does not comply with the medically indicated regimen, the question of whether the staff had become "too attached" to this patient, and the moral justifiability of using coercive measures with patients when all other efforts have failed. Because this committee views its role as advisory, and because the case was mooted by the patient's death, no clear resolution of these several problems was reached. Yet the nurses and social workers who brought the case to the committee expressed their gratitude, noting that the open discussion of the case in that forum raised considerations that they had not examined and that would be useful in dealing with similar problems in the future.

## Modes of Consultative Operation of IECs

The examples described in the foregoing section illustrate the different approaches to consultation that might be adopted by committees or even by a single committee operating under several different consultative models. Furthermore, the consultative function overlaps to a considerable extent with other functions; and it may be difficult to separate them from one another. There seems to be no good reason why only one mode of operation should prevail. However, it is worth describing briefly the successful model used by Dr. Cranford's committee at Hennepin County Medical Center in Minnesota. That committee is rather large, and after several years of operation it has a huge caseload. The committee meets in plenary session once a month, but its large caseload precludes dealing with all cases brought to it at the monthly meetings. Accordingly, its activities are carried out continuously by the use of subcommittees and groups of two or three members of the committee who are assigned responsibility for individual cases. These cases are brought to the committee chairman, usually by hospital personnel. The chairman himself is frequently a member of the small consulting teams, and consultations often take place at the bedside.

One consequence of this consultative model is instructive. Because of the large caseload and the resultant visibility of the IEC and its operation, physicians in the hospital have gained increasing familiarity with the way the committee works. This has led to greater confidence on the part of those physicians in their ability to handle new cases "the way the committee would handle them." Furthermore, since a large portion of the cases that come to that committee pose a range of similar problems—namely, whether or not to withhold or withdraw treatment—it is not surprising that the committee's consultative role has assumed features of an educational role. To the extent that an IEC does handle similar issues in the same manner (a measure of consistency is, after all, a virtue), physicians in the hospital can readily learn to approach those ethical dilemmas in the way the committee has handled them. There is little danger, however, that by enabling their consultative role to expand into an educational one, IECs will put themselves out of business. New cases will continue to arise, cases that may not fit the paradigms the committee has addressed in the past. Furthermore, entirely new classes of cases are also inevitable, given both the technological advances in contemporary medicine, and other, unforeseen circumstances such as the appearance of a new disease entity—for example, AIDS (acquired immune deficiency syndrome)—which may demand an institutional response of some sort.

One worry that has been voiced about the operation of IECs is that they will usurp the traditional decision-making authority of the individual physician. In response, it is worth emphasizing the distinction between a consultative role and a decision-making role. Just as the long-standing practice has been to seek an individual consultation when further medical expertise is needed in the clinical setting, so too can this function be performed by a larger group or a smaller subset of the entire committee. The model of consultation, then, is analogous to the practice of seeking advice from a subspecialist with expertise in a certain area. This consultative role fits the first category described earlier: the IEC as consultant to individual physicians or other health care workers in the institution. A second model of consultation, the "management consultant" model, best fits the second and third categories: the IEC as consultant to a department or service within the hospital, or to the hospital administration.

The possibility of distinguishing—both in principle and in practice—between a decision-making function and a consultative role should serve to allay some fears about the establishment of hospital ethics committees. Yet physicians may still feel threatened if they tend to be paternalistic, if they are suspicious about medical ethics in the first place, if they foresee a mandate to consult the committee instead of proceeding on a voluntary basis, or if they are worried about the prospect of whole committees trooping to the bedside. Enough has been said here, and in other papers in this volume, to dispel at least some of these fears.

In conclusion, the precise mode of operation of IECs may vary in different respects and for different reasons. First, the charge to the committee may stem from a mission conceived initially by the hospital administration. In that case, care must be taken to ensure that the committee's primary responsibility remains that of protecting patients and ensure that the IEC does not adopt another potential role, one incompatible with its function of protecting patients' rights and interests.

A second factor that may cause variations in committees' modes of operation is the strength and style of the chairman. A chairman may aggressively seek cases in the hospital to bring before the committee. The chairman may take steps to make the committee's existence and functions well known in the hospital, and may devote considerable time and effort to setting up the agenda at committee meetings and to seeking appropriate and important agenda items. These and other variations in the stance assumed by the committee's chairman could be attributable to individual style and personality, but they might also be characteristics consciously sought or developed in the interest of having the committee function in a particular way.

Finally, the operation of IECs may vary depending on whether other mechanisms exist in the hospital for addressing ethical problems that arise. Some examples are ethics rounds on particular services, such as pediatrics or neonatology; ombudsmen rounds; ad hoc case conferences attended by a philosopher-in-residence or ethicist; and individual consultations on an ongoing basis with a resident ethicist. Depending on the hospital's resources, whether or not it serves as a teaching institution, and whether it has ready access to someone with expertise in the field of biomedical ethics, the activities of an institutional ethics committee may be expanded or contracted to fit the institution's own needs for ethics consultations.

NOTES

1. Youngner, S. J., *et al.*, *A National Survey of Hospital Ethics Committees*, in DECIDING TO FOREGO LIFE-SUSTAINING TREATMENT: ETHICAL, MEDICAL AND LEGAL ISSUES IN TREATMENT DECISIONS (President's Commission for the Study of Ethical Problems in Medicine and Biomedical and Behavioral Research) (U.S. Gov't Printing Office, Washington, D.C.) (March 1983).
2. *See* Annas, G. J., ch. 5 of this text.

# 14

## Guidelines for Decision Making: Ethical Values and Limitations

### Leslie Steven Rothenberg

If one were to conceptualize the three legitimate roles of an institutional ethics committee as the components of a classical music trio (it is not a quartet because, with all due respect to Alex Capron,[1] I reject decision review and prognosis confirmation—à la tumor boards—as appropriate functions of such a committee), it is possible to visualize the educational role as the cello or piano with its continuity of smooth, rich sounds; the consultative role as the violin with its lyrical passages and opportunities for virtuoso performance; and the role of developing institutional guidelines or policies as a tuba—big, ungainly, and impossible to ignore.

The process of writing guidelines and policies is often a thankless and arduous task, not often given to lyricism, virtuosity, or even continuity. The very juxtaposition of the nouns *committee* and *guidelines* is sufficient to inspire drowsiness and even deep sleep in the most committed health care professional. Having paid homage to the goal of full disclosure, I now shall ask the reader to put aside your preconceived notions, suspend for the moment all value judgments regarding the virtues or vices of creating policies by committee, and permit me to try to convince you of the merits of the struggle to create guidelines which touch on ethical concerns.

I plead, first of all, guilty to the charge of having been involved in this activity. For the past three years, I have been cochairing the Joint Committee on Biomedical Ethics of the Los Angeles County Bar and Medical Associations. These two organizations comprise the largest local societies of lawyers and physicians in the world. In April 1981, the governing boards of those two organizations announced and distributed the first guidelines on the withdrawal of respirators from hospitalized incompetent patients.[2] While only a first step and far from perfect in their scope and articulation, these guidelines, which were also developed by the Los Angeles County Select Citizens Committee on Life Support Policies, have received international publicity and represent an interdisciplinary effort of no small measure.

Second, I plead innocent to the charge of lacking a proper respect for the educational and consultative roles of ethics committees. At UCLA Medical Center, where I serve on the medical faculty and, for the moment, as a one-person ethics committee, I do a significant amount of clinical ethics teaching each week with physicians, nurses, and other professionals, both formally and informally. In addition, I am under contract to provide 24-hour-a-day, 7-day-a-week on-call consultations to all services of the UCLA Hospital, and do an average of four to six consultations a week at the request of attending physicians. Despite my activity in the educational and consultative roles of ethics committees, I firmly believe that the development of guidelines or policies by ethics committees is the most significant *institutional* function that such a committee can perform. Admittedly the least glamorous role, it is one which can shape the institution's responses (and those of its personnel) to ethical crises, can enhance the autonomy of patients and the morale of staff, and can provide the basis for thoughtful decision making in a clinical context with less of the paranoia, lawyer-phobia, and ethical "fuzziness" that often accompany decision making in settings where everything is *ad hoc* and nothing ethically important is put into writing. Additionally, the approval of such guidelines or procedures by the appropriate institutional authority strengthens the possibility that they will be followed, even if grudgingly, by staff, and that they will provide a standard which will pass legal and regulatory scrutiny.

DEVELOPING INSTITUTIONAL GUIDELINES

Perhaps it is symbolic of the complex and controversial nature of ethical decision making in medical settings that relatively few guidelines and procedures currently exist to guide institutional practice. When reviewing the policies on the forms to use in making requisitions for supplies, checking patient insurance coverage, or utilizing appropriate informed consent forms, one could literally weep over the sacrifice of trees to make the paper on which such policies are written. People seem more reticent to tackle issues on which a clear consensus is lacking, however, and many physicians are understandably wary of administrative policies that will hamper their free exercise of clinical judgment with regard to a specific patient. Yet the President's Commission for the Study of Ethical Problems in Medicine and Biomedical and Behavioral Research has endorsed the development of institutional policies to deal with decision-making dilemmas.[3] The opportunity thus exists for ethics committees, after they themselves become educated and experienced in dealing with the types of clinical dilemmas which are eased by the use of guidelines, to offer to staff and administration approaches which are thoughtful, pragmatic, feasible, and patient-oriented. The proverbial phrase, "Run it up the flagpole and see if anyone salutes," seems relevant here.

If a committee is performing its educational and consultative roles properly, it will find itself evolving notions of how to avoid "reinventing the wheel" in recurring ethical dilemmas. By developing credibility with the medical staff and hospital administration, the committee will find itself being asked to propose policies; if not, it should volunteer to try drafting a policy on a subject of general ethical concern. This "window of opportunity" often occurs after some decision-making crisis, particularly if the outcome is generally regarded as negative. Do not despair if the committee members are uncertain as to how to grapple with the issue, much less resolve it! It may seem as though a committee of the blind has been chosen to lead the blind, but the very fact that members of an ethics committee have an interest in considering such issues gives them a valuable qualification to initially address these questions and to consider useful methods and medically—and ethically— wise ways of resolving them.

PROCEDURAL SUGGESTIONS

Having accepted that challenge, the committee might wish to consider several suggestions that relate more to process than content:

1. Consider inviting members of the institution's staff, or persons from outside the institution, who can bring to the committee their experience, credibility, or prior thinking on the issue.

2. Keep in mind that ultimately the medical staff has to be convinced of the appropriateness and feasibility of the procedures or guidelines to be proposed. It helps to have one or more physicians on the committee who are widely respected among the medical staff, but it is equally important to make certain that the proposal is medically sophisticated, is clinically appropriate to the institutional setting involved (for example, recognizing the difference between decision making which takes place in the emergency room and in the intensive care unit), and lends itself to the time and personnel constraints imposed by a given setting or situation of the patient.

3.  Avoid the use of ambiguous terminology (for example, adjectives such as *imminent*), unnecessary professional jargon, and detailed statements that may "fix in concrete" rules which may be applied to changing treatment situations or scientific analysis.

4.  Encourage, through the guidelines or procedures, a collaborative and supportive approach to the resolution of ethical dilemmas among patients, physicians, nurses, and other hospital personnel.

5.  Assume that the institution's administration will want to have proposed policies reviewed by legal counsel, but concentrate first on reaching the committee's objectives in spelling out the policy. Concerns about lawyers, judges, licensing boards, or other entities should not divert the committee's focus.

6.  Evaluate the impact of any proposed policies on administrative personnel, the nursing service, and allied health professionals, as well as on patients. (For example, would you, as a patient, be pleased with or benefit from the proposed policy if it were in effect? If in doubt, reconsider the proposal!)

7.  Separate the policy from the set of implementing procedures in order that the two not be confused and that the procedures can be changed from time to time to accommodate new developments in treatment modalities and other relevant factors.

8.  Write the policy in English that is as clear as it is possible to be in a medical setting.

9.  Once the final policy has been approved by the institution's governing authority, use the committee's educational role to promote its use among the staff, and be alert to the need to revise it at a later date.

The business of writing guidelines is as frustrating and grueling an experience as one is likely to face during service on an ethics committee. The careful tightrope walk between the personalities and professional egos of committee members, the relentless pressure to take language and do wonders with it in a short period of time, the very real policy choices that have to be made in formulating guidelines—it may seem as though one is trying to swim through a pool of molasses.[4] Yet the satisfactions come not only when the proposal is found acceptable by the institutional governing authority, but more importantly, when the committee member first sees this imperfect, but functioning, guidelines or policies help a patient and staff cope with an ethical dilemma.

Last year, I was involved personally in the decisions to disconnect ventilators from more than 50 irreversible comatose patients whose families sought this decision not to treat. As I stood with the physicians and nurses at the bedside and watched those patients in their final moments of life, I often reflected on the collective efforts of the men and women who struggled to develop guidelines to deal with this treatment decision and the ethical issues surrounding it. I was enormously proud of their effort and grateful for their courage in offering physicians and families a way of providing the only beneficial assistance possible in that circumstance.

Your institution could benefit from collective efforts to deal with such issues as "do-not-resuscitate" orders, withholding or withdrawal of treatment, issues involving neonates with congenital abnormalities or extreme prematurity, the patient or family who wants the most aggressive therapy possible despite the pessimism of the medical and nursing teams, determination of death, and refusal of treatment. I urge you to utilize your existing ethics committee or to create one as a means of developing and promoting such guidelines for your institution.

## NOTES

1. *See* Capron, A. M., ch. 15 of this text.
2. Published in Section III of this text.
3. PRESIDENT'S COMMISSION FOR THE STUDY OF ETHICAL PROBLEMS IN MEDICINE AND BIOMEDICAL AND BEHAVIORAL RESEARCH, DECIDING TO FOREGO LIFE-SUSTAINING TREATMENT: ETHICAL, MEDICAL AND LEGAL ISSUES IN TREATMENT DECISIONS (U.S. Gov't Printing Office, Washington, D.C.) (March 1983) at 4, 5, 164.
4. For mechanical guidance in the formulation of policies, see K. M. COUNTRYMAN, DEVELOPMENT AND IMPLEMENTATION OF A PATIENT'S BILL OF RIGHTS IN HOSPITALS (American Hospital Association, Chicago) (1980); DEVELOPING POLICIES AND PROCEDURES FOR LONG-TERM CARE INSTITUTIONS (American Hospital Association, Chicago) (1975).

# 15

## Decision Review: A Problematic Task

Alexander Morgan Capron

This is a very hard time for health care in America. Hospitals find themselves under many pressures—financial, administrative, medical, and legal. Some patients want care that they cannot afford, or that is unavailable to them; others receive care either that they regard as unduly burdensome or that threatens to swamp them financially. The families of patients, particularly those who are incompetent to make their own decisions, are confronted with awesome responsibilities about therapies both proven and experimental. The research community struggles to maintain a level of effort commensurate with the challenges of finding new, effective, and even—blessed be the thought— less expensive cures. Courts and legislatures find themselves drawn into areas for which they have little preparation or familiarity.

Among all these daunting prospects, why is it that one set of problems has of late achieved particular prominence? Why is it, in particular, that the question of decisions to forego treatment has come to absorb so much public and professional attention?

Each of us will have his or her own answer to these questions. It seems to me that this public attention exists because the congeries of issues around decisions about life-sustaining treatment epitomize and crystallize the social phenomenon of modern medicine: its reliance on complex technology and high specialization, resulting in atomization and alienation for provider and patient alike; the interweaving of a desire for personal choice with the inescapable fact of high uncertainty and abstruse facts that are difficult for most people to comprehend; and the frequent consequence of such treatment, that patients are often rendered incapable of participating in decisions, raising the sensitive issue of making choices for others whose lives are at stake.

As one way to deal with that set of problems—which have recently been thrown into stark relief by the Reagan Administration's proposed "Infant Doe" rules,[1] by the charges brought against two Los Angeles physicians,[2] and so forth—hospitals are increasingly turning to institutional ethics committees. As Stuart Youngner has reported, in the last decade almost 5 percent of the larger hospitals in this country have apparently set up bodies to aid in decision making in situations of doubt, typically those involving the treatment of incompetent patients, especially where the treatment in question is life-supporting.[3] Recently, the President's Commission for the Study of Ethical Problems in Medicine and Biomedical and Behavioral Research issued two reports that discuss the possible role of ethics committees.[4] The Commission recognized that ethics committees do not represent a miraculous cure for this problem that has of late so noticeably raised the public's temperature. Indeed, there is, I believe, simply no miracle to be found. The Commission voiced cautions about ethics committees and acknowledged that very little is known about them. We urged not only that different alternatives be tried, but also that they be carefully evaluated and compared, lest society rush prematurely to adopt a single, uniform formula:

> Very little is known . . . about the actual effectiveness of institutional ethics committees, especially in comparison with private, informal mechanisms or with judicial decision making for patients lacking decision-making capacity. The composition and functions of existing ethics committees vary substantially from one institution to another. Not enough experience has accumulated to date to know the appropriate and most effective functions and hence the suitable composition of such committees. If their role is to serve primarily as "prognosis committees" to pass on the accuracy of an attending physician's judgment, then committees composed largely of physicians would seem to be appropriate. If the ethics committees are supposed to reach decisions that best reflect the individually defined well-being of patients or the ethicality of decisions, however, it seems doubtful that an exclusively medical group would be suitable. And if the appropriate role of such review bodies should be to determine whether a surrogate decision maker is qualified to make medical decisions on a patient's behalf (and to set only outer boundaries on the nature of the decision reached rather than second-guessing the choice), the membership should be diverse.[5]

Events of the past year have caused those cautions to go unnoticed, something for which those of us who were closely associated with the Commission are largely responsible. At the time that the report on deciding about life support was issued, President Reagan and the Office of Civil Rights of the Department of Health and Human Services had just issued a regulation under Section 504 of the 1973 Rehabilitation Act that required the posting of warning notices in facilities caring for infants and that established a 24-hour, toll-free "hot line" so that anyone could report to Washington alleged instances of failure to provide "food and customary care" to a newborn.[6] Believing that approach to be unwise, and not wishing to sound merely critical, those of us who were called upon for comments growing out of the Commission's two-year study of the subject tended to stress that an alternative to the Section 504 regulation was available—namely, if the federal government wanted to be involved, it could encourage better decision making in hospitals, and specifically in neonatal intensive care units, through the use of devices like ethics committees.

Apparently the ruling on April 14, 1983, by Judge Gerhard Gesell in the federal district court in Washington, D.C., in which he indicated his negative view of the substance of the Section 504 regulation in the course of enjoining its enforcement on administrative law grounds,[7] was insufficient to discourage further attempts at federal regulation on this subject, since substantially the same rules were proposed in July 1983.[8] Nonetheless, I am still hopeful that both those within the department, who participate in the formulation of policy, such as Surgeon General Koop, and those from outside the department who influence it, such as the leaders of the American Academy of Pediatrics, will give serious thought to the recommendations of the Commission. Before they do so, however, I think it is appropriate to take this opportunity to remind ourselves about the cautions and concerns that the Commission voiced regarding ethics committees. It is clearly too soon for revisionist history of the operations of the Commission; indeed, it is too soon for any "history" at all. But it is not too soon to ask questions about ethics committees if—under the pressure of the federal government's desire to avoid bad medical decision making—they are about to become a standard feature of all hospitals.

It seems apparent, at the very least, that society is no longer comfortable with having certain decisions made behind closed doors. If the choice is between ethics committees and other less sensitive, less prompt, and less discreet mechanisms—be they routine reliance on trial judges or frequent involvement of federal civil rights or reimbursement regulators—I should say at the outset that my vote would be cast for the intrainstitutional mechanism. Nonetheless, it is worthwhile asking some questions about the committees, particularly in connection with the problematic task of decision review that they are apparently being asked to undertake. I relate my comments to four questions about ethics committees: *Why* do they exist? *When* should they function? *Who* should participate? and *How* should they operate?

## WHY SHOULD ETHICS COMMITTEES EXIST?

There are a number of things to be learned from our experience with the use of committees to promote ethical decision making in another area of biomedicine—namely, the development over the last two decades of Institutional Review Boards (IRBs). Certainly, one problem with which we have a good deal of experience in that context is the difficulty that arises when the review task of the IRB is perceived by different people as being undertaken for different reasons. The same sorts of questions arise in the case of institutional ethics committees.

As an analytic matter, it is important to distinguish the *function* of an ethics committee from the *purpose* of the committee. Those are both, in effect, "why" questions; but they are distinct in much the same way that "motive" and "intent," though similar, are distinct in the criminal law.

Other commentators have pointed to several functions of these committees: to educate; to improve communication among patients, families, and different members of the health care team; to consult on such matters as medical prognosis; to develop policies and guidelines; and to review treatment decisions. This last function is my particular topic, but I don't believe it can be discussed without paying some attention to other functions.

Moreover, these functions are, as I mentioned, distinct from the purposes of the committees. Depending on one's view, the major purpose might be articulated as protecting competent patients' choices, or as ensuring the well-being of patients, competent or incompetent, or as guarding from liability the hospital and those who practice there. I think there is a real danger in this area that institutions will regard the purpose of protecting hospitals and physicians as the primary one, just as they now seek protection through trips to the courtroom for an advance blessing on a particular course of treatment. (That was, after all, what caused the trouble in the "Infant Doe" case in Indiana in the first place.)[9] These problems arise not because hospitals are compelled to go to court to seek judicial approval, but simply because they want the guarantee of immunity from any judgment sought against them after the fact.

Of course, one cannot object to an ethics committee on the ground that if it functions properly, it will indeed provide protection for hospitals and physicians. But that is not the same as saying that such protection is the primary purpose of the committee. After all, when physicians provide medical services, they attempt to do so with due care; however, their purpose in doing so is not, or ought not to be, the avoidance of legal liability, but to provide all the help to their patients that a careful, competent physician can provide in applying current medical knowledge. Yet in intervening in a careful and reasonable manner according to professional norms, they also protect themselves legally.

Looking at Dr. Youngner's study[10] and at other surveys and discussions,[11] it is my contention that of the functions that the ethics committees can serve—reviewing a case to confirm the responsible physician's diagnosis and prognosis; providing a forum for discussion of broad social and ethical concerns; formulating policy and guidelines; and, finally, reviewing decisions in individual cases—only the last is unique. I realize this is a contentious suggestion on my part, but I make it because I want to stimulate thought about just what makes an ethics committee an ethics committee. I conclude it is "decision review," because all the other functions are either adjunct to it or superfluous.

This is a strong claim. Let me try to defend it. First, it seems apparent to me that the educational function did not begin with ethics committees, and it is not necessary to have an "ethics committee" to have that function occur in the hospital. There are many forms of education, from those within a hospital to national, regional, and local conferences, continuing education, and, of course, journals—all of which can provide as much education as anyone's head can absorb. Morever, by setting up mechanisms for education in the sense of psychological sensitization and preparation for dealing with the problems that people face, it is possible through seminars on a cross-disciplinary basis to have nurses, physicians, and social workers sit down together and work through the problems that they are facing as individual human beings coping with these hard cases. Yet it seems to me unlikely that calling that an ethics committee tells you very much about it. Indeed, institutions that do that regularly do not denominate that function an "ethics committee." Thus, one doesn't need an ethics committee for the educational function.

What about the role of consultation, whether it is consultation with a physician to provide a confirmation of prognosis or consultation with a lawyer to talk about the hospital's legal liability? That is not uniquely the function of an ethics committee. If that function impeded what I regard as the unique function, I would say that one should get rid of it. Yet it is clear that some of the groups responding to Dr. Youngner's survey have what they term "ethics committees" that basically operate that way.[12] They are New Jersey-style "ethics committees"—which is to say, prognosis committees—involving, for example, skilled neurologists coming to a hospital to help with the determination of the permanence of a patient's unconscious state. Or they may be "committees" that never even meet as such, but rather are some "wise men" at the hospital who are called upon by the physicians (particularly house officers) caring for difficult cases and who, through their advice, help to shape "the decision" reached by the physicians handling the case. That is plainly not a function that is unique to ethics committees. Physicians have been doing that with each other, for each other, for a long time.

What about the function of simply improving communication among the staff and the patients—of making sure that people are talking about the same thing? Plainly, this is a very important function, but a lot of other people already do it. It is a role that many individuals have traditionally played. We all know from our experience with hospitals that there are certain people who are very good at that. Sometimes they are social workers; sometimes they are pastors; sometimes they are skilled nurses or physicians who are deeply involved in patient care, but are also very good at making sure that all the people involved are talking to each other.

Finally, there is the question of policies and guidelines. I quite agree with Les Rothenberg that from the caldron of deciding individual cases, certain common themes may emerge that could be written down. But an ethics committee is not needed to do that; medical staff committees and hospital boards of trustees can perform this function. It would be very odd, for example, if an ethics committee were to be the primary group responsible for drafting the policies on "no-code" orders in a hospital. That is not a function that is particularly suited to ethics committees, for it requires great involvement with the management of the hospital, to say nothing of the numerous technical, medical issues.

What, then, is left? It seems to me that what is central to ethics committees is the process of decision review. That is what a committee sits to do that is not and has not been done well before. That is why the President's Commission, in responding to the Section 504 regulation, did not say "business as usual" in America's hospitals. Some bad—perhaps even indefensible—decisions have been made; means must now be created to review decisions that involve life and death so that everyone will have greater assurance that such decisions, particularly when they involve incompetent patients, will respect the best interest of seriously ill patients.

The courts have recognized the "decision review" function of ethics committees, but have varied on the details. We have a wide spectrum, from the New Jersey courts[13] (which in effect said—perhaps not fully realizing it—"Don't come back to us regularly, but develop your institutional mechanisms for confirmation of prognoses and then go ahead and apply them") to the Massachusetts Supreme Judicial Court[14] (which has said that most of these decisions must be reviewed by the court in some way, although it realized that the judges do not have the flexibility and the time to decide every health care decision, as they at first suggested).

The argument in favor of an ethics committee is that the decisions in these difficult cases can be made in a locus that is close to the treatment setting where the facts are unfolding minute by minute or hour by hour among people who have more familiarity than judges with these cases. Both health care professionals, such as physicians and nurses, and "outsiders" who, through service on such a committee, will eventually become familiar with the decisions, are better decision reviewers than are judges and guardians ad litem. At the heart, then, of the role of the ethics committee is its function to insure that all interests of the affected parties, especially incapacitated parties, have been adequately represented and that the decision falls within the range of those that are found to be socially and legally acceptable.

One threshold issue that any ethics committee must face is whether the case before it is to be decided under standards for competent patients or incompetent patients. This means, in effect, that a committee must answer a question that turns on a judgment involving facts about a particular patient. It will have to decide whether it determines this on the basis of the record of other people's conclusions or functions like a judge who holds hearings at the bedside. I strongly favor the former because it is a process of reviewing a decision, rather than initial decision making. But it will be important for that decision to be made.

In many cases, of course, the determination of which standards to use ("incompetent" or "competent") is obvious because the patient is unconscious, is a child, or is otherwise incapacitated in a manner about which no one has any doubt. But in other cases, the question of competence is itself the central issue. In effect, if it is determined that the patient is competent, the range of review for the committee is greatly narrowed because society recognizes that (within certain parameters) the decisions of a competent patient have a force that the decisions of a surrogate do not.

## When Should Ethics Committees Function?

Let me turn to the question of when committee reviews should take place. The central fact about this review, if it is to be an improvement over the existing situation, is that it should be current, prompt, and prospective. The committee should be involved with decisions in the making that are of a type requiring review.

What will trigger review? It is exactly on this point that I think we have to be vague. We have to account for such matters as the diversity that is experienced in individual hospitals as a result of the mix of cases; the style of decision making that already characterizes the hospital; whether the hospital decisions primarily involve hospital staff—residents and interns and others who are on the staff—or primarily involve attending physicians who have a different role. The trigger may be different in those different cases, it seems to me.

In any case, this function should primarily be something that is prospective. However, when that is not possible, it would be advisable to insure that there is review after the fact—for example, as discussed by the Commission, in reviewing the treatment of a newborn where the decision has been made to forego treatment. Insuring retrospective review in such cases will remove any incentive that medical personnel would have for taking hasty action in treatment decisions in order to prevent prospective review, a course that would be disadvantageous to at least some at-risk newborns. Retrospective review cannot change what has happened in a particular case, but it can help to ensure the high quality of decision-making practices in the institution, as well as leading to censure, both internal and judicial where appropriate, of seriously erroneous decision making.

## WHO SHOULD PARTICIPATE IN DECISION MAKING?

Who ought to be involved in decisions? I suppose that by now it has become commonplace to declare that medical decisions are too important to be left solely to physicians. The first, and ethically most significant, response is that decisions ought to rest with patients—and are best arrived at through a process of mutual discussion and respect on the part of the professional health care providers and the patient, with the decision ultimately, of course, resting with the informed, competent patient who can make a voluntary choice.[15]

The second response has been to insist that those decisions not made by a patient should instead involve committees of review whose membership reaches out beyond physicians and nurses to include lawyers, clergy, social and behavioral scientists, and representatives of the general public. The Commission provided several reasons why institutions should seriously consider the advantage of a diverse membership for an ethics committee. First, having individuals from many different specialties, as well as those without professional specialization, can minimize the tendency to take the committee's task as essentially a technical one, which it is not. Second, diversity can prevent ethics committees from becoming uncritically accepting of, or adverse to, the views of any one professional or social group. Finally, since one of the central functions of ethics committees may be to advise within the context of decision review, many different perspectives should be available so that the advice can be communicated in a way that speaks to the varied needs and orientations of patients and practitioners.

Again, this strikes me as an issue about which some things can be learned by looking at our experience with IRBs. The membership required on IRBs has been gradually increased until today the federal regulations specify the categories of people who should sit on an IRB. Yet, during that process, there was no clear articulation of why we wanted that diverse membership. There are several alternative theories, but they are not necessarily compatible. It strikes me as very important, therefore, that as a hospital determines whether it will have an ethics committee and what its membership will be, diversity for diversity's sake ought not to be the goal. Instead, institutional officials ought to decide whether they intend to bring in a cross-sample of the community in order to replicate the sort of choice that a jury would make if this were a case that had gone to court. Alternatively, are they seeking diversity to obtain additional insights into technical questions (including the technical issues of ethics)?—in which case one would want a professor of philosophy or a theologian or whatever is necessary. In any case, my message is: decide why it is that you are looking for individuals other than physicians to be decision makers. Do not answer the "who" question with diversity for its own sake, but because of the specific functions you want diversity to serve.

## How Should Ethics Committees Operate?

The next rather central issue that has not been addressed adequately, in my view, is the question of "how"—that is, the relationship, in an administrative law sense, between the committee and others. Specifically, to what extent is it in effect an appellate tribunal? Reciprocally, to what extent ought the courts to defer to its decisions, and to what extent ought the courts to play the role of initial decision maker themselves?

Looking again to the IRB for an analogy, we see that these questions have not been clearly addressed by those who drafted the IRB regulations nor, so far as I know, have they been resolved by any court. An opportunity to review this issue arose—but ultimately was not resolved—in the recent Iowa case of *Head v. Colloton*.[16] In that case, a leukemia victim learned that the University of Iowa Hospitals and Clinics had in its bone marrow transplant registry the name of a woman who might, upon further testing, prove to be the most suitable donor of bone marrow for an experimental treatment of his leukemia. He brought suit under the state Freedom of Information Act to learn the woman's name so he could contact her directly or, alternatively, so that the hospital could contact the woman and explain his need for her marrow.

Previously, the IRB at the University of Iowa had specifically reviewed the research protocol involved and had decided that it would be proper to contact the woman, referred to as "Mrs. X," when the hospital records of her tissue typing became available to the university —to explain to her the existence of the registry, and to ask whether she was interested in being registered as a potential donor. When that was done, first by letter and then by a phone call, she replied that she was not interested and that she would only consider donating to a family member. On that basis the IRB had declined to allow the university to make her name available or to contact her further.

Rather than deferring to the IRB's judgment about the appropriate way to protect privacy and to respect the rights of the woman, the Iowa district court ruled in the plaintiff's favor.[17] On appeal, that judgment was reversed by the Iowa Supreme Court, but the reversal rested not on the deference owed to the IRB, but on the different reading the higher court gave to the exemption in the Iowa Freedom of Information Act that shields from disclosure "hospital records and medical records of the condition, diagnoses, care, or treatment of a patient or former patient, including outpatients."[18] Reversing the lower court, Judge McCormick ruled that this exemption applied to Mrs. X, for while she had not, herself, been treated when she was tissue-typed, a broad definition of the word *treatment* would encompass her role as a potential donor for a member of her family.[19]

The relevance of *Head v. Colloton* for institutional ethics committees is that we have a long way to go to develop, in a clear fashion that draws on socially accepted norms, those standards by which such committees will operate. In the absence of such standards and their acceptance by society, I do not expect to see courts deferring to the judgments of ethics committees.

Having stressed the role of ethics committees in decision review, I want to recognize a drawback to that. The drawback is undue interference and bureaucratization of the decisions. If at the moment we see ourselves faced with the prospect of mounting judicial interference in decisions—with the accompanying delays, rigidity, and, often, publicity —an ethics committee may seem a very attractive alternative. But the question always arises, "compared to what?" If we are comparing ethics committees to a system of more informal decision making that has not been cumbersome, but has rather been fairly responsive in most cases, and if the movement toward ethics committees has occurred merely because of a few cases involving abuses, then we should be sensitive to the fact that the ethics committee might turn out to be the worst of all worlds: it might be less burdensome than the courts—but, therefore, used more frequently—while at the same time being much more burdensome than decision making on a more informal basis, which it would supplant since it would be seen as more protective against legal liability.

In the end, I think that some protection against bureaucratization lies in ensuring that ethics committees deal primarily with issues of process rather than content so that they find themselves neither second-guessing every decision nor articulating the sort of substantive decisions that we expect of courts of law. Instead, they should focus in each case on the question of whether the interests of all parties, particularly the "silent" ones, have been adequately represented, and whether the relevant considerations have been taken into account—while recognizing that, in many cases, there will be a range of ethically acceptable decisions.

Of course, it is also imperative for an ethics committee to know that there is an outer limit to the range of ethically acceptable decisions. If that limit is crossed, it is then appropriate for the committee members to attempt to persuade the participants to change an initial decision because the committee's review of that decision indicates that the relevant factors were not all taken into account, or that the various interests were not adequately represented by decision makers free from the effects of conflicting interests. If the ethics committee is not successful in persuasion, it is appropriate at that point for it to refer the matter to an authorized agency, to petition a court to name a substitute decision maker, or to find some other appropriate remedy.

In conclusion, I would not want movement toward institutional ethics committees to occur too quickly; we should try to avoid the situation we now have with IRBs, which have a specific federal mandate without full articulation of the major premises. There are many unresolved issues about the functions of IRBs, and it seems to me that we also have many unanswered questions about ethics committees, including basic questions about how urgently they are needed and for which particular problems. These issues are best sorted out by experience—rather in the way the common law developed, by slow accretion of ideas and by the sharing of those ideas through conferences such as this. I hope that by taking a strong stand, I have provoked at least Les Rothenberg, since I have declared that his musical trio—education, consultation, and guideline formulation[20]—is playing outside in the lobby, while the real decisions are being reviewed inside.

## NOTES

1. 48 Fed. Reg. 30,846 (July 5, 1983) (to be codified at 45 C.F.R. §84.61).
2. People v. Barber, No. A 025586 (Los Angeles Municipal Court, Los Angeles County, Calif., March 9, 1983).
3. Youngner, S. J., *et. al.*, *A National Survey of Hospital Ethics Committees*, in DECIDING TO FOREGO TREATMENT, *infra* note 4.

4. PRESIDENT'S COMMISSION FOR THE STUDY OF ETHICAL PROBLEMS IN MEDI-
   CINE AND BIOMEDICAL AND BEHAVIORAL RESEARCH, MAKING HEALTH
   CARE DECISIONS: THE ETHICAL AND LEGAL IMPLICATIONS OF INFORMED
   CONSENT IN THE PATIENT-PRACTITIONER RELATIONSHIP (U.S. Gov't
   Printing Office, Washington, D.C.) (October 1982) [hereinafter referred
   to as MAKING HEALTH CARE DECISIONS]; PRESIDENT'S COMMISSION FOR
   THE STUDY OF ETHICAL PROBLEMS IN MEDICINE AND BIOMEDICAL AND
   BEHAVIORAL RESEARCH, DECIDING TO FOREGO LIFE-SUSTAINING TREAT-
   MENT: ETHICAL, MEDICAL AND LEGAL ISSUES IN TREATMENT DECISIONS
   (U.S. Gov't Printing Office, Washington, D.C.) (March 1983) [hereinafter
   referred to as DECIDING TO FOREGO TREATMENT].
5. MAKING HEALTH CARE DECISIONS, *supra* note 4, at 187–88.
6. 48 Fed. Reg. 9,630 (March 7,1983). *But see* Fed. Reg. 17,588 (April 25,
   1983) (invalidating interim final rule in compliance with court order, *infra*
   note 7).
7. American Academy of Pediatrics v. Heckler, 561 F. Supp. 395
   (D.D.C.1983).
8. *Supra* note 1.
9. New York Times (April 15, 1982), at D21, col. 5.
10. Youngner, *et al.*, *supra* note 3.
11. Levine, C., *Hospital Ethics Committees: A Guarded Prognosis*, HASTINGS CEN-
    TER REPORT 7(3):25 (June 1977); Veatch, R. M., *Hospital Ethics Committees:
    Is There a Role?*, HASTINGS CENTER REPORT 7(3):22 (June 1977).
12. Youngner, *et al.*, *supra* note 3, at 447.
13. *In re* Quinlan, 355 A.2d 647 (N.J. 1976), *cert. denied*, 429 U.S. 922 (1976).
    Many commentators have suggested that the "ethics committee" described
    by the *Quinlan* court is actually a mechanism for confirmation of medical
    prognosis. *See, e.g.*, Robertson, J., Ch. 7 of this text. *See also In re* Colyer,
    660 P.2d 738 (Wash. 1983) (where the Washington Supreme Court criti-
    cized the hospital ethics committee composed of diverse membership, as
    recommended by the *Quinlan* court, in favor of an all-physician prognosis
    board to confirm prognoses only).
14. *In re* Spring, 405 N.E.2d 115 (Mass. 1980) (orders to withhold life-sustain-
    ing treatment from an incompetent hemodialysis patient are the ultimate
    responsibility of the court); Superintendent of Belchertown State School v.
    Saikewicz, 370 N.E.2d 417 (Mass. 1977) (order withholding chemotherapy
    from incompetent and profoundly retarded leukemia patient at State
    School should be subject to judicial scrutiny). *Compare In re* Dinnerstein,
    380 N.E.2d 134 (Mass. App. 1978) (declaration that validity of order not to
    resuscitate patient with Alzheimer's disease did not depend on prior court
    approval).
15. MAKING HEALTH CARE DECISIONS, *supra* note 4, at 2–6.
16. Head v. Colloton, 331 N.W.2d 870 (Iowa 1983).
17. *Id.* at 872.
18. Iowa Code Ann. §68A.7 (West Supp. 1983–84).
19. Head v. Colloton, *supra* note 16, at 876.
20. *See* Rothenberg, L.S., ch. 14 of this text.

# Audience Discussion

## David L. Jackson, Moderator

DAVID L. JACKSON, M.D., PH.D. (at present Director of Health, state of Ohio): It has struck me in the discussion of the educational roles of IECs and how IECs operate that so frequently the critical issues are immediate. The incidents occur at two o'clock in the morning, or there is a limited time during which the IECs (or any process) can be helpful to the patient, the family, and the staff. IECs also can serve long-range functions (e.g., developing guidelines and policies, and broader educational activities). But I would like to see committees become more involved with individual cases in real time, where the immediate dilemmas concern family and staff. Having health professionals bring cases to these committees is the first step in increasing useful input from a group of concerned individuals. I also think that committees ought to include lay members, as well as members of the health professions. If one is really concerned about true patient autonomy and the use of substituted judgment for patients by family members, then patients and families should be able to "bring" these issues to the committees.

This raises, however, a logistical dilemma. We encountered this in Cleveland when we tried to add to the guidelines for our institutional review committee that patients and family could bring cases to the committee. I think that this could be an important feature, but it is meaningless if patients and families do not know that this institutional mechanism exists, and do not understand when to use it and what it can (and cannot) accomplish. Are there ways that committees interested not only in serving individual health professionals who bring their cases to a committee, but also in reaching out to patients and families, could facilitate this bringing of cases to the committee? How can we approach our patients and their families with uniformity about how our institution approaches the difficult ethical issues so frequently encountered in high technology medicine today? When a committee begins not only to serve the "needs" of the health professionals, but also to be responsive to the individual needs and requests of patients and families in crises, does this change the consultative role and function of the committee?[1]

CORRINE BAYLEY, C.S.J. (conference faculty): I'm not sure how helpful my response will be, but it will be very candid. I think that at this point, the committees need to develop their own comfort level with dealing with these things. It is too early to say to the hospital community, "We are here to help you do this." I think committees should do that eventually. However, because most committees are new, because they themselves disagree about issues, and because they are sometimes not even sure what an ethical issue is, much less how to resolve it, they are uncomfortable in offering help to other members of the hospital. On a few occasions, the committee of which I am a member has done this, and it has worked out nicely for the most part—helping people to come to a better decision. To be frank, I think that not even our entire staff, much less our patients, know we have a committee. Perhaps this is because most of us have more "internal" work to do before we advertise our services widely to the "external" community.

RUTH MACKLIN, PH.D. (conference faculty): I find myself ambivalent about this kind of circumstance. On the one hand, I am not in favor of secrecy, and I do not like discussing things behind people's backs. Yet I can foresee a lot of problems, not only where a committee is divided, but also where there may even be disagreement among family members. I am thinking of adult family members who may be quarreling about what is best for an elderly parent, and some actual cases come to mind. In one case, the two middle-aged sons were waiting outside the door while the physician brought the case to the ethics committee. Despite the protestations of the chairman of the committee that the committee did not make decisions, that it was only advisory, it was clear that this physician was waiting for our answer. It involved the removal of fluids and other continued life supports from the patient, and the sons were quarreling with each other over this issue.

In addition to the shortcomings that Corrine just mentioned, existing committees and newly formed committees lack expertise in counseling and in the kinds of sensitive concerns that may confront the committee. The specter of a patient or a patient's family bringing a matter of life and death before a bunch of haranguing, wrangling, debating, quarrelsome verbal types sitting in a committee could be very distressing. When I think of the few cases in which families were involved, either where family members disagreed or where there were some questions about the motivations of the family in wishing to withdraw treatment from an elderly relative, I realize that there are many problems that we have to consider before we make committees open and invite patients and families to sit in on meetings in which their concerns are deliberated.

DR. JACKSON: I do not think it follows, "as the night follows the day," that if families can call the meeting they would choose to do so or would be present at the discussions. My committee lets all families know that such a discussion is going to take place, even if they have not requested it. None of them, in the 15 or so cases I have personally brought to our committee, have asked to participate in the discussions.

DR. MACKLIN: I see. In that case, then, most of the threat goes away.

ELLEN COVNER WEISS, J.D. (Children's Hospital, Boston): I had thought originally that I should ask this question yesterday, but Dr. Jackson's question makes me feel that it is appropriate to ask now. Has anyone given any consideration to the role of a patient relations representative, a patient coordinator, or a patient rights advocate? It strikes me that some of the discussions at this meeting relate to responsibilities or functions that are being fulfilled by patient representatives. This last discussion suggests to me that there might be some benefit in using a patient representative to assist families in getting at least some reassurance that their concerns are being heard. I think that some of the issues that go to ethics committees or to patient representatives reflect a lack of communication between the patient and the family, or the patient and the physician. I wonder if you would comment on that.

SISTER BAYLEY: I would agree that we should use the patient's representative in that way. We need all the help we can get. The ethics committee is not there to usurp the roles of other departments, such as pastoral care or social services, or to take unto itself all these issues. I think we need to sensitize the entire institution to the issues, and we have been doing that in lots of ways. The ethics committee came along because we had some very troublesome issues for which a patient representative sometimes needs to know the institutional policy.

DR. MACKLIN: I agree, and on one of the committees on which I serve, one committee member is a representative from the patient relations office. I have also noticed that not all patient advocates operate uniformly. Patient relations offices may serve functions other than that of straightforward patient advocacy. Very often, the patient relations office is called on to deal with a recalcitrant patient, to try to get a patient to sign when the patient has not signed the consent form; and the question arises as to just what advocacy requires in such situations. It is not clear that the people from the patient relations office are always acting in the role of the patient's advocate, even though it is called the patient relations office. That title is sufficiently ambiguous to suggest that the office has to do with relations that may come out on the hospital's side sometimes, and not always on the patient's side. However, I agree with what Corrine said.

The functions of the committee may vary from one institution to another depending upon what other mechanisms exist for consultations and for addressing ethical issues. So, in one of the hospitals with which I am affiliated, my colleagues and I engage in ethics rounds, omsbudsman rounds, case conferences, and bioethics bag lunches. There is much education about ethics in the hospital. To the extent that there are other activities that also serve an educational role, including the work of the patient relations office, they do not usurp the work of the committee, but complement it.

DR. JACKSON: I would only add that the role of the advocate should not be left to the patient relations office. It is really something that is, I hope, shared by physician, nurse, social worker, and all of the individuals involved in the care of the patient. In our unit, we specify a senior social worker who has *carte blanche* to institute consultation on every patient in the unit without being asked by anybody to serve as an advocate. I hold to my own view that, as a physician, I am one of the primary advocates for my patients; and when we lose sight of that, it blurs communications.

JOHN B. REINHART, M.D. (Children's Hospital of Pittsburgh): Sister Bayley has said this morning that one should not combine the institutional review board (IRB) and the institutional ethics committee. We have done that for a number of years, and I wonder, what have we been doing wrong and why is it so dangerous?

SISTER BAYLEY: I think it is not dangerous, but the two types of committees have some different kinds of functions. The IRB has been formed to do very specific things; its membership is very specific, and, most important, it is all mandated by law.[2] I think this may inhibit the interdisciplinary, multidisciplinary interaction that we would like to have on an ethics committee. I have not seen it combined successfully, but that does not mean that it cannot be.

DR. MACKLIN: I agree that the functions of an IRB and of an IEC are very different. The IRB is clearly making decisions, and the nature of its decisions is very different from any decision that an ethics committee might make. One should also consider the load of cases. My IRB can barely get the work done that it has to do every session. It would never have the time to attend to the kinds of problems that require slower deliberations. So there are both practical barriers and other types of difficulties stemming from their different functions.

DR. DOLORES DOOLEY (CLARKE) (on sabbatical at the University of Notre Dame, Notre Dame, Indiana, from the Department of Philosophy, University College, Cork, Ireland): The whole tone of the discussion up to now has been based on the assumption that institutional ethics committees share a broad ethical framework but are in fact pluralistic in terms of their composition. My question is very specific, and affects a large number of institutions—religiously denominational hospitals. What do you think the composition of the ethics committees for religious-run hospitals should be? Within that kind of an institutional framework, are there not a priori constraints on what kinds of questions can be brought to the ethics committee? For example, consider a woman who has had her ninth child, and whose doctor has said that she should not have more children. The woman is 35, and a hysterectomy would be premature. Should she have a tubal ligation? Often, a woman will be moved from a Catholic hospital to a nonreligious one for the tubal ligation. This is occurring increasingly. My permanent base is Ireland, and it is a recurring question there. As Dr. Macklin points out, this case raises concerns at all levels—the institutional, the departmental (obstetrics/gynecology, for example), as well as the specific patient level.

SISTER BAYLEY: To answer your question about composition, I have noted very little difference between Catholic and non-Catholic hospitals.[3] The committees are multidisciplinary. I would say that most committees are composed of one-third physicians, one-third nurses, and one-third other individuals, e.g., social workers, chaplains, administrators, ethicists, or theologians.

You are, of course, correct that there are certain policies that all Catholic hospitals are expected to follow because of their religious sponsorship (though probably not as many policies as many people think.) One of the most difficult of these is the issue you raise—sterilization. There is considerable difference of opinion with the official teaching of the church, as expressed by the American bishops, theologians, health professionals, and others struggling with these issues on a day-to-day basis. The official teaching is that sterilization may not be done. Many of us feel this formulation is far too harsh and rigid. There are times, for example, when a medical condition of the woman makes tubal ligation the best medical and moral choice. This can be done without compromising the principle underlying the church's teaching: respect for life. We must continue the dialogue with the bishops on this to arrive at a more reasonable policy. Ethics committees can help with this.

FREDERICK ABRAMS, M.D. (Center for Biomedical Ethics, Rose Medical Center, Denver): I want to add a few things to the educational recommendations that Sister Bayley made. It took a year of education before our committee became operational. We insisted that all 25 members of our committee have a course in biomedical ethics or a comparable background. Some of our theologians already had an excellent ethical background. We used Beauchamp and Childress's book and went through its principles.[4] When everybody had finished that, we split the educational and the operational parts. The operational part functions as a forum to aid in decision making. Discussing cases, of course, continues the educational process. The educational part presents programs to raise the consciousness of ethical problems among health care workers as well as the community at large.

We found another excellent resource to be the public broadcasting series, "Hard Choices." Those films are a great starting point for understanding problems in allocation of resources, death and dying, and genetic screening. Each time we have discussed an operational problem, the first thing that we have settled is whose decision this is. Resolving this question has broken up the questions of micro-allocation and macro-allocation, which sometimes get confused. In this regard, ultimately, when the question becomes whose choice it is, the patient's choice, if he or she is competent, should be respected.

Lastly, concerning the involvement of the lay public, in all our meetings we have tried to reach the public by inviting the nonacademic and the nonmedical community. Representatives from colleges and institutions have come to our lectures on biomedical ethics, and they have disseminated information to the public. Also, the nonmedical religious community has been very interested and has participated actively. Since this is a community hospital, we have invited our board of trustees to take our ethics courses, and many of them have. We have invited all the charitable donors to the hospital to attend the big ethics programs—half-day programs in which nationally known speakers discussed current ethical dilemmas. The community is becoming informed. We have talked to local church groups and local schools. We are almost ready to put an item into the hospital's admissions procedures that will inform patients that the ethics committee is available.

S. BRYANT KENDRICK, JR. (North Carolina Baptist Hospital, Winston-Salem): I coordinate a course in biomedical ethics for medical students and consult with physicians when various crises arrive. Consequently, I am very interested in what Dr. Macklin suggested was a fundamental purpose of groups such as ethics committees, that is, assisting in making morally right decisions. I would like to ask Dr. Macklin if she could describe the criteria that must be met in order for a decision to count as a morally right one.

DR. MACKLIN: The answer, of course, requires a whole course in biomedical ethics. I am sure that the questioner realizes the difficulty of developing such criteria not only to be briefly articulated here at a meeting, but also in general. That's something that religious thinkers and Western philosophers have been grappling with for years. I can give a short and curt answer, which is to say that "a morally right decision is one that results in a refusal to violate anybody's rights," but that is just as empty as saying "morally right decision" in the first place. So if you are focusing on the problem of ethical dilemmas that exist in the bioethical, biomedical realm, I certainly agree that ethical dilemmas, by their very nature, have no one clear, right answer. But if there are two or more choices, no one of which is entirely satisfactory from a moral perspective—or alternatively, each of which is flawed in some way— then at least you will not do something blatantly wrong by opting for either horn of the dilemma. We will not get a clear or simple criterion as long as we have different principles and different ethical and religious traditions. The best we can do is to make students and others who are confronting such choices aware not only of what the dilemmas are, and thereby raise their consciousness, but also what principles are available for resolving them.

DR. JACKSON: One of the issues that has struck me from the clinical perspective is the fuzziness of the word *consultative*. It means different things to different people, and I have been a little confused about precisely what we mean by it. Consultative could mean a "prognosis" committee—the technical judgment by a senior health professional whether, for example, the bedside team's judgment that a patient's coma is "irreversible" is correct. If this were its role, I would agree with Alexander Capron that this is not the most useful function of an optional ethics committee.

As a clinician, one views consultation as going beyond one's own perspective to receive, from either an individual or a group, a review of the decision process and the options that may be available. For example, I consult an infectious disease specialist to determine whether I have overlooked any key factors in my choice of antibiotics. One should approach an institutional ethics committee to ensure that the process by which difficult decisions are made honors patient autonomy and/or gives appropriate consideration to the balancing inherent in the use of substituted judgments for incompetent patients. It is that broader definition of consultation that, I think, we agree, is the central function of ethics committees. Are there questions from the audience?

BARBARA S. EDWARDS, R.N. (Georgetown Hospital, Washington, D.C.): I am not familiar with the function and makeup of IECs or IRBs, but I am familiar with committees. By their nature—that is, because of the multiple representation that often occurs on committees—they produce decisions that are either so watered down or so eclectic that they are often unhelpful. My question, for both Mr. Rothenberg and Mr. Capron, is whether this has been a problem with IECs or IRBs?

LESLIE STEVEN ROTHENBERG, J.D. (conference faculty): I think that we can only speak from our anecdotal experience in our particular settings. Little research has been done on the sociological dimensions of these committees' performances. I have not found reticence to be a quality associated with the people on ethics committees with whom I have discussed issues. Indeed, there is a certain self-selection by which people volunteer to be on the committees, and that lends itself to getting people who are outspoken and who have strong interests in this area. The IEC is often viewed as a different kind of committee, and maybe that is only because of the early moments of enthusiasm for the concept. Ten or 15 years from now, we may be dealing with the traditional committee dilemmas. My own experience has not suggested, however, that there is a dilution of concern or an unwillingness to speak out even if other people on the committee might have a different viewpoint, or an unwillingness even to speak out against the consensus.

ALEXANDER M. CAPRON, LL.B. (conference faculty): In the case of IRBs, as here, there is ultimately a choice to be made, and so it is hard to water it down beyond a certain point. It is possible to water down reports and rules and guidelines infinitely, but that is not the case with review of actual cases. Whether it is called consultation or decision review, what basically happens then is that someone says, "We're facing a choice with this patient. This is how we got to where we are; please review that, help us with it." And so there has to be some kind of outcome. That outcome may not be helpful, however, and that is why I am cautious about advocating ethics committees. We do not know how helpful they are.

SISTER AURELIA SHUSTER (St. Mary's Hospital, Milwaukee): I'd like to address my question to Mr. Capron. You mentioned that it was important that the concerns of all of the people involved are represented on the committee, and I stretch that to mean that the needs of the institution would also have to be addressed and represented. Could you comment on what I think would be a very practical problem of a conflict between the patient's concerns or decisions, and the institution's ethical framework, particularly in a religious-affiliated hospital? Euthanasia would probably be a very good example. If the patient were sincere in coming to that decision, and that really were in direct conflict with the ethical principles of the hospital, it does not seem that the committee would have the flexibility to disregard the ethical framework. Would you comment on that, please?

PROFESSOR CAPRON: I do not see that a hospital ethics committee has any greater authority than any other person within the hospital. If the hospital has particular policies that would be contradicted by a decision which either a professional or a patient wishes to see go forward, then that decision cannot go forward in that hospital. There may be some need for a temporary accommodation in order to protect the patient from being abandoned, but the choice faced by the patient then is whether or not to transfer to another hospital if the restriction or the limitation is one that the patient cannot accept.

RONALD MILLER, M.D., (St. Joseph Hospital, Orange, California): Does the term *decision review* mean something retrospective?

PROFESSOR CAPRON: No. I specifically said that I believe that for the most part, this is review of a decision at relevant points in the decision process. When necessary, because events have overtaken the decision, there should be retrospective review of at least a certain category of decisions. The example I have given is the death of a newborn after the withdrawal of treatment. You would not want to conduct a review only when you have a live newborn, and withhold review when you have a dead one. Such a rule would give improper incentives. These are controversial matters that people are sensitive about having reviewed. The incentive would be to not treat quickly, so as not to have to face review. This would probably be a very bad incentive to give.

DR. MILLER: I have another semantic problem. If decision review can be prospective, then how does that differ from consultation? Are you advising against decision making by the IEC?

PROFESSOR CAPRON: Yes. Committees should be consulted by individuals who present the decision that is being made about the problem, not the action taken on that decision. This is why the committee's function seems problematic. There can be conflict between patient and doctor and conflict within the family. Other situations may deal with an incompetent patient, and those concerned are not sure about the judgment they made about the best interests involved. Whatever the question that is presented to the committee, it boils down to whether it is morally or legally acceptable within the understanding of the members of this committee. That is the decision that the committee is ready to reach. The question then is, have the interests been adequately represented? Are the relevant issues on the table? The committee may decide that the individuals involved have neglected a set of issues. For example, a parent may not seem to be informed about the treatment that is available for handicapped children. Therefore, the committee would decide that the child's best interests have not yet been considered fully, and that the decision of the individuals involved in the care of that child should not be acted upon.

DR. JACKSON: Would you add the caveat that if the individual does not take your advice and you feel that there is a moral or legal wrong, you have to intercede? Does the committee have the power of decision making, or is it only advisory?

PROFESSOR CAPRON: The function as I describe it here is an advisory function with the potential for triggering a court review. It does not seem to me that a hospital could choose to say that this committee is a decision-making committee against which no one can go. It seems to me that this distorts what is most likely the IEC's best function. Every member of that committee acts as a citizen; the hospital does not give them any further authority. Every member has a responsibility to bring to the attention of the authorities any act about to be taken that is clearly detrimental and harmful to a helpless patient. You should not keep quiet about a felony you know is about to happen. We were talking here, instead, about a recognized function of the committee, which is triggering that judicial review. One begins with the parents as the appropriate decision makers. But when something about the process of decision making indicates that they are incapable or unwilling to take the best interests of the child into account in making the decision, another guardian should be appointed. The committee does not have the authority to appoint guardians, only the juvenile court or the probate court or some other court of that jurisdiction does, and it is to the courts that the case should be referred at that point.

ROBERT FRASER (National Institutes of Health, Rockville, Maryland): It seems to me that we are working with two separate models here. One of them was suggested by Professor Capron. It involves the point in the process at which we enter the decision review. It seems to me that you are suggesting that there is an adversarial relationship between the patient and the care providers, because of the conflict. This idea suggests, then, a legal review type of model. We can pick up the process at a different place or view it in a different way. Let me suggest this way of looking at it. The patient and the physician and the care institution begin their relationship in a partnership, a partnership of trust. Because of the patient's illness, because of his or her condition, and because of the expertise and authority of the institution, a state of inequality can occur. The IEC, then, is a body which can help to nurture and renew the equality which was there in the initial stage of the partnership. To make one final illustration, a married couple enter into marriage as partners, and try to maintain a state of equality. When they have conflict, they may go to a counselor for advice and support in order to restore the equality that was there at the beginning. If the marriage breaks down, they go to lawyers who relate to them and act as representatives in an adversarial relationship. The positions taken earlier, with regard to the guidelines and some of the other functions of the committee, suggest to me that those speakers were talking about the committee entering the scene when attempts are being made to restore and nurture the equality between patient and physician.

PROFESSOR CAPRON: I see nothing in the function of guidelines that does that at all. At this conference, I have taken it for granted that everyone is familiar with the materials prepared by the President's Commission, which discussed a nonadversarial relationship.[5] Let me reiterate: We are not talking about a necessarily adversarial relationship. We are talking about a situation in which an apparent dilemma or choice is troublesome to people, including physicians and nurses, because they are not sure that the patient is capable of making the decision, or they are not sure that those who are making it on behalf of the patient are capable. You could have a situation, as the Commission notes, in which the physician and the parents of the newborn agree completely. Yet, it was the Commission's advice that if the decision is to forego treatment, the case should get another look, a review if you will, from an institutional ethics committee.[6] That does not put people in an adversarial relationship. It does say that it helps to have someone else look over the decision and review it, to see whether all the factors and all the interests have come into play. People with regular familiarity with these kinds of issues will be aware of what has worked before, what has been important before, and the implications for the institution of this decision on future decisions. But I do not see that function as involving or creating an adversarial relationship. This is not a divorce proceeding.

MR. ROTHENBERG: The speaker's comments do deserve some consideration in the context of the realpolitik and the reality of a hospital setting in particular. I have found myself frustrated by the attempts of others to do right by pounding people over the head with a club that is labelled "right," with the hope that each pounding will achieve some success as, figuratively speaking, the lump grows. I must admit, although it is embarrassing to do so in a group of people who are interested in ethical things, that I have read the writings of Machiavelli and that I often practice what I call guerrilla ethics. I try to sneak ethical ideas into the thinking of people who might not wish to say, because of their own biases or, often, fears and insecurities, that they are focusing on ethical dilemmas. What concerns me is that if we gradually move, either by outside or inside pressure, to what John Robertson labelled the mandatory/mandatory review process for certain types of cases,[7] we will further alienate the physicians. I focus on the physicians, in particular, because they are, after all, generally the only people who can write orders. I am afraid that the end result of the process is going to be even worse for the patient. I am also concerned that the patient may then have to be told on admission that his or her care providers' decisions may be overriden directly or indirectly by a committee if certain situations evolve in that patient's care.

Now, I do want to reinforce what Alex just said. The President's Commission has made a strong point of urging people not to adopt an adversarial posture or to rush into court all the time with these problems. Physicians are already upset about the infringements on their practice resulting from changing power relationships in hospitals, as administrations and boards of trustees take over what was formerly thought to be medical turf in running the hospital. I am fearful that if we impose yet another structure, even an inside structure, to sit in judgment on even a select group of situations, what may result in the long term will not be ethically beneficial to patients.

PROFESSOR CAPRON: I want to discuss this further because I think it is at the heart of the matter. The pressure is not in this room. It is not the people here who are insisting that ethics committees change the relationship between the hospitals and the physician. That change is occurring independently. What we are addressing here, however, is that set of issues, out of all the issues in the hospital, which is probably the most important to have handled in a good fashion. I think Les illustrates my point about the educational function. Those who serve this function work as a presence in the wards, on the rounds, in the trenches, educating and sensitizing physicians and nurses about these ethical issues. That probably means that the decisions that percolate up from that context should trouble us very much less often that they would without that process, if the process is at all worthwhile. But it does not have to be a committee that does that. It would be good if the committee, by its posture, could continue to communicate its ideas to people in a way which is not threatening to them, and is likely to be accepted by them. I think that is terrific. But you do not have to have a committee to serve that function.

AUDIENCE PARTICIPANT: One of the problems, though, is that you deal with such a diverse group of people—patient, family, medical and nursing staff, and others—that if you expect unanimity or consensus, 99.9 percent of the time you are going to be disappointed. This is what happened when I set up a system in our unit seven years ago; it was run like a New England town meeting. We tried to get the patient, the family, and everybody to agree on what was to be done. When external consultative review is needed, and when dichotomous choices need to be made, somebody will be upset with the decision process, no matter what the decision, no matter what process the committee goes through. We did a study that looked at the diversity of attitudes involved, and we're now broadening it to the patient's family as well as the professional staff in the intensive care unit. When one looks at the diversity of ethical traditions that people have in this polyglot society, to expect unanimity is really unrealistic. The only thing that we can hope for is to make sure that the process is right and that some majority consensus is reached with adequate protection for the minority opinions.

HAMILTON SOUTHWORTH, M.D. (board member of Concern for Dying, Inc. and member of Critical Care Committee, Columbia-Presbyterian Medical Center, New York): The small committee in our hospital operates, at the moment, only on the medical service, and, perhaps through its smallness and limitation, it has some advantages. We find we are more useful when we are approached before the decisions really are made than when we are approached for a formal consultation later. On the ward service, an attending physician or a resident will come to one of us and say that he or she has a problem. Then one or two of us go to the ward and coach the physician on how to handle it. We also see the patient. This has proven to be very successful. I just want to mention this as a technique that seems to save time and trouble.

FRANK J. BRESCIA, M.D. (Calvary Hospital, Bronx, New York): I would like an opinion on the question of whether or not there is a danger of elitism in terms of shifting the paternalism from the physician to a committee. It seems to me that the committee needs to have a great deal of punch, both in terms of policymaking for the hospital and decision making, and therefore you need the most influential people at the institution on this committee. It also seems to me that the most influential people at a hospital may not be the most rational. Is there a need for a mechanism to monitor the IEC, and if so, how do you do that? Secondly, what should the threshold be in terms of what is brought to the committee? Medicine is filled with odd kinds of things on a day-to-day basis, and who decides what ought to be brought to the committee? If, indeed, an issue is brought by a health care professional such as a nurse, what immunity does he or she need to be protected in her position—something which may be very difficult in institutions?

MR. ROTHENBERG: I think these are two very separate issues. John Paris is standing in the back of the room and one takes great risks in paraphrasing John at any time, but I recall his mentioning a suggestion with regard to the composition of ethics committees which has always appealed to me, and which will, I assume, never be done. The idea was, in order to get the view of the non-health care professional and the nonprofessional, and something closer to the view of the person on the street, each hospital ought to select one person from the custodial staff and one person from the kitchen crew to serve on the committee. Over time, of course, you would have to keep switching, since they too would become conditioned. I think his point was well made. We all come with certain preconceived notions and biases, and of course there is a built-in elitism just as there is when we talk about notions like rights and interests. We all know that ordinary people in the supermarket do not usually use that kind of lingo.

The second question is very important. That is, how can we make sure that no one suffers from bringing a case to the attention of the IEC? We are particularly concerned with the patient or the patient's family, but we are also concerned with the nurse, other health care professionals, and even the physician, in terms of peer pressure. One has to begin with the governing authority in the hospital. There needs to be some basic support for the notion of an entity working within the institution, which is designed to benefit all of the parties. There has to be some commitment in principle to the notion that no one will suffer, even if someone brings something to the committee which later proves to be embarrassing, or uncomfortable, or any one of a number of adjectives that you could think of. This is more easily said than done, particularly in the tough cases. But I want to tell you that a lot of the cases that have gone to court in my experience have gone to court precisely because someone was unhappy with the lack of receptivity within the institutional setting to dissonant points of view. The inability to be heard and to have serious consideration given to another point of view forces someone to leave the institution and seek help from some other source. By beginning within the institution to sensitize people to the issues, and hopefully to reach that glorious day in the future when we do not need an ethics committee because people have already become educated and know how to deal with these issues, we have to allow for that ferment that requires people coming forward without sanction.

## NOTES

1. For a discussion of patient attitudes towards one institutional ethics committee, see Youngner, S. J., *et al.*, ch. 6 of this text.
2. For a discussion of the contrasting functions and attributes of IRBs and IECs, see Glantz, L. H., ch. 11 of this text.
3. For a discussion of ethics committees in Catholic health institutions, see *Ethics Committees and Ethicists in Catholic Hospitals*, HOSPITAL PROGRESS 64(9):47 (September 1983).

4. T. BEAUCHAMP, J. CHILDRESS, PRINCIPLES OF BIOMEDICAL ETHICS (Oxford Univ. Press, New York) (2d ed. 1983).

5. PRESIDENT'S COMMISSION FOR THE STUDY OF ETHICAL PROBLEMS IN MEDICINE AND BIOMEDICAL AND BEHAVIORAL RESEARCH, DECIDING TO FOREGO LIFE-SUSTAINING TREATMENT: ETHICAL, MEDICAL AND LEGAL ISSUES IN TREATMENT DECISIONS (U.S. Gov't Printing Office, Washington, D.C.) (March 1983), at 160–70.

6. *Id.* at 227.

7. *See* Robertson, J., ch. 7 of this text.

# Part IV

## Practical Problems Facing Institutional Ethics Committees

# 16

# The Decision to Withdraw Life-sustaining Treatment and the Potential Role of an IEC: The Case of *People v. Barber and Nejdl*

John J. Paris

The case of the two California physicians, Drs. Neil L. Barber and Robert J. Nejdl, who have been charged with murder for withdrawing intravenous (IV) nourishment from an irreversibly brain-damaged patient, is a fascinating and frightening one. It has seriously disrupted the practice of good medicine by creating a reign of terror among physicians in California and throughout the country.

The case has not been settled, and its effects are still being felt. For example, physicians are treating patients whom they believe ought not to be treated, lest charges be brought against them as were brought against Drs. Barber and Nejdl. The case can, however, illustrate the important educational and consultative role an ethics committee could have served.

## BACKGROUND OF THE CASE

The case initially involved a very simple procedure, an ileostomy repair, which was performed without difficulty by Dr. Nejdl, the chief of surgery at Kaiser-Permanente's Harbor City Hospital. After some 48 minutes in the hospital's recovery room, the patient, Clarence Leroy Herbert, was observed to be cyanotic and not breathing. During resuscitation efforts, he suffered a cardiac arrest. By the time he was resuscitated, massive brain damage had occurred and the assessment by the neurologist was that the damage was probably irreversible. When the family was told the prognosis by the attending physician, Dr. Barber, they asked that all heroic measures be stopped. Barber asked the family to put in writing their desires for Herbert's care. The wife and eight children signed a statement saying, in their own words, "We would like all machines off that are sustaining life."[1]

On the third day post-arrest, Dr. Barber removed the respirator and, somewhat to his and the family's surprise, the patient began to breathe on his own. Clarence Herbert now had the potential to become another Karen Ann Quinlan—a nonresponsive, irreversibly brain-damaged patient being maintained with IV feedings and antibiotics. Two days later, on the fifth day post-arrest, the doctors acceded to the family's request that the IVs be removed.

Sandra Bardenilla, the supervising nurse in the ICU at Harbor City, objected to the fact that there was no misting machine provided for Mr. Herbert after the removal of the respirator. Dr. Nejdl, who had performed the operation on Mr. Herbert, now anticipated that Herbert would soon die and specifically ordered that there be no misting. Nurse Bardenilla, believing that such an omission violated good nursing care and standard clinical procedures, had the head nurse ask a house officer to write an order to mist Mr. Herbert. A few minutes later Dr. Nejdl met the house officer and asked him, "Have you pronounced Mr. Herbert yet?" Far from having pronounced him dead, the resident told Nejdl that he had just ordered a misting machine for him. Nejdl phoned Nurse Bardenilla and demanded to know why she had gone behind his back to change his orders. A furious fight ensued on the telephone. Shortly afterwards, Bardenilla began gathering data, Xeroxed all the records, and began complaining to various members of the hospital staff, including the director of nurses and the chief of staff. During this time, Clarence Herbert died—five days after the removal of the IVs.

Three weeks later, Bardenilla went to the Los Angeles County Department of Health Services, and then to the district attorney, claiming that the doctors had starved Herbert to death, or more specifically, had dehydrated him. After an investigation lasting several months, the district attorney agreed, and charged the doctors with murder in the first degree—"the deliberate, intentional taking of the life of another."

A preliminary hearing was held before a Los Angeles municipal court judge to determine if there was probable cause for an indictment on the charge. That hearing extended over 13 days, during which time 31 witnesses testified, including neurosurgeons, pathologists, and anesthesiologists. I was called by the defense as an expert in medical ethics.

After extensive testimony, which covered over 1,300 pages of transcript, Judge Crahan determined that the actions of Drs. Barber and Nejdl were the appropriate response to the patient's condition. In the course of his opinion the judge quoted me several times, sometimes inaccurately. For example, he said, "Father Paris testified that these are strictly medical decisions." If you understand that phrase in the context of the President's Commission's report entitled *Deciding to Forego Treatment*,[2] any decision involving the physician's diagnosis and recommendation, the patient's psychosocial values, and community standards is a medical one, and he is correct. It is not correct, however, to say, as Judge Crahan did, "It is left to the physician in his or her best judgment to determine whether heroic or nonheroic care should be given to patients in comatose or brain-dead situations."[3]

At the end of the lengthy preliminary hearing, Judge Crahan dismissed the charges. In doing so, he ruled that there had been no breach of the physicians' duty of care, since "the duty to treat ceases when there is no further 'potential for recovery.' " Given Clarence Herbert's medical status, Judge Crahan decreed that the care due him by the physicians was "to comfort, to console, to treat with objectivity." To do otherwise, he stated, "is to concede one's surrender to the will of a machine." Crahan concluded his comments with the observation that "in severely terminal cases, the community understanding is clear; that is, termination of all life-support systems is indicated at some point during the dying process." The district attorney appealed and on May 5, 1983, a superior court judge ruled that under California statutes, the intentional shortening of the life of another is homicide.[4] The only exceptions are statutory: life-support systems may be removed upon a finding of brain death or the execution of a valid living will. Since Mr. Herbert did not meet either criterion, the actions of the physicians were potentially criminal and they must stand trial on the charge of murder.

The legal fees are already well in excess of $650,000; the personal and professional lives of the physicians have been disrupted by the trauma of a criminal indictment; and the case has seriously hampered the practice of good medicine in the area. There are, for example, instances of physicians refusing to stop the respirator on brain-dead patients or refusing to offer families the option of terminating aggressive therapies on clearly dying patients. The most adverse consequence of the superior court's action is to reinforce the idea already rampant in the minds of many, that not doing everything to extend life as long as is physically possible is equivalent to killing the patient. Perhaps the most dramatic example of that mind-set is found in a *Newsweek* "My Turn" column, where a nurse tells of a young, pain-racked, terminally ill cancer patient who, despite his pleas to let him die, was resuscitated 52 times until, in desperation, the nurse took it upon herself to refuse to call a Code Blue when the patient once again stopped breathing.[5]

## THE ROLE OF AN ETHICS COMMITTEE

The question facing us is whether some of these issues would have been alleviated if there had been an in-house ethics committee functioning at Harbor City Hospital. Consider the following:

One of the precursors in the *Barber/Nejdl* case was dissatisfaction on the part of some of the health care givers—especially Nurse Bardenilla—with the treatment and practices that were occurring. Bardenilla went to the director of nurses and to the chief of staff; both told her things were under control and, as she described it, "to be quiet." In fact, she was told to apologize to the surgeon for her rude behavior during the phone conversation over the misting device. She got very angry, and angry people can do a lot of damage. Moreover, Nurse Bardenilla subsequently stated that her major problem was that there were no guidelines for the nurses and consequently no legal protection for them when a patient was removed from life-supporting machinery. There were also no guidelines for removal of patients from ICU. Without such guidance, she maintains, nurses are placed in an untenable legal bind.[6]

Some, the judge in the preliminary hearing among them, questioned whether the actions of the physicians were precipitous. Did they have an adequate factual basis on which to determine that Mr. Herbert's condition was irreversible? While pathology reports subsequently indicated that their assessment was correct, questions over how much time ought to have been allowed for a proper assessment seem appropriate.

The patient's wife has filed a $25 million malpractice suit against the physicians and the hospital. Her attorney, Melvin Belli, insists that Mrs. Herbert was told that her husband was brain-dead. He maintains that if she had known that that was not the case, she would never have consented to the removal of the life-support systems. Hence, we have a question as to how adequately the family was informed of the patient's condition.

The legal counsel for Kaiser Hospital had prepared a statement informing staff physicians that the removal of life-supporting systems could involve legal issues and that therefore they should consult with the counsel before effecting such a procedure. Drs. Barber and Nejdl did not do so. How does one proceed when there is legal ambiguity about the procedure?

The district attorney's theory is that the physicians or the hospital were guilty of malpractice in the recovery room. To cover up their actions, the prosecutors claimed, the doctors lied to the wife, telling her that her husband was brain-dead. On the basis of that misinformation, they then obtained her permission to remove the life-support systems. Would there have been the basis for charges of a cover-up had the issue been openly discussed at an institutional forum?

There is ambiguity in the medical records as to the exact neurological condition of the patient at the time the initial decision was made to disconnect the respirator. The findings of the judge at the preliminary hearing indicate that the patient's prognosis at that time was "not absolutely clear." An institutional ethics committee conference involving the neurologist would have produced clear distinctions between brain death, severe hypoxic-ischemic encephalopathy, and a persistent vegetative condition. It would also have clarified the shift in prognosis from "poor" to "nil" and most likely would have demanded a more definitive prognosis than "poor" before authorizing termination of treatment.

I recently received a letter from Dr. Bruce Zawacki (noted for his fine article in the *New England Journal of Medicine*, "Autonomy for Burn Victims") reflecting on the Kaiser case. He wrote:

> One of the great advantages of an ethics consultation service in a hospital is to prevent such precipitous decision making and to allow all of those concerned, including unhappy nurses, to be heard fully in the open. Open discussion between physicians, nurses, patients, and family is trust-building, whereas closed, hushed-up, behind-the-door decision making breeds the kind of distrust which leads to Infant Doe Hotlines. Such a hotline would be a grave disservice as it would institutionalize distrust and diminish dialogue between care givers and care receivers.

The *Barber and Nejdl* case, as Zawacki pointed out, brings to the fore the conflict of two possible approaches to the problem of determining when to discontinue life-sustaining treatment. It is arguable that either a hotline or an ethics committee would have been an appropriate forum for Nurse Bardenilla to bring her complaint. The issue is simply which of these is more desirable. Regardless of which is chosen, the *Barber and Nejdl* case makes it clear that *some* measures must be taken shortly.

## NOTES

1. Magistrate's Findings, People v. Barber, No. A 025586 (Los Angeles Municipal Court, Los Angeles County, Calif., March 9, 1983) at 3 [hereinafter referred to as Magistrate's Findings].
2. PRESIDENT'S COMMISSION FOR THE STUDY OF ETHICAL PROBLEMS IN MEDICINE AND BIOMEDICAL AND BEHAVIORAL RESEARCH, DECIDING TO FOREGO LIFE-SUSTAINING TREATMENT: ETHICAL, MEDICAL AND LEGAL ISSUES IN TREATMENT DECISIONS (U.S. Gov't Printing Office, Washington, D.C.) (March 1983).
3. Magistrate's Findings, *supra* note 1, at 7.

4. People v. Barber, No. A 025586 (Superior Court of California, County of Los Angeles, May 5, 1983).
5. Huttmann, B., *A Crime of Compassion*, NEWSWEEK (August 8, 1983) at 15.
6. Kirsch, J., *A Death at Kaiser Hospital*, CALIFORNIA MAGAZINE (November 1982) at 79.

# 17

## Limitations on the Family's Right to Decide for the Incompetent Patient

Allen E. Buchanan

This essay explores the role that an institutional ethics committee can play in decision making for incompetent patients.[1] An individual may be incompetent to decide whether to accept or reject medical treatment because he or she is comatose, mentally retarded, psychotic, senile, or simply because he or she is a young child.

### THREE MODELS OF DECISION MAKING FOR INCOMPETENT PATIENTS

The question of who should decide for the incompetent patient has been hotly disputed in the literature and in the courts. Elsewhere I have criticized two rival models of decision making for the incompetent patient: medical paternalism and legal imperialism.[2] Medical paternalism is the view that it is essential to the physician's role to be the primary decision maker and to make treatment decisions for the good of the incompetent patient. Legal imperialism identifies judges (or, more recently, makers of administrative law, as in the federal "Infant Doe" regulations) as the primary decision makers for incompetent patients, at least in cases in which the patient's basic rights and interests are at stake. The main objections to medical paternalism are that it overestimates the physician's knowledge of the patient's interests and values, while underestimating the ability of the patient's family to make decisions, and that it confuses medical judgments, which physicians' special training uniquely qualifies them to make, with moral decisions, for which physicians possess no special credentials. For example, the judgment that Karen Quinlan is in a persistent vegetative state is a medical judgment, but the judgment that *because* she is in a persistent vegetative state it is permissible to remove her from life support is a moral judgment. Legal imperialism is equally flawed. By judicializing treatment decisions for the incompetent patient, this model of decision making routinely requires cumbersome and unnecessarily adversarial procedures, while failing to recognize the special role of the family as decision maker.

Dissatisfaction with both medical paternalism and legal imperialism has led some to espouse what might be called the family autonomy model.[3] This model is based on the presumption that the incompetent patient's "family" is the appropriate decision maker and should be allowed to accept or refuse medical treatment on the patient's behalf. There are two main grounds for this presumption. First, the family is *in general* both more concerned about the patient's interests and more knowledgeable about his or her preferences and values. Second, because the family as a personally fulfilling, intimate relationship requires privacy, society ought to be reluctant to intrude into the family's decisions concerning its own members. By the patient's "family," I mean not necessarily his or her closest biological relations or spouse but rather those with whom he or she is most closely associated. This point is especially important at this stage in our society's history, when alternatives to marriage and the nuclear family are becoming more common.

The presumption that the family should decide is, however, rebuttable, and this is what the family autonomy model fails to recognize adequately. In emergency situations it will sometimes be necessary for the health care professional to make decisions without even consulting the family. And even in nonemergency situations, adequate protection of the patient requires limitations on the authority of the family to decide. For these reasons, the extreme family autonomy view must be rejected. The problem, then, is to develop a model for decision making which avoids the excesses of the extreme family autonomy view without lapsing into either medical paternalism or legal imperialism. My suggestion is that an institutional ethics committee should play an important role in arrangements designed to recognize the family's presumptive, though not unlimited, authority to decide for the incompetent patient. In what follows I sketch a proposal for how an institutional ethics committee might serve as a check on the family as decision maker and yet do so in the least intrusive way compatible with adequate protection of the incompetent patient.

## THE NEED FOR INTERVENTION PRINCIPLES

Crucial to my proposal is the distinction between guidance principles and intervention principles. Guidance principles are those which the surrogate decision maker—in this case, the family—is to follow in deciding for the incompetent patient. The two most widely accepted guidance principles for surrogate decision making are (1) the best interest principle and (2) the substituted judgment principle. The former states that the surrogate is to choose what is in the patient's best interest, after weighing the benefits and "costs" of each of the options to the patient. The latter requires the surrogate to choose what the patient would choose, if competent.[4] Increasingly, a third guidance principle is being recognized in the law and in medical ethics. This is the principle that the patient's advance directive, if there is one, should guide the treatment decision. Advance directives are of two main types: living wills, which specify certain forms of treatment the patient does, or does not, wish to have; and durable power-of-attorney documents, by which the individual designates a surrogate to make decisions in the event that individual becomes incompetent. Respect for individual autonomy, which requires that the right of self-determination of a competent patient should take precedence over the duties of others to benefit him or her, also lends support to the conclusion that we should follow the patient's advance directive. If there is no applicable advance directive, then respect for the individual's former autonomy speaks in favor of using the substituted judgment principle, because this principle attempts to base the decision on the distinctive values and preferences of the individual when he or she was competent. If there is no applicable advance directive and if it is not possible to determine what the patient, if competent, would choose, then the best interest principle should guide the surrogate's decision.

Intervention principles, on the other hand, state the conditions under which it is appropriate to challenge the surrogate's decision. Here I will be concerned primarily with stating principles that specify the conditions under which a health care professional or other person involved in the care of an incompetent patient should challenge the family by invoking review by an institutional ethics committee. In other words, I shall endeavor to shed light on the thorny problem of *when* the committee's review should be invoked. Clearly, it should not be invoked for most decisions, nor even for every life-or-death decision.

I wish to emphasize that referral to the committee does not imply that the committee itself is to assume the role of surrogate and attempt to make treatment decisions. Instead, the role of the committee is to function as an informal, consultative body to aid the surrogate decision maker in choosing so as to serve the interests and respect the rights of the incompetent patient. In exceptional cases the committee may find it necessary to seek court intervention. If the committee concludes that recourse to the courts is the only way to protect the patient, it should seek appointment of a guardian, perhaps with judicial review of the guardian's decision, rather than attempting to foist the responsibility of actually making the treatment decision onto the judge. The role of the institutional ethics committee is not to perpetuate the illusion that judges are generally best equipped to make treatment decisions.

It is important to emphasize that what is appropriate as a guidance principle may be inappropriate as an intervention principle. For example, in most cases the guidance principle that parents should follow in making decisions for their child is the best interest principle. However, it would be unreasonably intrusive to authorize child welfare workers to intervene in the family, perhaps to remove the child from his or her natural parents, simply because the parents failed to *maximize* the child's good. In what follows I will attempt to articulate intervention principles that impose suitable limitations on the family's use of the best interest and substituted judgment guidance principles.

## THREE TYPES OF INTERVENTION PRINCIPLES

Plausible intervention principles fall into three types. First, there are those that specify conditions that disqualify the family from the role of surrogate decision maker altogether. The family should be disqualified if there is abuse or neglect, if there is a conflict of interest likely to bias their decisions against the patient's rights and interests, or if the family itself is incompetent to decide. If a member of the health care team or anyone else involved in the care of the patient believes any of these disqualifying conditions is satisfied, he or she should notify the institutional ethics committee. If the institutional ethics committee concurs with the judgment that the family is disqualified, then the committee may seek court intervention to see that a suitable guardian is appointed.

The second type of intervention principle specifies certain classes of cases as deserving special scrutiny, either by virtue of the especially vulnerable position of the incompetent patient or because of the momentousness of the consequences of the decision. The former subcategory would include (1) incompetents who are candidates for removal of tissue or organs for transplantation, and (2) incompetent patients who are long-term residents or inmates of institutions such as mental hospitals, state institutions for the retarded, or prisons. The latter subcategory would include two types of "momentous decisions": first, decisions that are likely to result in a preventable and considerable shortening of the patient's life (for example, when parents refuse to sign a surgical permit for correction of the blocked intestine of an otherwise healthy Down syndrome baby); and second, decisions that are likely to result in permanent loss or impairment of important physical or psychological functions (for example, sterilization or psychosurgery). If a case falls into any of these special scrutiny categories, referral to an institutional ethics committee should be mandatory.

So far we have discussed two types of intervention principles: those that state the conditions that disqualify the family from being the decision maker and those that single out certain types of cases as deserving unusual safeguards. In addition to these, a third type of intervention principle may be distinguished. This type of principle focuses on the decision the surrogate makes and specifies the very general conditions which the surrogate's decision must satisfy.

There is at least one condition which the family's decision should always satisfy. Regardless of whether the decision is made by following the patient's advance directive or according to the substituted judgment or best interest principles, the medical option the family or guardian chooses must be within the range of medically sound alternatives, as determined by appropriate medical community standards. To deny this is to make the mistake of viewing the physician as a passive vendor of services and to overlook the physician's right to refuse requests for bad medical care. But so long as the family's choice of a particular treatment falls within the range of medically sound options, physicians should not insist that the particular option they favor be employed; nor should they seek intervention by the institutional ethics committee to challenge the family's decision. If competent medical opinion is divided as to which of two or more options for achieving a therapeutic goal is best, due recognition of the family's role as decision maker requires noninterference. If physicians' personal standards forbid them to employ what they take to be second-best means or if they have serious moral objections to the procedure, they should see that the patient is transferred to the care of another physician.

The additional conditions which the family's decision must satisfy may differ depending on which guidance principle is being employed. If the appropriate guidance principle is the best interest principle it is tempting to assume that any departure from the single most beneficial course is sufficient for intervention. This, however, would be a mistake, for reasons I alluded to earlier. Neither the law nor commonsense morality dictates that society should intervene whenever the family's treatment of its dependent member merely fails to *maximize* his or her interests. For example, intervention by the state to transfer a child to the custody of a richer family simply because this would maximize his or her interests in higher education would be wholly inappropriate.

The fact that a decision concerns medical treatment does not itself prove an exception to this general policy of allowing some latitude in the family's determination of what is best for its incompetent member.

It is one thing to acknowledge that in employing the best interest principle the family should sometimes be allowed to depart from what would, strictly speaking, maximize the incompetent's interest. It is another to say that what counts as the best interest of the incompetent should be left wholly to the judgment of the family. In general, the degree of latitude that should be accorded to the family's determination of the incompetent's best interest should be governed by two distinct types of factors: first, the severity of the harm (or the magnitude of the foregone benefit) that might result from the family's decision and the likelihood that the harm will actually occur (or that the benefit will actually be lost); and second, the strength of the evidence that most reasonable and informed persons would choose differently from the family in applying the best interest principle.

The greater the harm (or loss of benefit to the patient) and the more likely its occurrence, the stronger the case for intervention. But even if the likelihood that the family's choice will result in harm to the patient is small, intervention may be appropriate if the severity of the harm is very great and if there is strong evidence that most informed and reasonable persons, in applying the best interest principle, would choose differently.

If there is a consensus, among reasonable persons who are informed about the relevant facts of the case, that the family's choice is *not* in the best interest of the incompetent, then intervention may be appropriate. Even where such a consensus exists, however, intervention would not be appropriate if the harm (or loss of benefit) to the patient that would result if the family's choice were respected is rather slight and very unlikely to occur.

If the surrogate decision maker simply executes a properly prepared and documented, unambiguous advance directive set out by the patient when he or she was competent, there would seem to be no ground for intervention. For if there is no doubt about the nature of the instructions, their application to the decision at hand, or the patient's competence when he or she issued them, then it is difficult to see why in general the advance directive should not have the same moral and legal force as a competent patient's informed consent to, or refusal of, treatment. Both the law and the prevailing view in medical ethics now recognize that the competent patient has the right to decide whether to accept or reject medical treatment, even lifesaving medical treatment (except where important health interests of others are threatened, as in the case of refusal to accept treatment for a communicable disease). Similarly, it could be argued that the qualified surrogate's accurate execution of the explicit and unambiguous, well-documented instructions of a formerly competent patient should not be overridden even if it will result in an avoidable shortening of the patient's life.

In the case of substituted judgment, however, additional safeguards are needed and a different intervention principle will be appropriate. This is because substituted judgment, a judgment about what the patient would want if competent, is *speculative*; it is a hypothetical statement constructed from evidence about the patient's past preferences and values. As such, it does not carry the same moral weight as the actual choice of a patient when he or she is competent, nor even the same moral force as a clear and well-documented advance directive. There are at least two conditions under which it is appropriate to intervene in the family's exercise of substituted judgment. First, if there is a consensus among reasonable and informed persons that the family's construction of what the patient, if competent, would choose is an unreasonable inference from the evidence about his former general preferences and values, then the family's decision should be challenged and the case should be referred to the institutional ethics committee. In applying this intervention principle, it is important to emphasize that there may be a *range* of reasonable interpretations of the patient's prior instructions, rather than *one* uniquely reasonable interpretation. If there is no consensus among reasonable and informed persons as to what the range of reasonable constructions is, then substituted judgment should not be attempted and the best interest principle should be employed.

Second, even if the family's attempt to decide according to substituted judgment falls within the range of reasonable inferences from the evidence about the patient's former values and preferences, it may still be challenged if the decision is likely to result in severe harm to the patient. This restriction, like the first, reflects the fact that substituted judgment does not carry the same moral force as the informed decision of a competent patient, nor of an advance directive.

Nonetheless, it does not follow that a family's attempt to use substituted judgment should be challenged whenever it yields a decision that is not strictly in the patient's best interest. Instead, the same latitude should be tolerated here as in the application of the best interest principle, so long as the decision made according to substituted judgment falls within the range of reasonable inferences from the evidence of the patient's former general preferences and values. The reasons for allowing this latitude in the family's application of the two guidance principles are the same reasons that ground the presumption that the family is the appropriate decision maker: the fact that the family is generally more knowledgeable about the patient's preference and values and more interested in his or her good, and the need to protect the family from unnecessary intrusions.

In this discussion, I have deliberately limited myself to intervention principles designed to protect the rights and interests of the *patient*. I have not considered ways in which the family's application of the best interest or substituted judgment principles or their attempts to follow an advance directive might legitimately be limited by the rights and interests of those other than the patient. It seems clear that the problem of rationing expensive health care resources will become exacerbated as the incidence of chronic illness increases. And since many who suffer chronic illnesses become incompetent, an acceptable institutional framework for decision making for incompetent patients will eventually have to take into account the fact that treatment decisions affect others besides the patient. Whether at some time in the future institutional ethics committees could play a useful role in a system for fairly rationing scarce health care resources is certainly an open question. However, at this early stage of their evolution, I believe it would be a serious mistake to endanger their primary role—that of protecting the vulnerable, incompetent patient—by attempting to impose any sort of rationing criteria on the family's decision.

Rationing decisions are in fact made every day by hospital administrators—though often without explicit recognition of the ethical issues they raise. The institutional ethics committee might serve a very useful function by advising administrators on the ethical implications of institutional policies.

I have offered a set of principles specifying the conditions under which the family's role as decision maker for the incompetent patient ought to be brought to the attention of an institutional ethics committee. I have said less about what action the committee ought to take. This omission was deliberate. I believe that it would be premature to attempt to specify precisely the conditions under which institutional ethics committees should seek recourse to the courts or use other institutional sanctions to attempt to override the surrogate's decision, if persuasion fails. Nonetheless, I think it is reasonable to expect that even if such formal action is quite rare, the mere fact that a case comes under the scrutiny of an institutional ethics committee itself may improve the decision-making process, if only by requiring the decision makers to articulate their ethical and factual assumptions and to explain the basis for their decisions to others.[5]

## NOTES

1. For a useful discussion of the various roles an institutional ethics committee may play, as well as a summary of survey data on the functioning of such bodies, see PRESIDENT'S COMMISSION FOR THE STUDY OF ETHICAL PROBLEMS IN MEDICINE AND BIOMEDICAL AND BEHAVIORAL RESEARCH, DECIDING TO FOREGO LIFE-SUSTAINING TREATMENT: ETHICAL, MEDICAL AND LEGAL ISSUES IN TREATMENT DECISIONS (U.S. Gov't Printing Office, Washington, D.C.) (March 1983) at 160–70.

2. Buchanan, A., *Medical Paternalism or Legal Imperialism: Not the Only Alternatives for Handling* Saikewicz-*Type Cases,* AMERICAN JOURNAL OF LAW & MEDICINE 5(2):97–117 (1979).

3. The family autonomy view is advocated in the following articles: Duff, R. A., Campbell, A. G., *Moral and Ethical Dilemmas in the Special Care Nursery,* NEW ENGLAND JOURNAL OF MEDICINE 289:855 (1973); Duff, R. A., *On Deciding about the Care of Severely Handicapped and Dying Persons: With Particular Reference to Infants,* PEDIATRICS 57:487 (1976). While the view is explicitly applied only to the case of infants, the rationale for it—in particular, the claim that the parents should decide because they will bear the consequences of the decision—applies equally to cases in which the dependent, incompetent member of the family is not an infant.

4. For a detailed examination of the scope and limits of the best interest and substituted judgment principles, see Buchanan, A., *Our Treatment of Incompetents,* in BORDER CROSSINGS: NEW INTRODUCTORY ESSAYS IN MEDICAL ETHICS (T. Regan, D. VanDeVeer, eds.) (Random House, New York) (forthcoming). For a critical survey of the legal issues, see Capron, A. M., *The Authority of Others to Decide about Biomedical Interventions with Incompetents,* in WHO SPEAKS FOR THE CHILD? (W. Gaylin, R. Macklin, eds.) (Plenum Press, New York) (1982) at 115–52.

5. I am grateful to Deborah Mathieu for her comments on an earlier draft of this paper, which was presented at the conference on institutional ethics committees sponsored by the American Society of Law & Medicine, Washington, D.C., April 1983.

# 18

## Health Care Professionals and Ethical Relationships on IECs

Mila Ann Aroskar

The purposes of this chapter are to discuss some concerns about the ethical relationships of health care professionals that may enhance or impede the dialogue on institutional ethics committees and to suggest ethical principles that might underlie issues of access to and interaction within an IEC. Throughout this chapter, I use nurse-physician relationships for purposes of discussion, recognizing that many of the same issues arise for clergy, social workers, and other health professionals. Concerns about power and authority are significant in the development and effectiveness of IECs, as are other social mechanisms that arise to deal with the profound ethical questions facing health care institutions today. The relationships of health care professionals serving on IECs must be considered within a context of the increasing use of complex technologies in patient care and in recognition of the power differentials that exist between those individuals who participate in, and are affected by, the decisions that are made with and for them.

### UNDERSTANDING THE ROLES OF PHYSICIANS AND NURSES

A better understanding of nurse-physician roles and relationships is essential to all IEC members, as even nurses and physicians do not always have a clear understanding of the others' roles. The National Commission on Nursing, composed of nurses, physicians, and administrators, reported in 1981 that a major issue in nursing is the need to develop and foster collegial "relationships among nursing, medical staff and hospital administrations, including the nurse's ability to participate through organizational structures in decision making as it relates to nursing care. . . ."[1] My view of IECs is that they are (or should be) face-to-face communities of dialogue, to which members of the health care institution can bring their professional concerns and dilemmas for discussion and some degree of resolution. Committees do not make "the decision" about individual patients, their care, and their treatment; rather they serve a consultative and educative function for those individuals such as nurses who do make patient care decisions. While nurses do not write orders, they constantly make decisions that affect patient welfare, such as whether or not to bring a patient's condition and questions to the physician's attention when the patient is unable to do so.

There are many fears about ethics committees. Some fear that an institutional ethics committee may become a grievance committee for nurses. A related issue is the possibility that nurses and physicians would disagree in a patient care situation and become locked in adversarial positions. Yet another concern relates to individual expertise in dealing with ethical questions. While individual members have their own areas of technical and professional expertise, they may not have any formal preparation or skills in ethical inquiry. Professional expertise does not automatically translate into expertise in dealing with moral problems in medicine and health care. A physician recently sounded a poignant note when she said that after medical school she knew a great deal about electrolyte problems in children, but very little about how to deal with the profound ethical questions confronting her in practice. Uncertainty about duties and obligations in patient care situations, such as transplant surgery and termination of treatment, are sometimes overwhelming for health care professionals, patients, and their families.

In 1975, the National Joint Practice Commission, sponsored by the American Medical Association and the American Nurses' Association, adopted a definition of joint practice for physicians and nurses collaborating to provide patient care. Collegial relationships were described as follows:

1. Nurses and physicians mutually agree on the goals of patient care.
2. There is equity in status and personal interactions.
3. There is a shared base of scientific and professional knowledge with diverse skills and practices that are complementary.
4. There is mutual trust and respect for each other's competence.[2]

Shared responsibility for patients means equality in making decisions with and for patients; it requires an administrative structure that supports collaborative practice. Even if this appears to be an overly idealistic goal in many settings, it reminds us of the need for a more collegial attitude as IECs become face-to-face communities of dialogue fostering decision making that focuses on the interests of the patient.

## The Rules of the Game

Robert A. Hoekelman, a physician, notes that mutual respect does not always exist in physician-nurse relationships and that cooperation is often obtained by playing the "doctor-nurse game."[3] This game allows nurses to participate in medical decision making without seeming to do so, and without sharing in the responsibility for those decisions. The major rule of the game is that open disagreement must be avoided at all costs. If you play well, you win the respect and cooperation of the other discipline. The penalty for not playing correctly, the loss of respect and cooperation, is a particular hazard for nurses (primarily women) who seek their sense of self-worth and validation from physicians (primarily men). The penalty for physicians who do play the game is self-deception; for nurses, it is the suppression of initiative and the risk to their own integrity. The penalty for both is dishonesty in professional relationships.

There are other major impediments to collaborative and respectful relationships between physicians and nurses. One is that most nurses are employed in hospitals. Nurses who have been educated for professional practice and decision making find themselves struggling against bureaucratic rules that impede professionalism. Some give up and leave nursing. Those who stay risk losing their individual integrity. One nurse told this author recently that she was very close to leaving nursing altogether, mainly because of her sense of powerlessness in relation to ethical issues. She was simply unable to accept her role as implementer of physicians' decisions into which she had had no input. Instead of recognizing that they are victims of an organizational problem, nurses attempt to reduce their anxiety by blaming physicians. Physicians, who are not trapped by the same organizational demands, respond with anger and reciprocal blame. The result is a no-win situation for everyone.

Another impediment is poor communication resulting in misinterpretations, lack of follow-through, and failure to write down orders given verbally. The demands on both nurses and physicians due to increased patient loads and cost-containment efforts are excessive. Instead of working on these problems together, however, physicians and nurses often fight with each other. Hoekelman specifically mentions the male-female syndrome as an impediment to collegial relationships and a cause of the basic lack of understanding that each discipline has for the other's role in health care delivery. Physicians for the most part think only in terms of the "physician's helper" role of the nurse,[4] while nurses often view physicians as authoritarian and paternalistic. Yet, ironically, in viewing themselves as patient advocates, nurses run the risk of replacing physician paternalism with nursing maternalism.

Timothy Sheard, writing from his background in nursing and medical sociology, claims that nurses and physicians work in worlds that contrast in terms of underlying logic and experience.[5] To ignore these differences is to assume incorrectly that nurses and physicians inhabit identical work worlds. Individual nurses and physicians may experience any or all of the differences described by Sheard to varying degrees depending on their own work setting and individual sensitivity. These differences, actual or perceived, explain further the often expressed frustrations of both nurses and physicians, and can lead to adversarial positions in patient care decision making. These frustrations contribute to stress, may cause further conflict, and jeopardize patient welfare.

Sheard cites six dimensions of the work world where nurses and physicians differ: sense of time, sense of resources, unit of analysis for decision making, work assignment, rewards, and sense of mastery.[6] According to Sheard, physicians have a sense of time that constricts and expands to match patient problems. Time is measured not in hours, but by reference to the course of the illness as a patient moves toward recovery, stabilization, or death. This contrasts with a nurse's sense of time, which is strictly scheduled, with work organized around the performance of discrete tasks. In addition, nurses often have too much work to complete in the time available, so they try to eliminate those tasks that appear unnecessary. Interruptions in work routines, such as orders from physicians to give medications at odd times, are resented, and nurses may end up giving such medications late or at routine times to facilitate the flow of their work. Physicians rarely appreciate what a stat order may mean since they do not think in terms of a rigid work schedule.

Nurses experience hospital resources as limited and frequently difficult to obtain. The physician, who views institutional resources as abundant, writes orders in the patient's chart with little sense of the time and difficulty involved in carrying them out. There are several reasons for this, including the lack of sanctions against physicians who request or perform unnecessary tests or treatments and the fact that physicians write orders with little or no involvement in executing the task.

Physicians use a more global unit of analysis for decision making than nurses. Physicians organize all data around individual patients while nurses use a particulate unit of analysis, with more emphasis on completion of scheduled tasks than on the patient's overall health problems and progress.

Work assignments differ greatly. Physicians deal with patients as individual "cases," whereas nurses are assigned geographically, with less opportunity for achieving continuity of patient care (primary nursing to the contrary). This type of geographical nursing assignment, along with shorter hospital stays, effectively prevents nurses from developing any ongoing therapeutic relationship with patients.

Physicians and nurses also differ significantly in terms of rewards within the system. Inequalities in status and compensation are often difficult to justify in terms of the responsibilities of both the medical and nursing professions.

Lastly, nurses and physicians differ in terms of their sense of mastery over their work. Physicians' relatively strong sense of mastery is derived from the more integrated structure of their work, which is organized around individual patients. Nurses have a weaker sense of mastery over their work, as a result of the difficulties in administering the institution's bureaucracy on behalf of patients, their focus on tasks rather than patients, and their often shifting assignments.

The failure to understand the differences in the ways in which physicians and nurses experience their work worlds probably contributes more than many of us realize to frustration and conflict in physician-nurse relationships. Increased sensitivity to and understanding of these differences by all members of IECs may serve to clarify some of the difficulties encountered in the committee process and help identify strategies for dealing with differences that impede committee effectiveness.

## THE HEALTH CARE TEAM

The health care team concept is often viewed as a model for a multidisciplinary ethics committee, since this concept is familiar to most people in health care institutions. However, it is dangerous and misleading to assume that everyone uses "health care team" terminology in the same way. In fact, unexamined use of the team concept may serve as a barrier to achieving more respectful and collaborative relationships among health care professionals. While the notion of "the team" has been praised in the business world, the concept may be used coercively to limit the behaviors and ideas of team members.

Edmund Erde, a philosopher, explains some of the problems in using sports jargon to describe teams in health care, where goals, norms, and roles are not necessarily congruent with the variety of ways in which teams can be characterized.[7] He suggests that teams may be categorized by type of work as Type I or Type II teams. Type I teams are concerned with work that is highly specific to a particular task. Membership on a Type I team requires specialized technical training; an example is a surgical team. Functions are highly differentiated; the surgeon is in charge and gives orders to other team members, and there are few territorial or jurisdictional disputes. However, there may be ethical disputes when issues such as patient welfare are at stake. In contrast, a Type II team is organized around work that two or more persons from different backgrounds, professions, or roles can do equally effectively. An example is a pediatric nurse practitioner and a pediatrician providing well-baby care. This kind of situation can lead to many conflicts. Assignments are based not so much on skill as on negotiation over such factors as available time, costs, and the nature of the care required. Territorial and jurisdictional disputes are much more frequent on a Type II team.

In the sports team model, social norms differ from moral norms, and these norms will frequently conflict. For example, an ethical issue for nurses is whistle-blowing on a team member. Social norms require that team members support each other and this includes the possibility of hiding certain things that occur in the course of the team's work. Moral norms, on the other hand, may require blowing the whistle on another team member when patient welfare is in jeopardy. This moral norm is supported unequivocally in the American Nurses' Association *Code for Nurses with Interpretive Statements* (1976).

Erde states that team talk seems to hide the real need for change in many hospitals by suppressing feelings of alienation and by manipulating people to feel guilty while the causes of alienation are allowed to continue. Playing the "doctor-nurse game" can also contribute further to feelings of guilt and alienation. Erde also mentions the need to truly respect the different interests and contributions of everyone involved in patient care.

In summary, although a team approach may exist as hospital rhetoric or ethos, it is not appropriate as a model for the relationships of ethics committee members. In fact, if the members of the IEC hold different views of "the team," the concept may impede the effectiveness of the committee as it seeks to deal with profound and difficult issues fraught with ambiguity and uncertainty.

## ETHICS FOR IEC RELATIONSHIPS

Considering, then, the different work worlds of physicians, nurses, and other health care professionals, difficulties with the team model, and the issues raised about collegial relationships in the report of the National Commission on Nursing as recently as 1981, I think there are three principles that could be considered as guides to an internal norm or ethic for relationships on an IEC:

1. The interests and rights of patients are uppermost and take precedence over the competing rights and interests of health care professionals or institutional interests.

2. There is mutual respect among all members of the IEC based on the inherent worth of each individual person.

3. Following from principle #2, there is explicit recognition that each member of an IEC has perspectives and expertise that contribute to the consultative, educative, and policy-recommendation processes involved in working through ethical dilemmas in patient care.

Members and prospective members of IECs should discuss openly and have some commitment to these principles. They cut across committee functions and have the potential for facilitating more collegial, ethical relationships. They may also serve to generate new perspectives on institutional structures or mechanisms for dealing with ethical concerns in such highly specialized patient care units as oncology research units and neonatal intensive care units.

Explicit recognition that such principles enhance committee effectiveness may also modify fears that the IEC will function as a grievance committee, and will leave the committee open to consider issues that might be brought to its attention by patients and families as well as health care professionals. Dealing with ethical issues and concerns has many dimensions that health care professionals need to consider in concert with patients, families, and members of other disciplines. Existing committees and institutions contemplating the development of IECs should be clear about their functions and what constitutes an ethical issue or dilemma. Once these considerations have been dealt with openly and clearly, the question of *who* brings issues to the committee can be recognized as the political question that it is. Otherwise, members may not be able to move on to the major tasks of education and consultation in the interest of better decision making related to the ethical aspects of patient care. An IEC should have the burden of demonstrating why an individual or profession should *not* have access to the committee, and should not attempt to draw up a definitive list of those who are automatically included or excluded by virtue of professional position or expertise alone.

My hope is that these comments will illuminate some areas that need reflection in connection with facilitating more ethical relationships among members of IECs. With these considerations in mind, an IEC can serve as an effective means to the goal of responsible and thoughtful decision making in painful and complex situations where the ethical aspects predominate, whether these situations involve individual patient care or policy making.

# NOTES

1. NATIONAL COMMISSION ON NURSING, INITIAL REPORT AND PRELIMINARY RECOMMENDATIONS (The Hospital Research and Educational Trust, Chicago, Ill.) (1981) at 5.
2. Smoyak, S., *Problems in Interprofessional Relations*, in THE NURSING PROFESSION (N. Chaska, ed.) (McGraw-Hill, New York, N.Y.) (1978) at 323–29.
3. Hoekelman, R., *Nurse-Physician Relationships: Problems and Solutions*, in THE NURSING PROFESSION, *supra* note 2, at 330–31.
4. *Id.* at 332–33.
5. Sheard, T., *The Structure of Conflict in Nurse-Physician Relations*, SUPERVISOR NURSE 11:14–15, 17–18 (August 1980).
6. *Id.*
7. Erde, E., *Notions of Team and Team Talk in Health Care*, LAW, MEDICINE AND HEALTH CARE 9(5):26–28 (October 1981).

# Panel Discussion:
# Implementing and Utilizing an
# Institutional Ethics Committee

## Ronald E. Cranford, Moderator

RONALD E. CRANFORD, M.D.: Let me start by stating my concern that an ethics committee should remain a grass-roots organization that will be built up by the institution. I have a great concern that the federal government is going to become prematurely involved with this and mandate certain procedures without really knowing what is going on. I think that such a course would be very harmful to the movement at this stage in its development.

A lot of you have shared with me your concerns and your experiences, and let me assure you that you are going through the same painful and slow growth process that others of us went through three, five, even ten years ago. There's no doubt that in each institution, there is a group of dedicated individuals who are sincerely interested in trying to cope with these dilemmas in a realistic and humane way and to translate societal values into specific case decisions. The American Society of Law & Medicine has agreed to attempt to facilitate information sharing in this area, and to encourage the development of these committees through experience and on-the-job training.

I will now open the discussion for comments from any of the panelists, after which the entire audience is invited to join the discussion.

DAVID L. JACKSON, M.D. (conference faculty): I would like to make one observation on our definition of terms. I'm not sure there is anything intrinsic in the team concept that is necessarily negative or disrespectful of diversity of opinion. I think systems reflect values and people. If by "team" you mean a group run by an arbitrary and capricious dictator, then obviously that team will not be sensitive to the kinds of issues that institutional ethics committees need to be sensitive to. But if you look at the sports analogy again—which I didn't bring up but will refer back to—I think in many situations the specific roles and the mutual respect that can be engendered in a team, based on appropriate values and mutual respect, can be a very useful model for certain aspects of the health care system, including dialogue. This is particularly true at the bedside given the diversity of professional disciplines necessary to take care of critically ill patients.

If there isn't mutual respect, whether in a team context or not in a team context, the system won't work. Thus, with institutional ethics committees I'd like to reemphasize the need to set very clearly, and to define, your expectations. If that's not done, then no matter how the system works, people are going to have unmet expectations and will become disillusioned and disappointed. For example, it is important to recognize that you are not going to get a consensus on the tough cases, and this needs to be clearly understood by all the people working to set up these committees. You also have to understand that even if you could get decisional consensus, preserving patient autonomy and protecting patient rights are the primary functions of the institutional ethics committee. The clinical assessment of what patient autonomy means is likely to generate a fair amount of controversy and is also not likely to be unanimous. You can look at the debate in the literature between Imbus and Zawacki[1] and Youngner and others,[2] and discover that it's not always perfectly clear what "patient autonomy" means in the immediate clinical setting. Unless the people who are instituting an ethics committee understand that this is likely to be a contentious point, they will probably flounder in a sea of controversy and disagreement without understanding that this kind of disagreement is to be expected and there have to be mechanisms to deal with it—it has to be institutionalized.

RUTH MACKLIN PH.D. (conference faculty): Let me pick up on one point that David Jackson mentioned, something that has not been adequately addressed as a possible role for the institutional ethics committee. What about the marginally or questionably competent patient who may be expressing wishes or desires regarding treatment, whether it is a treatment refusal or perhaps some demand for treatment—for example, an elderly patient exhibiting the signs of a dementing illness. Dr. Joanne Lynn mentioned determinations of competency as one of the possible areas where an institutional ethics committee might work. Clearly, a whole committee is not going to make the determination of competency. Very often, at least in my experience, psychiatry is called in by a primary care physician who finds that the patient is refusing treatment, and the physician wants to get an assessment of mental competence. I think it is important that we address what role, if any, the institutional ethics committee might play in adjudicating competency determinations, in trying to protect the patient in the face of possible disagreement about the patient's competency, and whether to support the judgment of incompetency in the absence of a legal determination. I find this a gray area, especially if we're talking about patients in extended care facilities, and also with regard to a growing number of patients in the acute care hospital setting. What role, if any, should the IEC play either in the determination of competency or in advocating for the patient when those issues arise?

ROBERT M. VEATCH, PH.D. (conference faculty): As I understand it, the panel this afternoon is supposed to focus on the practical problems of implementing and utilizing an IEC. I am the designated ethics theorist, or one of them, on the panel, and I don't pretend to possess a wealth of practical experience, especially with IECs. Nonetheless, I have one comment that might be relevant to the initial phase of implementation and utilization. This pertains only to what I would refer to as clinical or patient-centered IECs, those not involved in such issues as resource allocation. It's a plea to take seriously the possibility that the purpose of an IEC is to serve the patient and to protect the patient's rights and welfare. I was a bit distressed on several occasions during the conference when lists were put forward of possible groups to whom an IEC might be accountable. Ruth Macklin named the physician, the department chairman, and the administrator as three plausible candidates. This is a naive theorist's plea to at least add the patient to that list as a possible person to whom an IEC might really be accountable. However, to do so requires that the patient or the agent for the patient play some substantial role in the structuring and in the implementation of the way IECs work. For example, as David Jackson mentioned, patients may be notified that their case is to be discussed and either they or their representatives really need to sit in on those meetings and be a very central part of them whenever possible.

I think this would probably have four implications for these committees. It would mean that patients would be involved, whenever possible, as members of the IEC, and would participate as individuals when their own cases are going to be discussed. It would mean that the IEC probably would not get involved in making substantive decisions for or against, say, resuscitation. When the IEC is involved in guideline writing, the guidelines are going to end up being procedural, rather than substantive, and it means that IECs ought to be very careful about getting involved in larger social ethics questions such as resource allocation.

JOHN A. ROBERTSON, J.D. (conference faculty): I just want to make a couple of comments. One is that I think John Paris's account of the prosecution and trial of Doctors Nejdl and Barber in Los Angeles[3] shows the need for ethics committees, at least of the optional/optional variety. If such a committee had existed in their institution, I think the chances are very good that the whole episode could have been avoided.

I'd also like to clarify a few points concerning my optional/ optional ethics committee. First, if a physician invokes an optional/ optional committee and the committee essentially agrees with the physician's course of action, that would be added protection against later legal repercussions because the committee's decision would be further evidence that the physician acted reasonably in the case. On the other hand, if the optional/optional committee views the matter differently than does the physician, and the physician at his or her option chooses not to follow the advice of the committee (it being advisory and merely optional), would that have any effect on legal liability? I do not think it would, because the fact that the physician does not follow the advice of a merely advisory committee does not in itself show that the physician's actions are negligent or reckless. The underlying question in such a case would be whether there is a duty to continue to treat or not to treat the patient. That is a question that exists independently of what the committee has advised, and as long as there is not a well-established custom of having to follow the committee, I think the physician would still be free to disregard its advice. The underlying issue in any later legal proceeding would be whether the physician's action was reasonable, not whether he or she followed the committee's advice. Thus, I do not think there is much danger that the optional/optional committee may really evolve into an optional/mandatory committee.

JOHN J. PARIS, S.J. (conference faculty): One area I'd like to raise some questions about is Bob Veatch's emphasis upon autonomy, and particularly the involvement of the patient or the proxy in the consultation process. I think it's very premature to do that. Very often, the physician has doubts or ambiguities or uncertainties which he wants to have clarified well before making a recommendation to the family as to how treatment ought to go. If we get the notion into our heads that we must involve the patient, or the patient's family, in the consultation process when the attending physician is seeking clarification, then we are going to create untold anxiety on the part of families, which is not necessary and ought not to occur.

My second warning is that when you begin these committees, be very careful not to allow the lawyers to have too dominant a role. It would cut very much against Ruth Macklin's insistence, and I think correct insistence, that it's the patient and the patient's concern and interest that must be the focus. The lawyer, particularly the legal counsel for the institution, is not necessarily a representative of the patient's interests. The lawyer has a wholly different agenda which may in fact be quite detrimental to the patient's best interests. Ethics committees ought to bear in mind and heed the warning of that great constitutional theorist, Edmund Burke, who said, "It is not what a lawyer tells me I may do; but what humanity, reason, and justice tell me I ought to do."[4]

CORRINE BAYLEY, C.S.J. (conference faculty): I have very little to say except that I wonder why you people are here and what issues or forces have directed you to think about having such a committee. We've talked about some of them, but I'm not sure we've really explored them carefully enough, as Alex Capron's earlier points about function and purpose made clear, at least to me. As I talk about function, I have to keep remembering why we felt this need for an ethics committee in the first place. Maybe there are some alternative ways to meet some of those needs. So I'd be interested in your response about what remaining concerns, questions, and ambiguities this conference might address.

Just one other issue: I've heard people say we've got to have some way to resolve these problems. I think it is important to recognize that the ambiguities will remain; in fact, the more the issues are examined, the more complicated things sometimes get. So try not to make that mistake, which I've made myself.

MILA A. AROSKAR, R.N., ED.D. (conference faculty): As attention is focused on the development and implementation of institutional ethics committees, I think it is important not to lose sight of the needs of all the individuals who work in health care institutions or groups such as boards of trustees to become sensitive to the ethical aspects of their work and decisions. They also need opportunities for education about and discussion of ethical issues and dilemmas related to patient care and to policy decisions. These opportunities and mechanisms could be viewed as complementary to the work and purposes of an IEC, e.g., ethics rounds on patient care units and explicit discussion of ethical dimensions of the decisions and recommendations made by an institution's governing body.

ALEXANDER M. CAPRON, LL.B. (conference faculty): I just want to say how pleased I am that, when Ron Cranford began by describing his ten years of experience in this field, he decided not to cast himself in the role of the Elisabeth Kübler-Ross of institutional ethics committees, laying out the prescription as to the stages of development that you can all expect to encounter—for example, denial and anger. I also wonder if we don't have to develop some new vocabulary. I cannot imagine us continuing to take the time that it takes to say, as John Robertson does, "optional/optional." Like Sister Corrine Bayley, I found the earlier questions from the floor enormously illuminating, and rather than take the time for more comments from those of us you've already heard, let's turn the floor over to questions.

MARY LOGAN, C.S.J. (Second Vice President, Sacred Heart Hospital, Allentown, Pennsylvania): Earlier someone said that perhaps the Barber/Nejdl case in California would not have come up if the hospital had had an ethics committee. I wonder if perhaps the case would not have come up if they—that is, Drs. Barber and Nejdl—had communicated better with the nurse. I want to ask Father Paris: From what I've read about the case, the first communication seemed to be when the nurse wanted to do the misting of the endotracheal tube. Was she alerted to the fact that the doctor had written permission from the family and things of that nature?

FATHER PARIS: Yes. She knew that, and interestingly enough she did not object to the removal of the respirator and she did not object to the removal of the IVs when that happened. What she objected to was what she thought were poor nursing care orders being issued to her staff, and that's how the battle began.

SISTER LOGAN: I see. The report I read did not bring that out too clearly, and I thought perhaps she was not aware of all the conditions. Nonetheless, I do think communication between the physician and the nurse certainly needs a great deal of attention before we even attempt to have a committee communicate.

FATHER PARIS: I think you are correct, but let me make two points. First, sometimes the way in which we facilitate communication is by having a place where the nurse can go instead of fighting with the physician. Second, of course, the difficulty in that case was that once the allegation was made, it was the district attorney who went forward on the murder charge. His insistence was that the withholding of fluids and nutrition violates community standards, that it's starving. An enormous misunderstanding of the medical activity exists there, I think. If you had a committee which had established that course of action, there would have been greater evidence, at least for the district attorney, that in certain, limited circumstances this is appropriate medical behavior. Instead, he thought of it as the reckless action of malicious doctors.

SISTER LOGAN: I can certainly see the difficulty came when the nurse didn't have anyone to turn to within the institution.

One final comment concerning Mr. Robertson's earlier point, on the optional/optional group: My feeling is that if a doctor were brought into court and he had gone against the decision of the ethics committee, the jury would think it was most unreasonable to go against the decision of what I'm sure they would perceive as a group of experts, even though the doctor had no obligation or pressure on him to follow their opinion.

MR. ROBERTSON: Just a quick response to that. It may not even be possible for that evidence to be presented if the committee is set up in such a way that its proceedings are confidential. Even if it were admissible in court, the question would be, has the doctor deviated from an appropriate standard of care in not following the committee? That would depend to some extent upon accepted medical practice, and there is no clear custom of following such committees. Failing to follow the committee's advice would not in itself show that the doctor had acted in a reckless manner in the case.

SISTER LOGAN: I believe you are correct; even though the doctor may consult with a committee, his or her obligation remains the same: to follow the appropriate standard of care.

DR. JACKSON: There's one clinical note that I'd like to add. When the primary physician gets a consultation from any subspecialty, he or she can either take the advice or not take it. But you do have an obligation to explain in the chart and to the patient why you chose either course. Sometimes you get conflicting advice—e.g., from pulmonary medicine and infectious disease—and you choose some different pathway. But I do think there is a presumption of having to explain why you chose not to accept expert advice. It may be a perfectly rational reason. Occasionally committees can be wrong, believe it or not. But I do think there's a presumption of having to explain yourself.

D. I. WRIGHT, M.D. (Naval Hospital of Bethesda, Bethesda, Maryland): My understanding of what Mr. Capron said was that the function of the ethics committee was to assure quality in the decisions, and that the mechanism for this was concurrent review, problem identification, and problem solving. In those terms, it sounds like it's right out of the JCAH manual for quality assurance.[5] Do you feel that this committee should be a part of the overall hospital quality assurance program?

MR. CAPRON: As I understand the quality assurance mechanism, I think the level of questions that are dealt with is similiar but the questions are not at all identical. Part of the process that is going on goes beyond the kind of review that is brought about by quality assurance. Now whether that means that you want, within a particular hospital, to mandate this under the board of trustees in the same fashion as the quality assurance program, using the medical staff, having a committee of that sort, and having some form of communication between these two bodies, I think depends on the kind of hospital you're talking about. I might note that the President's Commission does recommend that accreditation bodies give consideration to the existence or nonexistence of some IEC-type mechanism in the hospital in considering whether or not the hospital should be accredited.[6]

WALTER ZUCKERMAN, M.D. (thoracic surgeon, Mt. Auburn Hospital, Cambridge, Massachusetts): An area of concern which brought me to this conference is the extreme overutilization of resources used in the extension of the life of a patient who predictably cannot survive hospitalization or whose life is devoid of quality. At any one time there are several patients in our institution who are receiving excessive care. I am sure many here share this experience. This is a major problem which ethics committees should address. Unhappily, the issue is often avoided because of potential (real or perceived) legal implications and justifiable concern for the wishes of the family and patient. We must face the problem even though it may be emotionally difficult to accept. I am looking for recommendations as to possible mechanisms by which the issue can be addressed.

MR. CAPRON: In a certain way, in fact, I was a little uncomfortable that we were focusing so much of the ethics committee discussion around decisions to forego treatment, usually because the treatment is regarded either as not wanted by the patient or too burdensome and disproportionate to the benefit that's being provided. In a way the ethics committee is a mechanism which has a broader use, but, as I tried to say, I think that is what has generated interest in it right now, particularly in light of the Section 504 regulations.[7] Generally, this is the area where conflicts most often arise within the hospital, where the hospital feels most under scrutiny by the legal authorities, and so on; so I do not feel we've sidestepped it. In a way this is a mechanism which can be very responsive to concerns that there is overtreatment.

DR. CRANFORD: I think overtreatment is rampant in hospitals. It is a major problem, and I don't think we are really sidestepping it.

WILLIAM C. GARDNER, Q.C. (attorney for Health Sciences Center, Winnipeg, Manitoba, Canada): I represent a large health unit in Winnipeg of about 1,100 beds. I've enjoyed very much, as I'm sure everybody has, all the speakers here to date, and I have a far better understanding of the theory of an IEC. But I'm a little concerned and a little confused about how the actual practical application works. I've got all the disciplines here at the moment, including the lawyers who are suffering a little bit by being told not to be too involved. The confusion arises a little bit from the timing, and I guess I'd like to suggest that we consider that the IEC would be mandatory/mandatory, that it would be a decision-making process as well as an educational and consultative one. Sister Corrine Bayley spoke of an old lady in a nursing home, I think she was 83 years old, who had a temperature of 103°-plus. If that patient was to be the subject of any consultation within an IEC, one of the speakers yesterday said, perhaps you can get an opinion and get everybody together in seven days. Mr. Rothenberg said this morning that he does four to six such consultations a week. But I wasn't absolutely clear with whom he was consulting, whether it was with the patient, the doctor, or the family, but he did mention standing by a bedside. I'm wondering if anybody would care to comment on the actual practicality of an ethics committee in an emergency situation, where there is going to be not only consultation, but perhaps a decision which would also be binding, as I understand it, on the physician in charge.

SISTER BAYLEY: One of the first things I wanted to say when you started to talk is that I don't think there's any one right way to begin. If you go back to your hospital tomorrow and start to work on developing an ethics committee, what I would suggest is that you take into consideration things you have heard here. We obviously haven't had sufficient experience to have a "right way" to go about it. I think that there are some cautions that people have suggested and certainly you'd want to consider those, but those of us who have experience have a little different perspective. So I guess my concern is, what are the issues in your hospital? How do you think you and your institution can best deal with these issues? Again, I worry about making too many rules and regulations before we've had some more experience.

On the issue of the incompetent patient and decision making, it seems to me that a committee can be very useful in developing principles, and we've talked about those, such as patient preference—what would the patient want? Do we use the best interest test or the substituted judgment test? We ask these questions in fear and trembling with an incompetent patient because we're never sure what the patient would want. I shouldn't say we're never sure; we're sometimes not sure. And in that particular case that I mentioned this morning, the physician did indicate in his article that he knew what the patient would want; that she had once said to him, "Don't do anything to prolong my life if I'm no longer responding." So he at least had that principle, but he was still reluctant, and I think it was a real cry for help. I think we can begin to sort out what these principles might be. The President's Commission report has detailed some of them very carefully.[8] So, I don't see the committee, personally, making a decision, telling the physician that he or she should institute antibiotics or should not. But to outline some of the principles—patient preference, patient benefits—

to weigh burdens and benefits; these decisions are difficult, and they'll always remain difficult. But to make them in isolation I think is even more burdensome, for physicians and others.

DR. CRANFORD: I might mention that some of us have had a fair amount of experience in consultation, and we can move quickly when necessary. At our hospital, we've had a variety of consultations, perhaps 50 to 100, in the last several years. In an emergency situation we do it informally; an attending physician or house officer can pick up the phone and call us, and one of us can be there in five or ten minutes. We had a consultation a few weeks ago on a Monday. It was referred to our entire committee on Tuesday since we recognized it as a major ethical dilemma. On Thursday we had 15 of the 20 members of our committee meeting with 15 staff persons concerned with the case. We discussed the case for two hours, came to a resolution, and over the weekend the patient was allowed to die. Many members of the committee participated in that decision and its implementation. We visited with the patient and the family, and talked with the health care team. So a committee can be activated rapidly.

MR. GARDNER: I have one more very brief question concerning the medical fraternity losing some control. At our health care unit we have an internationally known neurosurgeon. When we were drawing up, eight or nine years ago, a protocol for a transplantation service, one of the things that he was asked was to permit a consultation to make sure that the patient was dead. Well, the discussion took place inside the hospital at that time, and he said, "I've never had any difficulty in pronouncing a patient dead. None of them have ever come back from there," as he pointed to the morgue. So do you have any difficulty with doctors agreeing to this form of consultation? Are there any suggestions by any of the faculty on experiences they've had on that matter?

DR. JACKSON: I think it would be unrealistic to pretend that there is no resistance in the medical profession to outside consultation on these difficult issues. What we found in our experience in Cleveland is that as physicians gain experience in using a consultative committee, they begin to view it as an adjunct, as a service, as a communication tool that diminishes their legal concern, or even if it really doesn't do that, at least they perceive that it does. It diminishes staff conflict because there are good mechanisms for communication that are set up in advance. And it is hoped that it is also directed at making sure that the patient's rights are protected by due process, and then the resistance slowly fades. Some people are enthusiastic from day one, others come on board slowly, and, to be frank, some continue to feel that they can tell when a patient is dead and don't need a committee to help them with that, and I'm not sure I'll ever dissuade them from that view.

DR. MACKLIN: Let me just add one point, that this may be a process of slow evolution rather than very rapid change. Young, new physicians, perhaps more aware of these issues, are coming up through the ranks. Once institutional ethics committees are in place and are visible within the institution, and people see what kind of work they do, that they are not a threat to the primary roles that physicians have as decision makers or care givers, then some of the fears will be allayed. Of course, there is the matter of peer pressure, and although there may always be recalcitrant or arrogant individuals, that is what the world is like in every enterprise. I remain hopeful that if there is a success story with the use of these committees, it may even change the kind of resistance that you mentioned, which is all too well known to most people; it may even change that practice through an evolutionary process, especially with younger physicians availing themselves of it. One of the things that struck me—at least on the one committee that I serve on, to which house officers have access—is that a house officer actually served on the committee for a while, and, on two separate occasions, house officers brought cases to the committee. This is a hopeful sign, perhaps, that a new generation of physicians is emerging.

FATHER JAMES BURYSKA (St. Mary's Hospital, Rochester, Minnesota): I direct this question to the panelists, particularly those who have hands-on experience with institutional ethics committees. I'd be interested to hear your comments on the interplay between professional roles and personal attitudes and values—for instance, about the crucial issues of life and death—as you experience them in the members of the committees that you're familiar with. What kind of conflicts or harmony or whatever happens under those sorts of circumstances?

DR. CRANFORD: I'll make one comment, although I'm not sure I fully understand your question. I think the committees are multidisciplinary by nature, and so you have a multitude of perspectives. The very nature of the committee would be to bring different value systems into interplay, and to respect the differences of opinion and to discuss them. You would then develop a working dialogue and a working relationship in the committee so you would fully expect diverse value systems and opinions to come into play as you make decisions.

FATHER BURYSKA: Maybe I'm asking the question at one level of value deeper than that. For instance, the individual who has personally reflected upon or faced the prospect of his or her own death is bound to have a different perspective than the person who is in a state of denial about death. The professional, be it a doctor, clergyperson, or whoever, has another perspective on death. That is the level of interaction that I'm inquiring about.

SISTER BAYLEY: I had a feeling you were making a statement when you asked the question in the first place, and maybe that is what you're doing. Clearly, people who have come to terms with their own death, whatever that means, will have a little different perspective about withholding and withdrawing treatment than those who have not. I don't know what to say about it except that yes, that's true. You may also be wondering whether people of that ilk are more likely to serve on committees like this, and I would say that's probably true also.

PETER MCSHANNON, JR., J.D. (Keck, Mahin & Cate, Washington, D.C.): I'd like to go back to the legal issues. One of my clients is a large metropolitan hospital. As outside counsel, responsible to the board of directors, my primary concern remains the patient, but I am still concerned about liability for the institution. As I understood Professor Robertson's descriptions of the optional/optional and optional/mandatory committees, he seems to be saying that if a doctor were to go to an optional/optional ethics committee, it would be an indication that he had exercised a reasonable standard of care, whereas if he went to an optional/mandatory committee and did not follow its advice, there would be no legal implication. I respectfully submit that you cannot have it both ways. From other standpoints it might be best to have a very loose committee, an optional/optional committee; but from a liability standpoint, where you have fewer guidelines and fewer standards, no review process and no decision-making process as such, then there is, in my opinion, little protection for the doctor who goes to an optional/optional committee. The looser the committee, as far as the courts are concerned, the less value and the less deference they would give to a doctor going to that committee. Maybe I'm alone in disagreeing with you on this, but I personally believe you are too sanguine in your evaluation of the legal protections for a physician arising from use of an optional/optional ethics committee.

MR. ROBERTSON: What I mean to say is that I do not think it's going to hurt the doctor, and it might possibly help. In either case, if you take just civil liability—we can put aside criminal liability—the issue will be, has the physician acted with due care? That question will really be independent of whether he has gone to the committee or not. The fact that he had gone to the committee would, I think, support a claim that the doctor had acted in good faith and with due care because he sought out the opinion of others. That's where they end up agreeing with him. I think that will help the case a little bit. I'm not saying that it would necessarily put on it a stamp of approval; that would be giving total immunity. But it would be some support for the notion that the physician was acting with due care.

On the other hand, if a committee is purely advisory, I don't think anything flows from the fact that the physician has not gone along with what it advised. The underlying question will still be, is the physician acting with due care? And again, I think that's independent of what the committee recommends. The question you're really asking is, then, does it become an independent indicator of lack of due care if a physician does not go along with the advice of a committee? I would submit that as long as a kind of customary standard of practice is applied here, as long as there's not a custom of all physicians or most physicians going along with a committee opinion, failure to do so would not in and of itself show a lack of due care.

MR. CAPRON: I share the questioner's concerns, and it's an example of why I hope that we will give more thought and proceed with a little more caution with ethics committees than we did with institutional review boards (IRBs). Even though IRBs have been around a long time and are even mandated by federal law, and even though we have every indication that the Iowa IRB was behaving in a very reasonable fashion, yet it got zero deference from the court.[9] I was somewhat surprised, frankly, because of the kinds of assumptions that John Robertson just voiced. It seems to me that when a physician goes to an optional/ optional committee, the major benefit will be improving the quality of the decision that is reached. It's the same way with an IRB. The major impact of IRBs is encouraging a process of self-scrutiny on the part of investigators: "Someone is going to be looking at this protocol and asking what perhaps are embarrassing questions to me, and I'd better have thought it through pretty carefully before I submit this, because the people who are going to be looking at it are not just my peers, who are going to be looking at research design, but people who are going to say, this isn't consent, or you haven't considered the risk/benefit ratio well enough. So I want to think that through, and I want to explain it. I'm going to have to put it down in writing or I'm going to have to answer questions or both." Institutional ethics committees may turn out to be beneficial in provoking that same sort of advance thinking and in helping physicians through their own thought processes so that their decisions are less likely to lead, after the fact, to problems.

Suppose you turn to an optional/optional committee, and the prosecutor or the plaintiff's attorney has the doctor on the stand and says: "Doctor, this committee—you chose to go to it, right? You weren't required?"

"That's right."

"You also weren't required to follow its advice, were you?"

"No."

"Now they agreed with you in this case, right? And if they hadn't agreed with you, you would have gone right ahead anyway, wouldn't you?"

What's the answer to that? Indeed, the lawyer may even have indications from past cases where that happened. In other words, he says, this was window dressing. The attorney submits to the court that this didn't mean anything: the doctor appeared to be rolling the dice but he couldn't lose. If the committee supported him, fine; if they didn't he was going to ignore them. I think we have to think through those questions, and figure out the possible ramifications, especially since I do not see the major purpose of the committee as being to protect the hospital or the doctor, but to improve the quality of the decision.

MR. McSHANNON: I agree with you.

MR. CAPRON: I'm not bothered by the fact that it doesn't have that binding effect, but I think you were right. If we are going to go and sell this to physicians and hospitals, in effect as a form of insurance, as a form of risk management, then these kinds of questions will become predominant, and I don't think we have adequate answers to them yet.

MR. ROBERTSON: Just one quick comment to properly clarify the thrust of my remarks. The legal implications here do not cut against establishing such a committee but at least go in favor of it. How far they push in favor is something we could debate about, but if anything, they're positive rather than negative.

MR. CAPRON: While I'm sure you do not want to hear me argue with John forever, he made one comment in passing that I think is very important to explore. That would be the question of whether a hospital ethics committee would come under whatever law your state may have that immunizes and protects certain hospital committee records. Some of those state statutes, it seems to me, would not cover the kinds of committees we are talking about. They are designed to cover a tissue committee or the like, and to permit the hospital to engage in good internal discipline. If the ethics committee did not come under the statute, then that information would not be immunized. Thus, in regard to the earlier questioner who asked about the introduction of an adverse report, the answer is that the records of the committee would be introducible in court. Then you would have to start arguing to the jury why they should not regard it as an indication of negligence or worse. But, on the face of it, it would depend upon your state law on that issue.

MR. VEATCH: I, too, noticed that "you-can't-have-it-both-ways" problem with John Robertson's original formulation. Let me comment not on what the law is going to do with regard to hospital ethics committee;

I have no idea. But I do have a sense of the way I think the law ought to treat an opinion of a hospital ethics committee. I'm very concerned that ethics committees will too quickly gain too much standing to either support or refute the judgment of a patient and his or her clinician. In particular, I envision a situation which I think we already have with IRBs, that if the local committee is given the standing to protect an individual in any signficant way at all, the reputation of the IRB or institutional ethics committee will quickly spread. And there will be particularly lenient or particularly rigorous committees, and these will be well known. It seems to me the most you could get from an ideal hospital ethics committee is that it would reflect the ethical consensus of the management and administration, the sponsoring agency for the institution. I see no particular reason why that consensus ought to be given any deference at law. I would expect, for example, that if committees were given such deference, the word would get around that there is one particular committee that tolerates stopping treatment on newborns or on the senile or on the retarded. It may in fact reflect the actual consensus of that institution. But the mere fact that the committee reflects the consensus of the institution should not give any particular insulation for the practitioners within that institution in a court of law.

HELEN MARR MITCHELL, M.D. (Augusta, Maine): I'm a pediatrician in Augusta, Maine, and I teach in the Maine-Dartmouth Family Practice Residency Program. My question is stimulated by Alan Buchanan's paper. I was impressed with his idea that the family should be the primary and preferred unit to speak for an incompetent patient, under the conditions he outlined, and as he defined a "family." That definition was reminiscent to me of the family as defined by the pediatrician Mary Howell in her book, *Helping Ourselves: Families and the Human Network*.[10] I don't know if the judicial system is particularly conservative or traditionalist in Maine, but we have repeatedly been frustrated when a blood relative of an incompetent patient, one who was estranged from the patient, maybe even really alienated from that patient, was apparently automatically given the right to speak for that patient over people who would be considered "family" as Buchanan defined it this morning. I'm just wondering, is there evidence that our legal and judicial confreres are, in some places, conceiving of and defining the family as those persons with whom a person lives and interacts most closely?

MR. VEATCH: In Virginia, just this last month, we passed a statute that clearly establishes which family members are presumed to have priority, and it follows the rather standard notions of degree of kinship: designated agent or power of attorney first, then spouse, then adult children and parents, and so forth.[11] I get the sense that we spend too much time agonizing over the problem of whether we can always trust family members. After all, parents today routinely have the responsibility of consenting or refusing to consent to care for their children. If once in a while parents do not perform in ways that seem responsible, we have mechanisms to review that judgment and to have someone appointed in their place. I suspect that the only plausible way to go is not Alan Buchanan's scheme of seeking out the relative who is really in sympathy with the patient; that would come only if the patient has designated that relative as a decision maker, as the designated agent. But we're going to have to go with something that is far more objective, following degrees of kinship, and then use the standard procedures that are well in place to overturn decisions of those next of kin in cases where they don't appear to make sense and seem inappropriate.

DR. MACKLIN: I think that Bob Veatch is right about the questions regarding children. The bigger problem that I see is with the elderly. The decision maker will, in many but not all cases, be a spouse. In other cases, however, it will be adult children. Do you then look at the birth order of the adult children? Is that next of kin? Do you look at the one with whom the relative may have lived before being placed in a nursing home, even though that may be the younger of two siblings? But most importantly, what do you do when two or more siblings are in conflict about the decision? This is something I think that we have not agonized over too much. Perhaps it has not been given enough thought because these problems—for any of you who may work in settings with the elderly, whether it's an extended care facility or a hospital—are the problems that seem to be intractable, and there's no guideline that I've seen or heard of, either from anyone who's written about it or, strictly speaking, from the law. Now I may be ignorant of what the law says in those kinds of cases, but it's not clear. It has been observed that many people in our country live in very remote areas, and that their next of kin may have very little to do with that elderly person during the later years. So I think that this is a problem that deserves attention, and since we are so uncertain about what to do in those cases, I would look to guidance from my fellow committee members and hope that collective wisdom may be better than individual judgments.

DR. MITCHELL: Actually, that's correct. My questions did stem more from cases involving elderly patients, reflecting my general role in the family practice residency rather than my pediatrics role.

DON GIBBONS (*Medical World News*, New York): I've repeatedly heard people say that you have to allow institutions to develop their own model for an IEC and then allow it to mold to the institution and evolve into a working format—and to do so fairly quickly in order to avoid the legislative or regulatory route that the IRBs or the PSROs went. Those two went that route largely because the medical establishment either dragged its feet or totally balked on those issues. On this issue, the American Hospital Association [AHA] has yet to come out in favor of ethics committees. They're continuing to study it. The American Medical Association [AMA] won't say yes and won't say no. The American Academy of Pediatrics has said, well, start a temporary committee until we can study it. Can you move quickly enough to get this movement going, to avoid legislation without that establishment backing?

DR. CRANFORD: That's a profound question and I do not know the answer.

MR. GIBBONS: Is anybody on the faculty doing anything to try and get that establishment backing?

DR. CRANFORD: We all are. That is what we are here for; that is why this first national conference is being held, with more conferences planned.

MR. GIBBONS: Were any people from AHA or AMA invited to come?

DR. CRANFORD: I've worked with the AMA; it took us three years to get them to reverse their position on brain death legislation; it took intensive lobbying, hundreds of hours, and pressure from the specialty societies. I think a strong position on ethics committees could take ten years with the AMA.

MR. GIBBONS: You don't think their foot-dragging on this issue will again end up with legislation?

DR. CRANFORD: That's the major problem. Can we do it at a grassroots level?

THE REV. JULIAN BYRD (Hermann Hospital, Houston, Texas): Recently, the American Hospital Association's organization for governing boards sponsored four workshops and a major address calling for hospital trustees to take the initiative in establishing ethics committees in their institutions. Representatives of institutions from 28 states and Canada attended that conference. Stuart Wesbury, President of the American College of Hospital Administrators and a contributor to this text, was, I believe, something of a catalyst for that workshop and symposium. I would say that the AHA is suggesting that its member institutions establish ethics committees.

MR. GIBBONS: If they're telling their trustees that, they are not telling it publicly because of the *Infant Doe* case. I asked them if they wanted the regulation. I also asked them if they backed the President's Commission on that issue, even though the Commission says something positive about review. They would not come out and back ethics committees.

DR. CRANFORD: These are rapidly accelerating events, and what you and he are saying is not incompatible if you know these organizations. I am pleased by what you have shared with us.

MONSIGNOR CHARLES P. KOSTER (St. Vincent's Hospital, Indianapolis): Having recently seen the movie *The Verdict*, I have recognized that there the doctors and the lawyers, and to some extent the clergy, took it in the neck, or whatever you want to say. I really feel it would be good for any IEC to include at least one or two members of the nonprofessional community, perhaps one businessperson and maybe one understanding person from the labor community. This would protect the professionals and preserve the viewpoint of the patients. I believe that the broader-based constitution of an ethics committee would in the long run serve to give greater credibility and insight to the committee.

DR. JACKSON: I was on the task force that set up our IEC at University Hospitals in Cleveland and I was the lone voice favoring lay representation on that committee. The vote was nine to one. I actually thought that the business community and the labor community both ought to be represented. I think that is coming, and if we do not want the courts involved in each individual decision, we're going to have to have a broad-based committee that can withstand the scrutiny of the courts—in terms of both its process and its composition.

UNIDENTIFIED SPEAKER: My question is for Mr. Capron. I understand the concept that you presented this morning in terms of the one unique role for the IEC. My question is: If the IEC does not first participate in the education role or guideline-development role, how does it establish the credentials and the basis for being involved in decision review?

MR. CAPRON: I suppose to a certain extent it depends upon the people who are on the committee and the respect that they command within the institution. My understanding, based on Stuart Youngner's study[12] and other data that we have, is that most of these committees are evolving, and they may well begin with a core of people who were already, like the Ron Cranfords or the John Parises, playing a consultative role as individuals. They then gather other people to them; they form a group that's going to give a seminar, and then they say, "We really could have an ongoing relationship in this institution." But I don't think that you have to have those other functions to have what is valuable and unique about the IEC. That is, the other functions can be performed by other groups. Certainly, if a group is capable of doing all those things, and if the other functions don't undermine, in the particular setting, the role regarding decision review, it does not matter whether you call it decision review or something else. Whatever it is that you are doing, how well you do it within the institution is largely going to determine your credibility—not whether you hold seminars, not whether you sit and hold hands when people are going through agony.

UNIDENTIFIED SPEAKER: My concern is that to be credible when you participate in decision review, you have to first go through a self-educational and developmental phase.

MR. CAPRON: I agree, but the educational function must be broader than just a well-informed committee. In the decision-review role, the IEC does not begin to exhaust what the hospital as an institution and its members also need in terms of education and psychological support and so forth. I just think that one committee is not likely to do all those things successfully.

DR. CRANFORD: The experience of well-established hospital ethics committees around the country has been similar to yours: that one has to perform the educational function in combination with consultation, in combination with development of guidelines, in building credibility, and then get into retrospective review of cases, which I think ultimately will be an important function. To do that initially would destroy the credibility of the committee. I think my experience, and the experience of hospitals around the country, has been similar to what you're saying now.

MR. CAPRON: My only comment on that is that we are not speaking as scientists when we say that. We're speaking as perhaps journalists or anecdotists. We do not have the comparative basis. We really do not know whether we are better off relying on a John Paris alone or you alone or on committees, or whether a committee that has educative functions is better than one without those functions. We just don't have a controlled study. So maybe this is like a lot of social experiments that occur in nature; we look back and try as best we can to examine them and make sense of the experience. We have an opportunity here, and I believe the NIH should be supporting research in this area. Since we are talking about things that mean a lot not only for the health of people, but also for the expenditure of funds on treatment, why not support research to see whether certain forms of committee functioning do a better job than others in improving the quality of decision making?

NOTES

1. Imbus, S. H., Zawacki, B. E., *Autonomy for Burned Patients When Survival Is Unprecedented*, NEW ENGLAND JOURNAL OF MEDICINE 297(6):1308–11 (August 11, 1977).
2. Youngner, S. J., Jackson, D. L., *Family Wishes and Patient Autonomy*, HASTINGS CENTER REPORT 10(5):21–22 (October 1980); Jackson, D. L., Youngner, S. J., *Patient Autonomy and "Death with Dignity,"* NEW ENGLAND JOURNAL OF MEDICINE 301(8):404–8 (August 23, 1979).
3. *See* Paris, J. J., ch. 16 of this text.
4. Burke, E., *Second Speech on Conciliation with America. The Thirteen Resolutions* (March 22, 1775), reprinted in THE WORKS OF EDMUND BURKE, vol. 2 (Charles C. Little and James Brown, Boston) (1839) at 15–85.
5. JOINT COMMISSION ON ACCREDITATION OF HOSPITALS, ACCREDITATION MANUAL FOR HOSPITALS, 1983 ed. (Joint Commission on Accreditation of Hospitals, Chicago) (1982) at 151–54.
6. PRESIDENT'S COMMISSION FOR THE STUDY OF ETHICAL PROBLEMS IN MEDICINE AND BIOMEDICAL AND BEHAVIORAL RESEARCH, DECIDING TO FOREGO LIFE-SUSTAINING TREATMENT: ETHICAL, MEDICAL AND LEGAL ISSUES IN TREATMENT DECISIONS (U.S. Gov't Printing Office, Washington, D.C.) (March 1983) at 7 [hereinafter referred to as DECIDING TO FOREGO TREATMENT].
7. 48 Fed. Reg. 9630 (March 7, 1983), *superseded by* 48 Fed. Reg. 30,846 (July 5, 1983).
8. DECIDING TO FOREGO TREATMENT, *supra* note 6, at 160–70.
9. Head v. Colloton, 331 N.W. 2d 870 (Iowa 1983).
10. M. C. HOWELL, HELPING OURSELVES: FAMILIES AND THE HUMAN NETWORK (Beacon Press, Boston) (1975).
11. VA. CODE § 54–325.8:1 *et. seq.* (1983) (Virginia Natural Death Act).
12. Youngner, S. J., *et al.*, *A National Survey of Ethics Committees*, in DECIDING TO FOREGO TREATMENT, *supra* note 6, at 443–49.

# Section II

# Descriptive Summaries of Extant Institutional Ethics Committees

Thomasine Kushner and Joan M. Gibson, Editors

## INTRODUCTION

This section is intended to provide the reader with a sense of the diversity and individualistic approaches exhibited in extant, functioning institutional ethics committees. The institutions selected represent the full spectrum of health care facilities and are located in a variety of geographical areas.

The individual reports were prepared by members of the various committees according to a set of questions sent to them by the editors. That outline follows.

# Outline for
# IEC Descriptive Report

*Committee Name.*

*Institution Name and Address.*

*Reported by* (please give your name and mailing address).

*Committee Chair:* If the preparer of this report is not the chairperson of your committee, please give his or her name, title, and address.

*Position within Institution:* What is the place of the committee in the institutional flow chart? What is the nature of the institution (i.e., religious affiliation, university-teaching hospital, etc.), and what does the institution perceive to be its role in the community?

*History:* Year formed; what prompted formation of the committee? Who (in terms of roles and functions) acted as impetus in its formation? What were the sources of support and resistance, and has this changed?

*Membership:* Composition by profession, total members, and how selected. If you do not have a community representative, have you considered adding one? Are meetings attended by persons other than committee members? If so, under what circumstances?

*Referrals to Committee:* Who can and who in fact does bring cases before your committee?

*Functions:* What are the functions of the committee and are they specifically outlined?

    a.  Educational

    b.  Policy-making

    c.  Consultative

*Operations and Activities:*

    a.  If the committee is educational, how is this accomplished—e.g., through seminars, grand rounds?

    b.  If the committee is policy-making, describe and send copies of any guidelines or by-laws developed by the committee.

    c. If the committee is consultative, is it advisory or binding? How many cases is the committee consulted upon per year? How are clinical emergencies handled? How are decisions reached, by majority vote or unanimity? Does the committee function prospectively or retrospectively?

*Success and Strengths:* How does the committee define success, and what have proven to be the particular strengths of the committee?

*Problems:* What problems have there been? What changes do you envision? Do you have any words of advice for other committees?

*Comments* (please limit to one typed page).

# BIOETHICS STUDY GROUP

St. Joseph Hospital
1000 W. Stewart Drive
Orange, California 92668

*Reported by:* Sister Corrine Bayley, C.S.J.
Director of Bioethics
Sisters of St. Joseph of Orange Health System
440 S. Batavia
Orange, California 92668

*Committee Cochairs:* Peter Hinckle, M.D.
1201 W. La Veta Avenue
Orange, California 92668

Deborah Pugh, R.N.
Director of Clinical Education
St. Joseph Hospital

*Position within Institution:* The committee is an administrative committee, responsible through the administrator to the board of trustees. The institution is a Catholic community acute care facility that is highly visible and has an excellent reputation.

*History:* The committee was formed in April 1979, as the result of a growing need to discuss issues not adequately addressed in any other forum. The physician director of medical education and a consulting bioethicist were the proximate causes for the formation of the committee. We made a list of those we thought would be interested in membership, secured support from administration, and away we went. There was very little, if any, overt resistance. Support among those asked to serve as members was high. Support has continued to be high (among those who are aware of the committee's existence). Some resistance has surfaced recently as the committee has begun to serve in a consultative role. This is seen by some as an encroachment on traditional (administrative) decision-making prerogatives.

*Membership:* The committee consists of approximately eight physicians, eight nurses, and eight others (social workers, pastoral care representatives, administrative representatives, an ethicist). We do not have, nor have we considered adding, a community representative. Meetings are attended by persons other than committee members if their presence is helpful for a case under discussion or if someone wishes to address the committee for some other reason.

*Referrals to Committee:* Anyone can bring a case before the committee. Cases have been brought by physicians, nurses, social workers, and pastoral care representatives.

*Functions:* The description of our group includes the following purpose statements:

1. to serve as an advisory body for administration and professional staffs on the formulation of policies and/or guidelines dealing with ethical issues in health care

2. to serve as a resource for the medical staff, nursing and allied health staff, and patients and/or families, in dealing with ethical questions related to hospitalization and treatment

3. to provide a forum for the discussion of ethical and moral questions and concerns that arise in the hospital but that are not dealt with systematically by any other committee

4. to encourage and assist in the development of educational programs for medical, nursing, allied health, and administrative departments in the areas of ethics and Catholic philosophy

5. to provide an opportunity for members of the committee, and through them other hospital staff, to become sensitive to and knowledgeable about ethical issues in medicine and the life sciences

*Operations and Activities:* The group has held seminars, workshops, and small group discussions. We have found it particularly helpful to hold educational sessions to explain and discuss any guidelines we develop. We have not used grand rounds as such, but plan to establish such a program in the near future.

The committee has just completed a second revision of do-not-resuscitate guidelines (see Section III of this text). We are in the process of revising our guidelines for foregoing other types of life-prolonging treatment. We have also developed a set of guidelines to assist health professionals in dealing with ethical dilemmas (see Section III of this text).

Consultation by the committee is advisory and not binding. The number of cases referred to the committee in the last few months has increased dramatically; however, prior to that time, there were fewer than half a dozen per year. Clinical emergencies are handled by gathering together as many members of the committee as can be located. We are still struggling with whether we should take a vote or simply try to arrive at consensus without the formality of a vote. The committee functions prospectively if asked to consult on a case; however, there are no types of cases at the moment which require committee review, either prospective or retrospective.

*Success and Strengths:* The committee defines success by the fact that we are now meeting twice a month instead of once a month! We have also written some guidelines and are working on some more that we feel will be helpful to the hospital at large. The particular strengths of the committee seem to be the high interest level among its members, as well as their growing ability to recognize and work through an ethical issue.

*Problems:* The committee has recently run into some problems regarding the manner of scheduling "emergency" consultation meetings. Although the committee members and both physicians who brought the cases stated that they had been assisted by the committee's deliberations, others in the hospital were troubled by the fact that a meeting was called. Questions arose such as: Should all cases like this go to the committee? Why do we need a committee now when we never had one before? How many people should be present for a consultation, and who is authorized to call it? Hopefully, questions such as these will not hamper the consultative function of the committee in the future. It would also be unfortunate, in the opinion of this writer, if consultations became "over-formalized," i.e., voting procedures, quorum, etc. The purpose of a consultation is to assist the presenter in thinking through an ethical dilemma. In that sense, the *process* is as important as the product and should not be hampered by too many structures and procedures. However, we should make it more clear to the hospital at large what the consultative function of the committee is and how it can be of assistance.

# MEDICAL ETHICS COMMITTEE

University of California Hospitals and Clinics
University of California, San Francisco
San Francisco, California 94102

*Reported by:* Albert R. Jonsen, Ph.D.
Professor of Ethics
Health Policy Program
University of California, San Francisco
1362 Third Avenue
San Francisco, California 94102

*Committee Chair:* Albert R. Jonsen

*Position within Institution:* The University of California, San Francisco, is a campus of the University of California devoted entirely to health sciences education. It comprises schools of medicine, nursing, dentistry, and pharmacy, as well as a graduate division in biomedical sciences. There are on campus three hospitals and many outpatient clinics, all under a central administration. In addition, the San Francisco County Hospital and the San Francisco Veterans Administration Medical Center are staffed by University of California faculty.

The Medical Ethics Committee has an independent status, and is responsible directly to the president of the medical staff, who is an ex officio member.

*History:* The Medical Ethics Committee was instituted in 1978. It was originally a subcommittee of the Patient Care Committee, one of the standing committees of the medical staff. Its members were appointed by the president of the medical staff. Albert R. Jonsen, professor of ethics, was appointed Chair. The impetus for the formation of the committee was the suggestion of the medical officer on campus, a state official who reviews the cases being reimbursed by Medicaid (MediCal). He proposed that claims that patients should be treated in ways and for lengths of time that departed from medical standards be reviewed by an "ethics" committee and that he would be disposed to accept the judgment of such a committee.

In 1980, there was a general reorganization of the administration and medical staff structure of UC Hospitals and Clinics. At this time the Medical Ethics Committee assumed its independent status. Dr. Jonsen remains Chair.

*Membership:* Current membership consists of:

Six physicians (three internists, one pediatrician, one surgeon, one psychiatrist)

Two nurses (one from nursing administration, one staff nurse)

One social worker

The hospital chaplain

Hospital legal counsel (an employee of the university)

One representative of hospital administration

One ethicist

There is no community representative, nor has consideration ever been given to including one (there are community representatives on other committees, such as the IRB).

*Referrals to Committee:* The initial request for a consultation may come from a variety of sources, e.g., house officer, nurse, or social worker. The committee chair then contacts the attending physician who may then, according to stated policy, initiate a formal consultation request.

*Functions:* The Medical Ethics Committee serves two functions: policy-making and consultative.

*Operations and Activities:* With regard to policy making, the committee continues to develop guidelines for the hospital. For example, we have developed a no-code policy and, more recently, a response to the "Baby Doe" issue.

Much of the committee's activity revolves around its consultative function. If the issues in a case are particularly difficult or if there is disagreement about the appropriate resolution even after consultation, a meeting is summoned. This is done at the discretion of the chair. After discussion and, if necessary, further investigation, a recommendation is formulated. The committee has not, to the best of my recollection, ever taken a formal vote on a recommendation; majority opinion or consensus is usually achieved. Dr. Jonsen communicates the recommendation to the appropriate person, who is usually the president of the medical staff, the administrator of the hospital, or the chief of the service.

About two or three cases are referred each month; only a few of these need to be brought to full committee attention. On average, the committee will review three cases each year. Each of these seems to require a minimum of two meetings. On occasion, the committee invites the principals to meet with it. Other than that, non-committee members do not meet with the committee. Also, as a matter of policy, the committee does not meet with patients or family, since it believes this communication is the responsibility of the attending physicians. On occasion, one or another member will do so to gain necessary information.

*Success and Strengths:* During its four years, the committee has worked with relative success. Success is defined as the ability to reach agreement about how to proceed on a case and the willingness of responsible parties to accept the committee's advice. We do not know of any overt resistance to the committee's existence or operation; in fact, we have occasionally been gratified by the reaction to its work. We do not, however, know how many cases do not come to our attention and we do note, from time to time, cases that might have been dealt with more reasonably and efficiently had they come to our attention. The fact that there is a full-time faculty member in medical ethics, whom it consults regularly on many services, means that certain cases that might be material for committee consideration are dealt with informally at the staff level. In the judgment of the chairperson, the committee is well accepted and the members work together well.

*Problems:* Because of conflicting time commitments, there is always the problem of getting the full committee together.

Advice: The most important advice we would have for other committees is to devise a working methodology, a way of analyzing cases with clarity and consistency.

# ETHICS AND HUMAN VALUES COMMITTEE

Rose Medical Center
4567 East Ninth.Avenue
Denver, Colorado 80220

*Reported by:* Fredrick R. Abrams, M.D.
Director, Center for Biomedical Ethics
Rose Medical Center

*Committee Chair:* Fredrick R. Abrams

*Position within Institution:* The committee is a standing hospital committee which reports its activities to the Medical Executive Committee. The institution, Rose Medical Center, is a community hospital which is nonsectarian, but endowed in great part by the Jewish community of Denver. It has a formal affiliation agreement with the University of Colorado Medical College, and is well established as a teaching hospital with interns and residents rotating through the university and Rose Medical Center in the majority of the programs. The institution perceives its role as a community hospital which provides excellence in medical care. It is primarily a specialist hospital which is trying to build its family practice program to equal status. The feeling is that its affiliation with the medical college enhances the quality of the medicine practiced there.

*History:* The committee was organized on an ad hoc basis as part of the Critical Care Coordinating Committee, because of a series of issues which had puzzled the staff. These issues culminated in the case of an elderly patient, irreversibly and terminally ill with recurrent respiratory failure. This patient was put on artificial life-support systems and placed in the ICU, where she expired several weeks and more than $30,000 later. This case caused concern over whether it was proper to allocate an ICU bed to a hopelessly ill patient who might tie the bed up for weeks and who would use up diminishing resources. At the urging of several of the nurses involved in intensive care, the chairman of the department of critical care was instrumental in organizing the committee. It became apparent to the members of the committee that much of their discussion and opinion were "gut reactions," and they felt that some formal preparation and discussion would enable them to begin dealing with these problems with a common language and more sympathetic listening to people with opposite views. A staff physician with a particular interest in biomedical ethics had studied independently, following initial training at a National Endowment for the Humanities Seminar and an intensive refresher course at the Kennedy Institute for

Ethics at Georgetown University. He was called upon to lead seminars and discussions in some formal philosophical approaches to these problems and, using Beauchamp and Childress's book, *Principles of Biomedical Ethics*, took about a year to educate the members of the committee. At the end of that year, they adopted a recommended format, and began petitioning the medical executive board of the hospital for acceptance as a standing hospital committee. Subsequently, the Medical Executive Committee endorsed the Ethics and Human Values Committee as an official hospital standing committee which reports to the Medical Executive Committee.

*Membership:* Committee membership consists of:

Seven RMC physicians (two ob/gyn, one neonatologist, one cardiologist, one internist, one pulmonary specialist, one general surgeon)

Nine RMC nurses (one mental health specialist, one enterostomal therapist, one surgical ICU nurse, two hospital ward head nurses, one critical care coordinator, one patient representative, two staff nurses)

Two RMC chaplaincy clergymen (one Jewish, one Protestant)

One RMC attorney (the vice president for legal affairs)

Four social workers (two members of the RMC department of social service, two clinical social workers in private practice)

Two RMC laypeople (one cabinet shop foreman from the department of engineering, one administrative secretary from the department of emergency medical services)

We have spelled out what we feel would be an ideal, but not mandatory, composition:

> The committee would optimally be composed of an equal number of physicians and nurses, including three physicians, preferably from different fields, plus one resident or intern; three nurses, preferably from different fields, plus one student nurse; one clergyman from the in-house chaplaincy staff; one member of social service; one administration or finance representative; one secretary; and one other representative of the community from outside the hospital. Pharmacy, finance, legal, and/or other community resources may be called upon in consultation.

Our current community representatives are both social workers who are independent and not employed or affiliated with the hospital. They were elected to membership on the committee after being proposed and recommended by persons who were already on the committee. Meetings may be attended by persons other than committee members. They are open to all hospital staff, and would be open to others, but currently its activities are not publicized widely enough to attract other people interested in attending. We have had guests from other institutions who wished to see how we function.

*Referrals to Committee:* Staff and family may bring cases before the committee. In fact, we have had no family members use the committee directly in consultation, although members of the committee in their capacity as, for example, chaplain, social worker, or mental health nurse, have consulted and been consulted by family members. Cases have been brought before the committee, both prospectively and retrospectively, by physicians, nurses, and other members of the staff.

*Functions:* The functions of the committee, so far, are educational, policy-making, and consultative. Aside from the educational role played each time there is a consultation, the educational arm has been split off and designated as the Center for Biomedical Ethics at Rose Medical Center. This group has sponsored programs which included outside speakers and panelists. They have presented medical grand rounds with ethical interpretations of medical cases, with involved medical staff, as well as members of the Ethics and Human Values Committee, participating. The Center has put on two programs on the structure and function of hospital ethics committees in Colorado, with the assistance of staff at the University of Colorado Health Sciences Center and the members of the Ethics and Human Values Committee. In addition, ongoing short courses involving the essentials of biomedical ethics have been taught to Rose Medical Center staff, as well as other professionals in the community from other institutions, and interested laypersons. Two sets of evening seminars have been held, and our participants have included libertarians, judges, lawyers, representatives of every medical specialty, physicians' assistants, Ph.D. professors, philosophers, and interested laypersons. We have used the public television series "Hard Choices" as the basis of two of our series. Several of our participants have returned to their institutions to establish ethics committees. One- to two-hour programs on the subject of biomedical ethics have been given to interested groups and to help with the formation of discussion groups and/or active committees. These have been primarily in hospitals, but programs have also been given in religious institutions and adult education courses. Our primary target has been postgraduate education groups for practicing members of the health care community.

*Operations and Activities:* Our policy-making duties at the hospital administration's request have included a study of the ethical issues involved in a proposed *in vitro* fertilization program and a hospital policy for "do-not-resuscitate" orders. The project that the committee is currently studying, in conjunction with the department of newborn medicine at this institution, is a procedure for evaluating and determining the treatment of severely compromised newborns. Although it was somewhat tangential to our usual concerns, a group of physicians brought the issue of hospital support for a nuclear freeze to the Ethics Committee as well, for a hospital position statement. Although we have discussed this issue, whether or not our committee will make a statement or recommendation is still under advisement.

Finally, our consultative role has been undertaken in specific cases. Initially, these were brought to the whole committee, but it soon became obvious that the committee in its entirety could not be called together on such short notice, and the second mechanism that was determined was to divide ourselves into a group of five "on-call" members who would act as swiftly as possible, and certainly in no more than 24 hours, depending on the urgency of the consultation. We have functioned only as a forum, and we do not offer an "official" opinion. Therefore, we do not vote on issues. The committee functions both prospectively and retrospectively. Although we probably get only one or two official calls per month, many members of the committee are called upon for informal discussion in the elevators and hallways. Further, by consciousness raising, many questions which might formally demand committee involvement have now been settled by careful consideration with the involved parties, without the need for "outsiders" to guide the discussion. By continuing ongoing education we envision that many of the reasons for which we were called formally will no longer exist.

*Success and Strengths:* The committee defines success much as we have noted above in answer to questions 7 and 8; that is, by raising the consciousness of the staff to ethical issues, much more consideration is given to problems of competency, consent, promotion of autonomy, etc. Because many of the questions have been brought out into the open, the friction between medical and nursing staff has decreased significantly, because of willingness to ask and to answer questions involving patient care. I believe the particular successes of the committee and the Center for Biomedical Ethics have been in raising consciousness and maintaining an awareness of ethical issues by ongoing programs and classes. We are aware of cases which have been redirected by staff members asking, "What do you think the Ethics Committee would say about this projected course of therapy?"

True success would be such widespread knowledge and sensitivity that there would be no need for such a group.

*Problems:* The problems the committee has experienced have primarily revolved around the apprehension that it would be a "policing" group, rather than a forum for advice and discussion which serves as a mechanism to decrease tension rather than increase it. I believe this is the first point to get across to resistant staff when an ethics committee is being proposed. It should be made clear that no one is going to take over patient care or force it into a particular mold. Usually a grand rounds in a medical format to which the physicians are accustomed (bringing out the ethical issues, the choices, and the dilemmas with sympathy toward those involved in both giving and receiving care) is a good way to introduce the value of this type of program in a hospital. The most important advice I would give to any institution which is planning on organizing such a committee is to take a reasonable amount of time as a discussion group, and to invite people who are knowledgeable in formal methods of ethical consideration to address them. It is necessary that they become aware of ethics as a separate discipline which is being applied to a particular context. There is value in learning the basic language of ethics, and in reviewing competing ethical theories with special emphasis in comparing and contrasting deontological and utilitarian approaches to problems. Basic ethical principles such as autonomy, beneficence, nonmaleficence, and justice, as discussed by Beauchamp and Childress, should be a minimal curriculum. Care must be taken that the group does not get lost in philosophical reflection, because it is a fact of medical life that decisions often must be made quickly and with incomplete information. A logical guideline for making ethical decisions in a hospital environment necessarily includes:

1. Whose decision is it to make?
2. Who else is involved in the case, and what are the values?
3. What are the medical facts in the case?
4. What principles and values apply, and what is their priority?
5. Who else on the medical staff or the auxiliary services can add information?
6. What are the unique human variables of the case which may put weight on a particular side of the decision when there are conflicting values?

# AD HOC COMMITTEE ON CLINICAL ETHICS

Northwestern Memorial Hospital
Superior Street at Fairbanks Court
Chicago, Illinois 60611

*Reported by:*  Norma Shaw Hogan
Director, Patient Representative Department
Northwestern Memorial Hospital

*Committee Chair:*  John Serkland
Chaplain Coordinator of Clinical Ethics
and Research
Department of Pastoral Services and Education
Northwestern Memorial Hospital

*Position within Institution:* The Clinical Ethics Committee remains an ad hoc committee and is not on the institutional flow chart, per se. Northwestern Memorial Hospital is a not-for-profit, tertiary care, teaching hospital affiliated with Northwestern University Medical School. The institution perceives its role in the community as: (a) providing comprehensive health care to the sick and injured; (b) mobilizing community support and resources to serve the comprehensive health care needs of the community; (c) providing medical and educational programs; and (d) encouraging research to save human lives, minimize suffering, and improve health services.

*History:* In 1976 one of our attending nephrologists found himself in an ethical quandary when a patient who desired abortion counseling was referred to him. Because this physician has strong moral views about abortion, he decided to seek advice but could find no readily identifiable resource within the institution. He therefore called Holy Name Cathedral and requested the services of an ethicist. Although there was no ethicist at the cathedral, the rector not only gave expert and practical advice, but he referred the physician to a priest/lawyer who is an expert in the broad field of ethics.

   The question that the physician posed to the rector caused several of the priests to question their ministry to the ministers of health and prompted the rector to ask the physician if other care givers would be interested in a forum to discuss ethical issues. After ascertaining interest, the priests offered the Archdiocese Auditorium and their support for the proposed discussion.

   Publicity was disseminated via word of mouth and an informal memo to "interested parties." When the scheduled workshop convened, instead of the 20 or 30 attendees anticipated, there was standing room only and the auditorium was packed. The physician and priests coordinated several other meetings which also played to full houses.

The high level of interest in ethical issues encouraged the physician to approach the executive vice president of the hospital to discuss institutional sponsorship of ethical workshops. The executive vice president was enthusiastic and agreed it would be appropriate to have the workshops at the hospital. The physician coordinated several more workshops. Participation and assistance came from nurses, social workers, therapists, and technicians. Physician involvement was minimal.

After successfully launching the first workshops, the physician passed on his coordinating role to the director of pastoral services and education because he wanted to assure the multidisciplinary attraction of the topics discussed and at the same time institutionalize the committee's role and sponsorship.

Coincidentally, some students at Northwestern University Medical School were approaching the dean with a request for a course on medical ethics as a means of helping them with the dilemmas they faced. The course was established in 1977 with the priest/lawyer as the principal facilitator.

After the first educational ethics program at the hospital in 1977, physician support increased. At the present time physician participation varies, depending upon time available for meetings and interest in the program being presented. There has been some interest expressed in changing the status of the committee from ad hoc to standing, but the issue has never been fully addressed.

*Membership:* The Clinical Ethics Committee is chaired by a chaplain; thus, the department of pastoral services and education coordinates and administratively supports the work of the committee. Because the director of pastoral services and education reports to the executive vice president of the hospital, institutional support for the committee is implicit.

Committee membership includes physicians, nurses, social workers, chaplains, administrators, and the director of patient representatives. Membership is attained by invitation and nomination by a committee member. There is a core group of approximately 20 people who divide into subgroups to plan programs, recruit members, suggest topics, etc. The committee meets at least 12 times a year.

Discussions about community representatives on the committee have generated a negative response from the majority and have been tabled as "an idea whose time has not come."

From time to time, staff who express an interest in a particular topic are invited to attend the planning meetings to explore the feasibility of participating in workshops.

*Referrals to Committee:* Members of the committee propose subjects for discussion and bring individual cases before the committee. Usually these cases are illustrative of dilemmas that care givers have faced and are cases which are presented, retrospectively, at clinical ethics grand rounds.

*Functions:* The Ad Hoc Clinical Ethics Committee's function is educational.

*Operations and Activities:* Seminars/grand rounds/workshops using the case presentation method seem to be the favored format. A list of topics presented to date is as follows:

> Ethical Problems of the Terminally Ill Patient
> "Do-Not-Resuscitate"/The Right to Die
> A Patient's Right to Medical Care vs. Cost
> Ethical Considerations of Human Investigation
> Who Shall Survive?
> Rights and Responsibilities—The Right to Refuse, Deny, or Mandate Medical Treatment
> Aggressive Prolongation of Life vs. Cessation of Medical Treatment
> Who Controls the Health Team's Ethics?
> Informed Consent—Moral and Legal Perspectives
> Ethical Considerations in the Care of the Premature Infant
> Free Care, Research, and Education within NMH: Who Pays for It; Who Should Pay for It; Who Should Decide?
> The Last Available Bed
> When Ought an Attending M.D.'s Word to Be Final?
> Informed Consent: Medical Tokenism/Legal Necessity
> Challenges to Confidentiality

The high visibility of committee members has resulted in individual members receiving "ethical consultation" requests from care givers and practitioners. We have not kept records on how many times a year each individual committee member has been consulted.

*Success and Strengths:* Attendance at the workshops/seminars/grand rounds has been excellent. We are pleased that nursing and medical students, house officers, nurses, technicians, patient representatives, social workers, and administrators are dependable workshop attendees, but distressed at the proportionally small numbers of attending physicians who show up.

We view as a particular strength the diversity of professions represented on the committee, the passion of the members, and the energetic, informal discussions that result from differing points of view.

The respect and esteem of the committee members for each other are also viewed positively.

*Problems:* We define our major weakness as the lack of financial resources. Appropriate funding would enable the committee to have at least half-time administrative and clerical help to coordinate all committee activities and offer honoraria to outside speakers.

The American Society of Law & Medicine conference in April 1983 has generated discussion as to whether the committee's focus should remain educational, with committee members continuing to be available to give advice, being alert to opportunities to discuss relevant issues, and providing a forum for addressing timely issues, or if the committee should tackle the consultative, decision-making role.

*Comments:* Interest in the subject of clinical ethics is exceedingly high at NMH. DRGs, the proliferation of literature, media exploitation, consumer awareness, and technology are causing an increasing number of dilemmas for all of us. Our focus has been mainly educational because there are so many issues that generate the need for more information. The committee has periodically surveyed the attending medical staff and house officers to ascertain interest in topics and willingness to serve on the committee and/or present information. The response has been gratifying.

A new survey asking for suggestions for topics for the committee's all-hospital ethics rounds will be sent out shortly, as we are concerned with maintaining awareness of currently relevant issues.

We are also seeking means of becoming more closely aligned with the medical school ethics course.

Recommendations from the President's Commission report cause us to question the appropriateness of formalized ethical consulting and the feasibility of decision making for committees such as ours. An informal reading of physicians in this institution suggests that they are vehemently opposed to a committee having decision-making powers.

The majority of the members of the committee sit on other hospital/medical staff committees which make policy. Some have expressed the opinion that because of that involvement and input, the role of institutional ethics committees should be confined to education.

# ETHICS COMMITTEE

Hebrew Home of Greater Washington
6121 Montrose Road
Rockville, Maryland 20852

*Reported by:*  Shulamith Weisman
 Director of Human Services
 Hebrew Home of Greater Washington

*Committee Chair:*  Rotates every two years

*Position within Institution:* The committee is one of 20 committees of the board. The president of the board chairs its meetings, thus making it a very high status group. It is considered an honor and a privilege to be a member of the committee. The institution is a long-term care nursing home. A short-stay rehabilitation and respite care unit is part of the facility. We believe that we are the first nursing home to have such a committee. The Hebrew Home is a 550-bed sectarian (Jewish) facility. The mission of the Hebrew Home is to care for the frail, infirm members of the Jewish community of greater Washington in consonance with the Jewish value of caring for the old and sick.

*History:* In 1979, the medical director approached the president of the board, asking him to form an ethics committee. As the director of human services, I volunteered to staff the committee. The committee was constituted as a board committee and was appointed by the president of the board.

*Membership:* The members of the committee are:

A forensic physician who teaches law and medicine in several universities

An ethicist who is an adjunct professor at the Georgetown University Kennedy Institute of Bioethics

A physician who is *not* part of the Home's medical staff

A judge

Two rabbis

The Home's medical director

The director of nursing

The director of social work

The executive director

The director of human services

The president of the board (a lawyer)

Two vice presidents of the board (both lawyers)

*Referrals to Committee:* Any member of the staff and any family member can bring cases before the committee. In fact, the medical director, social workers, and family members all have brought cases to the committee.

*Functions:* At first the committee was educational, but now it is largely consultative. We have found that each case is so different that we could not set policies down on paper, although in a more subtle way policies have been shaped by the discussions and consensus reached at meetings.

*Operations and Activities:* The committee's deliberations are advisory. During the first two years of the committee's existence there were about four cases each year. In the past year there has been only one case. When a case is brought to me as the person staffing the committee, I arrange a meeting within 24 hours. A real clinical emergency would be sent to the hospital and would not be handled within the nursing home. Decisions are reached by consensus. The committee usually functions prospectively; however, there have been some cases which were reviewed retrospectively.

*Success and Strengths:* The committee defines its activities as successful if the proceedings are perceived as being in the patient's best interest, and as having given comfort to the family members who have experienced emotional conflict, and if the Home's staff physician has been helped to work through an ethical dilemma. The strengths of the committee are that it has broad representation—i.e., many points of view and many disciplines are well represented. The fact that the Home views itself as a Jewish institution adds to its commitment to serious study of its ethical responsibilities. The management of the Home is very supportive of the committee.

*Problems:* The problems of the committee are:

a. The staff physicians are reluctant to bring cases to the committee since they see it as a loss of control and they do not like a committee "looking over their shoulders" and asking "Why?"

b. One very strong, articulate individual is sometimes able to sway the group (not the same individual at each meeting). Rabbis tend to have more influence than other members. Doctors are the next most influential group.

*Comments:* A paper entitled "An Ethics Committee Deals with Moral Dilemmas in a Long-term Care Facility," written by Shulamith Weisman, is available upon request.

# ETHICAL ADVISORY COMMITTEE

Holy Cross Hospital
1500 Forest Glen Road
Silver Spring, Maryland 20910

*Reported by:* Thomas R. Golden, L.C.S.W.
Psychiatric Social Worker
Holy Cross Hospital

Mimi Rigney, R.N., M.B.A.
Staff Development Instructor
Holy Cross Hospital

*Committee Chair:* Leonard Wisneski, M.D.
Holy Cross Hospital

*Position within Institution:* Holy Cross Hospital of Silver Spring, Maryland, is one of nine hospitals sponsored by the Sisters of the Holy Cross. The Ethical Advisory Committee is a board committee and, as such, is responsible to the board of directors of the hospital.

*History:* In early 1982, in response to the desire of the Holy Cross Health System, the Ethical Advisory Committee was established in order to ensure an ongoing mechanism to deal with ethical/moral issues.

*Membership:* Emphasis has been placed on maintaining diversity in the main committee's composition. The membership now includes:

The hospital president

Six physicians

The director of human resources administration

An ethicist

Two pastoral care representatives

One social worker

Seven registered nurses

The vice president of nursing

The patient representative

*Referrals to Committee:* Issues can be brought to the committee by any patient, physician, or hospital staff member. The procedure for this is to contact one of three members of the executive committee of the Ethical Advisory Committee (hospital president, committee chairman, ethicist).

*Functions:* The purpose statement which describes the function of the committee is as follows: "The Ethical Advisory Committee exists to assure the preservation of fundamental attitudes, values, and patterns of human response consistent with the congregation's philosophy on health care."

The committee began as a task force in early 1982 and developed six proposed goals:

1. educate the hospital community
2. promote interdisciplinary exchange and dialogue
3. provide a basis for unity by bringing various disciplines together
4. preserve patients' rights
5. serve as an advisory committee for hospital policy
6. advise the Holy Cross Health System about ethics issues that have systemwide applicability

The full committee first met in June 1982, and began discussing the above goals and defining issues which needed to be addressed. The committee compiled a list of priority issues and divided this list into five distinct categories:

1. no-code policy and living wills
2. termination of life support and quality of life
3. obstetrical concerns
4. patients' rights and hospital philosophy
5. employee relations

For each category a subcommittee was established, composed of Ethical Advisory Committee members as well as members of the hospital and medical staffs. The subcommittees have generally become the starting point for discussion of specific topics, and their reports, recommendations, or requests for further direction are then brought back to the main committee.

*Operations and Activities:* The committee perceives itself as a resource to the hospital community. One unique aspect of this role is the committee's focus on ethical issues as they relate to the employee in the workplace. The committee has also facilitated hospital-wide seminars on ethics issues, and has served in an advisory capacity in developing hospital policy on no-code guidelines. It is currently working on other guidelines, including a patients' rights document.

The committee addresses issues both prospectively and retrospectively. It is expected that the number of issues that are presented will increase as a result of greater awareness of the committee and its purpose.

*Success and Strengths:* We were greatly aided in getting started in the right direction by having the help of a professional ethicist who continues to act as a consultant.

*Problems:* Although we have moved ahead in forming a no-code policy and are currently working on a patients' rights document, the committee feels frustrated in that progress sometimes seems slower than we would like. In this regard, we have found subcommittees particularly helpful in focusing on specific topics and getting work done.

# MEDICAL MORAL COMMITTEE
(may change to Ethical Committee)

St. Joseph Hospital
215 North Avenue
Mt. Clemens, Michigan 48043

*Reported by:* Sister Ann Fidelis
 Ministry Effectiveness
 St. Joseph Hospital

*Committee Chair:* John Corbett, M.D.
 Orthopedic Surgeon
 225 South Gratiot
 Mt. Clemens, Michigan 48043

*Position within Institution:* The committee is an administrative or hospital committee, as opposed to a medical staff committee. Our institution is a 468-bed acute care facility sponsored by the Sisters of Charity. We see ourselves as an acute care facility mainly, but are developing programs in psychiatry and substance abuse.

*History:* The committee was begun in 1977 at the direction of Sister Anna Suttman, president of St. Joseph Hospital, largely in response to the Karen Quinlan case. The key people were: Akemi Takekoshi, M.D. (neurologist); Sister Anna Suttman; and Sister Ann Fidelis, nurse clinician. We had and still have administrative support. The greatest fear seemed to be that the committee would be telling the M.D.'s what they could or could not do. This group is beginning to see the committee as a strong support.

*Membership:* Our committee has been very large and is interdisciplinary. We are restructuring and membership will include:

 Four to five physicians

 An ethicist

 The CEO

 A pastoral care representative

 A social services representative

 A nurse

 A consumer

 A risk management representative

 A quality assurance representative

The medical director

A patient representative

A ministry effectiveness representative

The members serve by invitation of the CEO. We will probably have 16 members. A consumer or community representative has been a member the last four or five years. The meetings (five scheduled/year) are open but observers have no vote. They may, however, question or comment. This seems to be one way of meeting the interest of personnel.

*Referrals to Committee:* In the past it was the physician who referred cases, usually at the suggestion of the nursing staff. We hope to allow anyone to bring cases to the committee, including patients or their surrogates.

*Functions:* Our committee functions in all three areas: education, policy making, and consultation. We hope to strengthen all areas in the proposed restructuring.

*Operations and Activities:* In the past we have cosponsored with the Department for Continuing Medical Education (CME) a yearly program. We hope to be able to do our own in 1984. We also plan to prepare short articles on our work or on issues, to be published in the physicians' newsletter and in the employee newsletter. Policies and proposals on "Guidelines for Withholding Cardiopulmonary Resuscitation," "Guidelines in Brain Death," "Guidelines in Irreversible Terminal Illness," and "Guidelines in Irreversible Coma" are available upon request and are reprinted in Section III of this text. We have served in a consulting role which is advisory only. We average two cases per year. Emergencies have been handled by calling two to three members of the committee who have been in the facility at the time. This activity is evolving. Decisions are reached by unanimity, and the committee functions both pro- and retrospectively. Usually the case is discussed after the fact as a part of regular meetings.

*Success and Strengths:* We measure success by the acceptance of our policies and in terms of prognosis if we arrive at an amiable agreement and outcome.

*Problems:* Advice: Be flexible. Address issues current to your own institution. Expect change. Develop membership in work and task committees from outside the regular committee. Have the chairperson be a member of the regular committee.

*Comments:* The growth and development of our committee have been very rewarding. When we started we knew little, but through workshops and reading we grew. Our structure has changed four times since 1977. In September 1983 our committee became smaller. We meet regularly five times per year (January, March, May, September, and November) for about 1–1½ hours. Work committees meet as often as needed to complete their tasks. Over and beyond the goals of the committee we develop goals for each year for the five meetings. We have always addressed issues that are pertinent to our institution. Early on we addressed brain death and patient rights. These are reviewed yearly. Requests for tubal ligations are not addressed by this committee, but another committee from ob/gyn handles these.

In trying to satisfy the desires of many persons to be involved, over the last few years we have:

1. opened regular meetings to anyone interested.
2. developed work or task committees from outside the regular committee. The chairperson is always from the committee. We look for persons with expertise in the area being studied.
3. sponsored with CME a program open to all interested parties.

We are considering doing an institution-wide survey of attitudes and needs with the plan to develop a task force to study identified problems. From the task force we will develop a policy-making committee.

# BIOMEDICAL ETHICS COMMITTEE

Hennepin County Medical Center
701 Park Avenue South
Minneapolis, Minnesota 55415

*Reported by:* Ronald E. Cranford, M.D.
Associate Physician in Neurology
Hennepin County Medical Center

Paul A. Goldstein, M.S.W.
Associate Director, Social Service Department
Vice Chairperson, Biomedical Ethics Committee
Hennepin County Medical Center

*Committee Chair:* Ronald E. Cranford

*Position within Institution:* The Biomedical Ethics Committee is a medical staff committee responsible to the medical director of the hospital. Our institution is an academic, acute care county hospital with a university affiliation.

*History:* Prior to the formal establishment of the Biomedical Ethics Committee in November 1979, the hospital had established a Thanatology Committee in 1971. From the time of its inception through November 1979, the Thanatology Committee was involved primarily in issues related to death and dying. During the course of its work, the committee members became increasingly aware of recurrent bioethical themes that covered a broad range of ethical dilemmas, and not just termination of treatment issues. It was also felt there was a need to move the committee in a new direction, and make it more representative of the views and interests of the facility. While the Thanatology Committee normally consisted of about 10 members, the new Biomedical Ethics Committee was expanded to the present complement of 23 members. It is felt that the current committee is more representative of the general views throughout the hospital.

*Membership:* A number of the original members of the Thanatology Committee became members of the Biomedical Ethics Committee. There are currently 23 members, which represents only a small increase since the inception and the actual selection of members in late 1979 and early 1980. These include ten physicians, seven nurses, two clergy, two social workers, one administrator, and one respiratory therapist. It was important to have a variety of specialties represented. For example, the physicians come from neurology, family practice, emergency medicine, psychiatry, surgery, pediatrics/emergency medicine, laboratory medicine, internal medicine, and nephrology; there is also a house officer who is a resident in medicine. Similarly, the nurses include a nursing supervisor and representatives from medicine, surgery, pediatrics, neonatology, nephrology, and nursing administration. Currently, there are no outside people serving on the committee. In 1982 a temporary decision was made not to have anyone from outside the institution as a member of the committee. We have discussed this issue a number of times, and while we feel there are positive reasons for having an outside person on the committee, we have not yet chosen to take that step. At times invited guests, usually administrators with a particular interest in ethical issues, have attended our meetings.

*Referrals to Committee:* Procedures for requesting a committee meeting have never been formally written. Although we have had numerous consultations and requests for advice and consultation, no one has formally requested a meeting of the entire committee. Current practice dictates that referrals be generated by medical staff and directed to any member of the committee. Access to our committee is an ongoing topic of discussion, with a subcommittee currently addressing this issue. The general consensus is that, over time, referrals will be encouraged by any health professional within the institution and ultimately by families and patients.

*Functions:* We have never formally stated in writing the exact purposes of our committee, but have decided to proceed in an informal manner. This was deliberate on our part because we felt that if we became too formal in our stated objectives and procedures, there might be negative repercussions from the physicians and others in the hospital who have a misunderstanding of the functions of this type of committee. We felt that to formalize our objectives prematurely might be counterproductive to the work of our committee. Bearing in mind the desirability of informality, we decided early on in the deliberations of the newly formed Biomedical Ethics Committee that our primary functions were, in order of priority, education, policy making, and consultation.

*Operations and Activities:* The committee has sponsored a number of educational sessions over the years. As an example, the Biomedical Ethics Committee and United Theological Seminary have cosponsored a course in biomedical ethics, usually given every other year since 1975. This course uses a case-based approach, with the vast majority of cases being ones in which our ethics committee served in consultation. We have found the case-based approach a valuable teaching tool for health care professionals. We have also brought in various outside speakers of national prominence to interact with interested groups in the hospital (a partial list includes Don Harper Mills, Robert Veatch, Les Rothenberg, Harmon Smith, Melvin Krant, and Eric Cassell). Another important educational activity for our committee involves acting as a general source of information by maintaining a current bibliography and by having available reprints of key articles which are sent to station personnel after consultations on related cases.

Our committee has formulated policies on brain death and do-not-resuscitate orders. After policies were formulated on these two issues, our committee recommended to the executive committee that they be adopted as hospital policy, and the executive committee approved this action. As the criteria for brain death have been updated and modified, our committee has made further recommendations to the executive committee that these newer standards replace the old standards, and the executive committee has always approved our recommendations. Currently the standards for the determination of death are those established by the medical consultants to the President's Commission for the Study of Ethical Problems in Medicine and Biomedical and Behavioral Research. The current standards for do-not-resuscitate orders are similar to the standards adopted by the Board of Trustees of the Minnesota Medical Association in January 1981. Thus, the brain-death standards reflect national standards and the do-not-resuscitate standards reflect statewide standards.

The Biomedical Ethics Committee acts in an advisory and consultative capacity, although a specific written policy on this matter has never been formulated. Typically, referrals come to the committee through the following process. The physician calls a member of the committee who, after conferring with the physician, evaluates the case and decides whether he/she can resolve the issue at hand or needs to call in additional members of the committee for consultation. If a resolution cannot be achieved after a meeting between the staff requesting the consultation and the representative group of the committee, the case is then referred to the committee as a whole. The overwhelming majority of consultation requests are resolved to the satisfaction of requesting staff at this level. It is not nearly as common for the entire committee to meet on a consultation.

We feel it is unwise to handle every consultation in the same stereotypical fashion. As our committee has gained experience and credibility, the number of requests for consultations to individual members of the committee has also increased. These requests range from written requests to informal telephone calls. Some consultations have been handled in a matter of hours, others require days, and there have been some consultations which extended over a period of months. Indeed, one consultation lasted almost two years. Our committee does not normally issue a written response because it is felt that most of these cases can be handled most effectively in an informal manner through our interactions with the medical and nursing staffs. However, physicians are requesting with more regularity that opinions or comments from the committee be written into the patient's medical record.

We continue to find that the most effective way to educate our hospital staff is through the consultation process. In consulting we are, at the same time, educating people in working with ethical dilemmas. In a clinical sense it becomes obvious that there are recurrent themes for which policies and appropriate methods of decision making need to be developed. We believe subcommittees are useful in providing mechanisms, procedures, and other means for decision making in the frequently faced issues such as: "How should the hospital staff respond when respirator-dependent patients who are alert and competent request termination of treatment?" A subcommittee task force can make an important contribution by making specific recommendations as to appropriate medications to give. We have never formally decided how our committee would make a decision. This remains a controversial matter. Again, our committee felt it was better in the early stages to evolve in a more informal fashion and we have tried to do this without formulating rigid procedures which might be counterproductive in the long run. Thus, we have never tackled head-on exactly how to make a decision on extremely controversial cases, but have elected instead to handle these by informal discussion without pressing for a formal vote. We recognize that there is a definite possibility that in the future there will be controversial cases with a wide variety of opinions among the committee members and that it may be necessary to decide whether our committee will take a position by simple majority or unanimous vote. It seems likely that our decisions will represent a simple majority while allowing for dissenting opinions from individual committee members.

*Success and Strengths:* The success and strengths of our Biomedical Ethics Committee can be measured by the benefits derived by nurses, physicians, and patients' families. The nurses who are closest to ethical dilemmas, especially in terms of the feelings and suffering of the patient and family, have received support from the ethics committee in terms of hospital and educational activities, sessions on individual units, and consultation in numerous cases. Physicians have been educated on the ethical dimensions of their decisions and have also benefited from support, advice, and consultation on critical dilemmas. Also, our committee has facilitated the dialogue between the hospital staff and the patients' families, and the committee has consulted with patients' families when requested to do so. Members have expressed satisfaction with the progress of the committee and the positive effect that it has had on the care of patients and the needs in the institution. However, we feel that as ethics committees evolve over the years, as their importance becomes increasingly recognized, as the committee members gain experience and credibility, and as the hospital becomes more aware of the committee's functions, we will have an even greater impact.

*Problems:* The problems we face are undoubtedly shared by other committees. There is an important practical limitation to the functioning of the committee in that committee members, no matter how interested and committed, simply do not have enough time to devote to building up the required expertise for the committee to fully develop its potential. Also, there continues to be a misperception of the role of our committee. Many physicians at the hospital—and this is not unique to this institution—still view the committee with a great deal of apprehension and skepticism because of their concern that the committee will usurp the traditional decision-making prerogatives of the medical profession.

# BIOMEDICAL ETHICS COMMITTEE

University of Minnesota Hospitals and Clinics
420 Delaware Street S.E.
Box 39, Mayo Memorial Building
Minneapolis, Minnesota 55455

*Reported by:* Diane Bartels, R.N., M.A.
Associate Director of Nursing
University of Minnesota Hospitals and Clinics

*Committee Cochairs:* Diane Bartels

Theodore Thompson, M.D.
Director of Neonatology

*Position within Institution:* The committee is a standing committee of the Medical Staff-Hospital Council. We are a university teaching hospital. The institution perceives its role in the community as a leader in teaching, research, and service; in furthering knowledge; and in providing for the needs of the citizenry.

*History:* The committee began in 1975 as a Thanatology Task Force appointed by the Hospitals' general director and chief of staff. It was established as the Thanatology Committee upon recommendation of the Task Force Report of 12/1/75. Its focus has changed as the needs have changed, and in 1982 the focus was broadened and the name was changed to Biomedical Ethics Committee.

*Membership:* Current committee membership includes:

> Eight physicians in areas such as psychiatry, neurosurgery, surgery, neonatology, and oncology
> Eight registered nurses
> One chaplain
> One social worker
> One hospital administrator
> One professor of mortuary science
> One patient relations representative
> The hospital attorney

We are looking into the possibility of adding a community representative. Persons other than committee members attend meetings as appropriate, to give information, perspective, or recommendations to the committee.

*Referrals to Committee:* Any employee of the Hospitals and Clinics could bring cases before our committee. To date, however, we have had only committee members present cases to stimulate discussion rather than becoming involved in decision making. (In the early days, the Thanatology Committee was involved in consultations and the committee is considering offering this service again.)

*Functions:* The functions of our committee are as follows:

1. educational—develop a data base for ethical issues, advancing technology, and its implications; sponsor talks; provide a network of communication for local, state, and national seminars

2. policy-making—keep abreast of pending legislation and its possible consequences

3. consultative—not a formal function at this time, but offering this service is being discussed

*Operations and Activities:* The committee has sponsored speakers and programs in the past. It is hoped that our subcommittee on education will work on this in the future. The grand rounds possibility is being discussed as a valuable tool for learning. While the committee is not formally a policy-making committee, we did work extensively on the Hospitals' "do-not-resuscitate" policy, and we do so for other policies where appropriate. The committee is strictly advisory. As mentioned in #7 above, the committee is considering a broader consultative role.

*Success and Strengths:* The committee will be convening in the near future to assess precisely what they see as success (i.e., accomplished goals). The particular strengths at this time are a quiet growth in credibility and visibility as a nonthreatening, supportive body.

*Problems:* Problems of the committee include time limitations for discussion, and keeping the committee focused yet flexible to respond to the needs of those it serves. Words of advice: Start quietly, slowly. Develop your own member bonds and expertise. Keep a multidisciplinary membership.

# BIOETHICS COMMITTEE

Mount Sinai Hospital
2215 Park Avenue
Minneapolis, Minnesota 55404

*Reported by:* D. Gay Moldow, B.S.N., M.S.W.
Human Services Department
Mount Sinai Hospital

*Committee Chair:* D. Gay Moldow

*Position within Institution:* The committee is chaired by the coordinator of the Care in Crisis Program. The Care in Crisis Program is administratively under the human services department, which is administratively under the vice-president for human resources (flow chart available upon request). Mount Sinai Hospital has a Jewish affiliation and is a university teaching hospital. Its community role is to provide health care to the entire community, regardless of religion, in a private, non-profit, multispecialty acute care facility with multiple ambulatory services.

*History:* The present committee was established in 1980. A multidisciplinary committee called the Care in Crisis Committee had been in existence since 1975. That committee originated to educate hospital staff about specific psychosocial and physical care needs of dying patients and their families. Psychosocial counseling for patients and families and chemotherapy for patients were also initiated. A third function of this committee was bimonthly care conferences attended by committee members, hospital staff, patients, and families. Care of dying patients was planned, and communication between hospital staff, patients, and family members was enhanced. In 1980 committee members representing medicine, nursing, social service, hospital administration, clergy, and the law requested a change in emphasis in the committee, to include more education regarding bioethics, more policy formation, and more consultation to hospital staff regarding bioethical issues.

The committee has received hospital support since 1975. Some old resistance was based on the concern that the committee was advocating active euthanasia. Since the change in name and function in 1980, the committee has received no specific resistance. However, it has taken approximately two years to educate committee members so that they feel qualified to handle consultations. Thus, publicity about the renamed committee has been in circulation for only about six months, and requests for consultations have only recently begun to be received again.

*Membership:* The Bioethics Committee has 25 members, including:

Five physicians (three internists, one neurologist, one director of medical education)

Nine nurses (director of nursing education, two head nurses [surgery, ICU/CCU], three assistant head nurses [neurology, outpatient, oncology], one professor of nursing from the University of Minnesota, two staff nurses [medicine, ICU])

Three social workers (one committee chair, two medical/surgical)

Two administrators (vice president of patient care services, director of human services)

One patient representative coordinator

Two clergy (One Jewish, one Lutheran)

One ethicist, also a Unitarian clergyperson

One theology student

One attorney

Membership selection: Existing committee members periodically discuss committee membership and make recommendations. Chair or members invite candidates to join.

Community representatives: We do not have a "consumer" community representative. However, our attorney, three clergy members, theology student, nurse academician, and one physician are all community members. We feel their expertise greatly enhances our committee.

Committee attendees: Hospital professional staff attend to present and discuss their ethical concerns, e.g., should we be subjecting patients who are going to nursing homes to die to the placement of gastrostomy tubes? When consultations are requested of committee members, hospital staff and patients and families meet together. Anyone can attend a meeting.

*Referrals to Committee:* Anyone can bring a case to the committee. Usually physicians, nurses, and social workers initiate consultations. The departments of rehabilitation and respiratory therapy have also requested assistance.

*Functions:* Education, policy/guideline development, consultation.

*Operations and Activities:* In-Hospital Education—The committee holds conferences/workshops for nurses and physicians, although interested others have attended. Examples of topics include "Ethical-Legal Issues in Nursing Care of the Terminally Ill" and "DNR and Living Will Guidelines" and their use within our institution. We also sponsor all-personnel hospital conferences (e.g., "A Jewish Perspective on Death and Dying" and "Hospital Ethics 1973–Hospital Ethics 1983," using the audiovisual feature "Please Let Me Die"). Orientation lectures on the Bioethics Committee and on current bioethical issues are given to all new nursing personnel and all medical students who rotate through the institution. The committee also sponsors in-service education to nursing units throughout the hospital and one-to-one education for hospital staff when discussing patient care.

Community Education—A multidisciplinary group from the committee makes presentations to community organizations and conferences (e.g., "Eight Weeks to Live, Eight Weeks to Die," a University YMCA course, and an Oncology Social Workers Conference). Consultations are offered to other hospitals who are originating programs, usually by the committee chair but sometimes by a group of committee members. The committee chair also coordinates a Minnesota Institutional Ethics Committee Network that meets bimonthly using an educational forum, and writes and edits a bimonthly IEC publication.

Policy Formulation—The committee has developed do-not-resuscitate and living will guidelines (available upon request; also see Section III of this text). To date these guidelines have not become hospital policy. The DNR guidelines are widely used, with little resistance currently. The committee intended to draft a DNR policy in the fall of 1983. Living will guidelines were recently approved, but education regarding usage is not completed at this time.

Consultation—The committee's role is definitely advisory. However, because committee members are well educated with respect to legal issues, physicians have recently looked to the committee for a "current standard of medical practice" kind of legal approval before taking definitive steps, e.g., withdrawal of life-support equipment.

We have received three official requests in the past 12 months. Committee members, especially nurses, social workers, and the patient representative coordinator, have informally consulted/educated on approximately 15–20 additional cases.

We have received no requests for emergency consultation. Individual committee members provide consultation in emergency situations, e.g., a social worker counsels family/staff in not initiating life support during a surgical crisis. A care conference involving the entire committee, hospital staff, and family members usually takes several days to arrange.

We do not vote. Conferences have been led by either the referring physician or the committee chair and a conclusion is not drawn until the leader feels that all questions and concerns have been raised. A sound consensus has, to date, always been possible.

Originally, both pro- and retrospective cases were seen bimonthly. During our two-year self-education hiatus, most cases have been retrospective. Also, because the issues are so "hot" and staff persons so involved, cases are often best used retrospectively for educational purposes. Recently, we have received requests for consultations on specific, current ethical issues.

*Success and Strengths:* We define success as staff attending workshops, conferences, etc., and putting the knowledge and skills they learn to work. For example, we have seen significant growth in the sensitivity and skill of ICU nurses in handling ethical issues. Hospital staff have also utilized the DNR guidelines we drafted.

Strengths have been the long-standing participation on the committee by a multidisciplinary staff: physicians, attorney, nurses, social workers, clergy. Community professionals who volunteer their time have been very helpful.

*Problems:* Problems include not enough time to educate committee members and hospital staff, and current funding cuts that limit the time the chair has for self-education and creative leadership of the committee. Advice: It's slow going at first, so don't get frustrated. Develop supportive administrators, attorneys, and physicians—i.e., the "power people" in the institution.

# ETHICS COMMITTEE

Morris View Nursing Home
West Hanover Avenue
Morris Plains, New Jersey 07950

*Reported by:* Rev. Dale H. Forsman
Chairman, Morris View Nursing Home
Pastor, Chatham United Methodist Church
460 Main Street
Chatham, New Jersey 07928

*Committee Chair:* Rev. Dale H. Forsman

*Position within Institution:* The Morris View Nursing Home Ethics Committee is appointed by the chairperson on the board of social services at its annual meeting. The full board confirms this appointment. The board administers Morris View Nursing Home, a fully Medicaid nursing home of Morris County, N.J. We see ourselves as the primary Medicaid nursing home of the county; our services are supplemented by private nursing home admissions of Medicaid-eligible patients.

*History:* The committee was formed by the Morris County board of social services, then welfare board, in 1976, in response to the New Jersey State Supreme Court decision of March 31, 1976, *In the Matter of Karen Quinlan, an Alleged Incompetent.*

This decision was made by the board of social services immediately upon the admission of Karen Ann Quinlan to our facility. The board acted to meet the qualifications as established by this decision. It did so without hesitation and with legal consultation.

*Membership:* The committee is currently composed of the following persons: two physicians, an attorney, a clergyperson, a social worker, a board member, and a citizen member. Seven members comprise the full membership of the committee. The chairperson of the board of social services, the director, and the medical director of Morris View have attended meetings of the committee when policy decisions or other such business suggested their attendance. Generally speaking, the meetings are closed to others.

*Referrals to Committee:* Thus far, only the family and representatives of the Karen Quinlan family have brought a case to the committee.

*Functions:* To this point, the committee has interpreted its role in the most limited fashion, that of its relationship to this one particular case. Our word was, I suppose, binding in that case. We consulted with the physicians, and if we agreed, the treatment of choice could move forward.

*Operations and Activities:* While no other persons have brought cases to us, one of the doctors on the staff has presented two particular concerns to us and these are about to come under consideration. First, he has raised the whole question of the "living will." He wonders if patients who are fully cognizant when entering the nursing home, and who have little or no family, might not be given the opportunity to express their feelings about the kind of care they wish, when and if the situation of critical care becomes operative later in their stay at the nursing home. Second, he wants us to explore the whole subject of the use of tube-feeding methodologies as a matter of routine choice. He apparently sees the potential for more and more persons being kept alive in nursing homes through the use of nasogastric tube feeding. We have not yet met to work on these issues, but are primed to do so. This will not be in a policy-making role, but in a consultative capacity only.

*Success and Strengths:* Keeping in mind that our purpose for being was originally tied to a particular case, success can be counted in terms of: (a) our continued existence and current discussions to expand our role and (b) the growth that has taken place in our membership with regard to the disciplines represented.

*Problems:* Because our committee was originally formed with such a specific mandate, we have been extremely conservative in nature. We have met, nearly annually, to review/reorganize. However, we have never moved away from this one particular case to discuss other issues or questions.

It appears that we may now be more ready to discuss other issues regarding the treatment of patients at our home. I believe that this discussion will remain in the area of general care questions, rather than specific cases. The current practice of the committee is, and will continue to be, to make itself available to the staff of the nursing home for consultation. I do not know what we would do if a family or patient requested our services.

# MEDICAL ETHICS COMMITTEE

St. Joseph Hospital
400 Walter N.E.
Albuquerque, New Mexico 87102

*Reported by:*   Father Edward J. Dietrich
Chaplain, St. Joseph Hospital
Vice Chairperson, Medical Ethics Committee

*Committee Chair:*   Joan M. Gibson, Ph.D.
Adjunct Associate Professor
University of New Mexico School of Law
and Medicine
1516 Rita N.E.
Albuquerque, New Mexico 87106

*Position within Institution:* The Medical Ethics Committee is a committee of the hospital and not of the medical staff. It flows from the local board of trustees.

*History:* Previously named the Bioethics Committee, this committee first met on November 25, 1975. Its suggested purposes included education, interdisciplinary dialogue, unity, channels of communication, and legislative watchdog. The committee met four times in the first 12 months. In 1977 the committee was assigned the responsibility of an institutional review board, and soon established the Human Research Review Committee as a subcommittee. The Bioethics Committee was established as a result of the interest of the Sisters of Charity, but did not meet from 1978 through 1981—apparently because of its size, scheduling difficulties, and lack of specific direction. The committee was reorganized in 1982 and has met almost monthly since then.

*Membership:* Current members include:

> Three physicians (nephrologist and president of the medical staff, senior vice president of medical affairs, and chief of gynecology section)
>
> One attorney
>
> President of St. Joseph Hospital
>
> Chancellor of the Archdiocese of Santa Fe
>
> Hospital chaplain
>
> Ethicist and professor of philosophy
>
> Director of pastoral care

Hospital counselor/therapist

Vice president of nursing administration

Senior vice president for corporate affairs

*Referrals to Committee:* Concerns and issues are brought before the committee by any and all members.

*Functions:* Education and policy making.

*Operations and Activities:* Educational activities include seminars and medical staff and hospital newsletters. Policies that are being developed include definition of death, policy and protocol for tubal ligation, support for amendments to New Mexico's right-to-die legislation, preparation of supportive-therapy-only (STO) policy, hospital DNR policy. This ethics committee participated in the preparation of the report by the President's Commission for the Study of Ethical Problems in Medicine and Biomedical and Behavioral Research.

*Success and Strengths:* The committee sees itself as having progressed in its willingness to deal with problems within the hospital, the medical profession, and the legal and political arenas. It enjoys openness and freedom of expression, professional competency, and interest—perhaps even excitement—on the part of committee members.

*Problems:* The committee recognizes the need to identify a specific purpose and direction, and to assign projects and homework to those members who are interested and willing to accept them.

*Comments:* Our earlier experience with the Institutional Bioethics Committee shows that a focused and clear statement of purpose, along with a willingness and interest to keep up in the area, will create an effective committee. We have found that there is a great deal of material both in the public domain and in the hospital environment to provide us with a considerable amount of material with which to work. Educational programs seem to be the most difficult for us to get into, but I suspect that this is due to the amount of work that we are doing in other (i.e., policy-making) areas. Our first educational program is scheduled for early 1984. It is our opinion that we ought to avoid individual case responsibility where at all possible. To date, no case referrals have been received. We believe that a working dialogue between patient (where possible), family, nursing staff, doctors, and pastoral care representatives is the best solution when dealing with individual problems and decisions.

# BIOETHICS COMMITTEE

The Hospital of the Albert Einstein College of Medicine
Division of Montefiore Medical Center
1825 Eastchester Road
Bronx, New York 10461

*Reported by:* Joan H. Bilder
Associate Director of Nursing
Cochair, Bioethics Committee
The Hospital of the Albert Einstein College of Medicine

*Committee Cochairs:* Joan H. Bilder
Martin Cohen, M.D.
Director of Medicine

*Position within Institution:* The Bioethics Committee was approved as a standing committee of the medical council and its purpose defined as follows:

> To act as a forum for ethical considerations in critical care decision making and for the diffusion of responsibility in clinical perspectives in patient care; and to recommend to the medical council, when indicated, consideration of policies related to medical ethics.

The Hospital of the Albert Einstein College of Medicine, a division of Montefiore Medical Center, is a 431-bed university teaching hospital. Clinical specialties include pediatrics, obstetrics and gynecology, rehabilitation, medicine, and surgery, a neonatal intensive care unit, a hemodialysis unit, an intensive care unit, and a coronary care unit.

*History:* The committee was formed in 1975 and its first meeting was held on December 4, 1975. The need for such a committee became apparent as questions arose in meetings and clinical areas relating to hospital practice that could not be formally referred anywhere in the hospital for resolution or discussion—for example, problems of life-sustaining measures. Dr. Maurice Greenhill, director of psychiatry, and Joan H. Bilder, associate director of nursing, requested approval from the medical council of the hospital to become a standing committee of that organization.

*Membership:* The composition of the committee has varied since its inception. The first chairman was Dr. Maurice Greenhill, director of psychiatric service, and he recruited members through departmental directors. Medicine was represented by an oncologist, a nephrologist, and an internist, and surgery by a cardiothoracic surgeon. There was a pediatric nephrologist and a neonatologist. The director of the anesthesiology department, who was also the director of the intensive care unit, was a member. The associate dean for educational affairs of the College of Medicine was a member. The associate director of nursing, the director of social services, the administrator for patient relations, the chief physical therapist, and another assistant administrator were also members.

Ex officio members were the president of the medical council, the medical director of the hospital, the director of nursing, and the hospital administrator.

Consultants were appointed to the committee from the department of social medicine at Montefiore Hospital Medical Center, the Kennedy Center, and the department of social psychology. A community representative was not on the committee, and this consideration was never addressed.

The membership remained fairly consistent, and there were monthly meetings until June of 1980. Then the chairman became ill and passed away. The committee did not meet again until December 1981, when it was reactivated with the associate director of nursing as cochairperson with the director of medicine. Current membership now includes a neurologist, a radiologist, a psychiatrist, a dentist, a bioethicist, the director of nursing, a pediatric nurse clinician, a critical care nurse clinician, the director of social services, and an assistant administrator. Appointments are also made to ad hoc committees concerning special issues.

*Referrals to Committee:* Cases are brought before the committee after being referred to individual members. They are screened for applicability and then presented. The majority of specific cases are identified by nurses rendering direct patient care, but physicians and social workers also bring cases to the committee.

*Functions:* At the first meeting on December 4, 1975, it was determined that the committee would serve several purposes:

1. The committee's work would be utilized for educational purposes. Residents in medicine, surgery, and pediatrics would be invited to attend.

2. The committee would consider problems related to patient advocacy.

3. The committee would investigate problems of communication between professionals and patients with the intent of attempting to improve them through policy decisions.

4. The committee would discuss problems of life-sustaining measures and absence of no-code criteria.

*Operations and Activities:* The educational role of the committee is confined to members of the committee and the dissemination of information through them. The committee is not policy-making, but does assist in guideline writing as issues are identified, subject to approval and adoption by administration. The committee functions in a consultative advisory capacity, and is not a decision-making body.

*Problems:* Lack of strong visibility; not enough physician-initiated cases.

# BIOETHICS COMMITTEE

Montefiore Medical Center
111 East 210 Street
Bronx, New York 10467

*Reported by:* Alan R. Fleischman, M.D.
           Montefiore Medical Center

*Committee Chair:* Alan R. Fleischman

*Position within Institution:* Montefiore Medical Center is a tertiary care teaching hospital affiliated with the Albert Einstein College of Medicine. It is the major clinical campus for the medical school, as well as being the major tertiary clinical locus. The Bioethics Committee acts as a committee of the president of the Medical Center and reports directly to him.

*History:* The MMC Bioethics Committee was formed in 1977. The committee was initiated by the then president and director of the institution, who sought to establish a group which could be used for consultation on ethical matters by the institution and its administration. A grant by the Philosophers in Medicine Program had brought a half-time bioethicist to the institution; and, with the impetus of some of the leadership of the Department of Social Medicine and Psychiatry, the committee was initiated. The Medical Center has continued to support the salary of the ethicist as well as the expenses of the committee.

*Membership:* The committee consists of 23 members:

Ten physicians (chairman of the committee, a pediatrician/neonatologist; chief resident, Internal Medicine; chief resident, Pediatrics; internist/oncologist; internist/nephrologist-intensivist; surgeon; psychiatrist; internist, Social Medicine; pediatrician; internist/voluntary physician)

Four nurses

Two social workers

Three administrators

One patient representative

Two ethicists

One lawyer (member of the Department of Social Medicine, not the hospital attorney)

There is no specific community representative. The committee has discussed having such, but has elected to consider the patient representative as advocating for the patient community at large. Meetings may be attended by persons other than committee members, upon invitation. Such persons are invited when specific issues relate to their area of expertise or involvement in the institution.

*Referrals to Committee:* The committee primarily serves a policy-making and guideline-writing function and utilizes cases to assist in generalizing institutional ethical dilemmas. Members of the committee, as well as any member of the institution, may bring a case before the committee. No patients or families have been invited to do so, although there are no policies which would preclude their bringing a problem before the committee.

*Functions:* The committee functions primarily as an educational, policy-making, and guideline-writing consultative committee responsible directly to the president of the Medical Center.

*Operations and Activities:* Educational programs have included bedside consultations, seminars, rounds, grand rounds, whole-day conferences, national conferences, and involvement in departmental educational seminars for nurses, residents, and attending physicians.

The committee has helped in establishing guidelines for consent and refusal within the institution, and has discussed "do-not-resuscitate" policies and procedures, policies concerning transfusions, living wills, disclosure to patients, allocation of scarce intensive care unit beds, the utilization of hospital resources for research activities, etc.

The committee has not primarily engaged in consultative clinical activity.

*Success and Strengths:* The committee has gauged success by the institution of its policies and guidelines by the Medical Center.

*Problems:* The committee, at times, has floundered because of a lack of clear direction. It has, at times, become a discussion group rather than a goal-directed committee. Furthermore, I would advise the involvement of bioethicists in an attempt to keep the committee, when engaged in policy writing, within the framework of ethical analysis and not far afield.

# MEDICAL ETHICS COMMITTEE

North Shore University Hospital
300 Community Drive
Manhasset, New York 11030

*Reported by:* William F. Finn, M.D.
1380 Northern Boulevard
Manhasset, New York 11030

*Committee Chair:* William F. Finn

*Position within Institution:* The committee is a special committee of the medical staff. The institution is a teaching hospital of Cornell University Medical School. The hospital is a tertiary care hospital which also has deep roots in the community.

*History:* The committee was founded in 1974 because of the feeling that dying patients and their relatives were not receiving proper treatment. The impetus for information came from two social workers, a psychiatric nurse practitioner, a psychiatrist, and an obstetrician/gynecologist.

*Membership:* Committee membership at present includes eight physicians from different departments of the hospital, a registered nurse, and a social worker. At times in the past we have had community representation, but at the moment we do not. All meetings of the committee are open to anyone. Occasionally the committee goes into executive session on sensitive issues.

*Referrals to Committee:* Any member of the hospital or the community can and does bring cases before the committee.

*Functions:* The committee has been educational and consultative on both patient care and hospital policies.

*Operations and Activities:* The committee organizes a monthly core curriculum lecture in ethics, ideas, and grand rounds; has had several seminars; and two or three times a year has guest speakers from the Hastings Center and nearby universities. The committee has considered guidelines on do-not-resuscitate orders, care of defective newborns, etc. The committee consultations are merely advisory. About ten cases per year are submitted for consultation. Clinical emergencies are handled on an ad hoc basis. It is difficult to consider the consultative aspect of the committee's decisions because the committee feels that its role is merely to explore the ethical options which exist in various circumstances.

*Success and Strengths:* Success is such a nebulous thing that it is difficult to define. However, the committee's decisions are increasingly accorded more respect by influential departmental chairman and members of the medical staff. Problems of committee and hospital policies have been evaluated with an impartial, nonjudgmental attitude.

# CRITICAL CARE ADVISORY COMMITTEE

University Hospitals of Cleveland
2065 Adelbert Road
Cleveland, Ohio 44106

*Reported by:*  Stuart J. Youngner, M.D.
Assistant Professor of Psychiatry
University Hospitals of Cleveland
2040 Albington Road
Cleveland, Ohio 44106

*Committee Chair:*  Stuart J. Youngner

*Cochair:*  Charlene Phelps, R.N.
Associate Director of Nursing

*Position within Institution:* We are a university teaching hospital. The Critical Care Advisory Committee is a committee of the medical council and as such is responsible to the chief of staff and president of the hospital.

*History:* The committee was formed in 1978, prompted by administrative concern following the Karen Ann Quinlan case, coupled with a desire to handle ethical issues in the most optimal way possible.

*Membership:* The committee is composed of 17 members—11 physicians; two nurses; one house officer; one chaplain; one social worker; one hospital administrator. We do not currently have a community representative, but have considered adding one. Members are selected by department chairmen. Meetings can be attended by anyone involved in a case being reviewed—including the patient, family members, clergy, etc.

*Referrals to Committee:* Anyone involved in a case can request a committee meeting. Most meetings are requested by physicians.

*Functions:* The functions of the committee are educational and consultative, as outlined in the formal policy establishing the committee.

*Operations and Activities:* The committee is not policy-making and, at present, the educational aspect is not active. We are operating strictly in an advisory capacity. Each year we review eight to nine cases.

Clinical emergencies are handled by convening the committee within 24 hours of a request. Decisions are reached by consensus. The committee functions prospectively.

*Success and Strengths:* The committee has been particularly helpful as a source of advice and support for physicians.

*Problems:* Committee problems include a lack of attendance secondary to short notice for meetings. We have no advice for other committees.

# MEDICAL MORAL COMMITTEE

United Hospital Center
P.O. Box 1680
Clarksburg, West Virginia 26301

*Reported by:* W. Delma Parris, Chaplain
United Hospital Center

*Committee Chair:* W. M. Walker, M.D.
United Hospital Center

*Position within Institution:* Currently, the Medical Moral Committee is a standing committee of the medical staff and the medical staff is responsible to the board of directors. United Hospital Center is a 380-bed, private community hospital. It is the result of a merger between a Roman Catholic hospital and a United Methodist hospital.

*History:* This committee was first formed in 1976 when plans were being made for a kidney dialysis unit. The dialysis unit never developed and the committee was never utilized. It was resurrected in 1981 when a couple of situations arose in which physicians wanted a consultation regarding termination of mechanical life support. At that time the committee was formed as an ad hoc committee of the medical staff and consisted of three physicians and the hospital chaplain. The hospital chaplain was then asked to develop a protocol for a permanent ethics committee. This protocol was accepted by the executive committee of the medical staff in August of 1982. During discussion of the protocol there was strong support from hospital administration, nursing staff, and those physicians who have a high volume of patients in the critical care areas. There was some resistance from family physicians, particularly older physicians, who felt that the committee might be making decisions for them.

*Membership:* The Medical Moral Committee is composed of three physicians, one nurse, and one member of the chaplaincy staff. At this point, no representatives of the community have been involved with the committee. There has been discussion of inviting a patient's own minister to participate. The protocol leaves it to the option of the committee to invite others to meetings as it is felt necessary.

*Referrals to Committee:* At this point, only the attending physician, a department chairperson, or the chief of staff can bring cases before the committee.

*Functions:* The functions of this committee are purely consultative at this point. Plans are being made for some educational programs. However, the educational nature of the committee has not been spelled out in the protocol.

*Operations and Activities:* The recommendations of this committee are only advisory in nature and are not binding. In the last two years the committee has reviewed about six cases per year. In all of the cases so far, the committee has acted prospectively and decisions have been unanimous.

*Success and Strengths:* This particular committee feels that it has been successful in securing the support of the majority of physicians by operating in such a way so as not to threaten their autonomy in making critical decisions in caring for their patients.

*Problems:* One of the major problems encountered by our committee is that its function is often confused with the function of the Brain Death Committee, which exists only for the purpose of determining brain death. Even though we expect to encounter some problems, we hope that in the near future we will include educational activities.

# CLINICAL ETHICS COMMITTEE

Royal Victoria Hospital
687 Avenue Des Pins, Ouest
Montreal, Quebec H3A 1A1
Canada

*Reported by:* F. J. Tweedie, M.D.
Council of Physicians and Dentists
Royal Victoria Hospital

*Committee Chair:* F. J. Tweedie

*Position within Institution:* The Royal Victoria Hospital, Montreal, is a major teaching hospital of the McGill University Faculty of Medicine, and as such carries out the traditional functions of clinical care, teaching, and research. Over the years it has been at the top level of research funding and specialty development among Canadian hospitals, and aspires to provide the highest quality of tertiary care to the community at large.

*History:* The Clinical Ethics Committee was established in September 1980. It was first proposed by the executive committee of the Council of Physicians and Dentists (medical and dental staff committee), and the need for and possible function of such a committee were discussed at several meetings. It was decided to make it a standing committee of the executive committee, and terms of reference were drafted as follows:

1. to foster the development of ethics in all areas of clinical practice at the Royal Victoria Hospital

2. to periodically establish and review the ethics of clinical practice in all patient care activities at the Royal Victoria Hospital

3. to develop and maintain an institutional definition of death and to assist with the incorporation of this definition into clinical practice at the Royal Victoria Hospital

4. in collaboration with the Ethics Subcommittee of the Research Institute, to ensure adequate review of the ethics of all clinical research at the Royal Victoria Hospital

5. to perform other duties as requested by the executive committee concerning the ethics of clinical practice at the Royal Victoria Hospital

The committee was formed in response to the need to consider ethical issues arising from rapid advances in medical science and technology, plus changing social attitudes, particularly in the last 25 years, with resulting public interest and discussion of ethical-legal concerns.

For many years, larger departments in the R.V.H. doing research projects involving patients have had ad hoc or standing departmental ethics review committees to study and approve research protocols, whether or not this is required by the funding body. In the last two years, such department committees have come under the supervision of the Ethics Subcommittee of the Research Institute, which also convenes IRBs when required. These department committees concerned themselves specifically with research protocols, and were not seen as being an appropriate mechanism for considering the many ethical issues which arise in clinical practice—hence, the need for and formation of the broad-based Clinical Ethics Committee.

As mentioned above, this committee reports to the executive committee, Council of Physicians and Dentists (medical-dental staff) on which also sit the executive director of the hospital, the director of professional services (medical director), and the director of nursing, lending potential for essential discussion, approval, and implementation of recommendations with a minimum of bureaucratic delay.

*Membership:* The membership has been broadly based from the beginning, with representation from medical and nursing staff, social service, the patients' representative, hospital administration and board, theology, law, and the lay community. Consultants in bioethics and philosophy have been named and attend on request. From time to time, other well-qualified persons have been invited to assess the committee—for example, senior physicians from cardiac and surgical intensive care wards were asked to contribute to committee discussion on ethical aspects of life-support systems.

The current membership of the Clinical Ethics Committee is listed below:

> one representative from the department of surgery
>
> one representative from the department of obstetrics and gynecology
>
> one representative from the department of psychiatry
>
> one representative from the department of medicine
>
> one representative from the department of social work services
>
> one representative from the nursing services
>
> one representative from the administration
>
> two representatives from the lay community

one representative from the Faculty of Religious Studies, McGill
   University

one representative from the Faculty of Law, McGill University

*Referrals to Committee and Committee Function:* To date our committee has
functioned primarily as a policy-recommending committee, and individual case problems have not been dealt with to any extent.

However, as a result of current discussions on life-support systems, it can be anticipated that the committee will offer consultative
services on request when difficult ethical issues or persistent disagreements complicate medical decisions. Such requests may arise from the
attending physician, the patient or his/her representatives, or others
involved in the problem, and it is likely that committee opinion will be
advisory rather than mandatory.

*Operations and Activities:* The committee has had discussions on ethical
aspects of life-support systems and DNR orders for the past year, and
shortly expects to have a final draft of guidelines on these subjects.
With respect to the functions of consultation and education, the committee early adopted the philosophy that they would first have to educate themselves and develop a "feel" for ethical issues before they
could presume to consult on problems or educate others. Three years
of discussion on various topics, reading, exchange of information, and
input by knowledgeable members have brought us to the point where it
is felt that the committee could perhaps make a significant contribution
in these areas, and this is now under discussion.

*Successes and Strengths:* The committee would define success of its
efforts in accordance with several parameters. The first element of success is that such a diverse committee is able to reach a consensus on policy matters or difficult problems which are presented. The second is
that they are able to get acceptance of their opinions by the executive
committee, medical staff, hospital administration, and board; and
finally, that approved decisions and policies are implemented in the
hospital.

Basic to these elements of success is the confidence that the work
of the committee and its judgments are identifying, promoting, and
advancing the best interests of the patient in medicine's most trying
problems, and thus contributing to patient welfare.

The strengths of our Clinical Ethics Committee would appear to
be its diversity, the experience of certain members in ethical-legal pre-
cedents and real-life medical problems, and the continuing interest and
progressive education of its members. Among the obvious weaknesses
are lack of follow-up to determine what impact its approved recommendations have had on both hospital functions and clinical care of
patients, and the limited educational benefits accruing from its work.

*Problems and Envisioned Changes:* In the future, we envisage an evolution of our committee function from its present base to give more emphasis to consultation and education, rather than any sharp change in direction. While we average approximately eight meetings per year, it takes time to develop a consensus on major topics with such a diverse membership, and there are no shortcuts. The committee work is therefore slow and deliberate, but no major obstacles have been encountered, and all recommendations have been accepted to date.

# Section III

## Sample Guidelines and Policies

### INTRODUCTION

Section III is a collection of policies and guidelines, issued by a variety of institutions and organizations, that address many of the issues that institutional ethics committees will face—orders not to resuscitate, discontinuance of cardiopulmonary and other life-support systems, the determination of death, living wills, supportive care, foregoing life-sustaining treatment for seriously ill newborns, and the appropriate care of permanently unconscious patients. The guidelines included in this section have been developed at various levels—national, state, local, and institutional. It is important to note that guidelines developed at higher levels must often be modified by individual ethics committees to meet the needs and circumstances of their institutions. A major activity of the local and regional networks of ethics committees that are being developed around the country is the coordination of efforts to develop guidelines that may be applicable to a particular region and its individual institutions.

We encourage the reader first to reflect on the motivations, forces, and interests that gave rise to the awareness that some written policy or guideline was necessary, and then to consider what the guideline actually says. The institution's perspective and situation should be considered, as well as the impact of such factors as state laws, political and religious realities, and medical sophistication.

In the future, institutional ethics committees will undoubtedly be responsible not only for formulating guidelines and policies, but also for educating the staff as to the meaning, scope, and implications of the guidelines; facilitating their implementation; collecting comments and criticisms from hospital staff; and then modifying the guidelines when appropriate. Thus, it is likely that an individual institution may produce several generations of guidelines on a specific issue (e.g., orders not to resuscitate), and it will be the responsibility of the institutional ethics committee to facilitate and lead this dynamic process.

We offer these guidelines as a resource to members of institutional ethics committees who will ultimately be asked to deal with similar problems and, frequently, to develop policies and guidelines for their own institutions. This section is intended to provoke thought and to provide guidance as we seek fair and just solutions to these difficult dilemmas.

# QUALITY OF LIFE

## Opinion of the American Medical Association Judicial Council

In the making of decisions for the treatment of seriously deformed newborns or persons who are severely deteriorated victims of injury, illness, or advanced age, the primary consideration should be what is best for the individual patient and not the avoidance of a burden to the family or to society. Quality of life is a factor to be considered in determining what is best for the individual. Life should be cherished despite disabilities and handicaps, except when prolongation would be inhumane and unconscionable. Under these circumstances, withholding or removing life supporting means is ethical provided that the normal care given an individual who is ill is not discontinued. In desperate situations involving newborns, the advice and judgment of the physician should be readily available, but the decision whether to exert maximal efforts to sustain life should be the choice of the parents. The parents should be told the options, expected benefits, risks, and limits of any proposed care; how the potential for human relationships is affected by the infant's condition; and relevant information and answers to their questions. The presumption is that the love which parents usually have for their children will be dominant in the decisions which they make in determining what is in the best interest of their children. It is to be expected that parents will act unselfishly, particularly where life itself is at stake. Unless there is convincing evidence to the contrary, parental authority should be respected.

---

Drafted June 1981. Submitted as an attachment to the statement of the American Medical Association, dated August 26, 1983, to the Department of Health and Human Services re Nondiscrimination on the Basis of Handicap Related to Health Care for Handicapped Infants, as published 48 Fed. Reg. 30,846 (July 5, 1983).

## NO-CODE GUIDELINES

Medical-Legal Interprofessional Committee,
San Francisco Medical Society and
San Francisco Bar Association

The Medical-Legal Interprofessional Committee, a joint committee of the San Francisco Medical Society and San Francisco Bar Association, established a subcommittee to develop guidelines for no-code procedures in institutions in San Francisco. The subcommittee was chaired by Albert Jonsen, Ph.D., of the University of California, San Francisco. Participating on the subcommittee were representatives from the medical society, the bar association, the West Bay Hospital Conference, the Health Facilities Association, the coroner and the district attorney's office. To date, this report has been adopted as policy by: San Francisco Bar Association; San Francisco District Attorney's Office; San Francisco Medical Society.

The No-Code Subcommittee has reviewed the policies of nine hospitals within San Francisco City and County. It is pleased to note that all general acute care institutions, with the exception of two which are parts of a larger national system (VA and US Army-Letterman), have stated a policy on this subject. However, the committee found considerable diversity in these policies. In light of current legal opinion and ethical considerations, the committee recommends that institutions review their policies for adequacy and accuracy. The elements of a model policy, which meets both legal and ethical requisites, are stated below with commentary. It is the opinion of the committee that every institutional policy should reflect these elements, even though the language and emphasis might be unique to the institution. The issues of primary importance in all policies should be the patient's wishes and medical condition.

1. A statement that "orders to resuscitate" is a standing order in the institution and that this procedure should be initiated unless there is an express order to the contrary.

   *Commentary:* Patients who are admitted to general acute care hospitals are to receive all procedures indicated for the treatment of their admitting diagnosis or complaint. If cardiac arrest occurs during admission, the standard of care requires full resuscitative measures, since this

Reprinted from *San Francisco Medicine*, pp. 9–11 (February 1983), with permission from the San Francisco Medical Society. Dated July 1982.

event will either be unexpected or the anticipated, but undesirable, effect of their condition. Thus, each institution should have procedures for prompt response to this event and the only condition which justifies withholding this response is a written order to the contrary. In certain institutions, such as hospices, the presumption in favor of resuscitation may not be appropriate. However, all institutions providing health care should have an explicit policy.

2. A statement regarding the patient's wishes.

*Commentary:* A competent patient has the legal and moral right to refuse medical treatment, even if it is lifesaving, at any time. Thus, such a patient may exercise this right by requesting "no-code" and this request should, as a general rule, be honored.

If the patient is competent, it is morally incumbent on the physician to inform the patient of the diagnosis of an irremediable condition and to discuss the eventuality of demise by cardiac or respiratory arrest. The patient, in such a situation, should be offered the choice to refuse resuscitation.

Occasionally, the physician may judge that a discussion of this sort would so distress the patient as to render him or her incapable of a rational choice. Such judgment should be reached after thoughtful and sympathetic discussion with colleagues and with the family or friends of the patient. Even if a direct approach to the patient is judged inadvisable, a general discussion concerning the patient's preferences, in advance of the critical situation, is highly advisable.

The medical situation that makes a DNR (Do Not Resuscitate) order appropriate (Section 3) will often be reached only after the patient has lost the ability to comprehend or express his or her wishes. This incapacity should be verifiable by a clinical assessment of mental and emotional status. If the patient has left advance directives, such as the directive to physicians in the California Natural Death Act, these should be honored, according to circumstances.

3. A statement of the medical conditions which should be present to justify an order not to resuscitate.

*Commentary:* DNR orders are appropriately recommended when the patient suffers from a known lethal disease and when further medical treatment of that disease will not, in all probability, revise the course of that disease toward the patient's death. The legal cases which have upheld no-code orders have noted that the condition of the patient should be such that death is imminent as a result of the disease. Thus, the physician makes a judgment that a point of medical futility has been reached and that any sort of intervention would, at best, only prolong the patient's dying. In a condition of such futility, an order to refrain from such stopgap measures is appropriate. Obviously, no medical judgment is absolutely certain, but the physician's experience and accumulated evidence should lend high probability to the determination that further medical treatment for the condition and resuscitation are useless in seeking the goals of medical care, such as restoration of health or satisfactory function. Thus, a policy should contain a phrase such as, "irreversible and irremediable condition," "imminent death," etc.

4. A statement regarding the role of family or close associates.

*Commentary:* In many situations, patients will be incompetent to participate in a choice. They will often be surrounded by family or friends. There are, at present, no legal grounds to require consent for DNR orders from such persons, unless one of them has been appointed legal guardian or conservator.

However, good clinical practice requires a thoughtful and compassionate discussion with them. In addition, family and friends may be able to provide evidence of the patient's wishes, expressed to them at an earlier time. Such evidence, either verbal or written (particularly in the form of the California Natural Death Act), while it must be carefully evaluated in the circumstances, can support the physician's recommendation not to resuscitate.

If there is disagreement among family members, or between family and physician, consultation should be sought as mentioned in paragraph 7.

5. A statement regarding the entry of the DNR order in the patient's record.

*Commentary:* All general acute care institutions in San Francisco now require the physician to enter the DNR order in the record. This practice, formerly avoided on the basis of fear of liability, is now universally recommended. The order and its reasons, together with comments about discussion with patients, colleagues and family, is, in fact, the best defense against liability. In addition, the order allows all who are responsible for the care of the patients to act with unanimity in this situation and avoids confusion and uncertainty. It is reasonable, also, to require some regular review of the order, should conditions change unexpectedly. The extent of regular review should be determined by the institution in a prudent and reasonable way.

6. A statement about the scope of the order.

*Commentary:* An order not to resuscitate refers strictly to the practice of cardiopulmonary resuscitation. When a patient is "full code," the entire range of procedures, as stated in Standards for Cardiopulmonary Resuscitation, (*JAMA 1980; 244:453*) should be followed. If the physician wishes to issue limited orders, these should be stated explicitly rather than in such cryptic and confusing terms as "partial code," "slow code," or "chemical code." Thus, if for some reason cardiac massage and ventilatory efforts are desirable, but intubation and pressors are not, this should be stated explicitly in the order.

Further, a DNR order does not imply a change in other clinical procedures. Thus, a patient receiving artificial ventilation or intravenous nutrition would continue to be so treated until these procedures are explicitly discontinued, and a "no-code" patient, who develops an infection, would be given appropriate antibiotics unless *there is a specific order not to do so.*

Finally, the modality of care subsequent to DNR order should be expressed. Namely, that all efforts to provide comfort and relief of pain will be provided. This is, of course, the highest obligation of health care professionals once their obligation to save life and restore health is extinguished by the inevitability of death.

7. A statement regarding the obligation of various persons responsible for the care of the patient.

*Commentary:* Physicians are obliged to inform others who are responsible for care of the patient about the decision not to resuscitate. The written order is only one part of the communication necessary in this case. In order to provide the best care for the patient, all who are responsible for the care of the patient should clearly understand the order and its rationale. These persons have the right to clear, definitive and written instructions. In addition, if there is a disagreement about orders, there should be an opportunity to resolve differences.

Since some cases in which the issue of nonresuscitation is raised are complex, it is advisable to institute a system to facilitate the seeking of advice and the reconciliation of differences. Some institutions have found it useful to establish a "medical ethics committee" for this purpose. Such committees can have a form and function suited to the needs and character of the individual institution.

# DO NOT RESUSCITATE (DNR) GUIDELINES

## Minnesota Medical Association

These guidelines have been drafted by the Ad Hoc Committee on Death of the Minnesota Medical Association. It is widely recognized that in some clinical situations the initiation of potentially life-prolonging treatment is inappropriate. While there may be a variety of situations in which it is justifiable to withhold or withdraw medical treatment, the guidelines presented here cover only one specific aspect of the dilemmas created by modern medical technology, issues surrounding the question of whether or not to initiate cardiopulmonary resuscitation (CPR) when the patient experiences an acute cardiac or respiratory arrest.

### DEFINITION

DNR (do not resuscitate)—In the event of an acute cardiac or respiratory arrest, no cardiopulmonary resuscitative measures will be initiated.

### CONSIDERATIONS

1. An appropriate knowledge of the patient's medical condition is necessary before consideration of a DNR order.
2. The attending physician should determine the appropriateness of the DNR order for any given medical condition.
3. DNR orders are compatible with maximal therapeutic care. The patient may be receiving vigorous support in all other therapeutic modalities and yet justifiably be considered a proper subject for the DNR order.
4. When the patient is competent, the DNR decision will be reached consensually by the patient and physician. When the patient is judged to be incompetent, this decision will be reached consensually by the appropriate family member(s) and physician. If a competent patient disagrees, or, in cases of incompetency, the family member(s) disagrees, a DNR order will not be written.

---

Approved by the Minnesota Medical Association Board of Trustees, January 24, 1981.

## IMPLEMENTATION

1. Once the DNR decision has been made, this directive shall be written as a formal order by the attending physician. It is the responsibility of the attending physician to insure that this order and its meaning are discussed with appropriate members of the hospital staff.
2. The facts and considerations relevant to this decision shall be recorded by the attending physician in the progress notes.
3. The DNR order shall be subject to review on a regular basis and may be rescinded at any time.

# REPORT ON DO NOT RESUSCITATE DECISIONS

## Committee on Policy for DNR Decisions, Yale-New Haven Hospital

In January 1978, Dr. Samuel O. Thier, Chairman of the Department of Medicine, appointed this Committee[1] and charged it to recommend to the Department a policy for making, communicating and implementing decisions to withhold cardiopulmonary resuscitation in terminally ill patients. In developing this report, the Committee: (1) surveyed the literature on the ethical and legal aspects of its mandate; (2) reviewed policies developed by other hospitals (and found none to be entirely suitable for YNHH); and (3) solicited the opinions of various members of the YNHH professional staff concentrating particularly on their perceptions of what current practices are and how they might be improved.

The Committee concludes that the most important obstacle to the making and implementation of decisions on withholding cardiopulmonary resuscitation is faulty communications. Some of the more important barriers to communication in the current system are:

1. It is sometimes difficult to identify the responsible physician, the individual who has the responsibility for seeing to it that decisions are made, communicated and implemented. This is particularly true in the Intensive Care Unit (ICU) when multiple subspecialists are involved in the management of a patient.

2. Some members of the health care team who have important information that is germane to a decision may not make that information available to the responsible physician because: (a) they are unaware that a decision is to be made or (b) some nonphysicians—e.g., nurses, social workers—feel that they may be perceived as overstepping their bounds if they initiate discussions of such decisions with physicians.

3. Some physicians believe incorrectly that writing a "Do Not Resuscitate" order will increase the likelihood of malpractice litigation. In fact, writing such orders in accord with the recommendations of this report will have the opposite effect.

Adopted by the Department of Medicine at Yale-New Haven Hospital in 1979. Copyright © 1984 by *Connecticut Medicine*. Reprinted, with permission, from *Connecticut Medicine* 47(8):477–83 (August 1983).

4. Discussions between the responsible physician and the patient are at times initiated much too late. Discussions initiated in the suboptimal conditions of the ICU often could have been anticipated by several months and conducted in a much more satisfactory setting.

5. The authority to accept or refuse resuscitation (or any other therapeutic maneuver) properly resides with the patient or the next of kin. The physician, on the other hand, is most capable of predicting the consequences of any therapeutic intervention. In some cases there are great differences between what the patient wishes and what the physician judges to be possible; such differences are likely to be associated with unsatisfactory communication.

6. In some cases in which a decision has been made to withhold resuscitation (or any other therapeutic maneuver), not all health professionals who might come into contact with the patient are aware of it. Consequently, such interventions may be performed when they are contrary to the expressed will of the patient. Parenthetically, this seems to be an uncommon experience in YNHH.

This report reflects the Committee's attempt to eradicate—or at least to minimize—the six specified barriers to communication; other barriers perceived by the Committee are implicit in our recommendations for dealing with them. This report provides no guidelines for determining what medical conditions are to be considered grounds for withholding resuscitation or other life-sustaining therapy. Rather, it identifies the personnel who should be held accountable for ensuring that such decisions are made and the procedures that they should employ to facilitate clear and unambiguous communications relevant to these decisions.

The recommendations are presented in the following order:

I. Identification of the responsible physician.

II. Communications between health care professionals.

III. Classification of approaches to management of the terminally ill.

IV. Communications with the patient and family.

V. The mechanics of writing *Do Not Resuscitate* orders and classification notes.

## I. IDENTIFICATION OF THE RESPONSIBLE PHYSICIAN

In March 1978, the Medical Board and the Board of Directors approved an updated version of the "Policies Governing Responsibility for Care of Patients" in Yale-New Haven Hospital. These policies specify that all patients admitted to Yale-New Haven Hospital are to be under the care of a member of the hospital staff who is designated the "responsible physician." The responsible physician has the overall responsibility, both medically and legally, for the patient's care. A detailed account of the duties of the responsible physician may be found in the policy statement.

In the care of patients who appear to be terminally ill, clear identification of the responsible physician is of paramount importance. If at any time the identity of the responsible physician is unclear to any member of the health care team, he or she should ask the house officer to identify the responsible physician. If the house officer is unable to do so, he or she should contact the chief medical resident who has the obligation to provide a prompt identification of the responsible physician.

The obligations of the responsible physician in the care of terminally-ill patients—in addition to those specified in the YNHH *Policies* —are as follows:

1.  Coordination of communications among various members of the health care team and with various professional consultants.

2.  Communication with the patient and/or the family with the aim of seeking an agreement to a specific management classification with or without a Do Not Resuscitate order.

3.  Writing the management classification with or without a Do Not Resuscitate order in the chart.

4.  In cases of irreconcilable disagreement, activating the appeals mechanism (*cf.* section II, *infra*).

## II. COMMUNICATIONS AMONG HEALTH CARE PROFESSIONALS

Although the ultimate responsibility for medical decision making rests with the responsible physician, other members of the health care team often have important information that they might contribute to the decision-making process. In order to assure access to all relevant information at the time of making decisions about management classifications as well as Do Not Resuscitate orders, the Committee makes the following recommendation:

When it becomes apparent to the responsible physician that a decision must be made about a patient's management classification, he or she should signal to all members of the health care team the intention to make such a decision by writing a note to that effect in the patient's chart. Such a note might be worded: "The condition of this patient is deteriorating and it is necessary to formulate plans with regard to future management. This will be done at (specify a time and place; e.g., tomorrow at work rounds)."

Such a note should alert all parties (e.g., physicians, nurses, social workers, chaplains, students, and so on) that a management classification decision is about to be made. In this way they are alerted to contribute any information they consider relevant to the decision-making process. They may either speak directly with the responsible physician or the house officer or they might plan to be present at the designated time for making the decision.

In general, health care personnel should refrain from initiating discussions with the patient or the family that seem to reflect a consensus on management classification until such a consensus is reached through appropriate discussions between members of the health care team.

It is a strong conviction of the Committee that any member of the health care team who considers that the management classification for a patient is inappropriate (or, in some cases, when there is no management classification, that there should be one) should report this opinion to the responsible physician; any health care professional holding such an opinion should consider it an obligation, not merely a prerogative, to report such an opinion to the responsible physician. Further, it is the obligation of the responsible physician to act upon such communications. The responsible physician has the right and the obligation to make final judgments with regard to the medical reversibility[2] of the patient's condition; in the event of irreconcilable disagreements between health care professionals, suitable consultation should be obtained. If the disagreements cannot be resolved with the aid of a consultant, the matter should be referred to the Chief of Service for arbitration or mediation.

In many instances, the physician having the best relationship with the family or the patient may be a member of the House Staff and not the responsible physician. Therefore, discussions with the patient or family that ultimately led to a change in management classification (with or without a Do Not Resuscitate order) may be conducted by that member of the house staff. However, these discussions should first be approved by the responsible physician; delegation of authority to conduct such discussions must be explicit.

The authority to write a Do Not Resuscitate order may not be delegated; it must be written personally by the responsible physician. However, house officers have the authority to cancel Do Not Resuscitate orders as appropriate. For example, such orders should be cancelled at the request of the patient or duly authorized member of the family (*cf.* section IV, *infra*). Further, an unexpected finding that suggests that the prognosis for medical reversibility has been substantially underestimated should signal the need for cancellation of a Do Not Resuscitate order. In the latter case, the order should be suspended temporarily while the house officer attempts to discuss the unexpected finding with the responsible physician.

In the absence of a house officer, nurses may be called upon by family members to perform cardiopulmonary resuscitation on patients for whom Do Not Resuscitate orders have been written. Under these circumstances, the nurse should contact either the house officer or the responsible physician as soon as possible. In the event the request to disregard a Do Not Resuscitate order is made during cardiopulmonary arrest, and no physician is available, the nurse is authorized to proceed with cardiopulmonary resuscitation. However, all professionals should be aware that—at the moment of cardiopulmonary arrest—members of the family who have previously carefully thought through decisions to authorize Do Not Resuscitate orders may respond to the immediate situation by saying, "Do something." Professionals who are experienced at working in intensive care units can ordinarily distinguish this reaction from a determination to reverse a previously well thought out decision. Commonly, at such times, the family member is more in need of attention than the patient.

## III. Classification of Approaches to Management of the Terminally-Ill

When patients either are or appear to be terminally-ill, some members of the health care team may not have clear understandings of the team's overall management objectives. In some cases, this is because these objectives have not been defined by the responsible physician; the necessary consultations and discussions may not yet have been accomplished.

In other cases, the objectives may be clear to the responsible physician but not clearly articulated to others who should be aware of them. In the absence of clear articulation of overall objectives there is the ever-present possibility that a health care professional might either initiate or withhold a therapeutic maneuver and by so doing, undermine the management objectives.

In this section we present a system for classification of overall management objectives. The purpose of this classification system is to provide an easily accessible reference for those health professionals who might be called upon to make judgments about implementation of various therapeutic maneuvers when the responsible physician is not available for timely consultation.

*Class A:* The general presumption in this Class is that patients are to receive all curative and functional maintenance therapies as indicated. (Definitions of these classes of therapy are provided subsequently in this section.) The primary goal is to achieve arrest, remission, or cure of the basic disease process. The aims of curative therapy take priority over those of functional maintenance which, in turn, hold a higher priority than those of comforting therapy.

*Class B:* The general presumption in this Class is that any curative therapy in progress (if any) will be continued until its outcome has been determined and, further, that no new curative therapy will be implemented. The goals of functional maintenance therapy take priority over the goals of comforting therapy. The responsible physician should specify limits—if any—to be imposed on functional maintenance therapy: e.g., if sepsis occurs, should it be treated with antibiotics?

Class B is further subdivided as follows:

> *B1:* In the event of cardiopulmonary arrest, the patient is to be resuscitated.
>
> *B2:* Do Not Resuscitate order is written.

*Class C:* The goals of therapy are to comfort the patient as he or she is dying. A Do Not Resuscitate order is written and comforting therapy dominates the approach to medical care. The limits of functional maintenance therapy should be specified.

DEFINITIONS

*Basic Disease Process:* This is the disease process that plays the dominant role in determining whether the patient's illness is "medically reversible" *(infra).* In some patients there may be two (or rarely more) basic disease processes.

*Medical Reversibility:* The medical reversibility of a basic disease process is strictly a technical judgment. In the hospital setting the personnel who are most qualified to render such a judgment are physicians. Judgments with regard to medical reversibility should include statements both to its probability and of its magnitude. A characteristic technical statement of medical reversibility is: If we implement therapy X there is about a 10 percent chance of inducing a 50 percent reduction in (e.g.,) the size of the tumor. In order to translate this technical statement into language that is of use to a patient and his or her family an elaboration is ordinarily required. For example, if we implement therapy X there is about a 10 percent chance that it will work. If it does, we might hope to see a substantial return of (e.g.,) cognitive function.

*Curative Therapy:* These are therapies that are directed at the basic disease process for the purpose of either arresting or reversing its progress, with the aim of inducing a partial or total remission. Implementation of a curative therapy presupposes that a judgment has been made that the basic disease process is potentially medically reversible.

*Functional Equilibrium:* This term refers to a physiologic status of the patient that is compatible with biological survival. In general, a patient is said to be in functional equilibrium if there is adequate ventilation, nutrition, perfusion of vital organs, excretory function, and so on. Impairments of any of these functions may be caused by a variety of phenomena which may or may not be labelled appropriately as diseases. For example, impairments in respiratory function might be caused by obstruction to the airways either by excessive secretions or by tumors. They may also be caused by pneumonia or by paralysis of respiratory muscles. Actions directed toward removing these detriments to respiratory function are performed in the interests of maintaining functional equilibrium, notwithstanding the status of the detriment as a disease or some other thing.

Pneumonia, e.g., may be viewed as either a basic disease process or a detriment to functional equilibrium. Its status is determined by virtue of its role in making global determinations of the potential reversibility of the patient's medical illness. Thus, in a patient having a basic disease process—e.g., a metastatic solid tumor—that has rendered him or her totally incapacitated and which—in the considered judgment of the health care team—is nearly devoid of potential for medical reversibility, treatment of pneumonia may be considered functional maintenance therapy. A decision to treat pneumonia in such a patient has much more in common with a decision to use a ventilator than it does with a decision to administer "curative" therapy.

*Functional Maintenance Therapy:* These are therapies designed to achieve or maintain functional equilibrium.

*Comforting Therapy:* These are therapies designed to achieve or maintain the patient's comfort.

Determinations of what constitutes functional equilibrium lie nearly exclusively in the domain of the physician. By contrast, when the patient is capable of communicating, determination of what constitutes comfort lie exclusively in his or her domain. Often, therapies designed to be curative or to maintain functional equilibrium (e.g., endotracheal tubes) will produce discomfort. Similarly, therapies designed to produce comfort may induce functional dysequilibria (e.g., morphine given for purposes of producing comfort may inhibit respiratory function or induce ileus). Thus, it is necessary to make clear statements as to whether producing comfort takes priority over maintaining functional equilibrium.

Although the patient or the physician may be most competent to make judgments as to what constitutes comfort or functional equilibrium, respectively, such judgments are to be distinguished from decisions to take action. Decisions to take actions—e.g., implementation or withholding of various therapeutic maneuvers—are to be done in accord with agreements reached through appropriate discussions between all concerned parties—health care professionals and patients and/or their families.

The general presumption is that all patients are in Class A unless otherwise specified. Patients are to be classified according to this system only when there exists some legitimate cause to suspect that a patient should be in either Class B or C. Writing in the chart that a patient is in Class A should be done only to signal the fact that the health care team has—with due deliberation and consultation—rejected classifying the patient as either B or C.

Patients should be classified in Class B only when there is a very low probability of achieving any consequential remission. In general, reasonable curative therapies have been tried and failed or have been rejected for good cause. For example, the patient may have refused some potentially curative therapies. For some patients in this class a curative may be in progress but there is little likelihood of success.

Class B is, in general, to be considered a temporary classification. Some of these patients will show surprising responses to curative therapy in which case they will be transferred to Class A. Most of them, however, will become suitable candidates for Class C.

## IV. Communications with the Patient and Family

When the responsible physician—with due consultation with other health care professionals—has reached a decision with regard to the medical reversibility of a patient's condition, a discussion should be initiated with the patient and/or the family with the aim of defining the overall management objectives. The ultimate authority to determine the overall management objectives resides with the patient and/or the family; this is elaborated subsequently in this section. The discussions should ordinarily be conducted by the responsible physician; however, when appropriate this responsibility may be delegated to a house officer (*cf.* section II, *supra*).

If the patient is conscious and competent, he or she has the clear right to refuse any treatment (including resuscitation) even if the consequences of such refusal may be death. Thus, if the patient, after discussion of the alternatives, is capable of understanding the situation and wishes not to be resuscitated, the physician is entitled to rely on such a decision; this entitlement obtains even when the decision is opposed by one or more of the patient's relatives. In general, if a competent adult patient refuses any therapy, that therapy may be given only when authorized by a court order. It should be noted, however, that in cases of attempted suicide, it is customary and legal to oppose the expressed wishes of the patient to refuse lifesaving therapy.

If a legally competent patient is steadfast in refusing any type of therapy and if in the judgment of the responsible physician, such refusal seems irrational, the Chief of Staff or Hospital Counsel should be consulted. It should be noted that the Hospital will almost never initiate incompetency proceedings based solely on the fact that a patient is refusing treatment.

If the patient is comatose or incompetent and a legal guardian (known in Connecticut as the conservator of the person) has been appointed, the conservator of the person has the right to make such decisions. Only a patient who has been so adjudicated by a court is legally incompetent; all other patients are to be considered competent as a matter of law. Ideally, the family should be urged to obtain a court order appointing a conservator prior to the time such decisions are to be made if the patient seems incapable of speaking for himself or herself; however, in many cases this is impractical.

Decisions to discontinue lifesaving therapies or to withhold resuscitation must be authorized by the patient or, when appropriate, the guardian. Failure to secure such authorization may impose legal liability on the physician. Consequently, when such decisions are contemplated in the course of management of comatose or incompetent patients, every effort should be made to contact an individual who is entitled to provide such authorization. If such a person cannot be located, the Chief of Staff and Hospital Counsel should be notified.

If the patient is comatose or legally incompetent, the following order of decision making should be followed: The spouse, if present and competent, has the clear paramount right over adult children to be appointed conservator of an incompetent patient and, even if not appointed, to make decisions about treatment. Where there is no spouse but there are adult offspring, in situations where there is consensus, any one sibling may act for all. If there is disagreement, Hospital Counsel should be called.

When the authority to make a decision resides in a group (e.g., of siblings), it is legally perilous to discontinue therapy while there is conflict among members of the group. At times it may be necessary to resuscitate the patient, perhaps several times, while awaiting consensus to develop.

Some legally incompetent patients may be capable of expressing their wishes about their management. When there are conflicts between the conservator and the patient, no decision to withdraw curative or functional maintenance therapies or to write Do Not Resuscitate orders should be made without authorization from the Chief of Staff and the Hospital Counsel.

In any case in which the physician believes there is a reasonable possibility of medical reversibility of the basic disease process and the patient is comatose or incompetent, the physician has the legal authority to treat the patient over the family's objection. One should be aware of the possibility of conflicts of interest between the patient and his or her relatives. In the event a family member is adamant in opposing a physician's plans to continue life-sustaining therapy, Hospital Counsel should be consulted.

In some cases in which the responsible physician and the patient and/or family are in irreconcilable conflict about the appropriate course of management, the physician may offer to withdraw. In these circumstances the responsible physician should also offer assistance in identifying and contacting another who will assume the role of responsible physician.

According to YNHH policy, therapeutic procedures should be implemented only with the informed consent of the patient. The agreements reached between physicians and patients and/or their families that result in management classifications with or without Do Not Resuscitate orders may, at times, be based upon discussions that can truly be considered as resulting in a condition known as "informed consent." In general, this term can be properly applied in cases where the discussions are begun several weeks or months before a Do Not Resuscitate order might be implemented. In such cases the negotiations for informed consent may result in a document known as a "living will." The Committee strongly encourages the early initiation of such discussions and the development of living wills. Such documents provide the most clear and unambiguous expressions of the patient's values rendered at times when the patients are relatively rational and autonomous and when there is time for due deliberation; their situations are substantially and relevantly different from what they will be in the ICU.

When discussions are initiated by physicians under circumstances in which it seems appropriate to enter a patient in management Class B or C, it is rarely possible to achieve informed consent. Ordinarily, the physician approaches the patient and/or family with a statement that there is no reasonable chance of medical reversibility; accordingly, they are asked to "authorize" a shift in management objectives to Class B or C. The Committee recommends that the term "authorization" be used to refer to such agreements. As much time and support should be given as is necessary for the patient and/or family to reach a decision and to seek consultation with such advisors as they may choose, medical and otherwise. In these cases, what is sought is the authorization of the patient or the family to a particular plan of management based upon the estimation of the health care professionals as to what medicine can and cannot achieve. However, the patient and/or family have the legal authority to require that a patient be managed according to Class B1 even when the physician believes that Class C management would be more appropriate; the physician is obliged to proceed according to these wishes.

In the event a patient meets the criteria for "brain death,"[3] the patient may be pronounced dead and then all therapeutic maneuvers discontinued notwithstanding any expressions of wishes to do otherwise.

## V. The Mechanics of Writing Do Not Resuscitate Orders and Classification Notes

Decisions to withhold resuscitation in the event of cardiopulmonary arrest are to be written on the *order sheet*. They should be spelled out; the abbreviation, DNR, is not to be used. Also not to be used are such euphemisms as: "No code" or "In case of CPA, page house officer, stat." Only the responsible physician may write the Do Not Resuscitate order. It is presumed that Do Not Resuscitate orders will be reviewed at least once daily and commonly more frequently. The Committee considered and rejected recommending that these orders have automatic expiration periods—e.g., 24 hours.

According to YNHH Policies, all orders are to be written. In emergencies it is acceptable for physicians to give oral orders for therapeutic actions other than Do Not Resuscitate orders. Usually, oral orders are appropriate in emergencies when it would be detrimental to the interests of the patient to wait for them to be written. This justification is never appropriate for Do Not Resuscitate orders; they must always be written.

The Committee recommends that the physician write on the order sheet a notification that a management classification note has been written in the progress notes. This should indicate the date on which it was written and identify the individual who wrote it. Substantive changes in the management classification should also be noted similarly on the order sheet.

In all cases in which a Do Not Resuscitate order is written, a management classification note is mandatory.

In the *Kardex*, the nurse should note prominently that a Do Not Resuscitate order has been written. In close proximity to that notation there should be an additional notation of when the most current management classification note was written in the progress notes. When applicable, there should also be a list of limitations of such things as functional maintenance therapies.

*Progress notes:* Management classification notes should provide a clear account of the rationale for the determination of the objectives of management. There should be an identification of the basic disease process or processes and an estimation of the probability and magnitude of its medical reversibility. There should be a statement as to whether the management objectives are those of Class A, B (1 or 2) or C. Limitations, if any, on functional maintenance therapies (or other therapies) that have been agreed upon with the patient are to be identified. Further, there should be a statement on the extent to which the objectives of comforting take priority over those of functional maintenance.

Finally, there should be a statement as to who authorized this approach to management—either the patient or the appropriate relative(s) or guardian. This statement should include a brief account of the information that was conveyed to the patient and/or family that formed the basis of the authorization.

In general, a competent patient should not be asked to document his or her authorization of a Do Not Resuscitate order when it appears that there might soon be a need for its implementation. Such a request might be considered appropriate following thorough discussions of the matter several weeks or months before it appears that the Do Not Resuscitate order might be implemented. Ordinarily, in the early stages of an inevitably fatal disease, it is preferable to suggest to the patient that he or she might wish to develop a "living will"; if the patient wishes, a copy of this document may be put in the chart.

Occasionally it is necessary to ask either the patient or a member of the family to sign an "authorization note" for a Do Not Resuscitate order. These are situations in which either (1) there is irreconcilable disagreement between the person having the legal authority to make the decision and one or more members of the family, or (2) strong disagreements between equally entitled siblings have recently been resolved. In these cases, the member or the family who takes responsibility for authorizing a Do Not Resuscitate order should be asked to sign (or, if they prefer, write) an authorization note in the medical record (progress notes). This should be a brief note indicating that the responsible person(s) understands and agrees to the Do Not Resuscitate order. The note should include the fact that the condition of the patient is terminal, that discussions have been held with the family (and, if appropriate, the patient) and that a decision has been made not to resuscitate that patient in the event that breathing or the heart stops.

While no set form for such a note is suggested by the Committee, each one should include a reasonably full statement of the rationale for the decision and a summary of the discussions with the patient and/or family. Those who prefer not to sign such notes should not be coerced to do so; in such cases the physician should record the fact that the individual(s) preferred not to sign; the reasons for this preference, if known, should also be recorded.

It is of utmost importance that the existence of a Do Not Resuscitate order be communicated effectively to all members of the health care team. It should not be difficult to assure awareness of such orders on the part of those health care personnel who are assigned to work on various shifts in the patient care unit. Occasionally, patients for whom Do Not Resuscitate orders are written are transported to other parts of the Hospital to receive some diagnostic or therapeutic service. Thus, they may come into contact with health professionals who will be unaware of the Do Not Resuscitate order unless appropriate precautions are taken. Therefore, the Committee recommends that it be made the obligation of the responsible physician (or the house officer to whom he or she delegates such responsibility) to communicate clearly with the personnel of the department (e.g., the X-ray Department) to which the patient is being transported that there is a Do Not Resuscitate order. Ideally, a professional from the patient care unit should accompany the patient to see to it that—among other things—Do Not Resuscitate orders are respected. However, at times when this is not feasible, the responsible physician—or his or her delegate—should communicate clearly on this matter with a health professional in the department to which the patient is being transported that there is a Do Not Resuscitate order. The individual on the receiving end of this communication should be one who will be responsible for seeing to it that this order is respected while the patient is in his or her department.

The Committee considered and rejected proposals to employ some standard identifying symbol affixed either to the patient, to the medical record, or to the bed or stretcher. The basis for this rejection was that it was too dangerous; such symbols might inadvertently be left on, for example, the stretcher, when a new patient used it. Similarly rejected was a proposal to write Do Not Resuscitate orders on requisitions for such services as X-ray; the grounds for this rejection was that the requisition tends not to remain in the immediate vicinity of the patient.

## NOTES

1. Committee Membership: Shirley Blood, R.N., Head Nurse, Clinical Research Center, Yale-New Haven Hospital. John F. D'Avella, M.D., Fellow, Section of Nephrology, Department of Medicine, Yale University School of Medicine; formerly Chief Medical Resident, Yale-New Haven Hospital. Constance T. Donovan, R.N., M.S.N., Assistant Professor, Medical-Surgical Nursing Program, Yale School of Nursing, and Clinical Nurse Specialist, Yale-New Haven Hospital. Thomas P. Duffy, M.D., Associate Professor of Medicine, Yale University School of Medicine. David C. Duncombe, M. Div., Ph.D., Chaplain, Yale University School of Medicine, and Assistant Professor of Pastoral Theology, Yale Divinity School. Angela R. Holder, LL.M., Counsel for Medicolegal Affairs, Yale-New Haven Hospital, and Associate Clinical Professor of Pediatrics (Law), Yale University School of Medicine. Robert J. Levine, M.D. (Chair), Professor of Medicine and Lecturer in Pharmacology, Yale University School of Medicine. Melvin Lewis, M.B., F.R.C. Psych., D.C.H., Professor of Pediatrics and Psychiatry and Director of Medical Studies, Child Study Center, Yale University School of Medicine. Kathleen A. Nolan, Yale Medical Student. Rosalind A. Reed, R.N., Staff Nurse, Medical Intensive Care Unit, Yale-New Haven Hospital. James A. Talcott, Yale Medical Student.

   A slightly edited version of the policy appears in DILEMMAS OF DYING: POLICIES AND PROCEDURES FOR DECISIONS NOT TO TREAT (Cynthia B. Wong, Judith P. Swazey, eds.) (G. K. Hall Medical Publishers, Boston) (1981).

   The recommendations presented in this Committee Report have been adopted as the policy of Yale-New Haven Hospital.
2. Defined in section III, *infra.*
3. *See* Black, P. M., *Brain Death*, NEW ENGLAND JOURNAL OF MEDICINE 299:338–44, 393–401 (1978).

# GUIDELINES FOR WITHHOLDING CARDIO-PULMONARY RESUSCITATION (CODE BLUE)

## St. Joseph Hospital, Mt. Clemens, Michigan

St. Joseph Hospital is dedicated to care of the sick, injured, and dying. The hospital offers all its human and technological resources to patients who come for help. In most situations, this means that every possible effort is made to cure the sick and rehabilitate the injured. However, for the dying patient, St. Joseph Hospital's goal is to support the person in dying rather than to prolong his or her life. Helping the dying to live the end of their lives in a responsible and dignified manner is a goal equal in value to preserving life and restoring health.

One of the means by which the life of a dying patient is prolonged is cardio-pulmonary resuscitation (Code Blue). The patients who are to be considered for the withholding of cardio-pulmonary resuscitation are:

1. Those with irreversible irreparable disease, illness, or injury, where treatment of the acute problem will not prevent the progression of his/her terminal condition.

2. Those in which advanced life support would only maintain a life of prolonged pain or a life where there is a little or no potential for human experience.

The No-Code Blue order deals only with the withholding of cardio-pulmonary resuscitation (Code Blue) and does not affect the ongoing nursing care or medical treatment of the patient; all tender and symptomatic care shall continue and reevaluation will be an ongoing process.

The patient is the primary decision maker for his/her own health care. The patient must be consulted and must approve the course of medical treatment.

If a patient is not conscious or competent, the decision of a no-code order should be discussed and approved by someone who is presumed to be acting in the patient's best interest. Usually that is the family. Those who are involved must be made aware of the patient's condition and the present state of the art of treatment of that condition. They must also be made aware of the implications of a no-code order and their desires should be documented in the medical record.

---

Dated September 1983.

Members of the health care team often assist the patient and family with this issue. Nursing Service, Social Service, Pastoral Care, and the Patient Representative are available as consultants to staff as well as the patient and family.

These disciplines will be responsible to communicate pertinent information among themselves and to the attending physician.

## DOCUMENTATION

1. When a determination has been made that the patient should not receive advanced life support as routinely performed by the Code Blue team, the order will be written as "No-Code Blue." Orders for anything less than a full CPR response must be written out in detail by the physician.
2. The physician may write the order or give the order verbally; however, as with all verbal orders, it must be countersigned and dated by the physician within 24 hours. All verbal orders must be taken and recorded on the medical record by a R.N.
3. Only the patient's attending physician may give the order to withhold cardio-pulmonary resuscitation. If more than one physician is involved with the patient's care, it remains the responsibility of the attending physician to make the decision. If the attending physician delegates this responsibility, it must be so documented in the patient's medical record.
4. "No-Code Blue" orders shall be communicated to the ancillary departments when the patient leaves the nursing unit by writing "No-Code Blue" directly under "examinations desired" on the requisition and on the top of the two travel cards.

# GUIDELINES FOR "DNR/NO-CODE" ORDERS

## Saint Joseph Hospital, Orange, California

The following statement was adopted at the National Conference on Standards for Cardio-Pulmonary Resuscitation and Emergency Cardiac Care held in May 1973, and sponsored by the American Heart Association and the National Academy of Sciences:

> The purpose of cardio-pulmonary resuscitation is the prevention of sudden, unexpected death. Cardio-pulmonary resuscitation is not indicated in certain situations, such as in cases of terminal, irreversible illness, where death is not unexpected, or where prolonged cardiac arrest dictates the futility of resuscitation efforts. Resuscitation in these circumstances may represent a positive violation of an individual's right to die with dignity. When CPR is considered to be contra-indicated for hospital patients, it is appropriate to indicate this on the physician's order sheet for the benefit of nurses and other personnel who may be called upon to initiate or participate in cardio-pulmonary resuscitation.

### DEFINITION

A "no-code" or "DNR" (do-not-resuscitate) order refers to the written order to suspend the otherwise automatic initiation of cardio-pulmonary resuscitation.

### PRINCIPLES

1. Competent adults have the right to direct the course of their own medical treatment.
2. Questions of when to withhold or withdraw medical treatment are not only medical questions; they involve personal values as well. Therefore, decisions in these matters are not to be made by the physician alone, but do involve the patient and those closest to the patient.
3. Biological life need not be preserved at all costs. There are times when it is more in keeping with respect for life to let it go than to cling to it.
4. A decision to withhold or withdraw treatment which is potentially lifesaving does not mean the staff has abandoned the patient, but rather represents the time for intensification of efforts to provide physical and emotional comfort.

---

Dated July 1983.

5. As stated in Chapter 7 of the March 1983 report of the President's Commission for the Study of Ethical Problems in Medicine and Biomedical and Behavioral Research, entitled *Deciding to Forego Life-Sustaining Treatment:*

> Any DNR policy should ensure that the order not to resuscitate has no implications for any other treatment decision. Patients with DNR orders on their chart may still be quite appropriate candidates for all other vigorous care, including intensive care. Thus, orders regarding supportive care that is to be provided should be written separately.

## GUIDELINES FOR NO-CODE ORDERS

1. Competent patients should be involved in the decision and their wishes followed.
2. For incompetent patients, the following steps are suggested:
   a. It should be determined by the attending physician that the patient has an irreversible or terminal illness.
   b. The decision not to resuscitate should be discussed with and concurred in by the guardian of the patient, if there is one. If there is no guardian, those closest to the patient should be consulted, and their concurrence obtained. Documentation that this discussion has taken place should be made in the chart.
   c. The no-code order must be written in the patient's chart.
   d. The order should be re-evaluated periodically to be sure it is in accord with the patient's condition.
3. Slow-codes or partial-codes (e.g., defibrillation without other resuscitative measures) are rarely if ever indicated. A slow code may represent a thoughtless or even dishonest effort to placate relatives or hospital staff without offering the patient a reasonable chance for successful resuscitation. Request for a partial code by a patient or his family may be honored if requested, but the physician should inform them that if resuscitative effort is appropriate, it should generally be unrestricted.

# GUIDELINES FOR DISCONTINUANCE OF CARDIOPULMONARY LIFE-SUPPORT SYSTEMS UNDER SPECIFIED CIRCUMSTANCES

Joint Ad Hoc Committee on Biomedical Ethics,
Los Angeles County Medical Association and
Los Angeles County Bar Association

A. The general principles which should govern decision making in this area are:

1. It is the right of a person capable of giving informed consent to make his or her own decision regarding medical care after having been fully informed about the benefits, risks, and consequences of available treatment, even when such a decision might foreseeably result in shortening the individual's life.
2. Persons who are unable to give informed consent have the same rights as do persons who can give such consent. Decisions made on behalf of persons who cannot give their own informed consent should, to the extent possible, be the decisions which those persons would have made for themselves had they been able to do so. Parents (or the guardian) of a minor child, or the conservator of an adult patient, must consent to the decision. Family members of adult patients should always be consulted, although they have no legal standing under present California law to make such decisions on behalf of the patient.
3. A physician may discontinue use of a cardiopulmonary life-support system (i.e., mechanical respirator or ventilator), and is not required to continue its use indefinitely solely because such support was initiated at an earlier time.
4. The dignity of the individual must be preserved and necessary measures to assure comfort be maintained at all times.
5. It is the right of individual physicians to decline to participate in the withdrawal of life-support systems. In exercising this right, however, the physician must take appropriate steps to transfer the care of the patient to another qualified physician.

B. Three sets of circumstances in which decisions to discontinue the

Adopted by the Council of the Los Angeles County Medical Association on March 2, 1981, and by the Board of Trustees of the Los Angeles County Bar Association on March 11, 1981. Reprinted with the permission of the Los Angeles County Medical Association.

use of cardiopulmonary life-support systems can be made without the necessity of prior approval by the courts are:

1. Brain Death

   Section 7180 of the California Health and Safety Code states: "A person shall be pronounced dead if it is determined by a physician that the person has suffered a total and irreversible cessation of brain function." This statute also requires that a second physician independently confirm the death and that neither physician be involved in decisions regarding transplantation of organs.

   a. The physicians should document in the medical record the basis for the diagnosis of brain death.

   b. The patient should be pronounced brain dead before disconnecting the respirator or ventilator.

   c. It is desirable to explain the brain death law to family members and other interested persons before this procedure is implemented.

2. California Natural Death Act

   Sections 7185 through 7195 of the California Health and Safety Code (the California Natural Death Act) provide that cardiopulmonary life-support systems must be withdrawn from patients who have signed a "valid and binding" Directive to Physicians. For further information, physicians should consult the Guidelines on the California Natural Death Act adopted by the California Medical Association and the California Hospital Association (CHA). These guidelines are reproduced in the CHA Consent Manual.

3. Irreversible Coma[1]

   Cardiopulmonary life-support systems may be discontinued if all of the following conditions are present:

   a. The medical record contains a written diagnosis of irreversible coma, confirmed by a physician who by training or experience is qualified to assist in making such decisions. The medical record must include adequate medical evidence to support the diagnosis;

   b. The medical record indicates that there has been no expressed intention on the part of the patient that life-support systems be initiated or maintained in such circumstances; and

   c. The medical record indicates that the patient's family, or guardian or conservator, concurs in the decision to discontinue such support.

   The comfort and dignity of the patient shall be maintained if death does not occur on discontinuation of cardiopulmonary life-support systems.

NOTE

1. While paragraphs B(1) and B(2), dealing with brain death and the California Natural Death Act, are based on provisions of the California Health and Safety Code, this paragraph, dealing with irreversible coma, is not based on any California statute or court decision, but rather reflects our view of good medical practice and the current standard of medical care in Los Angeles County.

# Guidelines for the Determination of Death

Report of the Medical Consultants on the
Diagnosis of Death to the President's Commission
for the Study of Ethical Problems in Medicine
and Biomedical and Behavioral Research[1]

The advent of effective artificial cardiopulmonary support for severely brain-injured persons has created some confusion during the past several decades about the determination of death. Previously, loss of heart and lung functions was an easily observable and sufficient basis for diagnosing death, whether the initial failure occurred in the brain, the heart and lungs, or elsewhere in the body. Irreversible failure of either the heart and lungs or the brain precluded the continued functioning of the other. Now, however, circulation and respiration can be maintained by means of a mechanical respirator and other medical interventions, despite a loss of all brain functions. In these circumstances, we recognize as dead an individual whose loss of brain functions is complete and irreversible.

To recognize reliably that death has occurred, accurate criteria must be available for physicians' use. These now fall into two groups, to be applied depending on the clinical situation. When respiration and circulation have irreversibly ceased, there is no need to assess brain functions directly. When cardiopulmonary functions are artificially maintained, neurological criteria must be used to assess whether brain functions have ceased irreversibly.

More than half of the states now recognize, through statutes or judicial decisions, that death may be determined on the basis of irreversible cessation of all functions of the brain. Law in the remaining states has not yet departed from the older, common law view that death has not occurred until "all vital functions" (whether or not artificially maintained) have ceased. The language of the statutes has not been uniform from state to state, and the diversity of proposed and enacted laws has created substantial confusion. Consequently, the American Bar Association, the American Medical Association, the National Conference of Commissioners on Uniform State Laws, and the President's

---

Commission for the Study of Ethical Problems in Medicine and Biomedical and Behavioral Research have proposed the following model statute, intended for adoption in every jurisdiction:

UNIFORM DETERMINATION OF DEATH ACT

An individual who has sustained either (1) irreversible cessation of circulatory and respiratory functions, or (2) irreversible cessation of all functions of the entire brain, including the brain stem, is dead. A determination of death must be made in accordance with accepted medical standards.

This wording has also been endorsed by the American Academy of Neurology and the American Electroencephalographic Society.

The statute relies on the existence of "accepted medical standards" for determining that death has occurred. The medical profession, based on carefully conducted research and extensive clinical experience, has found that death can be determined reliably by either cardiopulmonary or neurological criteria. The tests used for determining cessation of brain functions have changed and will continue to do so with the advent of new research and technologies. The "Harvard criteria" (*JAMA* 1968;205:337–340) are widely accepted, but advances in recent years have led to the proposal of other criteria. As an aid to the implementation of the proposed uniform statute, we provide here one statement of currently accepted medical standards.

INTRODUCTION

The criteria that physicians use in determining that death has occurred should (1) eliminate errors in classifying a living individual as dead; (2) allow as few errors as possible in classifying a dead body as alive; (3) allow a determination to be made without unreasonable delay; (4) be adaptable to a variety of clinical situations; and (5) be explicit and accessible to verification.

Because it would be undesirable for any guidelines to be mandated by legislation or regulation or to be inflexibly established in case law, the proposed Uniform Determination of Death Act appropriately specifies only "accepted medical standards." Local, state, and national institutions and professional organizations are encouraged to examine and publish their practices.

The following guidelines represent a distillation of current practice in regard to the determination of death. Only the most commonly available and verified tests have been included. The time of death recorded on a death certificate is at present a matter of local practice and is not covered in this document.

These guidelines are advisory. Their successful use requires a competent and judicious physician, experienced in clinical examination and the relevant procedures. All periods of observation listed in these guidelines require the patient to be under the care of a physician. Considering the responsibility entailed in the determination of death, consultation is recommended when appropriate.

The outline of the criteria is set forth below in boldface letters. The lightface text that follows each heading explains its meaning. In addition, the two sets of criteria (cardiopulmonary and neurological) are followed by a presentation of the major complicating conditions: drug and metabolic intoxication, hypothermia, young age, and shock. It is of paramount importance that anyone referring to these guidelines be thoroughly familiar with the entire document, including explanatory notes and complicating conditions.

## THE CRITERIA FOR DETERMINATION OF DEATH

An individual presenting the findings in *either* section A (cardiopulmonary) *or* section B (neurological) is dead. In either section, a diagnosis of death requires that *both* cessation of functions, as set forth in subsection 1, *and* irreversibility, as set forth in subsection 2, be demonstrated.

**A. An individual with irreversible cessation of circulatory and respiratory functions is dead.**

**1. *Cessation* is recognized by an appropriate clinical examination.**

Clinical examination will disclose at least the absence of responsiveness, heartbeat, and respiratory effort. Medical circumstances may require the use of confirmatory tests, such as an ECG.

**2. *Irreversibility* is recognized by persistent cessation of functions during an appropriate period of observation and/or trial of therapy.**

In clinical situations where death is expected, where the course has been gradual, and where irregular agonal respiration or heartbeat finally ceases, the period of observation following the cessation may be only the few minutes required to complete the examination. Similarly, if resuscitation is not undertaken and ventricular fibrillation and standstill develop in a monitored patient, the required period of observation thereafter may be as short as a few minutes. When a possible death is unobserved, unexpected, or sudden, the examination may need to be more detailed and repeated over a longer period, while appropriate resuscitative effort is maintained as a test of cardiovascular responsiveness. Diagnosis in individuals who are first observed with rigor mortis or putrefaction may require only the observation period necessary to establish that fact.

**B. An individual with irreversible cessation of all functions of the entire brain, including the brain stem, is dead.** The "functions of the entire brain" that are relevant to the diagnosis are those that are clinically ascertainable. Where indicated, the clinical diagnosis is subject to confirmation by laboratory tests, as described in the following portions of the text. Consultation with a physician experienced in this diagnosis is advisable.

**1. *Cessation* is recognized when evaluation discloses findings of a *and* b:**

**a. Cerebral functions are absent, and . . .**

There must be deep coma, that is, cerebral unreceptivity and unresponsivity. Medical circumstances may require the use of confirmatory studies such as an EEG or blood-flow study.

**b. brain stem functions are absent.**

Reliable testing of brain stem reflexes requires a perceptive and experienced physician using adequate stimuli. Pupillary light, corneal, oculocephalic, oculovestibular, oropharyngeal, and respiratory (apnea) reflexes should be tested. When these reflexes cannot be adequately assessed, confirmatory tests are recommended.

Adequate testing for apnea is very important. An accepted method is ventilation with pure oxygen or an oxygen and carbon dioxide mixture for ten minutes before withdrawal of the ventilator, followed by passive flow of oxygen. (This procedure allows $PaCO_2$ to rise without hazardous hypoxia.) Hypercarbia adequately stimulates respiratory effort within 30 seconds when $PaCO_2$ is greater than 60 mm Hg. A ten-minute period of apnea is usually sufficient to attain this level of hypercarbia. Testing of arterial blood gases can be used to confirm this level. Spontaneous breathing efforts indicate that part of the brain stem is functioning.

Peripheral nervous system activity and spinal cord reflexes may persist after death. True decerebrate or decorticate posturing or seizures are inconsistent with the diagnosis of death.

**2. *Irreversibility* is recognized when evaluation discloses findings of a *and* b *and* c:**

**a. The cause of coma is established and is sufficient to account for the loss of brain functions, and . . .**

Most difficulties with the determination of death on the basis of neurological criteria have resulted from inadequate attention to this basic diagnostic prerequisite. In addition to a careful clinical examination and investigation of history, relevant knowledge of causation may be acquired by computed tomographic scan, measurement of core temperature, drug screening, EEG, angiography, or other procedures.

**b. the possibility of recovery of any brain functions is excluded, and . . .**

The most important reversible conditions are sedation, hypothermia, neuromuscular blockade, and shock. In the unusual circumstance where a sufficient cause cannot be established, irreversibility can be reliably inferred only after extensive evaluation for drug intoxication, extended observation, and other testing. A determination that blood flow to the brain is absent can be used to demonstrate a sufficient and irreversible condition.

**c. the cessation of all brain functions persists for an appropriate period of observation and/or trial of therapy.**

Even when coma is known to have started at an earlier time, the absence of all brain functions must be established by an experienced physician at the initiation of the observation period. The duration of observation periods is a matter of clinical judgment, and some physicians recommend shorter or longer periods than those given here.

Except for patients with drug intoxication, hypothermia, young age, or shock, medical centers with substantial experience in diagnosing death neurologically report no cases of brain functions returning following a six-hour cessation, documented by clinical examination and confirmatory EEG. In the absence of confirmatory tests, a period of observation of at least 12 hours is recommended when an irreversible condition is well established. For anoxic brain damage where the extent of damage is more difficult to ascertain, observation for 24 hours is generally desirable. In anoxic injury, the observation period may be reduced if a test shows cessation of cerebral blood flow or if an EEG shows electrocerebral silence in an adult patient without drug intoxication, hypothermia, or shock.

Confirmation of clinical findings by EEG is desirable when objective documentation is needed to substantiate the clinical findings. Electrocerebral silence verifies irreversible loss of cortical functions, except in patients with drug intoxication or hypothermia. (Important technical details are provided in "Minimal Technical Standards for EEG Recording in Suspected Cerebral Death" [*Guidelines in EEG 1980*. Atlanta, American Electroencephalographic Society, 1980, section 4, pp. 19–24].) When joined with the clinical findings of absent brain stem functions, electrocerebral silence confirms the diagnosis.

Complete cessation of circulation to the normothermic adult brain for more than ten minutes is incompatible with survival of brain tissue. Documentation of this circulatory failure is therefore evidence of death of the entire brain. Four-vessel intracranial angiography is definitive for diagnosing cessation of circulation to the entire brain (both cerebrum and posterior fossa) but entails substantial practical difficulties and risks. Tests are available that assess circulation only in the cerebral hemispheres, namely radioisotope bolus cerebral angiography and gamma camera imaging with radioisotope cerebral angiography. Without complicating conditions, absent cerebral blood flow as measured by these tests, in conjunction with the clinical determination of cessation of all brain functions for at least six hours, is diagnostic of death.

## COMPLICATING CONDITIONS

**A. Drug and Metabolic Intoxication.**—Drug intoxication is the most serious problem in the determination of death, especially when multiple drugs are used. Cessation of brain functions caused by the sedative and anesthetic drugs, such as barbiturates, benzodiazepines, meprobamate, methaqualone, and trichloroethylene, may be completely reversible even though they produce clinical cessation of brain functions and electrocerebral silence. In cases where there is any likelihood of sedative presence, toxicology screening for all likely drugs is required. If exogenous intoxication is found, death may not be declared until the intoxicant is metabolized or intracranial circulation is tested and found to have ceased.

Total paralysis may cause unresponsiveness, areflexia, and apnea that closely simulates death. Exposure to drugs such as neuromuscular blocking agents or aminoglycoside antibiotics, and diseases like myasthenia gravis are usually apparent by careful review of the history. Prolonged paralysis after use of succinylcholine chloride and related drugs requires evaluation for pseudocholinesterase deficiency. If there is any question, low-dose atropine stimulation, electromyogram, peripheral nerve stimulation, EEG, tests of intracranial circulation, or extended observation, as indicated, will make the diagnosis clear.

In drug-induced coma, EEG activity may return or persist while the patient remains unresponsive, and therefore the EEG may be an important evaluation along with extended observation. If the EEG shows electrocerebral silence, short latency auditory or somatosensory-evoked potentials may be used to test brain stem functions, since these potentials are unlikely to be affected by drugs.

Some severe illnesses (e.g., hepatic encephalopathy, hyperosmolar coma, and preterminal uremia) can cause deep coma. Before irreversible cessation of brain functions can be determined, metabolic abnormalities should be considered and, if possible, corrected. Confirmatory tests of circulation or EEG may be necessary.

**B. Hypothermia.**—Criteria for reliable recognition of death are not available in the presence of hypothermia (below 32.2°C core temperature). The variables of cerebral circulation in hypothermic patients are not sufficiently well studied to know whether tests of absent or diminished circulation are confirmatory. Hypothermia can mimic brain death by ordinary clinical criteria and can protect against neurological damage due to hypoxia. Further complications arise since hypothermia also usually precedes and follows death. If these complicating factors make it unclear whether an individual is alive, the only available measure to resolve the issue is to restore normothermia. Hypothermia is not a common cause of difficulty in the determination of death.

**C. Children.**—The brains of infants and young children have increased resistance to damage and may recover substantial functions even after exhibiting unresponsiveness on neurological examination for longer periods compared with adults. Physicians should be particularly cautious in applying neurological criteria to determine death in children younger than 5 years.

**D. Shock.**—Physicians should also be particularly cautious in applying neurological criteria to determine death in patients in shock because the reduction in cerebral circulation can render clinical examination and laboratory tests unreliable.

NOTE

1. The guidelines set forth in this report represent the views of the signatories as individuals; they do not necessarily reflect the policy of any institution or professional association with which any signatory is affiliated. Although the practice of individual signatories may vary slightly, signatories agree on the acceptability of these guidelines: Jesse Barber, M.D.; Don Becker, M.D.; Richard Behrman, M.D., J.D.; Donald R. Bennett, M.D.; Richard Beresford, M.D., J.D.; Reginald Bickford, M.D.; William A. Black, Jr., M.D.; Benjamin Boshes, M.D., Ph.D.; Philip Braunstein, M.D.; John Burroughs, M.D., J.D.; Russell Butler, M.D.; John Caronna, M.D.; Shelley Chou, M.D., Ph.D.; Kemp Clark, M.D.; Ronald Cranford, M.D.; Michael Earnest, M.D.; Albert Ehle, M.D.; Jack M. Fein, M.D.; Sal Fiscina, M.D., J.D.; Terrance G. Furlow, M.D., J.D.; Eli Goldensohn, M.D.; Jack Grabow, M.D.; Phillip M. Green, M.D.; Ake Grenvik, M.D.; Charles E. Henry, Ph.D.; John Hughes, M.D., Ph.D., D.M.; Howard Kaufman, M.D.; Robert King, M.D.; Julius Korein, M.D.; Thomas W. Langfitt, M.D.; Cesare Lombroso, M.D.; Kevin M. McIntyre, M.D., J.D.; Richard L. Masland, M.D.; Don Harper Mills, M.D., J.D.; Gaetano Molinari, M.D.; Byron C. Pevehouse, M.D.; Lawrence H. Pitts, M.D.; A. Bernard Pleet, M.D.; Fred Plum, M.D.; Jerome Posner, M.D.; David Powner, M.D.; Richard Rovit, M.D.; Peter Safar, M.D.; Henry Schwartz, M.D.; Edward Schlesinger, M.D.; Roy Selby, M.D.; James Snyder, M.D.; Bruce F. Sorenson, M.D.; Cary Suter, M.D.; Barry Tharp, M.D.; Fernando Torres, M.D.; A. Earl Walker, M.D.; Arthur Ward, M.D.; Jack Whisnant, M.D.; Robert Wilkus, M.D.; and Harry Zimmerman, M.D.

The preparation of this report was facilitated by the President's Commission but the guidelines have not been passed on by the Commission and are not intended as matters for governmental review or adoption.

# CRITERIA FOR DETERMINING BRAIN DEATH

## St. Joseph Hospital, Mt. Clemens, Michigan

The determination of death will be made by the patient's Attending Physician, or physician in charge of the patient's care. Death is defined as that point in a patient's care where there is a determination that an irreversible cessation of spontaneous respiratory and circulatory functions has occurred. However, in those cases where artificial means of support have been instituted, the following criteria can be used in determining that there is a cessation of Spontaneous Brain Function.

These criteria are presented to assist the physician in determining that the brain is dead. These guidelines are not presented as a rigid set of rules, for no set of criteria can replace the physician's evaluation of the total circumstances surrounding a given case. Therefore, the final decision regarding the termination of life must continue to depend upon the physician's judgment.

I. The patient is comatose.

A. Not as a result of hypothermia (temp below 90°F or 32.2°C).

B. Not as a result of central nervous system depressant drugs.

C. Is not a child under five years of age.

II. Brain stem reflexes are absent.

A. Absent pupillary reflexes.

B. Absent corneal reflexes.

C. Oculovestibular reflexes are absent.

D. There is no gag reflex response to bronchial stimulation.

E. Apnea.

III. Electrocerebral silence. When the clinical criteria set forth above have persisted for at least six hours as confirmed by the patient's Attending Physician with the assistance of a neurologist or neurosurgeon, an EEG is to be performed for a minimum recording period of thirty minutes (carried out in accordance with the techniques currently specified by the American EEG Society Guidelines, EEG No. 1, Minimum Technical Standards for EEG Recording in Suspected Cerebral Death, revised).

---

Dated October 1983.

IV. All of the above criteria are to be reexamined and confirmed on a second occasion, at least six hours after the first determination. In any instance where there is a possibility of drug effect, or any question regarding the true nature of the intracranial process, or the patient is under five years of age, the existence of brain death may be verified by persistence of the above-described conditions for a period exceeding 48 hours.

# SUPPORTIVE CARE PLAN: ITS MEANING AND APPLICATION

## Recommendations and Guidelines of the Task Force on Supportive Care, St. Paul, Minnesota

### PREAMBLE

Several incidents involving the withdrawal of treatment and/or the ordering of supportive care for nursing home residents came to public attention in the spring and summer of 1981, raising serious concerns among advocates, attorneys, and health care professionals about the use of supportive care orders. It appeared that there was little consistency or consensus with respect to the meaning or application of the supportive care concept.

In response to such concerns, a task force of interested individuals —long-term care staff and administrators, consumer advocates, medical, legal, and social service professionals, and government agency officials—was convened to identify and discuss issues raised by the use of supportive care. The task set by the group was to make recommendations and propose a set of guidelines for the provision of supportive care in long-term care settings.

As used in this document, supportive care means the concept of providing care and medical treatment to preserve comfort, hygiene, and dignity, but not to prolong life. The DNR (Do Not Resuscitate) concept must be clearly distinguished from supportive care. While the phrase "supportive care" may have negative or misleading connotations, it was the consensus of the task force to use the term for want of any better one. It is hoped that a common understanding will develop through continuing re-examination and refinement of the concept, and by consistent usage.

It is acknowledged that decisions regarding the continuance or discontinuance of treatment are commonly made in long-term care settings. The need to make such decisions results from advances in medical technology and treatments which have increased the ability to prolong life, even in situations where the prognosis is hopeless and further treatment offers no benefit to the resident.

Such advances have raised serious questions about, and conflicts among, fundamental principles and values including:

---

Dated October 1983.

— the preservation and protection of life;

— the promotion of individual and familial autonomy;

— safeguarding the rights of all parties;

— maintaining ethical integrity and the highest standards of practice of health care providers;

— the affirmation of compassion and humane considerations; and

— the equitable allocation of resources.

Particularly difficult ethical and legal questions are raised when incompetent or not fully competent residents are involved.

We have agreed that certain principles are fundamental in all supportive care situations:

1. Any decision regarding supportive care must be made on a case by case basis with full participation of all parties, and a thorough discussion of all concerns. All supportive care plans must be individualized.

2. The resident who is competent has the final decision as to the extent of care, or withdrawal, withholding, continuance, or initiation of treatment. Regardless of the degree of competence, the resident should be involved in the decision-making process to the fullest extent possible.

3. The individual's values, religion, and life philosophy must always be respected.

4. Wherever there are serious doubts or questions, the balance in the decision making should be struck in favor of preserving life.

5. Finally, in all instances, the comfort, hygiene, and dignity of a resident must never be compromised, and personal decision making and individual choice must be paramount.

The task force further agreed upon the following:

1. We recommend a principled approach to decision making in advance or by proxy, such as the use of living wills, advance directives, proxy decision makers, or other means of conveying a person's wishes to his family and physician regarding the prolonging of life or the withholding of treatment.

2. We recommend the formulation and adoption of institutional policies and procedures to address the issues raised in the initiation and provision of supportive care.

3. We recommend that long-term care facilities establish interdisciplinary biomedical ethics committees to assist in developing and implementing supportive care policies.

This document is our first attempt to address some of the problems faced by those involved in a supportive care situation. It is directed to residents, their families and friends, health care providers, and long-term care facilities to provide a basis for discussion, and assistance in making and carrying out supportive care decisions.

We have addressed only those circumstances involving competent or formerly competent adults in long-term care settings. We do not address situations involving individuals who were never competent (newborns, mentally retarded), nor do we address supportive care in acute care settings—although similar principles and procedures may apply.

This document makes recommendations and proposes guidelines for discussion and decision making when a supportive care plan is considered. It first defines *what supportive care is,* by making a basic statement of philosophy and by outlining care and treatment which typically will be given or withheld under a supportive care plan. It then discusses *for whom supportive care might be considered* by outlining several major categories of medical conditions which may make consideration of a supportive care plan appropriate. Finally, the remainder of the document sets forth *procedures to be followed* whenever a supportive care plan is considered.

While this document does provide a guideline for decision making, it cannot eliminate the significant ethical, religious, medical, and legal questions inherent in supportive care situations, nor will its use assure certainty in complex medical or legal cases.

## WHAT IS SUPPORTIVE CARE?

A decision to provide supportive care to an individual means a decision to provide care and treatment to preserve comfort, hygiene, and dignity, but not to prolong life. Supportive care is not considered to be part of the concept of euthanasia or causing death, but rather should be viewed as not extending life in hopeless situations. See For Whom Supportive Care Might Be Considered.

Once it has been determined that supportive care is appropriate, after utilizing the decision-making procedures outlined below, written orders for the individual plan of care must be established. The primary aims of a supportive care plan should be to promote the dignity of the individual and to minimize pain or discomfort. There should also be active support for the psychological, social, emotional, and spiritual needs of the individual and family.

An individual supportive care plan for a resident in a long-term care facility should include consideration of the following guidelines:

1. A specific disease or life-threatening condition which could end life but which does not cause pain or discomfort normally would not be treated. For example, pneumonia not causing dyspnea or pleuritic pain would not be treated.

2. Specific medical conditions which compromise comfort, hygiene, and dignity would be treated. For example, oxygen would be provided to alleviate dyspnea; pneumonia causing pleuritic pain would be treated; a clear airway would be maintained as by suctioning; localized infections and fractures would be treated.

3. Specific nursing care for comfort, hygiene, bowel care, skin care, passive range of motion (PROM) and positioning, and catheter care would be given.

4. Hospitalization or more extensive medical intervention would not ordinarily be indicated. There may be exceptions to this (see #2 above).

5. In most cases, a resident with a supportive care plan would have a do not resuscitate (DNR) order in the medical record.[1]

6. Life sustaining nutrition and hydration needs would ordinarily be met. There is no consensus within the task force on the controversial issue of when and under what circumstances food and fluids may be withheld. We do agree, however, that the existence of a supportive care plan does not in itself predetermine whether artificial means of providing fluids and nutrition will be continued or discontinued. Each individual case must be given careful and sensitive consideration.

7. The resident and family shall have as much control as possible over the care and activity level of the resident.

## For Whom Supportive Care Might Be Considered

Residents in long-term care facilities who fall within the following major categories of medical conditions may be considered *potential* candidates for supportive care plans, when there exists clear documentation of the medical condition, and a high degree of certainty of the diagnosis and prognosis. Our intent in setting forth these categories is to limit rather than expand the numbers of long-term care residents who may be considered for supportive care plans.

1. *Terminally Ill and Imminently Dying*, for example, from cancer or cardiac disease.

2. *Severe and Irreversible Mental Disability*, where the resident demonstrates a significant inability to communicate, or to interact meaningfully with the environment, and an unawareness of self and/or the environment; for example, those with pre-senile and senile dementia (Alzheimer's disease) and cerebral vascular disease (strokes).[2]

3. *Severe and Irreversible Physical Disability*, where there may exist normal mental functioning but, because of pain and suffering, or severe motor impairment, the resident demonstrates a significant inability to interact physically in a meaningful way with the environment; for example, spinal cord injury, head trauma, emphysema, and amyotrophic lateral sclerosis.[3]

## PROCEDURES FOR INITIATION OF A SUPPORTIVE CARE PLAN

### WHEN A SUPPORTIVE CARE PLAN SHOULD BE CONSIDERED

There is no need for any haste in evaluating a resident for initiation of a supportive care plan. Time should be allowed to carefully and thoroughly consider all aspects of the resident's condition.

1. A supportive care plan is generally inadvisable as part of the initial admission care plan. Before the appropriateness of supportive care can be fully determined, a complete medical record, including a full analysis of rehabilitative potential, should be created within the long-term care setting itself. However, in some cases a supportive care plan on admission may be appropriate depending on the resident's condition, previous course of care, completeness of previous record, and so forth. The physician and the facility should be open to full discussion of the issue if it is raised at admission.

2. We recommend that the facility not affirmatively suggest the initiation of a supportive care plan. Such a plan is a very personal medical, religious, and ethical matter for the resident, family, and attending physician. However, we do recommend that the facility staff be open and receptive to discussions of death and the dying process. The facility staff may serve as a valuable resource to residents and families, but should also act as a champion for any rehabilitative potential that may exist.

3. If a resident is admitted to a facility with physician orders for a supportive care plan, we recommend that the order not be fol-

lowed without going through the decision-making process outlined below, or, at the very least, without thoroughly assuring, and carefully documenting, that a decision-making process raising all relevant issues had previously been undertaken. In all cases, the facility should clarify the orders received so that no ambiguity exists about the intentions of the physician and the resident.

PARTICIPANTS IN A SUPPORTIVE CARE DECISION

*Resident*

The resident must always be involved to the fullest extent possible, even if the resident is under guardianship. The procedures recommended here are intended to involve all interested persons to the fullest extent possible in the final decision so that all viewpoints are represented and thoroughly aired, and so that legal risks are minimized if the resident is unable to make the final decision.

Since supportive care may be viewed by some as placing a resident in a life-threatening situation, any such plan for an incompetent or questionably competent resident involves considerable exposure to serious legal risks. Such a plan may, however, be in the best interests of the resident if all viewpoints, including medical, religious, ethical, and personal, as well as legal, are weighed against one another.

There is some question under guardianship law as to whether a guardian of a person has the legal authority to consent to a supportive care plan. Therefore, while these guidelines recommend having a guardian appointed if at all possible, a guardian's consent is not an absolute guarantee of proper authority to undertake a supportive care plan.

1. *Competent Resident.* When the resident is clearly competent, the resident has the full authority to make the decision on a supportive care plan, one way or the other.

2. *Questionably Competent Resident.* When there are questions about the resident's competence, but the resident is not under guardianship and is still able to express his or her wishes, the following principles should govern:

   — If the resident does not want a supportive care plan, no plan should be initiated.

   — If the resident seems to want a supportive care plan, the initiation of a guardianship for the resident should be encouraged so that someone is legally designated to speak for the resident.

— If the resident seems to want a supportive care plan and if guardianship is not a viable alternative, a supportive care plan may properly be initiated after thorough family, physician, staff, and Biomedical Ethics Committee involvement, as outlined below.

3. *Incompetent Resident Not under Guardianship.* If the resident is clearly incompetent but not under guardianship, and the resident is unable to express himself or herself, the following principles should govern:

— Without a guardian, no one is legally authorized to speak for the resident. This situation involves serious risks for the physician, the facility, and the family. However, we all agree that an incompetent resident should not be deprived of the right to a supportive care plan merely because of incompetence. Therefore, we recommend the initiation of a guardianship for the resident, so that someone is legally authorized to speak for the resident.

— If guardianship is not a viable alternative, but a supportive care plan seems highly appropriate under all the circumstances, a supportive care plan can be initiated after the careful involvement of family, interested parties, staff, physician, and Biomedical Ethics Committee. Be aware, however, that such a situation does pose great risks to all involved.

— If there is no guardian and no family to involve in the decision-making process, but a supportive care plan seems highly appropriate, a physician and a facility should carefully consider whether to initiate a supportive care plan without receiving court approval. In this case, the involvement of the Biomedical Ethics Committee is particularly important and strongly recommended. Facilities and physicians are cautioned, however, that deciding against a supportive care plan in highly appropriate circumstances because of potential legal risks for themselves may in itself violate the rights of the resident, both legally and ethically.

4. *Incompetent Resident under Guardianship.*

— The consent of both the guardian and the resident should be obtained, if the resident can in any way express his or her wishes. The family should be involved as outlined below.

— A guardian may wish to seek probate court approval of a supportive care plan; however, at this point, it is not at all clear how the court would view such a request.

*Family and Interested Persons*

1. Whenever possible, unless the resident is clearly competent and forbids it, the family should be fully involved in the decision-making process. All family members who are involved with the resident's care and activities should be included, and all family members as close or closer in degree of relationship to the resident as the involved persons should be notified of the discussion. Any other family members who may reasonably wish to be included in the decision-making process should also be notified.

2. Other persons or groups involved in the resident's care and/ or activities, or in support of the family, should also be involved.

3. We recommend that the resident's attending physician take primary responsibility for the notification and involvement of family and others. Each physician and facility could, however, develop cooperative procedures in this respect.

*Resident's Attending Physician*

1. A supportive care plan should be initiated by orders of the resident's attending physician only, never by the facility medical director unless the medical director is the attending physician.

2. If the resident and family are strongly in favor of supportive care and the physician is not, they have the right to consult another physician whose philosophy is more akin to their own. However, the resident and family should be strongly encouraged to consider why the physician is opposed and we encourage the involvement of the Biomedical Ethics Committee.

3. If the physician questions a family's motivation for initiation of supportive care plan, or if there is irresolvable conflict among family members, the matter should be referred to the facility Biomedical Ethics Committee for additional guidance.

*Long-Term Care Facility Involvement*

1. *Administrative and Professional Staff.*
   — The Director of Nursing Services, the Resident Services Director, and the Social Services Director, or their delegates, should be involved in the discussion. Minimally, the

Administrator should be informed of the existence of the discussion.

— General supportive care policies should be developed, along with a basic evaluation sheet, to ensure that all relevant information is gathered and assessed.

2. *Direct Care Givers.* Input should be solicited from those directly involved in care of the resident as they may notice small details or patterns of significance in the condition of the resident. Careful note should be given to the observations and opinions of the direct care giver, particularly when they conflict with the recommendation of the resident or the physician that a supportive care plan is appropriate.

3. *Medical Director.* The medical director of a long-term care facility should not direct a supportive care plan unless he or she is also the resident's attending physician.

We recommend involvement of the medical director in each supportive care decision-making process, but do not see this as an absolute requirement. He or she should at least be informed of the existence and progress of the consideration, and should be available for counsel or conflict resolution, if necessary.

The medical director should participate in the development of, and ultimately approve, all general supportive care policies developed by the facility.

4. *Biomedical Ethics Committee.* We encourage consideration of each potential supportive care plan by an interdisciplinary Biomedical Ethics Committee. In most facilities, the beginnings of such a committee may already exist (e.g., Utilization Review Committee).

Even when it is quite certain that a competent resident may authorize a supportive care plan for himself or herself, we nevertheless would encourage committee review. In cases of questionably competent or incompetent residents, we feel it very important to have the committee's more objective involvement.

While the use of a facility's Utilization Review Committee as a Biomedical Ethics Committee may be reasonable for the present, we would recommend future development of an expanded committee to include lay, religious, medical, legal, and other professional representation.

SUPPORTIVE CARE DECISION-MAKING PROCESS

The decision-making process should be designed to encourage full discussion of all relevant facts and options so that the meaning and significance of supportive care are fully understood by all participants, and to ensure that all views are expressed and weighed, and so that full documentation of the plan will be possible. The following steps are recommended:

1. The issue is raised by the resident, family, or physician.

2. The attending physician and facility should obtain complete medical and psychosocial information from the resident's records, at both the hospital and the long-term care facility. Observations and other comments which may not be completely reflected in the medical records should be solicited from direct care givers.

3. The physician and/or facility staff should privately discuss the potential supportive care plan and the significance with the resident, if at all possible, so that an assessment can be made in the absence of any pressure by family members.

4. The physician should participate in a full discussion with family members and/or other interested and involved persons, with the consent of the resident if competent. Other family members should be notified of the discussions by the physician.

5. The resident's physician and facility staff should discuss the issue thoroughly among themselves. The facility should assure itself that full discussion between the physician and the resident and family has taken place.

6. All issues should be raised and discussed with facility staff in a care conference format.

7. The proposed plan should be considered by the Biomedical Ethics Committee, particularly if the plan is for an incompetent or questionably competent resident.

*General Admonitions*

1. Document *all* conferences carefully and thoroughly.

2. Do not force a final decision too soon after all discussions have taken place. Let all involved have time to mull matters over.

*Conflict Resolution Principles*

1. If the resident can express himself or herself and does not want a supportive care plan, it should not be initiated, or, if initiated by the physician, it should not be carried out by the facility.

2. If the resident and family want a supportive care plan and the resident's physician will not initiate one, the resident and family have the right to consult another physician. In such cases, however, the facility should ensure that the initial physician's concerns and viewpoints are fully considered.

3. If the resident is unable to express himself or herself and the family seems to be pressing for a plan, the physician and facility should carefully weigh all factors before initiating and carrying out the plan to ensure its appropriateness. The physician and facility should carefully consider the family's intentions and motivations and should refer the case to the Biomedical Ethics Committee before initiating the plan.

4. If there is an intra-family dispute over the appropriateness of a plan, we recommend careful consideration by the physician and facility as this poses a great risk of legal challenge. We also recommend utilization of the Biomedical Ethics Committee or other facility or community resources to resolve the conflict prior to initiating the plan.

5. If the facility staff, medical director, or Biomedical Ethics Committee do not concur with the resident, family, or physician on the appropriateness of a plan (for example, if the facility feels significant rehabilitation potential exists), the facility should forcefully express such opinion to the resident, family, and physician to ensure that its objections are heard and understood. The facility may choose to refuse to implement the plan and recommend discharge, or may even consider resort to the courts.

DOCUMENTATION OF A SUPPORTIVE CARE PLAN

1. Physician authorization for a supportive care plan should be a specific, *individualized* set of orders, stating explicitly what will and will not be done for the resident. It must be part of the medical record. An order saying just "Supportive Care" (unlike "DNR") is not sufficient.

2. Written authorization for the plan should be obtained from the resident whenever possible, even if under guardianship. The guardian should also authorize the plan.

3. Written acknowledgment of the plan should be obtained from those interested persons who have been involved in the decision-making process whenever possible.

4. The specific plan and the facility policies on supportive care should be given to the resident and family so that no ambiguity exists.

5. The decision, the nature of the plan, and other relevant matters should be thoroughly discussed with all staff involved with the resident.

RE-EVALUATION OF A SUPPORTIVE CARE PLAN

1. The plan must be re-evaluated whenever the facts or conditions which led to the initial plan change, or whenever the resident, family, or other involved person requests it. The same persons should be involved in re-evaluation as were included in the initial decision.

2. The supportive care plan should be reviewed periodically, when the general plan of care is reviewed. We recommend review on a 30-day basis, in any event.

3. We recommend that criteria and an input sheet be developed for re-evaluation, to ensure that direct care givers are given guidance on what changes in conditions to look for.

## Conclusion

The task force does not view these recommendations and guidelines as the definitive resolution of the dilemmas raised by the supportive care concept, but rather as part of an ongoing dialogue on supportive care issues and practices. Comments are welcome and may be directed to individual members of the task force.

The recommendations and guidelines set forth in this report represent the views of the signatories as individuals. They do not necessarily reflect the policy of any institution, professional organization, or governmental agency with which the signatory is affiliated.

Barbara J. Blumer, J.D.
Attorney at Law
Broeker, Hartfeldt, Hedges & Grant

M. Francesca Chervenak, J.D.
Attorney at Law
Legal Aid Society of Minneapolis

Ronald E. Cranford, M.D.
Associate Physician in Neurology
Hennepin County Medical Center

Julie L. Ditzler, R.N., B.S.N.
Resident Services Director
Cedar Pines Health Care Facility

Jenean Erickson,
R.N., F.A.C.N.H.A.
Administrator
Yorkshire Manor

Iris C. Freeman
Director
Nursing Home
Residents' Advocates

Paul Goldstein
Assistant Director of Social Services
Hennepin County Medical Center

F. Allen Hester, J.D.
Adjunct Professor of Law
William Mitchell College of Law

Grace Nelson
Long Term Care Committee
Minnesota Senior Federation

Pamela J. Parker
Former Long Term
Care Ombudsman
Minnesota Board on Aging

Arnold Rosenthal
Director of the Office
of Health Facility Complaints
Minnesota Department of Health

Lise Laffoley Schmidt, J.D.
Attorney at Law
Minnesota Legal Services Coalition

Jim Varpness
Long Term Care Ombudsman
Minnesota Board on Aging

## Notes

1. See the Minnesota Medical Association DNR Guidelines adopted by the MMA Board of Trustees in January 1981.
2. The life of a physically or mentally disabled person is just as valuable as that of a person described as normal or healthy. It is not appropriate to consider a supportive care plan on the basis of a physical or mental disability alone.
3. *Id.*

# A LIVING WILL

## Concern for Dying

---

### *To My Family, My Physician, My Lawyer and All Others Whom It May Concern*

Death is as much a reality as birth, growth, maturity and old age—it is the one certainty of life. If the time comes when I can no longer take part in decisions for my own future, let this statement stand as an expression of my wishes and directions, while I am still of sound mind.

If at such a time the situation should arise in which there is no reasonable expectation of my recovery from extreme physical or mental disability, I direct that I be allowed to die and not be kept alive by medications, artificial means or "heroic measures." I do, however, ask that medication be mercifully administered to me to alleviate suffering even though this may shorten my remaining life.

This statement is made after careful consideration and is in accordance with my strong convictions and beliefs. I want the wishes and directions here expressed carried out to the extent permitted by law. Insofar as they are not legally enforceable, I hope that those to whom this Will is addressed will regard themselves as morally bound by these provisions.

*(Optional specific provisions to be made in this space—see other side)*

---

*Durable power of attorney (optional):* I hereby designate _____
to serve as my attorney-in-fact for the purpose of making treatment decisions. This power of attorney shall remain effective in the event that I become incompetent to make treatment decisions for me in the event I am comatose or otherwise unable to make such decisions for myself.

| | |
|---|---|
| *Optional Notarization:* | Signed _____ |
| "Sworn and subscribed to | Date _____ |
| before me this ____ day | Witness _____ |
| of _____, 19____." | Witness _____ |

Notary Public
(seal)

Copies of this request have been given to _____

---

*(Optional)*   My Living Will is registered with Concern for Dying (No. ____)

---

## To Make Best Use of Your Living Will

You may wish to add specific statements to the Living Will *in the space provided for that purpose above your signature.* Possible additional provisions are:

1.  Measures of artificial life support in the face of impending death that I specifically refuse are:

    a.  Electrical or mechanical resuscitation of my heart when it has stopped beating.

    b.  Nasogastric tube feeding when I am paralyzed or unable to take nourishment by mouth.

    c.  Mechanical respiration when I am no longer able to sustain my own breathing.

    d.  _____

2.  I would like to live out my last days at home rather than in a hospital if it does not jeopardize the chance of my recovery to a meaningful and sentient life or does not impose an undue burden on my family.

3.  If any of my tissues are sound and would be of value as transplants to other people, I freely give my permission for such donation.

If you choose more than one proxy for decision making on your behalf, please give order of priority (1, 2, 3, etc.).

Space is provided at the bottom of the Living will for notarization should you choose to have your Living Will witnessed by a Notary Public.

R<small>EMEMBER</small> . . .

- Sign and date your Living Will. Your two witnesses, who should not be blood relatives or beneficiaries of your property will, should also sign in the spaces provided.

- Discuss your Living Will with your doctors; if they agree with you, give them copies of your signed Living Will document for them to add to your medical file.

- Give copies of your signed Living Will to anyone who may be making decisions for you if you are unable to make them yourself.

- Look over your Living Will once a year, redate it, and initial the new date to make it clear that your wishes have not changed.

———————————

The Concern for Dying newsletter is a quarterly publication reporting the most recent developments in the field of death and dying. It contains announcements of upcoming educational conferences, workshops, and symposia, as well as reviews of current literature. The newsletter is sent to anyone who contributes $5.00 or more annually to Concern for Dying.

Additional materials available to contributors:

> Questions and answers about the Living Will
> Selected articles and case histories
> A bibliography
> Information on films

## T<small>HE</small> L<small>IVING</small> W<small>ILL</small> R<small>EGISTRY</small>

In 1983, Concern for Dying instituted the Living Will Registry, a computerized file system where you may keep an up-to-date copy of your Living Will in our New York office.

What are the benefits of joining the Living Will Registry?

- Concern's staff will ensure that your form is filled out correctly, assign you a Registry Number, and maintain a copy of your Living Will.

- Concern's staff will be able to refer to *your* personal document, explain procedures and options, and provide you with the latest case law or state legislation should you, your proxy, or anyone else acting on your behalf need counselling or legal guidance in implementing your Living Will.

- You will receive a permanent credit-card size plastic mini-will with your Registry number imprinted on it. The mini-will, which contains your address, Concern's address, and a short version of the Living Will, indicates that you have already filled out a full-sized, witnessed Living Will document.

HOW DO YOU JOIN THE LIVING WILL REGISTRY?

- Review your Living Will, making sure it is up to date and contains any specific provisions that you want added.

- Mail a copy of your original, signed and witnessed document along with a check for $25.00 to:

  The Living Will Registry
  Concern for Dying
  250 West 57th Street, Room 831
  New York, New York  10107

  The one-time Registry enrollment fee will cover the costs of processing and maintaining your Living Will and of issuing your new plastic mini-will.

- If you have any address changes or wish to add or delete special provisions that you have included in your Living Will, please write to the Registry so that we can keep your file up to date.

# LIVING WILL GUIDELINES

## Mount Sinai Hospital, Minneapolis, Minnesota

These guidelines have been drafted by the Mount Sinai Hospital Biomedical Ethics Committee. Increasing numbers of patients want to make a statement regarding the care they wish when they are terminally ill, specifically, the decision to have life-sustaining or death-prolonging procedures withheld or withdrawn. It is recommended that the patient and physician discuss and plan for the terminal care period and record that plan in the event of the patient becoming incompetent. A suggested document that can be prepared and entered in the physician and hospital record is the Living Will. (A sample Living Will is shown in Figure 1.)

### DEFINITION

A Living Will is a written statement prepared by a competent adult that describes the medical care that individual would wish should he/she become terminally ill and possibly no longer competent or able to participate in the decision regarding his/her medical care.

### CONSIDERATIONS

1. A competent adult always has the fundamental right to refuse treatment.
2. A Living Will can serve as a clear statement of the competent person's intent to accept or refuse life-sustaining treatment during the terminal phase of life.

### IMPLEMENTATION

1. If the patient has a Living Will, a copy should be placed on the patient's chart. An identifying sticker will also be placed on the front of the chart stating, "This patient has a Living Will," and a statement to this effect will be placed in the nursing care plan.
2. The Living Will will preferably have been discussed with the physician prior to admission. If not, it is advisable to discuss it as soon

---

Drafted November 1982. Approved by Mount Sinai Hospital Medical Executive Committee, May 3, 1983.

thereafter as possible and/or at the time of significant medical changes or diagnoses. All facts and considerations pertinent to the decisions made should be recorded in the Progress Notes. The physician should then, when appropriate, write orders in the patient's chart in accordance with the discussion, e.g., DNR, comfort care only, no antibiotics.

3. Metro Senior Health Program Clinic patients should discuss their Living Will with Metro Clinic staff. A copy of the Living Will should be filed in the Metro Clinic chart with a report of the discussion regarding the Living Will written in the Progress Notes. Notification of a Living Will should also be placed in the inside front pocket of the Metro chart.

4. A Living Will may be revoked or changed at any time by a competent patient. Should the patient revoke the directive, the physician should record the time and date of the revocation and any other pertinent considerations to the decision in the Progress Notes. Subsequent order changes may also need to be recorded.

Figure 1: Sample Living Will

I, _____, believe that it is my right to control the decisions relating to my medical care. Being of sound mind, I wish to make known my desire that my life not be artificially prolonged should I have an incurable injury, disease, or illness known to be a terminal condition by my physician.

If the application of life-sustaining procedures would serve only to artificially prolong the moment of my death and if my physician determines that my death is imminent whether or not life-sustaining procedures are utilized, I direct that such procedures be withheld or withdrawn, and that I be permitted to die naturally.

In the absence of my ability to give directions regarding the use of such life-sustaining procedures, it is my intention that this Living Will shall be honored by my family and physician(s) as the final expression of my legal right to refuse medical or surgical treatment and I accept the consequences of such refusal. I have discussed this with my physician(s) Dr. _____. I have also made my wishes known to _____ whom you should contact in the case of my incompetence or inability to participate in medical decisions.

Special Instructions: _____

_____

_____

_____

_____

I understand that I can revoke the above Living Will at any time.

Living Will made this _____ day of _____.

Signed _____

Address _____

_____

Prepared by Mount Sinai Hospital, 2215 Park Avenue, Minneapolis, MN 55404.

# GUIDELINES IN IRREVERSIBLE TERMINAL ILLNESS

## St. Joseph Hospital, Mt. Clemens, Michigan

### STATEMENT OF VALUES AND BELIEFS

We believe that human life is a gift to be treasured, for it is a sharing in the very spirit of God.

We believe that we have a responsibility to promote the dignity of human life, that the dignity of human life must be protected from conception to death.

With this policy and all the accompanying guidelines, we affirm our intentions to protect the rights of human life in moments of illness, suffering, and death and re-affirm our opposition to euthanasia.

### OPERATIONAL DEFINITION

An illness is irreversible when no known therapeutic measures can be effective in reversing the course of illness and when the status of the patient is "irreparable" in the sense that the course of illness has progressed beyond the capacity of existing knowledge and techniques to stem the process.

### CLINICAL EXAMPLES

1. Carcinoma with advanced metastases to several body systems;
2. Failure to a major organ, such as the heart, the lungs, or the liver, with additional systems involved;
3. Under certain conditions, advanced age and debility of the patient.

### GUIDELINES FOR NONRESUSCITATIVE MEASURES

In accordance with sound medical practice, patients have the right to be treated in accordance with their own decisions and expectations. This means that the use of treatment to sustain or prolong life can be justified only by adherence to the dictates of both sound medical practice and the patient's right to elect or decline the benefits of medical

---

Dated September 1983.

technology. Among the factors that are reality-making in determining the management of the patient are his/her own freedom to die the death that he/she is in fact dying and the fact that he/she has already begun the process of dying. If the competent patient chooses the option of nonresuscitative measures, this choice may not be overridden by contrary views of family members. It is important to inform the family members of this choice, with the patient's permission and according to his/her directions.

The primary physician makes the decision, and may choose to make his/her decision in consultation with another physician, and only with the informed consent of a competent patient, or of the family or legal guardian if the patient is unable to make the decision. The physician should explain the course that will follow in the event of sudden cessation of a patient's vital functions to the family and/or the patient.

## Policy

This should be fully documented. The decision must be documented by a witness (nurse) and daily reviewed and documented by the physician.

Other health care professionals, especially Pastoral Care Department staff, may be called upon to support the patient and/or family in the dying process and/or the decision process regarding nonresuscitative measures.

# GUIDELINES IN IRREVERSIBLE COMA

## St. Joseph Hospital, Mt. Clemens, Michigan

### STATEMENT OF VALUES AND BELIEFS

We believe that human life is a gift to be treasured, for it is a sharing in the very spirit of God.

We believe that we have a responsibility to promote the dignity of human life, that the dignity of human life must be protected from conception to death.

With this policy and all the accompanying guidelines, we affirm our intentions to protect the rights of human life in moments of illness, suffering, and death and re-affirm our opposition to euthanasia.

### OPERATIONAL DEFINITION

Irreversible coma is not diagnosed by a physician before at least 100 days of persisting coma have elapsed. This amount of time is needed to help distinguish whether the coma is reversible or irreversible. In both, there is clinical evidence of brain stem function. In reversible coma, after the initial paralysis of the arousal response, the person does finally respond to the environment.

Irreversible coma deals with fragmented viability of brain stem, characterized by loss of the arousal response; there is a total unawareness of externally-applied stimuli. Even the most intensely painful stimuli evoke no vocal or other response, not even a groan, withdrawal of a limb, or quickening of respiration. Irreversible coma is also characterized by paralysis of some, but not all, of the other vital functions:

1. Pupillary constriction to light;
2. Extra-ocular movement in response to changing the position of the head (Doll's eye test);
3. Closure of the eye to touching the eye lid or cornea (pontobulbar reflex);
4. Eye movement response to caloric stimulation of the tympanic membrane;
5. Gag reflex;
6. Spontaneous respirations.

Dated September 1983.

The use of electroencephalograph (EEG) is optional.

## GUIDELINES FOR THE USE OF
## ARTIFICIAL SUPPORT SYSTEMS

The decision to use or continue to use artificial support systems for a person with irreversible coma should take into account these three (3) issues:

1. Ordinary versus extraordinary means;
2. Prolonging life versus prolonging the dying process;
3. Allowing someone to die versus direct killing.

### ORDINARY VERSUS EXTRAORDINARY MEANS

Ordinary means, in the technical definition as approved by the American Medical Association (AMA), are those measures of preserving life which offer a reasonable hope of benefit for the patient and can be obtained and used without excessive expense, pain, or other inconvenience to the patient.

Extraordinary means, in the technical definition as approved by the AMA, are those measures of preserving life which cannot be obtained without excessive expense, pain, or other inconvenience to the patient, or which, if used, would not offer a reasonable hope for benefit for the patient.

There is no moral obligation to utilize extraordinary means.

### PROLONGING LIFE VERSUS PROLONGING THE DYING PROCESS

The dying process is the time in the course of an irreversible illness when treatment will no longer reverse it. Our responsibility to the dying differs from our responsibility to the living or the potentially still living. Just as it would be negligence to the sick to treat them as if they were about to die, so it is another sort of negligence to treat the dying as if they were going to get well or might get well. Some things are done for patients not as a means of preserving life but as ways of caring. To care for the dying is often the only means by which we can express our faithfulness to the human person.

### ALLOWING SOMEONE TO DIE VERSUS DIRECT KILLING

Euthanasia consists of direct actions designed to terminate the life of an individual painlessly so as to end suffering. To choose to refrain from treatment which serves no purpose is not to cause the death of a human person. The person's death comes from the causes that it is no longer merciful or reasonable to fight by means of possible medical interventions.

NONRESUSCITATIVE MEASURES

To choose nonresuscitation in anticipation of cardiac and/or respiratory arrest, in the case of someone with irreversible coma, is to choose not to use an extraordinary means for a dying person. This choice is a more appropriate measure of caring for the dying person than resuscitative measures which would only prolong the dying process.

TREATMENT DECISIONS

Any decisions about treatment measures are to be made by the attending physician in consultation with the family or legal guardian of the patient. Other health care professionals, especially Pastoral Care Department staff, may be called upon to support the family in the decision process.

# DIFFICULT DECISIONS—LET US HELP YOU THINK IT THROUGH

## North Memorial Medical Center, Robbinsdale, Minnesota

We know that you are now facing a difficult time and some painful decisions. In order to help us arrive at the best course of action, we have put down some ideas and ways of thinking through this problem. No one need see this form. It is yours to use to help you process your thoughts. We recognize that though you must have facts and knowledge about the situation, it is also an emotionally difficult time, and we encourage you to express those feelings of sadness, sorrow, and anger. We will support you in every way that we can as we go through this together. This is especially difficult when your loved one is unconscious and cannot be involved in the discussion.

1. As you understand it, what is the problem? What exactly is the question we are trying to resolve? (This may seem obvious, but it helps to clarify your thoughts if you write it down. It also helps you to say the unsayable and think the unthinkable. Just saying the problem out loud helps.)

2. In your own words, what has the doctor told you about the situation?

3. Do you have all the facts you need? If not, list any questions that you still have.

4. Who else do you want to speak to? Chaplain, lawyer, another physician, relatives, counselor. It is important for us to gather all the information we can.

5. What do you think we should do?

6. Why do you think this? That is, upon what belief or value do you base this decision? (Again, now may be the time you need to speak to a priest, minister, rabbi, counselor, or lawyer. If so, ask us for help with this.)

7. Is this, as far as you know, your loved one's belief? What do you think that he or she would want you to do in this situation? (Keep in mind that during periods of grief and shock it is not uncommon to feel guilty, resentful, angry, or confused. It is easier when you recognize this and have help understanding your own reactions.)

8. Is this, as far as you know, the belief of others in your family? (Here is often where conflicts between family members will arise. You begin to examine why you feel as you do about certain things. You sometimes find out that your beliefs are different from those of people that you love. Now is the time we need to examine these feelings and beliefs of your family members.)

9. What do you think that your loved one would want you to do? Have you talked to your loved one about this situation in the past? What do you remember about that conversation? (These questions help you to realize that a patient may have often talked about what he would have liked done. It helps you get in touch with the rights of the patient.)

10. What would you want for yourself in a similar situation?

11. What is the best that could happen for your loved one?

12. What is the worst that could happen in your opinion?

13. What options do we have now to solve this dilemma? Let us examine every possible solution pro and con.

14. How do you see this decision being made?
    We will sit down together to discuss this information and these feelings and beliefs. We will do all that we can to help you come to a good decision.

We will arrange a conference with Dr. _____,

Chaplain _____, Nurse _____,

others _____ at _____.

North Memorial Medical Center
Hospice Unit

## IMPLEMENTING FAMILY DISCUSSION OF ETHICAL DILEMMAS AND DECISION MAKING IN A HOSPICE SETTING

Hospice traditionally has meant no extraordinary measures, so when we were asked by a neurologist if we could bring a comatose woman on a respirator to our unit in order to facilitate the decision to remove the respirator, we were understandably cautious. Were we setting a difficult precedent? Were we setting ourselves up for a long-term patient that would not be appropriate for the Hospice? The neurologist explained that he believed that the concept of family and patient as one unit of care is important and that though the woman was in a coma, her family was standing by in much anguish, and could we help?

North Memorial Medical Center Hospice Program is located in a 400-bed acute care community hospital, with strong emphasis on trauma care. It is our belief that a Hospice Program should meet the needs of the community it serves, and so it was that our original idea of pure Hospice care, with no extraordinary measures, was tested. The neurologist who asked us to help had the right idea. He knew that the decision to remove the woman from the respirator was going to be difficult, and our staff would be equipped to help. It was at this time also that we began to discover that our own staff had problems describing their feelings and their reasons for feeling strongly about ethical decision making. We also discovered that the physicians involved were not exactly clear about their own basis for decisions, other than the clinical ones. We first used this form with the staff to clarify the problem and help us to understand the best way to help, and then decided we should use it with families so that we could all approach the situation with the facts as straight as we could get them.

Using this method, a decision was made, the family was comfortable, and the physician was comfortable with what was decided. The woman was weaned from the respirator and died in about one week, with the family intact and supported.

Since that time we have had 14 patients transferred to Hospice in order to help facilitate the family decisions about what was to be done. These dilemmas have included decisions about food and fluid, respirators, and further treatment. This is not a traditional role of Hospice, but I believe it is an appropriate one. We have learned that a collegial approach, adequate time spent, a comfortable place to be while the family is working it through, a staff that accepts expression of a wide range of emotion, the availability of information and good clinical data, even when there is not the luxury of much time, can make the difficult a little easier, can allow everyone to voice their opinions and insure that the best decision that can be made will be made. We have learned also the importance of allowing families time to process and rage and grieve.

We have learned that the team approach, including staff, family, counselor or chaplain, and any other people the family feels necessary, provides an arena in which much healing happens. We have seen, also importantly, that we are able to support each other through the phases of this decision-making process, and each time we do it, we learn something new.

After a family has had some time to think through the ideas about what should be done, discussed it with each other, gone over their ideas and thoughts, a conference must be arranged. The object of the conference is first to be sure that all information needed is given. It is important to discuss all aspects of the situation with the team before you meet with the family. Do not assume that the physician has all the information he needs; often there are family situations that he or she is not aware of. In fact, we have seen one of the most important steps may be to help the physician examine how he or she feels about the situation. It will be much easier for a physician to deliver bad news and state the true facts if he or she has discussed it first with the team, or at least one member of the team. We learn that physicians appreciate the support that they receive during this process. It is also important to allow the expression of feeling to happen throughout the conference. Sometimes this takes hours.

This form is used informally and is not a part of our chart; however, it could be adapted for documenting informed consent. The form is not intended to take the place of discussion, but to implement and guide it. It has been a beginning for us in learning to help people through very hard days. In speaking with families many months after having gone through these discussions, many have commented about how helpful it has been. We believe that decisions about ethical dilemmas are best made with care and responsibility by the people involved.

Kitty Kotchian Smith
Hospice Coordinator
North Memorial Medical Center
November 4, 1983

# GUIDELINES FOR HEALTH PROFESSIONALS IN DEALING WITH ETHICAL DILEMMAS

## Saint Joseph Hospital, Orange, California

### PREAMBLE

Saint Joseph Hospital is committed to a philosophy which places a high value on integrity and justice for all individuals: patients, families/ friends, volunteers, personnel, medical staff, the larger community. Personnel are expected to be aware of their own rights and responsibilities and the rights and responsibilities of others and to take action when valid rights are being threatened. Unfortunately, many ethical issues go unresolved because they are either not recognized or are ignored.

### INTRODUCTION

The following principles and guidelines are intended to provide health professionals employed by the Hospital with a framework for analyzing and resolving ethical conflicts and ambiguities which arise in his or her professional life. We refer to questions which usually involve "What is the right thing to do?," "How can I fulfill my obligations to be an advocate of the patient and families, a co-worker of physicians, a Hospital employee?," "How should I respond when I am faced with conflicting loyalties and responsibilities?" We recognize, at the outset, that the health professional is in a unique position, located at the interface of patient, family, doctor, hospital, and self. Dilemmas often arise when there are conflicts of values, obligations, and loyalties among and within these various groups.

---

Approved April 5, 1983. Bioethics Committee members included D. Baker, L.C.S.W.; R. Ball, M.D.; H. Burney, R.N.; R. Casciari, M.D.; S. Condon, R.N.; L. Cooper, M.D.; Sister Corrine; Sister Frances; A. Goldstein, M.D.; P. McMillan, R.N.C.; D. Halcrow, M.D.; P. Hinckle, M.D.; R. Lau, M.D.; G. Markham, D.Min.; Father McNamara; R. Miller, M.D.; Sister Phyllis; D. Pugh, R.N.; B. Redmond, R.N.; L. Sas, L.C.S.W.; K. Stoff, R.N.; Sister Teresa; A. Tracy, R.N.; D. Wynn, R.N.; and V. Wittstock, R.N.

## DEFINITIONS

A. Ethics—the study of how people ought to behave toward each other.
B. Bioethics—the study of ethical issues in health care.
C. Dilemma—conflict of obligation, loyalties, or values, in which every choice has both good and bad elements.

## EXAMPLES OF ETHICAL DILEMMAS

A. What should you do if you feel a patient and/or family's wishes regarding treatment are not being respected?
B. What should you do if you think a physician isn't giving patient and/or family adequate information for them to make a decision regarding treatment?
C. What should you do if family members request that certain information be withheld from a patient?
D. What should you do if you are asked to participate in something you have ethical objections to—i.e., placebo therapy, electroshock therapy, codes, etc?
E. What should you do if you think a patient is being mismanaged by a physician or a co-worker?
F. How should you handle physicians being openly derogatory about other physicians?
G. What should you do if a physician's behavior is inappropriate—e.g., abusive language?
H. What should you do if staff members are reading charts inappropriately?
I. What should you say if a patient asks about alternative forms of treatment to the one he or she is currently receiving?
J. What should you do if a patient asks what you think of his or her doctor?

## STEPS IN RESOLVING ETHICAL DILEMMAS

A. Recognize yourself as an ethical person whose decision making reflects your personal values, education, and experience.
B. Realize that ethical dilemmas often involve several individuals and points of view; therefore, it is important to discuss matters with others.
C. Get the facts about "the dilemma." Verify the appropriate details of the case; for example: medical, legal, Hospital regulations, religious, who is involved, how are they involved, who has the right to make decisions, what values and principles are involved?

D.  Consider and analyze each possible course of action with regard to its acceptability to you, its accordance with Hospital philosophy, and its short- and long-range consequences.

E.  Decide which course of action is true to you and fair to others.

Figure 1: Directions for Action in Resolving a Bioethical Dilemma

This diagram suggests the direction of action an individual might follow in resolving a particular issue. It is not intended to indicate the required course of action, but rather to suggest optional possibilities, emphasizing that the Bioethics Committee is readily available to lend assistance in any phase of resolution of the problem.

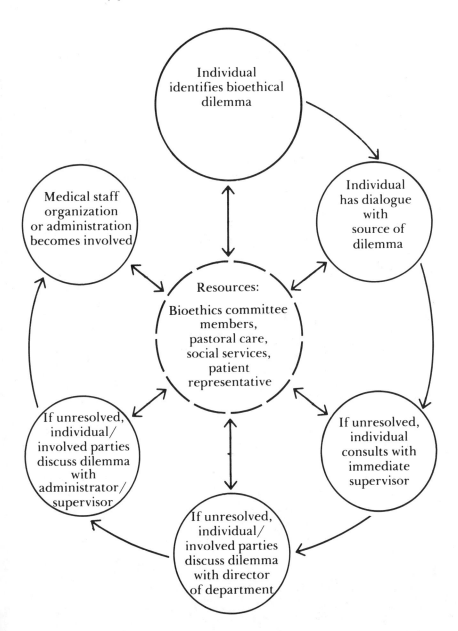

# FOREGOING LIFE-SUSTAINING TREATMENT FOR SERIOUSLY ILL NEWBORNS: ETHICAL GUIDELINES FOR DECISION MAKING

## Committee on Evolving Trends in Society Affecting Life, California Medical Association

*Note:* The following guidelines are advisory. The issues addressed by these guidelines are currently the subject of legislative debate, and may be affected by statutory or regulatory requirements.

1. Infants should receive all therapies that are clearly beneficial to them. Life-sustaining intervention should not be omitted simply because an infant is retarded.
2. Therapies expected to be futile need not be provided. When intervention would simply prolong a terminal condition, the natural process of death should be allowed to occur. However, basic, humane, and dignified care to ensure the infant's comfort should be provided under these circumstances.
3. Infants will always need a surrogate in the health care decision-making process. Parents should be the surrogates for a seriously ill newborn unless they are disqualified by decision-making incapacity, an unresolvable disagreement between them, or their choice of an action that is, in the opinion of the care givers, clearly against the infant's best interests.
4. Civil courts are ultimately the appropriate decision makers concerning the disqualification of parents as surrogates and the designation of surrogates to serve in their stead.
5. Families, health care institutions, and professionals should work together to make decisions for seriously ill infants. Recourse to the courts should be reserved for occasions when adjudication is clearly required by state law or as a last resort when concerned parties have disagreements that they cannot resolve over matters of substantial import.
6. The meaning of the diagnoses and the consequences of each treatment option must be conveyed to the parents or other surrogates.
7. When there is controversy about the appropriateness of diminishing care, the physician should consult with a member of the medical staff of the health care institution to establish the desirability of this medical decision.

---

Endorsed by the California Medical Association Council, July 1983.

8. When concerned parties have disagreements that cannot be resolved concerning treatment options, prior to recourse to the courts, mediation should be sought from an in-place, broadly based, multidisciplinary hospital ethics committee that is familiar both with the medical setting and with community standards. Such a consultative body, which would have an ongoing charge of establishing standards of treatment and issuing guidelines for the institution, would provide a framework for impartial and sensitive review of hard choices, and would guarantee that the interests of the patient were being considered without the formality and intensely adversarial character of a court proceeding. The purpose of such a committee would not be to make medical decisions or to become involved in clear-cut cases of surrogates refusing standard medical treatment, but rather to facilitate communication between concerned parties, assist in the decision-making process when ethical conflicts occur, and retrospectively review decisions for the purpose of policy making.

# DECISION MAKING FOR CRITICALLY ILL AND HANDICAPPED NEWBORNS

Twin Cities Committee for
Neonatal Life Support Policy

## INTRODUCTION

During the past several years, national attention has been focused on the difficult ethical problems faced on a daily basis in newborn intensive care units. In response both to growing public concern and to governmental policy changes at the state and federal levels, neonatologists representing all six metropolitan newborn intensive care units formed The Twin Cities Committee for Neonatal Life Support Policy. Two specific goals of the committee were (1) to formulate principles on which to base ethical decisions in the field of newborn medicine and (2) to formalize principles of decision making in newborn intensive care units. Over the past six months, this committee has drafted two documents entitled "Ethical Principles in the Care of the Newborn" and "Principles of Decision Making in a Newborn Intensive Care Unit." These principles have been written not only for use within newborn intensive care units, but also as a means to educate other interested individuals about decision-making processes affecting critically ill or defective newborns.

These working drafts have relied heavily on material taken from two documents, *Deciding to Forego Life-Sustaining Treatment*, by the President's Commission for the Study of Ethical Problems in Medicine and Biomedical and Behavioral Research (revised draft of October, 1982); and the article by A.R. Jonsen, R.H. Phibbs, W.H. Tooley, and M.J. Garland, "Critical Issues in Newborn Intensive Care: A Conference Report and Policy Proposal," *Pediatrics* 55:756–768, 1975. These working drafts are offered for your review and critique. The committee recognizes that these issues require input from many disciplines and further revision is intended in response to that input. Your comments and criticisms are therefore solicited. Please address them to: Dana E. Johnson, M.D., Ph.D., University of Minnesota Hospitals, Box 211 Mayo Memorial Building, 420 Delaware St. S.E., Minneapolis, MN 55455.

---

Working draft completed March 2, 1983.

ETHICAL PRINCIPLES IN THE CARE
OF THE NEWBORN: A WORKING DRAFT

1. Each infant born possesses an intrinsic dignity and worth that entitles the infant (within constraints of equity and availability) to all medical and special care that is reasonably thought to be conducive to the infant's well-being.
2. The parent(s) bear the principal moral responsibility for the well-being of their infant and should be the surrogates for their infant, unless disqualified for one of the following reasons: decision-making incapacity, unresolvable disagreements between parents, or choosing a course of action that is clearly against the infant's best interests.
3. The attending physician must take all reasonable medical measures conducive to the well-being of the infant.
4. When the burden of treatment lacks compensating benefit or treatment is futile, the parent(s) and attending physician need not continue or pursue it.
5. Therapies lack compensating benefit when: (a) they serve merely to prolong the dying process; (b) the infant suffers from intolerable, intractable pain, which cannot be alleviated by medical treatment; (c) the infant will be unable to participate even minimally in human experience.
6. In the care of an infant from whom life-sustaining support or curative efforts are withheld, certain provisions are necessary to continue to respect the intrinsic dignity and worth of that infant. These include: (a) warmth and physical and social comforting; (b) enteric feeding and hydration, if compatible with the above ethical propositions; (c) freedom from pain, even if administration of analgesia may inadvertently hasten death.

PRINCIPLES OF DECISION MAKING IN A NEWBORN
INTENSIVE CARE UNIT (NICU): A WORKING DRAFT

Because of the commitment to the principle of intrinsic dignity and worth of the infant's life, any decision which withholds therapy or discontinues life-sustaining therapy should necessarily involve a process that ensures deliberation, decision making, and action based on the above ethical propositions and the most current available medical information. Such a process acknowledges that a diversity of thoughts and values can be held by equally thoughtful and concerned individuals, but that through a careful process which always places the determination of the infant's best interests as the primary goal, an informed and thoughtful decision can be reached.

1. The decision to discontinue treatment requires sufficient observation, assessment, and parental involvement in the decision-making process.
2. All decisions will give primary importance to the intrinsic dignity and worth of the infant and to the infant's best interests.
3. As the parent(s) bear(s) the principal responsibility for the well-being of their infant, they are the primary decision makers. It is the parent's right to involve individuals of their choosing in a resource and/or support role. While the parent(s) may be unable or unwilling to make decisions, medical professionals should accept the principle that the responsibility should, if possible, be borne by the parent(s) and attempt to help, but not force, the parent(s) to make a decision.
4. The attending physician has the responsibility to be the primary medical consultant to the parent(s). In this role, the attending physician shall:
   a. Obtain consultation as needed to thoroughly assess and confirm the diagnosis and prognosis of the infant.
   b. Communicate this information to the family in a fashion they can understand.
   c. Counsel the parent(s) and provide access to others who may help them reach a decision.
   d. Involve nursing staff and any other individuals designated by the parent(s) in the assessment and information-gathering phase of decision making.
   e. Provide the parent(s) adequate time and an appropriate environment to reach a thoughtful decision.

## FUTURE PLANS

The next goal of the committee is to establish a workable system to monitor the decision-making process, a method which will assure the public that decisions are being made with "due process." This system as presently envisioned will consist of two components. The first is an ethics committee or decision review committee within each individual neonatal intensive care unit. This body of individuals will act as an internal resource to aid the medical and nursing staff and parents in reaching decisions and assure that good decision making is occurring within the unit using the above principles and guidelines. It is intended that the committee will be made up of individuals from many disciplines and backgrounds who share a practical knowledge of the special problems that are seen in a newborn intensive care unit. The second component will be the continuation of the Twin Cities Committee for

Neonatal Life Support Policy. This group will act as consultants to individual newborn intensive care units in matters of decision making. In addition, this committee will act as a liaison between the medical community and the general public, in order to assure the public that thoughtful decision making is occurring within newborn intensive care units.

# GUIDELINES ON THE FUNCTION, COMPOSITION, AND PROCEDURES OF AN INTRA-NEWBORN INTENSIVE CARE UNIT ETHICS COMMITTEE

## Twin Cities Committee for Neonatal Life Support Policy

### INTRODUCTION

The medical staff, administrators, and trustees of each institution that provides care to seriously ill newborns should take the responsibility for ensuring good decisionmaking practices. Accrediting bodies may want to require that institutions have appropriate policies in this area.[1]

Consistent with these recommendations of the President's Commission for the Study of Ethical Problems in Medicine and Biomedical and Behavioral Research, the Twin Cities Committee for Neonatal Life Support Policy supports the establishment of an ethics committee within each of the six newborn intensive care units in the Twin Cities area.

### FUNCTION

The primary purpose of a newborn intensive care unit ethics committee is to assure care in the best interests of each individual infant hospitalized on the newborn intensive care unit. Consistent with this primary purpose, the functions of the committee include:

1.  Adopting or modifying, as necessary, the above ethical propositions and decision-making principles developed by the Twin Cities Committee for Neonatal Life Support Policy and implementing their use on the newborn intensive care unit.

2.  Educating health care professionals and parents on accepted standards of care, current court decisions, federal and state regulations, public opinion, and surveys relevant to the decision making for and the care of infants hospitalized in the newborn intensive care unit.

---

Working draft completed August 12, 1983. Committee members included Mila Aroskar, Gary Atkinson, Ron Cranford, Dana Johnson, and Norm Virnig.

3. Consulting on cases within the newborn intensive care unit where appropriate.

4. Establishing a cooperative relationship with the existing institutional ethics committee.

5. Performing other functions deemed by the individual committee as consistent with the stated primary purpose.

By functioning in the above fashion, the committee will not only ensure the best care for infants hospitalized on the newborn intensive care unit, but will also assure the public that ethically sound decisions are being made within the units.

## COMPOSITION

In view of the specialized nature of newborn intensive care, the majority of committee members should be from within the newborn intensive care unit. The total number of individuals on the committee should generally be five to ten. The SUGGESTED composition is:

Two NICU Physicians

Two NICU Nurses

One NICU Social Worker

One Hospital Administrator

One Member of Institutional Ethics Committee

One Patient Advocate (The patient advocate should be from outside the unit, but from the hospital at large)

Additional Members from the health care team on the Newborn Intensive Care Unit, or from the institution at large

## PROCEDURES

### CONSULTATION

An institution should have clear and explicit policies that require prospective or retrospective review of decisions when life-sustaining treatment for an infant might be foregone or when parents and providers disagree about the correct decision for an infant. Certain categories of clearly futile therapies could be explicitly excluded from review.

Decisions should be referred to public agencies (including courts) for review when necessary to determine whether parents should be disqualified as decision makers and, if so, who should decide the course of treatment that would be in the best interests of their child.[2]

Consistent with these recommendations, the newborn intensive care unit ethics committee will meet as necessary to prospectively or retrospectively consult on all cases where it is elected to give less than maximal therapy or when health care providers and/or parents disagree on the appropriate level of care.

1.  Under most conditions, where (a) strong consideration has been given to provide less than maximal therapy or (b) parents and/or health care providers disagree on therapy, a full prospective consultation by the ethics committee should occur prior to changes in the treatment plan. ("A full consultation" is defined as a review of the care by a simple majority of the committee.)

2.  In emergency situations, a consultation consisting of a review of the case by three members of the committee is satisfactory. If possible, this should include the patient advocate. If there is no consensus among these three members, maximal therapy should be initiated or continued pending a full consultation by the committee.

3.  Each committee may list medical conditions where there is a committee consensus that treatment lacks compensating benefit, or treatment is futile, and that parents and attending physicians need not continue it or pursue it. Retrospective review of the case by the newborn intensive care unit ethics committee is adequate.

4.  Any member of the health care team or parent(s) can initiate a consult from the ethics committee on an individual patient.

5.  While parent(s) may request to appear before the committee, the committee need not involve them in all deliberations.

6.  The opinions of the ethics committee are nonbinding on the parents and/or the attending physician and are advisory only.

7.  The attending physician may not chair the session when his/her patient is discussed. However, he/she may continue to serve as a member of the committee.

## GENERAL PROCEDURES

To accomplish its primary purpose, to ensure care in the best interests of each infant hospitalized on the newborn intensive care unit, the intra-newborn intensive care unit ethics committee is free to develop its own procedures consistent with the above ethical propositions and decision-making principles.

NOTES

1. PRESIDENT'S COMMISSION FOR THE STUDY OF ETHICAL PROBLEMS IN MEDICINE AND BIOMEDICAL AND BEHAVIORAL RESEARCH, DECIDING TO FOREGO LIFE-SUSTAINING TREATMENT: ETHICAL, MEDICAL AND LEGAL ISSUES IN TREATMENT DECISIONS (U.S. Gov't Printing Office, Washington, D.C.) (March 1983), at 7.
2. *Id.*, at 7–8.

# GUIDELINES FOR HEALTH CARE FACILITIES TO IMPLEMENT PROCEDURES CONCERNING THE CARE OF COMATOSE NON-COGNITIVE PATIENTS

## Department of Health, State of New Jersey

In order to assist and guide the medical profession and the governing authorities of health care facilities[1] in the implementation of the procedures required by the New Jersey Supreme Court for cases similar to that of Karen Ann Quinlan, the formation and operation of the requisite Prognosis Committee is described herein. The term, Prognosis Committee, recognizes the court's view that "the focal point of decision should be the prognosis as to the reasonable possibility of return to cognitive and sapient life."

The basic decision-making procedure, as paraphrased from the Court's conclusions, would be as follows:

> Upon the concurrence of the family, and in cases where required by law, the guardian[2] of the patient, should the responsible attending physicians conclude that there is no reasonable possibility of the patient's ever emerging from a comatose condition to a cognitive, sapient state and that the life-support apparatus being administered to the patient should be discontinued, they shall consult with the Prognosis Committee (or like body) serving the institution in which the patient is confined. If that consultative body agrees that there is no reasonable possibility of the patient's ever emerging from a comatose condition to a cognitive, sapient state, the life-support system may be withdrawn and said action shall be without any civil or criminal liability therefor on the part of any participant, whether guardian, physician, hospital, or others.

A Prognosis Committee, which will facilitate the decision-making process outlined by the Court, should be established or arranged for by those health care facilities which receive inpatients who are or may become comatose and non-cognitive. The Committee should function in the manner indicated by the following guidelines.

---

Dated January 27, 1977.

## RESPONSIBILITY FOR FORMING THE PROGNOSIS COMMITTEE

The Board of Trustees, or responsible governing authority of the facility, shall have the responsibility to select those physicians who will form the Prognosis Committee. The physicians shall be designated to serve for a specified term and one of these physicians shall be selected by the governing authority to chair the Prognosis Committee.

## COMPOSITION OF THE PROGNOSIS COMMITTEE

1. A standard complement of medical disciplines shall be represented on the Prognosis Committee. These disciplines will be: General Surgery; Medicine; Neurosurgery or Neurology; Anesthesiology; and Pediatrics (if so indicated by the type of patient). At least two (2) additional physicians from any appropriate disciplines shall be selected from outside the staff of the facility to serve on the Prognosis Committee.
2. It is highly desirable that the physicians serving on the Prognosis Committee be Board Certified in their respective specialties.
3. At the time that the Prognosis Committee is required to consider a case, the family, guardian, or attending physician can request that the Prognosis Committee consult with a specific physician named by any of them. The medical specialty of such physician should be predicated upon the particular characteristics of the patient's case. The Prognosis Committee shall accede to this request. The family may also designate a physician, other than the attending physician, to be present throughout the Committee's proceedings.
4. Under no circumstances should any of the physicians serving on the Prognosis Committee have been the attending or treating physician on the case under consideration.

Note: In order to proceed with the establishment of the requisite Prognosis Committees some facilities, because of staff limitations, may need assistance in this effort or may desire to act cooperatively with neighboring institutions. For example, the regionalizing (or sharing) of a Prognosis Committee to serve several health care facilities is recommended as a practical approach. It is suggested, therefore, that health care facilities seek assistance in developing and coordinating such arrangements from the New Jersey Hospital Association as well as the professional medical organizations (the Medical Society of New Jersey, and the New Jersey Association of Osteopathic Physicians and Surgeons).

### Activation of the Prognosis Committee

1. The patient's family or guardian, or the attending physician acting on behalf of the family, may, in writing, request the health care facility's chief executive officer (administrator) to activate the Prognosis Committee to begin its work on a case. In the event that this request is made by the guardian of the patient, such individual shall present legal documentation so designating his status to the chief executive officer of the health care facility. The administrator has the responsibility to ensure that all of the required physician selections are made and to notify the Chairman of the Board of Trustees, or other responsible governing authority, as to the status of the Committee's composition.
2. The administrator shall advise the designated Chairman of the Prognosis Committee to have the group proceed promptly and with due diligence to come to a conclusion either supporting (concurring) or rejecting the prognosis of the attending physician.
3. The administrator shall also make readily available to the family the counseling and support services of the health care facility, or of the surrounding community.

### Prognosis Committee Functions and Reporting Requirements

1. The Committee shall review all relevant patient records, with the family's consent, and shall seek additional medical information concerning the patient from those nursing personnel and other professionals it deems appropriate to the case under consideration. The Committee shall also determine which member or members will conduct a complete examination of the patient.
2. During the course of its deliberations, the Committee should arrive at a clear consensus with respect to the prognosis of the patient although the Supreme Court's decision does not expressly require unanimity. It is recognized that professional standards dictate caution in the determination of the prognosis.
3. The Chairman of the Prognosis Committee shall summarize and report the Committee's conclusion, in writing, to the chairman of the hospital's Board of Trustees, or other responsible governing authority, the attending physician, the administrator of the hospital, the patient's family, and when appropriate, the patient's guardian. The report shall consist of the Committee's findings concerning the prognosis of the patient, supplemented by a summary of the information considered including professional consultations, if any, and the reasons supporting their conclusion. The report shall identify

each of the participating members of the Committee and their respective specialties and which member or members performed the complete examination of the patient. Finally, the Committee shall make a specific written finding in the report as to whether there is no reasonable possibility of the patient's ever emerging from a comatose condition to a cognitive, sapient state. The report shall be retained and preserved by the health care facility as part of the medical record of the patient.

## THE CONTINUING RESPONSIBILITY OF THE ATTENDING PHYSICIAN

It should be recognized from the foregoing that the function and responsibility of the Prognosis Committee is limited to the application of specialized medical knowledge to a particular case in order to arrive at a determination of concurrence or non-concurrence with the prognosis of the attending physician. Once that determination has been made and reported, the Committee has thereby discharged its responsibility. The attending physician, guided by the Committee's decision and with the concurrence of the family, may then proceed with the appropriate course of action and, if indicated, shall personally withdraw life-support systems.

## NOTES

1. In this context, "health care facility" means an institution or facility as defined in the Health Care Facilities Planning Act (N.J.S.A. 26:2H-2a).
2. The term guardian as here used refers to the "guardian of the person of the incompetent." This individual may be designated by a court to make decisions for the incompetent concerning the incompetent's physical state and bodily integrity, such as the acceptance or refusal of various types of treatment. Such guardians are bound by traditional fiduciary duties, and must act in the perceived best interests of the incompetent.

    This form of guardianship is contrasted with the "guardian of the property of the incompetent" who may be designated by a court to make decisions for the incompetent concerning dispositions of the incompetent's realty and personalty. Such guardians have no control over the disposition of the incompetent's body, i.e., person, and are not involved in any decisions concerning the incompetent's medical treatment.

# GUIDELINES FOR
# INFANT BIOETHICS COMMITTEES

## American Academy of Pediatrics


### BACKGROUND

In recent years a widespread public debate has developed on issues surrounding the care and treatment of critically ill infants. One aspect of this debate concerns the procedures which should be available to ensure that difficult treatment decisions regarding such infants are always made in the most effective manner possible. The American Academy of Pediatrics believes that hospital-based "infant bioethics committees," consisting of both physicians and non-physicians, can provide consultation and review, ensuring sensitive treatment decisions made in a reasoned, informed and caring manner. Infant bioethics committees can provide education, develop and recommend institutional policies, and offer consultation to providers and families facing a range of ethical problems or questions about medical treatment of infants. The Academy urges all hospitals to establish such committees either on their own or in conjunction with other hospitals. This document is intended to assist those individuals and institutions who elect to engage in this process.

The American Academy of Pediatrics has been involved in discussion of ethical issues surrounding the care and treatment of critically ill infants since 1982. In 1983 the United States Department of Health and Human Services published regulations on this issue establishing federal law enforcement activities which were intrusive into patient care. The Academy successfully challenged that rule in court. Subsequently the Department of Health and Human Services issued regulations in the Federal Register (effective February 13, 1984, but currently in litigation) that, among other things, endorse the concept of infant review committees as suggested in comments that had been submitted by the American Academy of Pediatrics.

The Academy's recommendation that parents and physicians consult with an institutional ethics committee when decisions are contemplated to forego life-sustaining treatment is consistent with the conclusions of the President's Commission for the Study of Ethical Problems in Medicine and Biomedical and Behavioral Research set forth in the report entitled *Deciding to Forego Life-Sustaining Treatment* (U.S. Government Printing Office, Washington, D.C., 1983). As the Commission's report points out, institutional ethics committees have been established by a number of hospitals in recent years. Their use has been recommended by health care professionals, ethicists and many others, including the American Society of Law & Medicine. While experience with this approach in the context of seriously ill infants is relatively limited, much can be learned from the experience of those institutions which have developed multidisciplinary ethics committees to address the needs of their general patient populations.

The following guidelines are suggestions developed by a task force of the American Academy of Pediatrics comprised of Academy members knowledgeable about ethics committees as well as consultants from other organizations and disciplines.[1] In light of the wide diversity of institutions which would consider establishing infant bioethics committees, the task force has prepared guidelines for a model committee which may, of course, be tailored to the needs of each institution. The Academy expects that each hospital will structure its own committee in a manner consonant with other committees of that hospital and responsive to the overall needs of the institution and the community. Over time, the scope and functions of such committees will undoubtedly evolve and the range of ethical issues which they address will expand.

As hospitals develop more experience with these committees, the Academy would appreciate comments on their experience and expects to supplement these guidelines to incorporate the benefits of this experience.

## INTRODUCTION

The American Academy of Pediatrics recommends that the governing body, in consultation with the medical staff and administration, of each hospital that provides care for infants give serious consideration to the role an Infant Bioethics Committee may play in aiding decision making about the care of seriously ill infants. (For purposes of these guidelines, an infant is any person less than two years old.) Such a committee would serve the purposes of:

— providing an educational resource for hospital personnel and families of seriously ill infants;

— recommending institutional guidelines and policies concerning ethical principles in the care of infants; and

— offering consultation and review on treatment decisions regarding critically ill infants, especially when the foregoing of life-sustaining treatment is being considered.

In designing a process that is appropriate for its circumstances, the hospital should consider:

— the relationship of an infant bioethics committee to other existing processes for decision making of the hospital (including other ethics committees);

— whether the process should include a standing hospital committee, a procedure for empaneling ad hoc committees as need arises, or a group of advisors; and

— the possibility of cooperating with other institutions in establishing a joint committee, especially when the hospital does not treat enough critically ill infants to justify a separate committee.

## FUNCTIONS

In the context of ethical issues involving the care of infants, the Infant Bioethics Committee should perform the following four functions:

1. *Education:* The committee should educate hospital personnel and families about the means available within the hospital and in the community to assist them in making good decisions about treatment, about relevant ethical principles, literature and resources, and about community services for disabled persons.

2. *Policy Development:* The committee should develop and recommend hospital policies and guidelines which define ethical principles for conduct within the hospital's activities.

3. *Prospective Review:* The committee should provide consultation and review in cases where the foregoing of life-sustaining treatment is under consideration, helping to resolve disagreements among families and health care providers.

4. *Retrospective Review:* The committee should review medical records retrospectively when life-sustaining treatment has been foregone to determine the appropriateness of hospital policies and whether these policies are being followed.

## STRUCTURE

The precise organizational relationship of the Infant Bioethics Committee—whether a committee of the governing body, of the medical staff, or otherwise—will depend upon a number of factors, such as hospital bylaws and state law on confidentiality and discoverability of hospital records. One committee may serve several hospitals as part of a collective effort among the hospitals.

Appropriate clerical, legal and fiscal support should be provided to the committee so that it can fulfill its obligations.

## MEMBERSHIP

While the precise membership of the committee will depend on institutional needs and resources, it is important that the committee include members from various disciplines. A multi-disciplinary approach is recommended so that the committee will have sufficient expertise to supply and evaluate all pertinent information, and because representation of viewpoints of the community is desirable to contribute to better decisions.

An effort should be made to ensure that the committee has at least the following expertise available to it through members or advisors: medical, psychosocial, human service resources, nursing, social work, familiarity with issues affecting disabled persons, legal and ethical. The committee may wish to identify and have available other areas of expertise.

The committee size should be large enough to represent diversity, but not so large as to hinder candid discussions and deliberations. The following is a suggested list of "core" committee members:

— practicing physician
— pediatrician knowledgeable about the nursery
— nurse
— hospital administrator
— parent of a disabled child, representative of a disability group, or developmental disability expert
— social worker
— member of the hospital's pastoral care program or other clergy
— lawyer
— lay community member
— person trained in ethics or philosophy

## JURISDICTION

The Infant Bioethics Committee should not supplant other existing means within the institution for reaching good decisions about the care of critically ill infants. The processes of consultation and review established by the committee should seek to assure that all decisions, whenever possible, have had the benefit of prior appropriate consultations and discussion in patient care conferences. This is particularly important when there is disagreement between the family members and/or the health care providers. The clarification that such processes provide may allow resolution on factual grounds of what may have seemed initially to be ethical disputes.

## PROCEDURES AND FUNCTIONS

At the time the governing board decides to establish an Infant Bioethics Committee, decisions should be made as to how the members will be appointed and how the chairperson and vice-chairperson will be selected.

The committee should establish procedures about how often it will meet, attendance of alternates or substitutes, quorum requirements, and the like. It is anticipated that regular meetings will be needed for the committee to carry out its functions in educating hospital staff, infants' families, and the community; in recommending to the hospital's governing board policies for the care of critically ill infants; and in retrospective review. The committee may find it helpful to draw on the extensive literature and published policies on issues such as orders not to resuscitate and appropriate treatment of permanently unconscious patients. (See, for example, Appendices G through I in the President's Commission's report on *Deciding to Forego Life-Sustaining Treatment* and Section III, Guidelines, in *Institutional Ethics Committees and Health Care Decision Making* (Cranford, R.E., Doudera, A.E., eds.) (Health Administration Press, Ann Arbor, Mich.) (1984).

In addition, the committee should meet at the call of the chairperson to review individual cases. It should be recognized that there will be fewer occasions for such special meetings as the committee's policies and expectations become better known and understood within the institution.

### EDUCATIONAL FUNCTIONS

The committee shall act as a resource to the hospital staff, to families of infants, and to the community, as feasible, for information on ethical principles involved in medical decision making and about issues surrounding the treatment of critically ill infants and programs for disabled persons and their families.

Each hospital shall be expected to see that the existence and functions of the Infant Bioethics Committee are well known, including policies, procedures and the method of contacting the committee.

POLICY DEVELOPMENT FUNCTIONS

The committee should develop and recommend for adoption by the hospital, institutional policies concerning foregoing of life-sustaining treatment for infants with life-threatening conditions and guidelines for decision making in other specific types of cases or diagnoses, e.g., Down syndrome and myelomeningocele. It should also develop procedures to be followed in recurring circumstances such as brain death and parental refusal to consent to life-sustaining treatment.

In recommending these policies and guidelines, the committee should consult with medical and other authorities on issues involving disabled individuals, e.g., neonatologists, pediatric surgeons, county and city agencies which provide services for the disabled, and disability advocacy organizations. The committee should also consult with appropriate committees of the medical staff to ensure that the committee policies and guidelines build on existing staff bylaws, rules and procedures concerning consultations and staff membership requirements. When these policies and guidelines have been approved by the hospital, the committee should inform and educate hospital staff on the policies and guidelines it develops and should recommend the necessary measures to insure that the policies and guidelines are properly implemented.

CONSULTATIVE FUNCTIONS (PROSPECTIVE REVIEW)

*Discretionary Review*

Because it should aim for an atmosphere of collaboration with those who face difficult decisions about the care of infants in the institution, the committee should make clear that it expects many (or even most) of the cases it reviews prospectively to arise in a voluntary context. In these cases, the committee may meet as a whole or may, by established procedures, delegate to certain members, as an ethics consultant team, the responsibility of consulting with the concerned parties. The scope of the committee's discretionary review should include the following:

a. The committee may review the care of a hospitalized infant upon the request of any member of the hospital staff or member of the infant's immediate family, when a serious ethical issue is presented by a decision about the infant's care.

b. The committee may review any case of a hospitalized infant when serious ethical questions about the infant's care have been raised by a public agency.

The presumption—especially early in a committee's existence—should be that it will review all cases in which there is serious disagreement among the staff responsible for the care of an infant or between the attending physician and the parents.

*Mandatory Review*

The committee should review all cases in which the attending physician and parents propose to forego life-sustaining treatment for an infant. Review is not mandatory when an infant is imminently dying. In doubtful cases, the presumption should be in favor of review. The attending physician should be responsible for notifying the committee of a case requiring mandatory review.

The committee may wish to specify certain diagnoses, such as Down syndrome or myelomeningocele, for which a decision to forego treatment will always be reviewed by the committee.

*Requests for Review*

Ordinarily, the attending physician should forward requests for review, or the need for mandatory review, to the committee, but others may do so if necessary. The person requesting review should contact the chairperson or other designated committee member or hospital official. Although not encouraged, requests for Infant Bioethics Committee review may be anonymous. In any case, the hospital should have procedures to keep confidential the identity of persons requesting committee review and to protect those persons from reprisal.

*Initial Assessment*

Following a request for committee review by any of the above routes, an assessment of the situation will be made by the committee chairperson or his/her designee, including contacting the family and the attending physician, before determining whether to convene a committee meeting. After review of relevant considerations, a preliminary decision should be made as to whether the request for committee review is appropriate or inappropriate. An inappropriate request is one which clearly does *not* raise serious ethical issues, e.g., because the infant in question is not a patient at the hospital, because the infant is not seriously ill, or because the decision alleged to have been made about treatment or nontreatment actually has not been made. The presumption should be toward review by the committee.

At the regularly scheduled meetings, the chairperson should report to the committee on any requests for committee review which were denied on the grounds that they were inappropriate.

If the chairperson considers the request appropriate, a committee meeting should be convened. If not, the request can receive administrative disposition by the chairperson, with a later report to the committee. The person requesting the review should be informed of the disposition of the request.

*Invited Participants*

When there is deemed sufficient reason to convene a special committee meeting to consult on a case, the committee generally should invite those persons with interest in the case to the appropriate parts of the meeting, but not necessarily at the same time:

— the parents (family) of the infant;

— the attending physician, nurse, senior staff person, consultants, house staff assigned to the infant and others closely connected with the care of the infant;

— the person requesting the meeting.

The parents (family) may, if they wish, bring their own support persons, e.g., clergy. The family and others invited to the meeting need not attend the meeting if they do not wish to or may be appropriately excused from the deliberative portions of the meeting.

*Plan of the Meeting*

At the meeting, all concerned parties should have an opportunity to present their viewpoints and, as appropriate to the case, to hear the views of others. The first objective should be to elicit all pertinent facts and to clarify the issues raised by the case. The committee should then assess the alternative course(s) of treatment proposed or possible, with the objective of facilitating consensus about the interests of the infant. A collaborative atmosphere will usually remedy any deficiencies in the decision-making process so that the committee and all those concerned with the case can agree on an appropriate course of action. Every effort should be made to support the dignity and integrity of the family and health care providers involved in such decisions, as the interests of the infant are being defined.

*Recommendations*

The committee should recommend a course of action only when agreement cannot be reached among the committee, the family, and the health care providers and when it concludes that one, or more, of the proposed course(s) of action is(are) based on clearly unreasonable premises about, or inappropriate evaluation of, the interests of the infant, e.g., failure to correct an uncomplicated intestinal obstruction in an infant with Down syndrome.

Regardless of committee recommendations, if the family wishes to continue life-sustaining treatment and the attending physician disagrees, the family's wishes should be carried out until they are officially removed from their position as the infant's guardian or until treatment is ceased pursuant to existing hospital policies and procedures.

With the above exception, when there continues to be substantive disagreement between the principal parties and the committee concerning the appropriate course of action, the committee should follow established procedures to report its conclusions to the hospital official(s) responsible for reporting such cases to the appropriate court and/or child protective agency. Because of the gravity of this step, the committee should establish procedures for documenting the degree of consensus about its recommendation through a formal vote, conducted in a manner that allows each committee member to express his or her conscientious conclusions free of coercion from the group process (such as by anonymous, written ballot). Only members of the committee should be allowed to vote. Such formal procedures for identifying committee recommendations should be limited to those situations in which a consensus cannot be achieved and in which members of the committee feel the proposed course of action is contrary to the interests of the infant.

While legal proceedings are being instituted, it is expected that every effort should be made to continue treatment, preserve the status quo, and prevent worsening of the infant's condition, until such time as a course of action has been ordered by a person acting under the authority of the court.

The recommendations of the committee discussions should be promptly conveyed to the attending physician, who should see that an appropriate notation is made in the patient's record. To avoid misunderstanding, especially in difficult cases, the attending physician may request the notation to be made by the committee.

CONSULTATIVE FUNCTION (RETROSPECTIVE REVIEW)

The committee should adopt retrospective review procedures to determine whether cases that should come before the committee are being missed, to follow up on the outcome of the cases that have been referred to the committee, and to evaluate the effectiveness and acceptability of the policies which have been approved by the hospital.

In order to ensure that appropriate cases are being reviewed, some form of review of treatment of critically ill infants in the hospital should be performed. Examples of how this could be accomplished include reviewing the records of disabled infants born in, or admitted to, the hospital and reviewing the records of infants who have died in the hospital. A listing of all such cases should be regularly provided to the committee. The committee should have a procedure for determining whether to review every chart so listed, to review a randomly selected sample of charts, or to assign preliminary reviews to a subcommittee.

## RECORD KEEPING

The committee should maintain records of all its deliberations and summary descriptions of specific cases considered and the disposition of those cases. Committee minutes should be approved by the committee before they become final. Records should be kept in accordance with institutional policies on confidentiality of medical information. Hospital counsel should clarify for the committee the circumstances under which records must be made available to governmental officials or other persons, as required by state law.

## LEGAL ISSUES

Provision should be made for timely reporting by the committee to the hospital's governing body through appropriate mechanisms. The advice of counsel should be sought about the responsibilities imposed by state law on hospital officials to see that certain treatment decisions are reported to designated governmental officials as possible instances of child neglect or abuse so that consideration may be given by a court to the appointment of an infant guardian.

It is unlikely that committee members will face civil or criminal liability for actions taken in the course of committee proceedings. Indeed, state law may provide committee members with immunity from any such civil and/or criminal liability. Nonetheless, hospitals should indemnify committee members from liability for their decisions. In any case, careful decisions made by the committee in good faith should minimize any chance of liability.

## NOTE

1. The members of and consultants to the American Academy of Pediatrics Infant Bioethics Task Force included: William B. Weil, Jr., M.D. (Chairman); William G. Bartholome, M.D., M.T.S.; Alexander M. Capron, LL.B.; Ronald E. Cranford, M.D. (American Society of Law & Medicine); Thomas E. Elkins, M.D.; Richard L. Epstein, LL.B.; Norman C. Fost, M.D.; Judy Hicks, R.N. (National Association of Children's Hospitals and Related Institutions); George A. Little, M.D.; Robert H. Parrott, M.D. (National Association of Children's Hospitals and Related Institutions); Robert H. Sweeney (National Association of Children's Hospitals and Related Institutions); Ann W. Weisman, J.D.; and Jean D. Lockhart, M.D., Staff, American Academy of Pediatrics.

# GUIDELINES ON HOSPITAL COMMITTEES ON BIOMEDICAL ETHICS

Special Committee on Biomedical Ethics,
American Hospital Association

## INTRODUCTION

The growth of medical knowledge and the rapid expansion of medical capabilities and technology have generated unprecedented opportunities and challenges in the delivery of health care. At the same time, this growth and expansion have created increasingly complex ethical choices for physicians, health care professionals, patients, and the families of patients. Recent efforts to clarify biomedical ethical issues on the institutional level have focused on the use of hospital biomedical ethics committees. Such committees, sometimes called "ethics committees," "human values committees," "medical-moral committees," or "bioethics committees," hold promise for identifying the ethical implications of these problems and their possible resolutions, if they are established with a clearly defined purpose and an understanding of their capabilities and limitations.

Institutional ethics committees are one of several approaches to address medical ethical matters. If an institution chooses this approach, the following guidelines may assist in determining the organization, composition, and function of these committees. Because such committees are relatively new and largely untested, the guidelines are not intended to be prescriptive or directive.

## FUNCTIONS

Although institutional ethics committees may have one or more functions, they seem particularly suited to: (1) directing educational programs on biomedical ethical issues, (2) providing forums for discussion

The American Hospital Association's General Council created a Special Committee on Biomedical Ethics in 1982. This multidisciplinary committee prepared these guidelines as part of its charge to assist hospitals in developing institutional processes to deal with the educational and decision-making challenges presented by biomedical ethical issues. These guidelines were approved by the AHA General Council on January 27, 1984. This guideline document is intended to provide general advice to the membership of the American Hospital Association, as approved by the General Council. Copyright © 1984 by the American Hospital Association, 840 North Lake Shore Drive, Chicago, Illinois 60611. Reprinted with permission.

among hospital and medical professionals and others about biomedical ethical issues, (3) serving in an advisory capacity and/or as a resource to persons involved in biomedical decision making, and (4) evaluating institutional experiences related to reviewing decisions having biomedical ethical implications. Ethics committees should not serve as professional ethics review boards, as substitutes for legal or judicial review, or as "decision makers" in biomedical ethical dilemmas. An ethics committee should not replace the traditional loci of decision making on these issues.

Educational programs on biomedical ethics issues serve to heighten awareness and provide guidance on identification of cases where ethical problems may arise. Such programs may be offered to medical staff, the hospital staff, and the community. Forums for the discussion of these issues serve similar purposes by providing an opportunity for physicians, nurses, administrators, trustees, clergy, ethicists, and others to consider and discuss a number of diverse perspectives.

The use of ethics committees in an advisory role to assist physicians, other health care professionals, and patients and their families to make decisions when confronted with dilemmas is probably their most complex function. Ethics committees often may make recommendations at the request of an attending physician, another hospital professional closely connected with the case, the hospital administration, and the patient or the patient's family. Access to the committee should be open to all those involved in patient care decisions. Hospitals should design and implement systems to bring to the committee's attention certain kinds of issues and to address similar issues in a reasonably consistent manner.

## COMPOSITION

The members of an ethics committee should be selected in keeping with its objectives and represent a range of perspectives and expertise. It may be multidisciplinary and may include physicians, nurses, administrators, social workers, clergy, trustees, attorneys, ethicists, and patient advocates (representatives). Hospital legal counsel should be available at the request of the committee, and legal review of its recommendations may be necessary.

To be most useful and effective, an ethics committee should be a standing committee, and its members should be approved by the appropriate authority within the institution. This structure provides continuity and enhances the credibility of the committee. It also provides an opportunity for the committee to develop an understanding of the permissible range for discretion and latitude within which biomedical ethical decisions may be made. The committee should meet regularly and whenever necessary to provide advice and recommendations. As a general rule, no one who is personally involved in the case in question should serve on the committee while the case is being considered.

## DELIBERATIONS

Issues that may be brought to an ethics committee acting in an advisory capacity should relate to patient care.

If a recommendation is made by the committee, it should be provided as appropriate to the physicians, nurses, and other health care professionals involved in treatment, and should be offered to the patient and the patient's family or other surrogate.

The confidentiality of patient information and the patient's privacy should be respected. The circumstances under which documentation of the committee's recommendations should appear in the patient's medical records should be determined by each institution with the advice of legal counsel.

The manner in which the committee considers an issue or a particular case should depend on the individual circumstances. The committee may review and discuss materials submitted to it, or it may meet with the health care team involved and others as needed, including persons acting on the patient's behalf.

## CONCLUSION

Each institution should take the steps necessary to implement suitable mechanisms that will reasonably provide for sound decision-making practices and for responsible and timely assessment of medical and ethical issues.

# GUIDELINES FOR ESTABLISHING BIOETHICS COMMITTEES

## Committee on Evolving Trends in Society Affecting Life, California Medical Association

Each acute care hospital in California is advised to establish and support a bioethics committee. The committee should be composed of physicians and appropriate non-physician members such as nurses, clergy, ethicists, and laypersons interested in and informed about issues of medical ethics. The purpose of the committee would be to facilitate communication between concerned parties regarding treatment decisions, to assist in the decision-making process when ethical conflicts occur, and to retrospectively review decisions for the purpose of establishing guidelines. The committee would not make medical decisions nor become involved in clear-cut cases of surrogates or guardians of incompetent patients refusing standard medical treatment. However, the committee would have an ongoing charge of recommending standards of treatment in cases having bioethical implications and issuing bioethical policy guidelines for the institution.

The members of such a committee should be available on a consultative basis and at short notice when asked for assistance by physicians. The committee should also be available for discussion with patients, when appropriate, and with family members or other members of the health care team. Availability of such a committee might facilitate resolution of a conflict of opinion between concerned parties without recourse to the courts. The presence of lay members serves to increase the likelihood that understandable communication of treatment options and realistic treatment outcomes are being provided in both directions. Care must be taken to assure the confidentiality of information presented to the committee.

The following guidelines are intended to supplement the above policy statement by providing additional guidance to medical staffs undertaking or considering the establishment of a bioethics committee. The California Medical Association recognizes that there is currently no consensus within the medical community regarding how a bioethics committee might best be structured, and no body of data available from which conclusions can be drawn as to how such committees function best. The following guidelines are offered as suggestions and are not intended to discourage alternative approaches.

---

Endorsed by the California Medical Association Council, June 1984.

## THE CHARGE OF BIOETHICS COMMITTEES

Although a bioethics committee is expected to benefit the hospital and its staff, its role is ultimately to serve patients and their families. A bioethics committee might perform the following functions:

— Development of criteria and guidelines for the consideration of cases having bioethical implications.

— Development and implementation of procedures for the review of cases having bioethical implications.

— Development and/or review of institutional policies regarding care and treatment in cases having bioethical implications.

— Retrospective review of cases for the purpose of determining the usefulness of, and to further refine, institutional bioethical policies.

— Consultation with concerned parties when ethical conflicts occur in order to facilitate communication and provide a process for conflict resolution.

— Education of hospital staff regarding policies and issues of a bioethical nature.

A bioethics committee ought not usurp the decision-making ability of physicians in the care and treatment of individual patients. It is recommended that the committee's role be advisory and not judicial.


## THE STRUCTURE OF BIOETHICS COMMITTEES

It is recommended that a bioethics committee be constituted as a committee of the medical staff in order for the proceedings and records of the committee to be protected from discovery. Members of the committee would be selected in accordance with medical staff bylaws, and the committee would report to the duly constituted representatives of the medical staff. A bioethics committee should serve the entire hospital and not be limited to one discipline. In large hospitals, subcommittees focusing on specific issues may be advisable. It is recommended that the committee meet on a regular, publicized schedule, although a mechanism for emergency meetings of key members on short notice should be provided for.

If an alternative structure for a bioethics committee is selected, it is recommended that provision be made to protect from discovery any committee proceedings or records pertaining to the review of individual cases.

## COMPOSITION OF BIOETHICS COMMITTEES

It is recommended that all bioethics committees include physicians from the medical staff and nurses from the nursing staff of a facility, as well as lay persons representing the community. Depending on the standards and resources of the community and the preferences of the medical staff, committees might also appropriately include the following:

— social workers;

— clergy;

— ethicists;

— attorneys;

— hospital administrators; and

— hospital board members.

## THE ROLE OF MEDICAL SOCIETIES

It is recommended that medical societies become involved in facilitating the establishment of bioethics committees by making informational materials available to local hospitals and assisting in the identification of source persons. Medical societies might also consider sponsoring educational programs to promote the development of bioethics committees in their areas.

## LEGAL ISSUES AFFECTING BIOETHICS COMMITTEES

Bioethics committees and their members should be mindful of various legal considerations, including but not limited to the following:

— the legal liability of committee members;

— liability insurance coverage of the committee and its members;

— protection from discovery of committee records; and

— required changes in medical staff bylaws.

Proposed committees are urged to seek the advice of legal counsel regarding these issues. The following opinion was prepared by Hassard, Bonnington, Rogers and Huber, Legal Counsel for the California Medical Association.

The responsibilities assigned to bioethics committees prompt questions concerning the potential legal liabilities and the scope of legal protections for the committee and its work. Specific advice may be needed in specific circumstances. The following discussion addresses some of the common questions raised in this area in general terms.

1. **What is the potential legal liability of the members of bioethics committees?**

    A. Criminal Liability

    Members of bioethics committees may ask whether they can be charged as parties to a criminal homicide (or possibly to the crime of assisting a suicide) or as criminal conspirators. Such charges could be filed. Criminal liability cannot be imposed absent a showing of unlawful conduct, however.

    A California appellate court recently concluded in *Barber and Nejdl vs. Superior Court* that the action taken by two physicians in removing life-sustaining treatment from a comatose patient could not support a prosecution for murder or conspiracy to commit murder, the two crimes with which they were charged. The Court concluded the physicians' actions were not unlawful. The court based this conclusion on three factors:

    1. Physicians have no legal duty to continue to provide treatment which would be "disproportionate" given the particular circumstance, that is, when the burdens of the proposed treatment would outweigh the benefits;

    2. The prognosis in this case met generally accepted standards of medical practice in the community; and

    3. These physicians properly consulted with the patient's family and obtained the family's informed consent.

    The *Barber and Nejdl* case does not eliminate all uncertainty in this area, but the opinion does provide guidance which other courts are likely to consider. Therefore, members of bioethics committees will be best protected from criminal liability if they abide by the criteria established in the *Barber and Nejdl* case.

    If the committee believes care is being withheld inappropriately, the committee's legal obligation to take action is unclear. Liability generally is not imposed for failing to take action which might prevent harm from occurring. However, the rule is different in situations in which the individual fails to perform an action which the individual has a legal duty to perform. The courts may conclude in the future that bioethics committees have an affirmative legal duty to protect patients. Therefore, bioethics committees may be best advised to recommend judicial review of questionable cases and to document that such a suggestion was made.

B. Civil Liability

While the *Barber and Nejdl* opinion involved a criminal action, it is broadly worded and is likely to be followed in civil actions and administrative proceedings.

There are also statutory provisions which may protect members of bioethics committees. Civil Code Section 43.7 generally protects from civil liability (in California courts at least) members of medical staff committees reviewing the quality of medical care rendered in a hospital so long as the member "acts without malice, has made a reasonable effort to obtain the facts of the matter as to which he or she acts, and acts in reasonable belief that the action taken by him or her is warranted by the facts known to him or her after such reasonable effort to obtain facts." The statute does not require committee members to be members of the medical staff. Therefore, this statute should apply to protect *all* members of a bioethics committee as long as the committee is a formal medical staff committee and the members are appointed following procedures described in the medical staff bylaws.

2. **To what extent are the records of a bioethics committee protected from discovery?**

With some exceptions, the proceedings and records of medical staff committees responsible for the evaluation and improvement of patient care are protected from discovery by statute in California (Section 1157, Evidence Code). As long as a bioethics committee is a formal medical staff committee established and described in the medical staff bylaws, the protection of Section 1157 should apply. The fact that individuals who are not otherwise affiliated with the hospital may be members of a bioethics committee would not appear to change the result.

It is important to note that Section 1157, Evidence Code, does not completely immunize the records and proceedings of medical staff committees from discovery. The statute contains three express exceptions applicable to medical staff committees. The protection does not apply to:

1. statements made by any person in attendance at such a meeting who is a party to an action or proceeding the subject matter of which was reviewed at such meeting,

2. any person requesting hospital staff privileges, or

3. any action against an insurance carrier alleging bad faith by the carrier in refusing to accept a settlement offer within the policy limits.

With respect to the first exception, the most recent appellate court opinion interpreting this exception concluded it did *not* mean that statements made to a committee by a physician-defendant in a professional liability action could be disclosed. The court reasoned that to set aside the protection from discovery in professional liability actions "would not only achieve an absurd result, but would render sterile the immunity provisions of the statute." While this case has not been overruled, it is unclear whether this conclusion will be followed by other courts.

The application of this statutory protection in criminal actions is somewhat unsettled. As a result of the passage of Proposition 8, "The Victims' Bill of Rights," a "Truth-in-Evidence" provision was added to the California Constitution which appears to broaden the evidence which may be utilized in criminal proceedings. It is possible that Section 1157 is not affected by this constitutional change, but that issue has not been tested.

Finally, it should be noted that Section 1157, Evidence Code, is not binding in federal courts in some circumstances, or in actions undertaken by federal agencies.

A related issue in civil litigation concerns the confidentiality of patient's medical information. Medical information is generally protected from disclosure in California by the Confidentiality of Medical Information Act. Pursuant to the Act, medical information which identifies the patient usually may not be disclosed unless the patient or the patient's legally authorized representative has signed a written form authorizing the disclosure. There is a provision in the Act which permits the disclosure of patient records even without the patient's written authorization to "organized committees. . . . of medical staffs of licensed hospitals . . . if the committees . . . are engaged in reviewing the competence or qualifications of health care professionals or in reviewing health care services with respect to medical necessity, level of care, quality of care, or justification of charges." This provision should apply to permit disclosure of patient records to bioethics committees. Of course, as with all such information, the committee should establish procedures to protect the confidentiality of patient information in its possession.

3. **What changes would be necessary in medical staff bylaws to provide for bioethics committees as committees of the medical staff?**
   Because medical staff bylaws vary greatly, it is impossible to determine the particular changes which may be necessary to establish a bioethics committee without reviewing the bylaws of the medical staff in question. However, as a general matter, the bylaws would have to be amended following the procedure established in the

bylaws to create a formal "Bioethics Committee." Ordinarily, bylaws contain provisions which describe the composition, duties, and meeting requirements of each medical staff committee, and this approach should be followed for bioethics committees.

4. **Should regional or joint committees serving several institutions be constituted as a bioethics committee?**
Some concern exists about the use of regional or joint medical staff bioethics committees. Both California hospital licensing regulations and JCAH standards require that medical staffs be "self-governing." Although we are unaware of any express prohibition against the use of joint medical staff committees, it may be preferable to avoid permitting the confidential functions of a medical staff to fall into a combined agenda merely for convenience. Divergence from the customary format for medical staff committees may increase the likelihood that a court will refuse to grant the protections ordinarily covering medical staff committees and their members. This may be particularly true for bioethics committees, both because such committees are not traditional and because the issues considered by these committees are controversial. Courts may question the propriety of placing too much power in the hands of one bioethics committee. Moreover, the justification ordinarily advanced in support of regional medical staff committees, that individual hospitals in the area do not have a sufficient number of physicians to review certain specialties effectively, would not appear to apply with the same force to bioethics committees.

In the event a community is unable to develop sufficient interest for more than one bioethics committee, or there is some other substantial justification for the use of a regional committee, certain formalities might be followed. First, as discussed previously, the discovery and immunity protections applicable to medical staff committees apply only to "organized committees of the medical staff." Therefore, each medical staff which utilizes the services of the regional committee should describe and incorporate the regional committee in the medical staff bylaws. Second, to increase the likelihood that the Section 1157 discovery protections would apply, the minutes of any "regional" committee deliberations should be segregated by hospital, and each medical staff should retain only the portion of the committee's records which pertain to care rendered at their hospital. Finally, special care should be taken to ensure the confidentiality of the proceedings. The confidentiality of all discussions, patient records, minutes, and other confidential information must be protected.

# Selected Bibliography

BOOKS

G. BENTON, DEATH AND DYING: PRINCIPLES AND PRACTICES IN PATIENT CARE (Van Nostrand Reinhold, New York) (1978).

H. BRODY, ETHICAL DECISIONS IN MEDICINE (Little, Brown & Co., Boston) (1981).

BIBLIOGRAPHY OF BIOETHICS (L. Walters, ed.) (Macmillan Publishing Co., New York) (issued annually).

BIOETHICS: BASIC WRITINGS ON THE KEY ETHICAL QUESTIONS THAT SURROUND THE MAJOR MODERN BIOLOGICAL POSSIBILITIES AND PROBLEMS (T. A. Shannon, ed.) (Paulist Press, Ramsey, N.J.) (rev. ed. 1981).

BIOMEDICAL ETHICS AND THE LAW (J. M. Humber, R. F. Almeder, eds.) (Plenum Press, New York) (2d ed. 1979).

BIOMEDICAL ETHICS REVIEWS, 1983 (J. M. Humber, R. F. Almeder, eds.) (Humana Press, Clifton, N.J.) (1983).

J. CHILDRESS, WHO SHOULD DECIDE? PATERNALISM IN HEALTH CARE (Oxford University Press, New York) (1982).

CONTEMPORARY ISSUES IN BIOETHICS (T. L. Beauchamp, L. R. Walters, eds.) (Dickenson Publishing Co., Encino, Cal.) (1978).

DEATH INSIDE OUT: THE HASTINGS CENTER REPORT (P. Steinfels, R. M. Veatch, eds.) (Harper and Row Publishers, New York) (1975).

ENCYCLOPEDIA OF BIOETHICS (W. Reich, ed.) (The Free Press, New York) (1978).

ETHICAL ISSUES IN DEATH AND DYING (R. F. Weir, ed.) Columbia University Press, New York) (1977).

ETHICAL ISSUES RELATING TO LIFE AND DEATH (J. Ladd, ed.) (Oxford University Press, New York) (1979).

THE ETHICS OF RESOURCE ALLOCATION IN HEALTH CARE (K. M. Boyd, ed.) (Edinburgh University Press, Edinburgh, Scotland) (1979).

R. FOX, J. SWAZEY, THE COURAGE TO FAIL: A SOCIAL VIEW OF ORGAN TRANSPLANTS AND DIALYSIS (University of Chicago, Chicago) (1974).

FRONTIERS IN MEDICAL ETHICS: APPLICATIONS IN A MEDICAL SETTING (V. Abernathy, ed.) (Ballinger Publishing Co., Cambridge, Mass.) (1980).

I. JACOBOVITS, JEWISH MEDICAL ETHICS (Block Publishing Co., New York) (1975).

A. R. JONSEN, M. SIEGLER, W. J. WINSLADE, CLINICAL ETHICS: A PRACTICAL APPROACH TO ETHICAL DECISIONS IN CLINICAL MEDICINE (Macmillan Publishing Co., New York) (1982).

J. KATZ, A. M. CAPRON, CATASTROPHIC DISEASES: WHO DECIDES WHAT? (Russell Sage Foundation, New York) (1975).

G. H. KIEFFER, BIOETHICS: A TEXTBOOK OF ISSUES (Addison-Wesley Publishing Co., Reading, Mass.) (1979).

KILLING AND LETTING DIE (B. Steinbock, ed.) (Prentice-Hall, Englewood Cliffs, N.J.) (1980).

LEGAL AND ETHICAL ASPECTS OF TREATING CRITICALLY AND TERMINALLY ILL PATIENTS (A. E. Doudera, J. D. Peters, eds.) (Health Administration Press, AUPHA Press, Ann Arbor, Mich.) (1982).

MEDICAL ETHICS: A CLINICAL TEXTBOOK AND REFERENCE FOR THE HEALTH PROFESSIONS (N. Abrams, M. D. Buckner, eds.) (Unit Press, Cambridge, Mass.) (1983).

MEDICAL TREATMENT OF THE DYING: MORAL ISSUES (M. D. Bayles, D. M. High, eds.) (Schenkman Publishing Co., Cambridge, Mass.) (1978).

D. W. MEYERS, MEDICO-LEGAL IMPLICATIONS OF DEATH AND DYING (Lawyers Cooperative Publishing Co., New York) (1981).

A. S. MORACZEWSKI, J. S. SHOWALTER, DETERMINATION OF DEATH: THEOLOGICAL, MEDICAL, ETHICAL, AND LEGAL ISSUES (Catholic Health Association of the United States, St. Louis, Mo.) (1982).

PRESIDENT'S COMMISSION FOR THE STUDY OF ETHICAL PROBLEMS IN MEDICINE AND BIOMEDICAL AND BEHAVIORAL RESEARCH, DECIDING TO FOREGO LIFE-SUSTAINING TREATMENT: ETHICAL, MEDICAL AND LEGAL ISSUES IN TREATMENT DECISIONS (U.S. Gov't Printing Office, Washington, D.C.) (1983).

PRESIDENT'S COMMISSION FOR THE STUDY OF ETHICAL PROBLEMS IN MEDICINE AND BIOMEDICAL AND BEHAVIORAL RESEARCH, MAKING HEALTH CARE DECISIONS (U.S. Gov't Printing Office, Washington, D.C.) (1982).

PRESIDENT'S COMMISSION FOR THE STUDY OF ETHICAL PROBLEMS IN MEDICINE AND BIOMEDICAL AND BEHAVIORAL RESEARCH, DEFINING DEATH (U.S. Gov't Printing Office, Washington, D.C.) (1981).

J. A. ROBERTSON, THE RIGHTS OF THE CRITICALLY ILL (Ballinger Publishing Co., Cambridge, Mass.) (1983).

M. H. SHAPIRO, R. G. SPECE, JR., CASES, MATERIALS, AND PROBLEMS ON BIOETHICS AND LAW (West Publishing Co., St. Paul, Minn.) (1981).

R. VEATCH, CASE STUDIES IN MEDICAL ETHICS (Harvard University Press, Cambridge, Mass.) (1977).

R. VEATCH, DEATH, DYING AND THE BIOLOGICAL REVOLUTION (Yale University Press, New Haven, Conn.) (1976).

D. N. WALTON, ETHICS OF WITHDRAWAL OF LIFE-SUPPORT SYSTEMS: CASE STUDIES ON DECISION MAKING IN INTENSIVE CARE (Greenwood Press, Westport, Conn.) (1983).

C. WONG, J. SWAZEY, DILEMMAS OF DYING: POLICIES AND PROCEDURES FOR DECISIONS NOT TO TREAT (G. K. Hall Medical Publishers, Boston) (1981).

ARTICLES

I. An Introduction to Institutional Ethics Committees

Allen, P. A., *et al.*, *Development of an Ethical Committee and Effects on a Research Design*, LANCET 1(82–83):1233–36 (May 1982).

Annas, G. J., *CPR: When the Beat Should Stop*, HASTINGS CENTER REPORT 12(5):30–31 (October 1982).

Annas, G. J., *In re Quinlan: Legal Comfort for Doctors*, HASTINGS CENTER REPORT 6:29–31 (1976).

Annas, G. J., *Informed Consent and Review Committees*, in THE PSYCHOSURGERY DEBATE (E. S. Valenstein, ed.) (Freeman Press, San Francisco) (1980).

Annas, G. J., *The Quinlan Case: Death Decision by Committee*, NEW PHYSICIAN 28(2):53–54 (February 1979).

Annas, G. J., *Reconciling Quinlan and Saikewicz: Decision Making for the Terminally Ill Incompetent*, AMERICAN JOURNAL OF LAW AND MEDICINE 4(4):367–96 (1979).

Annas, G. J., *Refusing Treatment for Incompetent Patients: Why Quinlan and Saikewicz Cases Agree on Roles of Guardians, Physicians, Judges, and Ethics Committees*, NEW YORK STATE JOURNAL OF MEDICINE 80(5):816–21 (April 1980).

Bader, B., *Medical Moral Committees: Guarding Values in an Ambivalent Society*, HOSPITAL PROGRESS 63(12):80 (December 1982).

Baron, C. H., *Medical Paternalism and the Rule of Law*, AMERICAN JOURNAL OF LAW AND MEDICINE 4(4):337–65 (Winter 1979).

Bayley, C., *Terminating Treatment: Asking the Right Questions*, HOSPITAL PROGRESS 61(9):50–53, 72 (September 1980).

Bayley, C., *Clinical Setting Enhances Bioethics Education*, HOSPITAL PROGRESS 64(12):50–53 (December 1983).

Beresford, H. R., *The Quinlan Decision: Problems and Legislative Alternatives*, ANNALS OF NEUROLOGY 2:74–80 (1977).

*Biomedical Ethics, A Symposium*, VIRGINIA LAW REVIEW 69:405–561 (April 1983).

Buchanan, A., *Medical Paternalism or Legal Imperialism: Not the Only Alternatives for Handling Saikewicz-type Cases*, AMERICAN JOURNAL OF LAW AND MEDICINE 5(2):97–117 (Summer 1979).

Buchanan, A. E., *The Limits of Proxy Decision-Making for Incompetent Patients*, UCLA LAW REVIEW 29(2):391–96 (1981).

Capron, A. M., *The Quinlan Decision: Shifting the Burden of Decision-Making*, HASTINGS CENTER REPORT 6:17–19 (1976).

Capron, A. M., *A Statutory Definition of the Standards for Determining Death: An Appraisal and a Proposal*, in BIOMEDICAL ETHICS AND THE LAW (J. M. Humber, R. F. Almeder, eds.) (Plenum Press, New York) (2d ed. 1979).

Cebik, L. B., *The Professional Role and Clinical Education of the Medical Ethicist*, ETHICS, SCIENCE, AND MEDICINE 6(2):115–21 (1979).

Childress, J. F., *Who Shall Live When Not All Can Live?*, in CONTEMPORARY ISSUES IN ETHICS (T. L. Beauchamp, L. R. Walters, eds.) (Dickenson Publishing Co., Encino, Cal.) (1978).

Curran, W. J., *Quality of Life and Treatment Decisions: The Canadian Law Reform Report*, NEW ENGLAND JOURNAL OF MEDICINE 319(5):297–98 (February 2, 1984).

Denham, M. J., *et al.*, *Work of a District Ethical Committee*, BRITISH MEDICAL JOURNAL 2(6197):1042–45 (October 27, 1979).

Doudera, A. E., *Editorial: Section 504, Handicapped Newborns and Ethics Committees: An Alternative to the Hotline*, LAW, MEDICINE & HEALTH CARE 11(5):200 (October 1983).

*Editorial: The Decision to Die: Who Makes It?*, LAWYERS WEEKLY 6:596 (1979).

Fish, M. S., *Euthanasia: Where Are We? Where Are We Going?*, JOURNAL OF THE MEDICAL SOCIETY OF NEW JERSEY 778(12):812–15 (November 1981).

Guido, D. J., *Hospital Ethics Committees: Potential Mediators for Educational and Policy Change*, DISSERTATION ABSTRACTS INTERNATIONAL 43(11):3529-B.

Hamilton, M. P., *Role of an Ethicist in the Conduct of Clinical Trials in the U.S.*, CONTROLLED CLINICAL TRIALS 14:411–20 (May 1981).

Hirsch, H., *Interview: Establish Ethics Committees to Minimize Liability, Authority Advises*, HOSPITAL RISK MANAGEMENT 3(4):45–48 (April 1981).

Holmes, C., *Bioethical Decision-Making: An Approach to Improve the Process*, MEDICAL CARE 17(11):1131–38 (November 1979).

Keenan, C., *Ethics Committees: Trend for Troubling Times*, HOSPITAL MEDICAL STAFF 12(6):2–11 (June 1983).

MacIntyre, A., *Theology, Ethics, and the Ethics of Medicine and Health Care: Comments on Papers by Novak, Mouw, Roach, Cahill, and Hart*, JOURNAL OF MEDICINE AND PHILOSOPHY (December 4, 1979).

*Massachusetts Law—The Substituted Judgment Doctrine Expands beyond Life-prolonging Decisions—In re Guardianship of Roe, 421 N.E. 2d 40 (Mass.)*, WESTERN NEW ENGLAND LAW REVIEW 5:565–87 (Winter 1983).

Mazonson, P. D., *et al.*, *Medical Ethical Rounds: Development and Organization*, ROCKY MOUNTAIN MEDICAL JOURNAL 76(6):282–88 (November–December 1979).

*Medical-Legal Agreement on Brain Death: An Assessment of the Uniform Determination of Death Act*, JOURNAL OF CONTEMPORARY LAW 8:97–122 (1982).

Memel, S. L. *The Legal Status of "No Code Orders,"* HOSPITAL MEDICAL STAFF 7(5):1–8 (May 1978).

Noble, C. N., *Ethics and Experts*, HASTINGS CENTER REPORT 12(3):7–15 (June 1982).

Paris, J. J., *Terminating Treatment for Newborns: A Theological Perspective*, LAW, MEDICINE & HEALTH CARE 10(3):120–22 (June 1982).

Pinkus, R. L., *Medical Foundations of Various Approaches to Medical-Ethical Decision-Making*, JOURNAL OF MEDICAL PHILOSOPHY 6(3):295–307 (August 1981).

Pope John Center Staff, *How Can Medical-Moral Committees Function Effectively in Catholic Health Facilities?*, HOSPITAL PROGRESS 64(4):77–78 (April 1983).

Procaccino, J. A., *Life v. Quality of Life: The Dilemma of Emerging Medical-Legal Standards*, MEDICAL TRIAL TECHNIQUE QUARTERLY 29(1):45–60 (Summer 1982).

Rabkin, M., *et al.*, *Orders Not to Resuscitate*, NEW ENGLAND JOURNAL OF MEDICINE 295:364 (1976).

Randal, J., *Are Ethics Committees Alive and Well?*, HASTINGS CENTER REPORT 13(6):10 (December 1983).

*Report of the Surgeon General's Workshop on Children with Handicaps and Their Families* (Department of Health and Human Services, DHHS Publication No. PHS–83–50194) (December 1982).

*Right to Privacy, Removal of Life-support Systems:* Leach v. Akron General Medical Center, 426 N.E. 2d 809 (Ohio), AKRON LAW REVIEW 16:162–70 (Summer 1970).

Rothenberg, L. S., *Are Doctors Abdicating Responsibility for Medical Treatment Decisions?*, LACMA PHYSICIAN 110(16):30–32 (October 1980).

Sargeant, K. J., *Withholding Treatment from Defective Newborns: Substituted Judgment, Informed Consent, and the* Quinlan *Decision*, GONZAGA LAW REVIEW 13:781–811 (1978).

Scott, R. S., *Life Support: Who Decides? How?*, LEGAL ASPECTS OF MEDICAL PRACTICE 7(10):33–36 (October 1979).

Showalter, J. S., *Determining Death: The Legal and Theological Aspects of Brain-Related Criteria*, CATHOLIC LAWYER, pp. 112–28 (Spring 1982).

Strong, C., *The Tiniest Newborns*, HASTINGS CENTER REPORT 13(4):14–19 (Fall 1983).

Teel, K., *The Physician's Dilemma—A Doctor's View: What the Law Should Be*, BAYLOR LAW REVIEW 27(1):6–9 (Winter 1975).

Veatch, R. M., *Courts, Committees, and Caring*, AMERICAN MEDICAL NEWS, pp. 1–2, 11–13 (May 23, 1980).

Wallice-Barnhill, G. R., *et al.*, *Medical, Legal and Ethical Issues in Critical Care*, CRITICAL CARE MEDICINE 10:57 (1982).

II. Review of Existing Institutional Ethics Committees and Comparison with "Prognosis" and Research Committees

Cohen, C. B., *Interdisciplinary Consultation on the Care of the Critically Ill and Dying: The Role of One Hospital Ethics Committee*, CRITICAL CARE MEDICINE 10(11):776–84 (1982).

Esquada, K., *Hospital Ethics Committees: Four Case Studies*, HOSPITAL MEDICAL STAFF 7(11):26 (November 1978).

*Ethics Committees in Hospitals* (available from the Library of the Center for Bioethics, Washington, D.C.) (1983).

Freedman, B., *One Philosopher's Experience on an Ethics Committee*, HASTINGS CENTER REPORT 11(2):22 (1981).

Glaser, J., *A Model for Forming a Medical-Moral Committee*, ETHICS NOTES, pp. 1–6 (December 1981) (newsletter).

*Guidelines to Aid Ethical Committees Considering Research in Children: Working Party on Ethics of Research in Children*, BRITISH MEDICAL JOURNAL 280(6209):229–36 (January 1980).

*Guidelines to Ethical Committees Considering Research Involving Children*, ARCHIVES OF DISEASES OF CHILDREN 55(1):75–77 (January 1980).

Lestz, P., *A Committee to Decide the Quality of Life*, AMERICAN JOURNAL OF NURSING 77(5):862–66 (May 1977).

Levine, C., *Hospital Ethics Committees: A Guarded Prognosis*, HASTINGS CENTER REPORT 7(3):25–27 (June 1977).

Levine, M. D., *et al.*, *Ethical Rounds in a Children's Medical Center: Evaluation of a Hospital Based Program for Continued Education in Medical Ethics*, PEDIATRICS 60:202–8 (August 1977).

Levine, R. J., *Do Not Resuscitate Decisions and Their Implementation*, in DILEMMAS OF DYING (G. K. Hall, Boston) (1981) (Report on the Ad Hoc Committee on Policy for Do Not Resuscitate Decisions, Department of Medicine, Yale-New Haven Hospital).

Lisson, E., *Active Medical-Moral Committees: Valuable Resource for Health Care*, HOSPITAL PROGRESS 63(10):36 (October 1982).

*Optimum Care for Hopelessly Ill Patients: A Report of the Clinical Care Committee of the Massachusetts General Hospital*, NEW ENGLAND JOURNAL OF MEDICINE 295(7):362–64 (August 12, 1976).

Pattullo, E. L., *Institutional Review Boards and the Freedom to Take Risks*, NEW ENGLAND JOURNAL OF MEDICINE 307(18):1156–59 (October 28, 1982).

Somfai, Bela, *Moral Leadership in a Socialized Health Care System* (Part II), CHAC REVIEW 8(1):24–26 (January–February 1980).

Stalder, G., *Ethical Committees in Pediatric Hospitals*, EUROPEAN JOURNAL OF PEDIATRICS 136:119–21 (1981).

Younger, S. J., *et al.*, *A National Survey of Hospital Ethics Committees*, in DECIDING TO FOREGO TREATMENT: ETHICAL, MEDICAL AND LEGAL ISSUES IN TREATMENT DECISIONS (President's Commission for the Study of Ethical Problems in Medicine and Biomedical and Behavioral Research, U. S. Gov't Printing Office, Washington, D.C.) (1983).

III. Implementing an Institutional Ethics Committee: Roles and Functions

Allen, D. F., Fowler, M. D., *Cognitive Moral Development Theory and Moral Decisions in Health Care*, LAW, MEDICINE & HEALTH CARE 10(1):19–23 (February 1982).

Aroskar, M., *Anatomy of an Ethical Dilemma: The Theory*, AMERICAN JOURNAL OF NURSING 80(4):658–63 (April 1980).

Bayley, C., *Who Should Decide?*, in LEGAL AND ETHICAL ASPECTS OF TREATING CRITICALLY AND TERMINALLY ILL PATIENTS (A. E. Doudera, J. D. Peters, eds.) (Health Administration Press, AUPHA Press, Ann Arbor, Mich.) (1982).

Caplan, A. L., *Can Applied Ethics Be Effective in Healthcare and Should It Strive to Be?*, ETHICS 93:311–19 (January 1983).

Committee on the Legal and Ethical Aspects of Health Care for Children, *Comments and Recommendations on the "Infant Doe" Proposed Regulations*, LAW, MEDICINE & HEALTH CARE 11(5):203–9, 213 (October 1983).

Freeman, J. M., Rogers, M. C., *On Death, Dying, and Decisions*, PEDIATRICS 66(4):637–38 (October 1980).

Gutteridge, F., *et al.*, *The Structure and Functioning of Ethical Review Committees*, SOCIAL SCIENCE AND MEDICINE 16(20):1791–800 (1982).

Henry, C., *The Ethics of Ethics: Nurses' Participation on Ethical Committees*, NURSING MIRROR 156(24):30 (June 15, 1983).

May, W., *Composition and Function of Ethics Committees*, JOURNAL OF MEDICAL ETHICS 1:23 (1975).

Murphy, M. A., Murphy, J., *Making Ethical Decisions Systematically*, NURSING 1976 6:13 (May 1976).

Paris, J. J., Fletcher, A. B., *Infant Doe Regulations and the Absolute Requirement to Use Nourishment and Fluids for the Dying Infant*, LAW, MEDICINE & HEALTH CARE 11(5):210–13 (October 1983).

Shannon, T. A., *What Guidance from the Guidelines?*, HASTINGS CENTER REPORT 7(3):28 (June 1977).

Siegler, M., *Decision-Making Strategy for Clinical-Ethical Problems in Medicine*, ARCHIVES OF INTERNAL MEDICINE 142(12):2178–79 (November 1982).

Statement of the Biomedical Ethics Committee, Hennepin County Medical Center, on the Case of Sergeant David Mack (June 23, 1980).

Stevens, J. E., *Hospital Ethics Committees*, QUALITY REVIEW BULLETIN 9(6):162–63 (June 1983).

Van Leeuwen, G., *Natural Committee for Life: Accepting Death in Our Patients*, CLINICAL PEDIATRICS 12(2):64–65 (December 1973).

Veatch, R. M., *Hospital Ethics Committees: Is There a Role?*, HASTINGS CENTER REPORT 7(3):22–25 (June 1977).

IV. Practical Problems Facing Ethics Committees

Bader, B., Burness, A., *Ethics: Boards Address Issues beyond Allocation of Resources*, TRUSTEE 35(10):14 (October 1982).

Basson, M. D., *Choosing among Candidates for Scarce Medical Resources*, JOURNAL OF MEDICINE AND PHILOSOPHY 4(3):313–33 (September 1979).

Cushing, M., *Law for Leaders: "No Code" Orders: Current Developments and the Nursing Director's Role*, JOURNAL OF NURSING ADMINISTRATION 11(4):22–29 (April 1981).

David, P. P., *Psychiatric Consideration for the "Right to Pull the Plug,"* ILLINOIS MEDICAL JOURNAL 155(6):380–83 (June 1979).

*Decisionmaking for the Incompetent Terminally Ill Patient: A Compromise in a Solution Eliminates a Compromise of Patients' Rights*, INDIANA LAW JOURNAL, pp. 325–48 (Spring 1982).

*Ethics Committees and Ethicists in Catholic Hospitals*, HOSPITAL PROGRESS 64(9):47 (September 1983).

Fama, A. J., *Classification of Critically Ill Patients: A Legal Examination*, SAINT LOUIS UNIVERSITY LAW JOURNAL 24(3):514–53 (October 1980).

*How Can Medical-Moral Committees Function Effectively in Catholic Health Facilities?*, HOSPITAL PROGRESS 64(4):77–78 (April 1983).

Leenan, H. J., *The Selection of Patients in the Event of a Scarcity of Medical Facilities —An Unavoidable Dilemma*, INTERNATIONAL JOURNAL OF MEDICINE AND LAW 1(2):161–80 (Autumn 1979).

Levin, D. L., Levin, N. R., *DNR, An Objectionable Form of Euthanasia*, UNIVERSITY OF CINCINNATI LAW REVIEW 49:567–79 (1980).

Lo, B., *et al.*, *Frequency of Ethical Dilemmas in a Medical In-patient Service*, ARCHIVES OF INTERNAL MEDICINE 141(8):1062–64 (July 1982).

Miles, S. H., *et al.*, *The Do-Not-Resuscitate Order in a Teaching Hospital: Considerations and a Suggested Policy*, ANNALS OF INTERNAL MEDICINE 96(5):660–64 (May 1982).

Pope John Paul II, *A Patient Is a Person*, MEDICAL SERVICE 39(2):13–17 (February 1982).

Read, W. A., *Hospital Management of Resuscitation Decisions* (draft document, available from Office of Aging and Long Term Care, Hospital Research and Educational Trust, Chicago) (March 1983).

Rescher, N., *The Allocation of Exotic Medical Lifesaving Therapy, in* CONTEMPO-
RARY ISSUES IN BIOETHICS (T. L. Beauchamp, L. R. Walters, eds.) (Dicken-
son Publishing Co., Encino, Cal.) (1978).
Robertson, J., *Legal Criteria for Orders Not to Resuscitate: A Response to Justice Lia-
cos,* MEDICOLEGAL NEWS 8(1):4 (February 1980).
Roth, A. B., Wild, R. A., *When the Patient Refuses Treatment: Some Observations
and Proposals for Handling the Difficult Case,* SAINT LOUIS UNIVERSITY LAW
JOURNAL 23(3):429–45 (1979).
Rothenberg, L. S., *The Empty Search for an Imprimatur, or Delphic Oracles Are in
Short Supply,* LAW, MEDICINE & HEALTH CARE 10(3):115–16 (June 1982).
Rothenberg, L. S., *Evidentiary Hearing Required for Termination of Treatment,*
HOSPITAL LAW 13(11):3 (November 1980).
Shannon, T. A., *The Withdrawal of Treatment: The Costs and Benefits of Guidelines,
in* BIOETHICS: BASIC WRITINGS ON THE KEY ETHICAL QUESTIONS THAT SUR-
ROUND THE MODERN BIOLOGICAL POSSIBILITIES AND PROBLEMS (T. A. Shan-
non, ed.) (Paulist Press, Ramsey, N.J.) (rev. ed. 1981).
Westervelt, F. B., *The Selection Process as Viewed from Within: A Reply to Childress,
in* ETHICS AND HEALTH CARE POLICY (R. M. Veatch, R. Brawson, eds.) (Bal-
linger Publishing Co., Cambridge, Mass.) (1976).
Wussburg, C., Hartz, J. N., *Legal, Ethical Risks Make Doctors Hesitant to Stop Life
Support Systems,* HEALTHCARE REVIEW 12(6):64–69 (December 1979-January
1980).

# Table of Cases

# Index

Note: Roman page numbers refer to Section I; italic page numbers refer to Sections
II and III.

# About the Editors

RONALD E. CRANFORD is Associate Physician in Neurology and Director of the Neurological Intensive Care Unit at Hennepin County Medical Center in Minneapolis, Minnesota, and Associate Professor of Neurology at the University of Minnesota. He received his undergraduate degree in 1962 from the University of Illinois and his M.D. from the University of Illinois College of Medicine. Dr. Cranford serves as the Chairperson of the American Society of Law & Medicine's Institutional Ethics Committees Advisory Board and as the Chairperson of the Ethics and Humanities Committee of the American Academy of Neurology. He is also the Chairperson of the Biomedical Ethics Committee of the Hennepin County Medical Center.

A. EDWARD DOUDERA is Executive Director of the American Society of Law & Medicine. He received a B.S. in business administration from Boston University in 1972 and a J.D. from Suffolk University School of Law. Mr. Doudera is Executive Editor of both the *American Journal of Law & Medicine* and *Law, Medicine & Health Care*. He has coedited several texts, including *Legal & Ethical Aspects of Treating Critically & Terminally Ill Patients* and *Defining Human Life: Medical, Legal, and Ethical Implications*. Before joining the American Society of Law & Medicine in 1977, Mr. Doudera was Associate Administrator for Research at Tufts-New England Medical Center.